Thi
se

URBAN LIFESTYLES: SPACES · PLACES · PEOPLE

PROCEEDINGS OF AN INTERNATIONAL CONFERENCE ON CITIES
IN THE NEW MILLENNIUM
NEWCASTLE UPON TYNE/UNITED KINGDOM/14–16 SEPTEMBER 2000

Urban Lifestyles:
Spaces · Places · People

Edited by

John F. Benson & Maggie H. Roe
School of Architecture, Planning & Landscape, University of Newcastle upon Tyne, United Kingdom

A.A. BALKEMA/ROTTERDAM/BROOKFIELD/2000

Photo cover: Newcastle upon Tyne, June 1999; courtesy of Airfotos Limited, Newcastle upon Tyne, United Kingdom

The texts of the various papers in this volume were set individually by typists under the supervision of each of the authors concerned.

Published by
A.A. Balkema, P.O. Box 1675, 3000 BR Rotterdam, Netherlands
Fax: +31.10.413.5947; E-mail: balkema@balkema.nl; Internet site: www.balkema.nl
A.A. Balkema Publishers, Old Post Road, Brookfield, VT 05036-9704, USA
Fax: 802.276.3837; E-mail: info@ashgate.com

ISBN 90 5809 169 4
© 2000 A.A. Balkema, Rotterdam
Printed in the Netherlands

Urban Lifestyles: Spaces · Places · People, Benson & Roe (eds)
© *2000 Balkema, Rotterdam, ISBN 90 5809 169 4*

Table of contents

Theoretical approaches to transforming spaces and places

The practice of restoring spaces and places

Policy, planning and place-making

Poster summaries

Miscellaneous

Urban Lifestyles: Spaces · Places · People, Benson & Roe (eds)
© 2000 Balkema, Rotterdam, ISBN 90 5809 169 4

Editorial foreword

When Frank Lloyd Wright described life in modern cities as 'pig-piling', with the citizen aspiring to a 'sterile urban verticality, actually unnatural to him because he is upended, suspended, and traffic-jammed ...due to his own mad excess' (Lloyd Wright, 1958 pp. 22-23), he became one in a long line of critics and commentators from Aristotle to the present day who, exasperated at the inability of politicians, policy-makers, planners and designers to respond to the perceived needs of citizens, offered an alternative vision. Lloyd Wright's vision was a 'living city' which would restore grace, beauty, function and freedom to the city fabric and to the quality of life for citizens. Long before sustainability had become a buzzword, Wright also suggested the need for forests within urban areas to be 'held in trust for future generations' (Lloyd Wright, 1958 pp. 102-103).

Life in the city in the developed nations has changed considerably since 1958, but it seems we are still grappling with the problems identified by Wright and others. In ancient Greece, Aristotle believed that the awareness of difference occurs primarily in cities and that this should breed tolerance (Sennett, 1999). Today we are grappling with a quite contrary and growing problem which is that 'difference' often breeds intolerance, isolation and violence. Many cities around the world are now having to address the issue of how to accommodate shifting populations who bring new cultural values into old city spaces.

The complexity of issues faced by professionals and researchers in the urban context has become greater as the population of cities has expanded. Mercer (1974) gives an example of the massive changes in cities by citing Cardiff in Wales which from the Norman period to the late eighteenth century was a small walled city with a population of approximately 2000. He calculates that a person would have been acquainted – or at least 'on nodding terms' (p. 11) – with a significant proportion of these people, whereas by 1971 (less than 200 years later) in a small city covering 20,000 acres with a population of approximately 280,000, well over a quarter of a million of the people would be strangers to him. The questions which Mercer posed then are still valid today – 'Does all this matter? Do such factors make any real difference to people?' (p. 12).

Colin Ward's seminal book The Child in the City (1977) identified the plight of children and young people as being predominantly 'at war with their environment', as a result of ignorance and dullness on the part of designers and poor policy and planning on the part of politicians and professionals. The links between environments – particularly urban environments – and behaviour have become a rich area of study, speculation and controversy. Does the physical fabric really make a difference? How and in what way can we or should we change the structures, infrastructures and spaces in cities to provide a richer and more fulfilling existence for all citizens? Almost a century before, Ebeneezer Howard had already answered these questions in his proposal of the 'social city' which is of particular interest today to those promoting a more sustainable lifestyle in cities. Howard developed principles of conservation, balanced development, environmental quality and social equality (see Howard, 1889 & 1965) and these ideals were transformed into a physical form in the early Garden Cities (Blowers, 1993).

This volume of papers represents a sample of the concerns of a wide range of politicians, policy-makers, practitioners, commentators and academics who are today engaged with these and many other issues linked to life in the city. The title of the conference, Urban Lifestyles, on which this volume is based, was intentionally broad in the hope that a multiplicity of views, research and reports of current practice could be extracted and presented for a multi-disciplinary audience. Although organised under the auspices of the Landscape Institute North East Branch, there was participation and sponsorship from national, regional and local government, the private sector, research and higher education. The international and multi-disciplinary response to this conference indicates the importance given worldwide to the future of cities, urban lifestyles and quality of life. The Keynote speakers represent this broad view. The policy and strategic view is established by Sir John Harman, Chairman of the Environment Agency in the UK and Jonathan Blackie from ONE North East, the Regional Development Agency, whilst the conference was also addressed by the Rt Hon Hilary Armstrong MP, Minister of State for Local Government and the Regions. Tjeerd Deelstra from the Netherlands and Joanne Westphal from the USA use their own particular interests and experience to examine how urban lifestyles can become more healthy and how policy, planning and design can respond to the needs of the most vulnerable groups. In Deelstra's case the emphasis is on the environment and the resourceful, sustainable city, and in Westphal's case on the health of citizens. Terry Farrell is particularly well-known in Newcastle upon Tyne as the designer of major public buildings and master planner of much of the regenerated quayside. He develops the metaphor of the city as a large house as a way to understand the 'dynamics of the public realm and the wonder of scale' and the infinity of possibilities which emerge from the layers of richness and diversity in the city. Graeme Bell, Director of the UK's Town & Country Planning Association, also picks up on this theme of a 'portfolio of solutions' which is now required to solve inner city problems and create new, more balanced settlements. He emphasises the need to put people back into the heart of planning using Ebeneezer Howard's paradigm to develop the idea of a 'Social City Region'. Ken Worpole, an independent researcher and writer well known for his work with the Comedia and Demos Consultancies, picks up the theme of the 'kindness of strangers' and suggests that a successful public realm should entail a development of management and responsibility amongst the users and not rely simply on good design of the physical structure.

The cross-disciplinary nature of the subject has meant that separating the offered papers into discrete sections has been difficult and to a certain extent contrary to the aims of the conference. However, three main themes can be identified within the papers, which clearly indicate the overriding concerns and interest in cities worldwide – the physical spaces, the mechanisms which create places and a particularly strong focus on the contribution of 'people' to city life and functioning.

Within the theoretical focus on the physical fabric of the city, the potential for transforming existing space (Bassand & Zepf) and buildings (Dickinson) has a strongly behavioural and experiental theme (Abbazadegan, Durack, Thwaites). A number of speakers follow this up by reflecting on the experience of the practical restoration of spaces and places, from individual sites (Filor, Gowans, Juvara et al.) to research into the citizen's experience of the wider civic realm (Abrams & Ozdil, Soygenis), and how this should be fed into the practice of transformation and restoration.

The second theme examines policy, planning and place-making, and design and planning for sustainability. Examples which reflect the worldwide movement to provide healthy cities and improve quality of life are investigated (Howes, Evans & Bohrer) and the implications of changing lifestyles, markets and political structures on planning policy that in turn affect the physical fabric are examined (Cipriani & Kitchen, Dimitrova, Kathlene & Lynn). Issues of 'city greening' and the widely varying potential paths to more sustainable city lifestyles are the broad basis for Coles & Bussey, Farmer & Guy and Herrmann to put forward their views, with Turner and Woods providing some examples from practice.

The 'people' theme really runs through all the papers, but in particular there is a very strong focus on issues of perception and policy, culture and diversity. A number of researchers have examined the attitudes and needs of certain groups inhabiting areas within the city (Chung & Jones, Grimm-Pretner & Licka, Rezazedeh, Townshend) and the potential effects of these attitudes on policies and city planning (McCann, Varady & Walker). Exclusion of groups from the decision-making process and issues of local versus central governance are also examined (Cook & Ng, Foord & Evans). The issue of the integration of migrants which has become a political 'hot potato' in many countries, particularly within Europe and Asia, is reflected in papers exploring the challenges of providing an acceptable quality of life for different cultures both in terms of physical space (MacFarlane et al.) and appropriate governance (Ahmed & Thomas).

Overall the interest shown in the conference and the diversity of the papers should provide an additional stimulus for those working in this area, in particular to examine how the new political agendas based very much on 'people power' and sustainability can enrich and enliven city spaces, provide enhanced quality of life to excluded groups and help to retain and restore the beauty and richness of the urban fabric. The organisers hope that the conference will help to provide a stimulus for further dialogue between researchers and practitioners, policy-makers, politicians and planners which will in turn provide new thinking and practice concerning the multiplicity of ways to provide an improved quality of life and quality of environment for urban dwellers.

References

Blowers, A. 1993. The Time for Change. In: A. Blowers (ed.), *Planning for a sustainable environment, A report by the Town & Country Planning Association.* (London, Earthscan) pp. 1-18.

Howard, E. 1889. A Peaceful path to Real Reform, revised edition (1965) entitled Garden Cities of Tomorrow, Faber & Faber (London, Purdom).

Mercer, C. 1975. Living in Cities: Psychology and the Urban Environment, (Harmondsworth, Penguin).

Sennett, R. 1999. The Spaces of Democracy, Harvard Design Magazine, Summer issue, pp. 68- 72.

Ward, Colin 1979. The Child in the City (Harmondsworth, Penguin).

Wright, Frank Lloyd 1958. The Living City (New York, Mentor).

Organisation/Sponsors/Acknowledgements

A small group of landscape architects organised the Conference from which these papers have been drawn, ably and essentially assisted by many other volunteers. All volunteers have busy working lives and the Landscape Institute, on behalf of whom the conference was staged, wishes to go on record to express its thanks and appreciation for the considerable and sustained effort that has been committed to what will certainly be a superbly successful conference.

The Landscape Institute would particularly like to thank Tony Walker (Chairman), Harry Shipley (Treasurer), Liz Bray (Secretary), Tom Robinson (Coordination) and John Benson (Speakers and Papers) for their enthusiasm and drive, with additional and invaluable support provided by the North East Branch of the Landscape Institute, private landscape practices, local government departments, landscape professionals and the University of Newcastle upon Tyne.

The Chartered Landscape Institute, The Environment Agency and ONE Northeast (Regional Development Agency) must be mentioned not only for their substantial financial support, but also for their ongoing advice and assistance provided to the conference working group in the build up to the event itself. This main sponsorship was supplemented by a large number of other sponsors from the business, commercial and professional communities, to whom the organisers are immensely grateful.

At the time of finalising this note, the following individuals and organisations had contributed significantly through their time or financial support to the Conference:

Main Organising Committee: John Benson, University of Newcastle upon Tyne; Liz Bray, City of Newcastle; Tom Robinson, Robinson Penn; Harry Shipley, Gateshead Metropoliton Council; Tony Walker, Anthony Walker & Partners.

Other Assistance: Nancy Corbett, Robinson Penn; Mayda Henderson, RPS Consultants; John Hogger, The Environment Agency; Sue Jackson, Stockton Borough Council; Kevin Johnson, City of Sunderland; Gerry Kemp, Glen Kemp Ltd; Steve Laws, The Landmark Partnership; Maggie Roe, University of Newcastle upon Tyne; Eleanor Silk, The Landscape Institute.

Main Sponsors: The Landscape Institute; The Environment Agency; ONE Northeast.

Other Sponsors: Brambledown landscapes; Carfax Publishing (Taylor & Francis Ltd); English Landscapes; Government Office for the North East; J W S Landscapes; Lumsden and Caroll; Melcourt Industries; North East Branch of the Landscape Institute.

Editors' Acknowledgements: The proceedings of some conferences appear months or even years after the event. These papers were produced before the conference. This was only possible because of the willingness of the authors, with or without cajoling and threats from us, to produce their papers to a very tight deadline and we are very grateful to them all for their hard work and tolerance of our demands. Emma Reynolds in the School of Architecture, Planning and Landscape at the University of Newcastle undertook all the editorial and formatting corrections needed to make final production possible. Finally, we would like to thank A.A. Balkema Publishers, Netherlands, and especially A.T. Balkema and production coordinator Louis Dumoulin, for their faith in the project and their efficient handling of the production process.

John Benson & Maggie Roe
School of Architecture, Planning & Landscape
University of Newcastle upon Tyne
July 2000

Policy, strategy and urban lifestyles

Urban Lifestyles: Spaces · Places · People, Benson & Roe (eds)
© 2000 Balkema, Rotterdam, ISBN 90 5809 169 4

Urban lifestyles: The future

J. Blackie
ONE Northeast (Regional Development Agency), Newcastle upon Tyne, UK

ABSTRACT

One NorthEast is the Regional Development Agency set up by the Government in April 1999 to help the people of the North East to create and sustain jobs, prosperity and a higher quality of life. The Agency is responsible to the people of the North East and to the UK Government. The Agency has produced a Regional Economic Strategy which provides the framework for economic development in the Region. The Strategy sets out a vision for the North East:

"By 2010, the North East of England is a vibrant and outward looking Region with the aspiration, ambition and confidence to unlock the potential of all its people"

It is the role of the Agency to take a leading strategic role in taking forward the Regional Economic Strategy. All regional partners have agreed the Strategy.

The Regional Economic Strategy itself is based upon the simple idea that, to improve the quality of people's lives in the North East, we need to develop and invest in the Region: economically, socially and environmentally. The following priorities provide the framework to achieving the vision and aims of the Strategy:

B1   Creating wealth by building a diversified, knowledge-driven economy
B2   Establishing an entrepreneurial society
B3   Building an adaptable, highly skilled workforce
B4   Placing our Universities and Colleges at the heart of the North East economy
B5   Meeting 21st Century transport, communication and property needs
B6   Accelerating the renaissance of the North East

It is the role of One NorthEast working closely with key partners to deliver the priorities for the North East. There are 7 key immediate priorities: Creation of Key Partnerships, Clusters, E-business, Business Birth Rate, Regional Education Plan, Skills, Technology and Knowledge Transfer.

Change is a constant in our lives. We as individuals, and the world around us, are intrinsically linked, and what affects one will inevitably affect the other. At various stages in our lives we are exposed to both physical and social changes, and at this point of change, different people, at different stages in their lives, are affected at different scales and in different ways. Thus although as a mass we can be universally affected by the same change, the change itself can be highly individual.

When we are faced with a new situation which will cause a change in the way we live our lives, depending upon our particular lifestyle, change is either posed as a threat or an opportunity. By highlighting probable future changes and predicting their probable effect we are able to offset possible problems or conflict with possible solutions. It is as important to recognize possible changes before they occur, enabling preparation for each eventuality, as it is to both recognize and accept that we all go through change.

However although change is unique, we are able to categorize the effects of a change by focusing upon typical lifestyles at regular stages in a person's lifecycle. This prediction of the impact of change using lifestyle scenarios in the urban environment is a useful tool in promoting an individual's acceptance of change.

Urban Lifestyles: Spaces · Places · People, Benson & Roe (eds)
© *2000 Balkema, Rotterdam, ISBN 90 5809 169 4*

Creating an environmental vision

J. Harman
The Environment Agency, UK

ABSTRACT

The Environment Agency was formed in 1996 around a sustainability agenda and has a major role in helping the UK Government achieve its sustainable development aims. Since that time the thinking on sustainable development, both nationally and internationally, has moved on significantly and the Government has comprehensively redefined the scope and priorities for sustainable development in the UK, in its sustainable development strategy "A Better Quality of Life". In the broadest sense Urban Lifestyles must take on board the most current approaches to sustainability.

While, as the Environment Agency, we naturally focus on the environment we also recognise that protecting and improving the environment is fundamentally linked with social progress and wealth creation. Sustainable development is about maintaining a careful balance between all the forces which impact on our quality of life, whether urban or rural, local or international.

To achieve a more sustainable way of life and to support lifestyles desired by the community, whether urban or rural, will require us all to work together and to have common goals. The Environment Agency is primarily an environmental regulator but we are keenly aware of the need to work in partnership with others: planners, designers, funding organisations, private businesses, government, the public, etc., in order to make our country a better place to live.

There are many factors to be taken into account when planning for urban communities in the future:

- Predicted global temperature rise and changes in sea levels;
- Population growth;
- Transport demands;
- Management of liquid and solid wastes;
- Inefficient use of resources;
- Changing land use patterns and the need to more effective re-use land;
- Sustaining biodiversity;
- Linking environmental quality and human health;
- Aesthetic qualities: landscapes, light pollution, noise, smell;
- Changing demands for leisure use, with impacts well beyond the urban setting.

This is why we have taken the opportunity to develop a new 'Vision for the Environment'. This vision aims to make a real difference to the quality of life, and the lifestyles of all citizens, and we believe it is both visionary and inspiring. We will be seeking to ensure people can have peace of mind from knowing that they live in a clean, safe and diverse environment which they can use, appreciate and enjoy.

Planning, design and urban lifestyles

Urban Lifestyles: Spaces · Places · People, Benson & Roe (eds)
© 2000 Balkema, Rotterdam, ISBN 90 5809 169 4

Getting there: Working towards places that last

Tj. Deelstra
The International Institute for the Urban Environment (IIUE), Delft, Netherlands

ABSTRACT: Global population growth concentrating in cities and increased ecological foot-prints require a new planning and design concept: the resourceful city. The aim is to make effi-cient use of both natural and human resources. There is some experience with design principles on how to incorporate natural resource management in urban planning. Attempts are being made to formulate programmes for the economy of the resourceful city. About life style and values in the resourceful city a lot has been published, but theory is only marginally applied. Scenario's can be helpful to discuss and choose possible options on how we want to live in the resourceful city and which urban form and architecture will meet our aspirations.

1 SETTLEMENT FORM AND ITS REASONS

Looking into the history and development of human settlements can help us to understand the reason for form, economy (or settlement function) and lifestyle. Any typology of urban evolu-tion is of course an over-simplification. Keywords (table 1) however might provide a frame-work in which to discuss possible future developments. (Forde, 1934; Steward, 1955; Thomas, 1956; Rapoport, 1969; Wilkinson, 1973; Kostof, 1991; Sassen, 1991).

Table 1. A typology of settlement evolution

Type	Form	Economy	Lifestyle	Reason
temporary	windscreens, huts, trees, caves	hunting and gathering	nomadic	survival
semi permanent	villages and agro-towns	agriculture	egalitarian	comfort
permanent	towns, near har-bours, oases, crossroads	trade of surplus produc-tion of food and materials	specialist: administra-tion, religion, craftmanship, power, military defense	safety
permanent	cities	industry, accumulation of capital and human resources	mechanisation	production
permanent - virtual	networks or urban regions	global exchange: tech-nology, commerce and trade, transport, services and communi-cation	personal choice (neo-nomadic)	flexibility

2 URBAN RESOURCE USE

At the end of the last millennium, the world's population reached six billion, meaning that it had doubled since 1960, or in 40 years (United Nations Population Fund, 1999). The world's population is still increasing rapidly, by 77 million a year. It may grow to nine billion or more by 2050. Population growth (increase in the number of people per year) however, is slowing down in many places in the world. Growth is highest in the least developed countries and lowest in the more developed industrial countries. This implies that the regional distribution of the world's population is changing from day to day.

The process of urbanisation is strongly related to regional population growth. Cities grow faster than rural areas, because cities offer much more economic and socio-cultural opportunities. Economic wealth is increasingly interwoven with the phenomenon of urbanisation. Each year the world's urban population grows by more than 60 million. Today, over forty-five percent of the world's population already lives in urban settlements.

The proportion of people in developing countries which live in cities, has almost doubled over the past 40 years (from less than 22 per cent in the early 1960s to more than 40 per cent in the late 1990s). In more developed regions, the urban share has grown from 61 per cent to 76 per cent in these 40 years. Although the proportion of people living in cities in less developed countries (LDCs) was still much lower than in more developed regions in the 1970s, the LDCs are expected to catch up towards the middle of the twenty first century.

The majority of people in Asia and Africa still live in rural areas, but in these regions urban areas are currently facing an average annual growth rate of between three and four percent, which is faster than their overall average population growth (Deelstra et al., 2000).

Cities are great consumers of natural resources, that are needed for life and work in the city (Douglas, 1983). To supply growing cities with food, water, materials and energy, more resources are rapidly explored and exploited. However, the systems of transformation of resources into products and services in cities are not very efficient. Cities are main sources of pollution, local, regional and global. Pollution in the form of solid waste, fluid and gaseous waste, and heat, are in fact spoiled resources.

When settlements are small and technologies simple, the use of natural resources and pollution of the environment will remain within the restoration capacity of ecosystems.

Pre-industrial towns had environmental impacts, but catchment areas remained limited. Industrial cities were the first settlements that started to change the environment irreversibly. Urban planning tried to counteract and make living conditions in cities more healthy with remedies such as zoning and separation of the main urban functions of housing, working, recreation and transport. Urban environmental policies were to make 'higher chimneys'. Nowadays we know that dilution is not the solution to pollution. The 'curative' approach has to be replaced by preventative policies. The urban regions and megacities of today contribute so seriously to global ecological change, that new planning concepts are needed.

Ecological footprint analysis is an accounting tool that helps to estimate the resource consumption and waste assimilation requirements of a city in terms of a corresponding area of land (Rees, & Wackernagel, 1995).

With this in mind, the concept of the urban 'ecological footprint' has been developed. Ecological footprint analysis reveals the growing competing demands on natural capital. In less developed countries footprints are still limited. Delhi, India, for instance 'consumed' already twenty years ago 'only' three times its surface to produce the firewood which is brought into the city. When one calculates the area of land needed for Delhi's food and water more surface has to be added (Rajarajeswari, 1986). London in the U.K. has already a footprint of about 125 times its area.

The ecological footprints of cities nowadays do not necessarily coincide with their home regions. Many cities are now dependent on imports of resources and products from remote hinterlands. The earth's ecosystems have limited production capacity. If resources are harvested too rapidly, nature is not able to restore and will lose its resilience. Over-exploitation is a serious risk for urban development. It has been calculated, that if everybody should adopt a lifestyle as is common in North America, three globes would be needed to remain within the capacity of the earth's life-support system. General adoption of the more urban European or Japanese lifestyle would require two planet earth's. The different impacts of contrasting settlement form can also be illustrated by the level of use of fossil fuels. Cities in low-income countries use about a fifth of the volume of fossil fuels used in European and Japanese cities, and a tenth of what is consumed in North American cities.

Estimations of urban ecological footprints raise the issues both of equity and the long-term sustainability of production. The current systems of trade, monetary flows, production and consumption allows only a small group of people to increase their wealth. In the future, cities in non-industrialised countries will demand their part of global wealth. If footprints of cities can not be reduced, the growing demand on natural resources will lead to more conflicts (Mac-Donald, with Delft, 1997).

3 TOWARDS THE RESOURCEFUL CITY

A new urban concept, the 'resourceful city' aims to address the problems of urban growth and the needs to reduce the consumption of natural resources (Deelstra, & de Hoop, 1990).

Cities do not necessarily have to be such serious causes of environmental degradation as they are today. Not at all. Cities offer unique possibilities to contribute to sustainable resource management. Cities have the potential to combine safe and healthy living conditions and culturally rich and enjoyable lifestyles with relatively low levels of energy and water consumption, material use and waste production. However it requires good knowledge to wisely use the large volumes, and great variety of natural resources that are nowadays spoiled by cities.

The advantage of cities in comparison to dispersed settlement patterns is due to the large number of people working and living together in a relatively small area. The physical concentration can well be used for better resource management.

The first advantage that creates opportunities is the volume of production and consumption. This offers a great range of possibilities for efficient use of resources, through the reclamation of materials and water, and their reuse or recycling.

Second: high densities can lead to much lower costs for resource efficient public services in the water and waste management sectors. Think about the provision of piped, treated water supply from renewable sources, the collection and disposal of domestic waste or cleaning of waste water for re-use.

The third potential environmental benefit of cities is related to the possibility to reduce fossil fuels. Because of short distances waste process heat from industry or thermal power stations can provide indoor heating for homes and commercial buildings. Another opportunity is efficient co-generation of electricity and heat in residential areas. Cooling can also be organised much more efficiently when buildings are concentrated.

Benefit number four is that (densely built) cities have a much greater potential for limiting the use of motor vehicles, greatly reducing the fossil fuels they need (and consequently air pollution). Cities enable many more trips to be made on foot or by bicycle; opportunities for public transport are more efficient and economical. Thus, although cities tend to be associated with a high level of private automobile use, cities and urban systems also represent the greatest potential for allowing their inhabitants quick and cheap access to a wide range of locations, without the need to use cars.

The fifth advantage of high population concentrations, is the opportunity for innovations. The level of interaction leads to new ideas and the wide rage of economic activities to the exploration of all kinds of niches for new businesses. The accumulation of capital and human resources make investments and new kinds of enterprise easily possible, also in the resource management sector.

The sixth advantage of cities is that community involvement will have a large environmental impact, because of the massive number of people involved. In cities, people and communities are relatively easy to reach, which can make the dissemination of information (for example on health, environment and lifestyles) easy and quick. Awareness raising actions towards environmentally sound behaviour and resource conservation can accelerate change.

The final benefit to be mentioned is the reduced need of land for cities, in comparison with sprawl or a dispersed land use pattern. The concentration of people in cities limits the demand for natural resource area, relative to population. In most countries, the built-up areas of cities take up less than one per cent of the national territory. Of course, the ecological footprint of settlements is always larger than the built up area itself. But it is important to realise that the entire urban population of today's world would fit into an area of 200.000 square kilometres, if this was shaped similar to Europe's much valued inner-city residential areas. This is comparable to half of Finland's surface, or to the size of an average American state, such as Kansas for instance; it would be equal more or less to Gabon, Ecuador or Bolivia, just to give other examples.

4 SHAPING THE RESOURCEFUL CITY

Every type of ecosystem has its special scale, and requires policies attuned to that scale (Andruss, Van et al., 1990). The environmental component of air should be the subject of policies at the level of climate regions. Water should be managed at the watershed level, and soils at the level of regional landscapes.

The efficient re-utilisation of wastes from cities require also special scales. For instance, the reuse of mercury, which is not managed in large quantities, will need a substantial number of waste producers in order to become feasible. But organic household waste can be recycled at the level of individual households. Thus, we have to organise 'ecology's of scale'.

Urban regions or city networks with a few million inhabitants will provide optimum scales to organise the resourceful city (Lynch, 1991). In terms of land use, such urban regions should however be interspersed with voluminous green areas. These areas could be used for forestry or agricultural production, or could be shaped as marshland, combining water storage and waste water cleaning, recreation and nature conservation. Green areas and water are also important to make the urban micro-climate pleasant. The built up areas should be conceived as rather dense, with a mix of functions and types of inhabitants. These areas should be clustered along public transport lines. The urban region could consist of a mix of heritage cities and new towns, of smaller and larger concentrations, each with its own characteristics and environmental features.

It is possible to design a 'time path' for how to (re)develop such region and use moments when new investments should be made for the right decisions. A 'decision tree' will become instrumental for urban planning at this scale.

When it comes to the level of clusters of built environments key aspects of resource management are related to landscape, water, nature, transport, energy, materials and waste. They are not mentioned at random; the sequence reflects the phases of decision making on these subjects in an appropriate urban planning process. 'Landscape' is more determining of urban form than 'waste'.

A large range of urban ecological studies and observations is available; there is also tested experience with environmentally compatible urban planning. Theory and practise learns that some principles can be formulated to help design the resourceful city (McHarg, 1969; Spirn, 1984; Dawe, 1990; Van der Ryn & Calthorpe, 1991; Perks & Van Vliet, 1993; Downton & Munn, 1996; Expert Group on the Urban Environment, 1996; Zeiher, 1996; Daniels, 1997; Deelstra & Nijwening, 1997; Kennedy & Kennedy, 1997; Breuste et al., 1998; Deelstra & Boyd, 1998; Spiegel & Meadows, 1999; Williams et al., 2000).

4.1 Landscape

Geomorphology, soil and water are inextricably linked together, forming the basis of the landscape pattern. Building activities change this connection. But in most cases, even in the inner parts of cities where building activities over ages have radically transformed original landscapes, patterns and features will be recognisable. Think about relief and watercourses. Landscape elements, such as hills, forests, trees can provide orientation points and serve as 'living memory', but may also be valuable as natural habitats. The landscape pattern and its elements provide the basis of any urban design.

4.2 Water

Cities should physically be structured in relation to water courses. Water courses are directly linked with landscape form and soils. Water networks can be seen as arteries of the built environment. Resourceful water management depends on five interrelated principles: the efficient use of (expensive and scarce) drinking water, the preservation of (clean) existing water bodies for local functions, the prevention of pollution and possible reparation of natural water systems and the attuning of the form of the built environment to the demands of water flows (for instance by limiting the amount of non penetrable hard covered surface). Water management can support nature development. The micro climate in densely built urban areas can benefit from the presence of water; cities with water will have more balanced temperatures and humidity.

4.3 *Nature*

Cities can support the development of nature. In fact cities add a-biotic conditions to those at the original site, with new micro-climates, and more surfaces because of the articulated form of buildings. This gives opportunities for specific urban vegetation and wildlife. Urban agriculture and forestry is of great value for the city's climate management, food production and production of materials. The educational, recreational and experiential value of urban greenery should not be neglected. Through concentration and zoning of green areas: from intense use to less busy and more 'natural', and by creating green arteries in the urban fabric, functions can be compatibly combined.

4.4 *Mobility*

Mobility processes play an important role in urban development. The use of automobiles affects the environment at different levels. The effects are recognised in the form of air pollution, unsafe traffic situations, noise and smell hindrance and the confiscation of vast areas of land. Outside the local area, acidification and climate change are consequences of the greenhouse effect.

Appropriate planning entails; reduction of automobile usage; utilisation of public transport; stimulation of slow traffic (walking, bicycling).

Reduction of car usage can be stimulated by selective choice of building sites, so that these are easily connected to existing urban networks (access roads, public transport etc.). Further measures can be applied in the urban lay out to stimulate slow traffic, use of public transport and to discourage car usage. The best results are often achieved when these measures are combined with 'mobility management', meaning the creation of information systems for users, which help them to choose and combine ad-hoc modes of transport. Well structured public transport systems, as well as road systems for selective automobile use, will highly contribute to the liveability and resourcefulness of cities.

4.5 *Energy*

The use of non-renewable fossil fuels for energy services has local (air pollution) as well as regional/global (acidification, climate change) effects on the environment.

A strategy for more sustainable energy management - with consequently less environmental damage - is made up of three elements: a switch to renewable energy sources (hydropower, wind, earth warmth, biogas and the sun), reduced use of fossil fuels (wind screens, isolation, compact building, zoning in buildings and 'good housekeeping'), as well as efficiency improvement (co-generation, heat pumps, etc.).

In architectural construction knowledge of orientation towards or turned from the sun should be incorporated.

When building as compact, even and sheltered as possible, temperatures will be balanced; this reduces energy use. Efficient energy distribution infrastructures are good means to save fuels.

4.6 *Materials*

The construction of the built environment necessitates the use of large quantities of raw materials. Careful management of raw materials can be exercised in all phases of the (re)development process, such as selective use of non-renewable resources, by reuse of waste materials and by substituting dangerous and exhaustible materials for environment-friendly alternatives. One should not only think about buildings but also about infrastructures. Infrastructure includes systems of roads, bicycle paths, footpaths, street furnishings, bridges, viaducts and tunnels, parking places and also pipelines for water and gas, cables for telecommunication and electricity etc. The use of materials is reduced by means of shorter and more efficient networks, and the careful selection and reuse of materials.

4.7 *Solid waste*

Wherever people build, live and work unwanted waste is created. Much of this waste is damaging to the environment and public health, it can not be reused and must be dumped or incinerated. One of the causes of the huge flow of waste products is the inefficient use of resources and products: too many mixtures of plastics, paper and/or metals in a single product makes it unfit for recycling and it therefore has to be dumped or incinerated. A further cause of mounting waste is the inefficient infrastructure for the separated processing of waste, which also reduces chances of recycling. The prevention of waste cannot be achieved through urban planning. However, it is possible to stimulate the processing of this waste by incorporating efficient disposal, collection and recycling systems and the provision of (public) amenities for separated storage and recycling of waste.

5 ECONOMY AND THE RESOURCEFUL CITY

Sustainable development is a comprehensive phrase often used these days. It reflects the necessity to move from pure economic growth towards a balanced development, based on wise use of resources, a robust economy, a healthy environment and social cohesion (World Commission on Environment and Development 1987).

Urban areas are crucial to national and global economic development (Jacobs, 1984). Within a globalising economy cities will have to compete more and more (Brotchie *et al.*, 1994). The global economic role of cities is decisive for the future of their home regions. A major competition factor is the quality of the local living environment. This is essential to attract knowledge workers, and knowledge industry will certainly shape the future. Despite the advantages of new information technologies, face to face contact between people remains a key factor for economy and its underlying technological and societal innovation: mutual trust is the basis of any economic interaction.

A balanced urban development means the creation of a local economy, in which all those wishing to participate can do so. Economic development should allow people to take control of their future and achieve a better quality of life (Daly & Cobb, 1989). However, conventional wisdom states that the best indicator of a country's development is its level of Gross Domestic Product (GDP). Nevertheless, GDP offers little insight into the quality of life, being simply a measure of products bought and sold. It does nothing more than add up transactions, making no attempt to distinguish between transactions that add to the quality of life and those that diminish it. As a result, the GDP increases every time there is a car crash, a divorce, an oil spill or an earthquake, because all of these socially or environmentally negative events represent economic activity, of rescue services, health care services, legal services and so on. In other words, the link between social and economic inefficiency and problems such as crime, noise pollution, inequality and environmental degradation is underestimated. Recent work to compile alternatives to GDP provide better measures of a country's development – for example, the Sustainable Welfare Index and the Human Development Index – are to be welcomed (Deelstra *et al.*, 1999).

Environmental problems and social exclusion have made many people realise the need for a more balanced economic system. This system, a 'sustainable economy', would not only use human and natural resources efficiently, but would develop new technologies, taking account of social and ecological needs instead of only mass production and low costs. An important reason for employment growth in a sustainable economy would be the efficiency in material use and energy resources requiring technological change with far less emphasis on reducing labour inputs. In this economic concept, benefits for society take priority over lowering of costs by means of improved production technologies.

6 LIFESTYLE AND FORM OF THE RESOURCEFUL CITY

Lifestyle in the resourceful city will vary a lot. It makes great difference when shaping a city in Africa, Asia, the Arab world, Europe, Latin America, North America or Australia.

Not only climate, landscape and natural conditions differ, and the cities' economic role, but also values, perceptions and belief.

Cities should be shaped according to the aspirations of its inhabitants. Points of departure are concepts of how to make places liveable and good.

In many cultures, homes and also cities have, in addition to their practical and social function, also a spiritual dimension. In many cultures outside industrialised regions, gods, goddesses and spirits are supposed to be present in the landscape. Cities are then somehow comparable with the cloth of heavenly bodies. The location, lay out and time of building activities need therefore to be chosen properly according to rules. Homes should fit well into the great house of the city, cities should fit properly in the landscape around (Deelstra, 1990).

Examples of this concept are the traditional building codes of pre-industrial China, the Indian sub-continent and South East Asia (Gutschow & Sieverts, 1978). In many parts of these regions these building codes are still in daily use. In Europe, the art of building and planning was originally also supposed to be inspired by the 'genius loci' (Rykwert, 1976).

However, in the course of industrialisation, architecture and urban design were explicitly made 'rational'. Not only in Europe, but also in the cities of the 'new world', in North and Latin America, and in Australia. And, through training in western schools of architecture, also in the 'second' and 'third' world. This led to the twentieth century international style (Giedion, 1941). The idea was to formulate a universal recipe. This style was supposed to bring about safe and healthy urban living conditions on a global scale. The principles of the new functionalism were to be applied on every location.

In traditional building methods, much knowledge is incorporated about local climate (temperature, humidity, light, flows of water and wind) and the use of local energy sources and building materials. Traditional building methods may be attuned well and even support existing lifestyles and social relations. The question is whether we want to maintain traditions. Maybe social changes occur, by choice or through influences from outside (because of todays global scale of commerce and communication). The choice should be made as to how to link up todays urban development with images of the past (Lynch, 1972) and combine existing elements from lifestyle, and maybe belief and ritual with opportunities for the future. A general principle is that people have to be able to recognise something of themselves in their surroundings.

In industrialised urban regions are values that shape urban form, humanitarian by nature. This implies the right of personal expression of ideas and opinions (if these are not detrimental to others). In the built environment however, in most industrialised countries people are only marginally allowed to express their ideas. Consequently, people do not know the value of the art of architecture. Since they are not able to learn by experience what design processes are, they have to rely on impressions of what is possible in the professional studio's of urban designers, landscape planners and architects. The consequence is that many designers try to draw attention of the public with gadgets and fashionable features, in order to get commissions. This does not make fertile grounds for 'pattern languages' (Alexander et al., 1977) and more modest, though high quality ways of building. Quality is sought in the extreme. However 'it is not the quality that counts, but the quantity - of quality' (van Eyck, 1999).

If any value is shared in our cities of today, it is health. In the last decennium the common aim was to create 'health for all by the year 2000'. This goal has not yet been reached (World Health Organization, 1998). According to the World Health Organization, health is not the mere absence of illness, but means physical, social and mental wellbeing. This implies that the urban environment should not only be safe and clean, with minimal risks for accidents, but also support social life. The urban environment should create opportunities for people to be productive and creative, to meet and communicate, and organise things together (Herzberger, 1991). With respect to mental health it means, among other things, that the environment should pro-

15

vide stimuli for the senses; not only for the eye, on which most architecture focuses, but also for the ear, the nose, mouth and skin and for the body as a whole, allowing movement and orientation. Health in the city means for instance that children can play hide and seek, or observe the big dipper by night, and experience 'safe dangers' walking to school. It would mean that old people can freely go around. It would mean that one can experience the cycles of nature and the seasons. It would imply that one is able to observe and experience in the same neighbourhood the changing phases of human life from birth through growing up, and growing old to death. (Deelstra *et al.*, 1976).

One can speak of a really 'good' city if these kinds of things are possible. The degree to which the needs of the most vulnerable groups of the urban population are taken into account determines the quality of life in the city. This has to be taken as an indicator for good urban environments.

The literature on the subject is overwhelming. Think about the classical studies of Lynch (Banerjee & Southworth, 1990) or Alexander (Alexander *et al.*, 1987) just to mention a few. Unfortunately, these sources are not well studied and certainly not used in the day to day practise of decision making, planning and design.

7 SCENARIO'S

Lifestyle in the resourceful city is a question of choice. Very different ways of life are possible that are all equally beneficial to the environment. One lifestyle would be very dominated by technology. Think about a computer controlled electric car, or water saving shower. Another lifestyle would be more dependent on - perhaps time consuming - organisation. Think about car sharing, or using a dry toilet from which the compost has to be brought to the garden frequently. Both lifestyles are based on individual choices. They could be combined in one city, if the market provides the necessary technologies. But more collective lifestyles are also possible. Think about public transport and double piping systems for drinking water and household water. Inhabitants can choose, in full environmental awareness, for these solutions. These solutions include advanced technologies, whose maintenance is dependent on for instance the local authority. Inhabitants 'delegate' so to say activities to the more communal level. They could also choose for more 'soft' communal solutions, which require more organisational responsibilities. A neighbourhood bus, managed by volunteers, is an example from the area of transport. With respect to water they could for instance install a waste water cleansing pond in the neighbourhood, ask a school to combine the monitoring of water quality with nature education, and a group of elderly people to cut the reeds at the end of the season. Solutions of all kinds would require some time for negotiation, supervision and financial management and control.

An important part of the local planning process is to look ahead and decide which lifestyles we wish to develop in the future. In the rush of everyday life this can be difficult, but without reflecting on where development is aimed, it is hard to decide on how to arrive at this aim. Scenarios for the future can help to provide indications of how (parts of) the city should – or definitely should not – appear in say, 25 years time (The International Institute for the Urban Environment 1996).

Such scenarios can be developed along two axes:
– WHO should be responsible for solving each particular problem - individual households, local authorities, or something in between?
– HOW? What role should 'advanced' technology play in solving these problems - should we look to technical or to organisational solutions for the problems of sustainable urban development?

By plotting these two axes against each other a matrix can be arrived at providing four extremes (Figure 1). These extremes are not really intended as choices in themselves but more as a stimulus to help shift thoughts from daily concerns to a longer term view. The choices can be classified as:
– Individual versus collective i.e. problems are experienced one way or the other, solutions can be brought about individually or can be seen as a collective effort (solutions had to be conceived as the responsibility of only one organisation within a municipality, etc.).

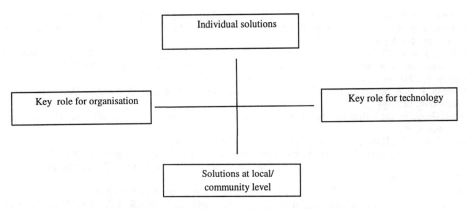

Figure 1: Four extremes make four possible scenarios

- (High) technology versus organisation i.e. problems could be conceived of in terms of degrees of technological sophistication either in utilising old techniques that may be fairly easily manageable without outside experts, or in employing the very latest of automated novelties requiring highly specialised operators.

To illustrate these extremes more concretely, four types of city can be conceived, each with its own characteristics. All four scenarios can result in a sustainable city but choices have to be made as to which scenario is desired and how that choice can be realised. For each scenario it is possible to identify issues to be considered in more detail (Bom, 1998).

When drawing up scenario's the skills of design experts are extremely helpful. Architects, landscape planners and urban designers can easily transform programmatic issues into imaginative images. And these are images that we have to share, when it comes to turning our cities into places in which we would like to be born, live and die.

REFERENCES

Alexander, C. et al. 1977. A Pattern Language. Towns, Buildings, Construction. New York: Oxford University Press

Alexander, C. et al. 1987. A New Theory of Urban Design. Oxford: Oxford University Press

Andruss, Van et al., eds. 1990. Home! A Bioregional Reader. Gabriola Island, BC: New Society Publishers

Banerjee, T. & Southworth, M. eds. 1990. City Sense and City Design. Writings and Projects of Kevin Lynch. Cambridge, Mass. & London: MIT Press

Bom, I. ed. 1998. Fleximodo. Manual on Urban Ecology, Urban Mobilty, Urban Information and Communication. European Awareness Scenario Workshop. N. pl (Luxemburg): European Commission DG XIII/D

Breuste, J. et al. eds. 1998. Urban Ecology. Berlin, Heidelberg, New York: SpringerVerlag

Brotchie, J. et al. eds. 1994. Cities in Competition. Melbourne: Cheshire

Daly, H. E. & Cobb, J.B. 1989. For the Common Good: Redirecting the Economy Toward Community, the Environment and a Sustainable Future. Boston: Beacon Press

Daniels, K. 1997. The Technology of Ecological Building: Basic Principles and Ideas. Basel, Boston, Berlin: Birkhäuser Verlag

Dawe, G. ed. 1990. The Urban Environment. A Sourcebook for the 1990's. Birmingham: Centre for Urban Ecology

Deelstra, Tj. et al. 1976. Beyond Shelter. In search of a better living environment. Amsterdam: Visual Arts Office for Abroad

Deelstra, Tj. & de Hoop, W. eds. 1990. The Resourceful City, Management Approaches to Efficient Cities Fit to Live in. Amsterdam: Royal Academy of Science of the Netherlands

Deelstra, Tj. (ed.) 1990. Human Settlements and Sustainable Development in the Third World. The Hague: Netherlands Ministry of Housing, Physical Planning and the Environment

Deelstra, Tj. & Nijwening, S. 1997. Environmental Sustainability of Cities. Management Issues and Experiences in Developing Countries. Den Haag: SNV Netherlands Development Organisation

17

Deelstra, T. & Boyd, D. eds. 1998. Indicators for Sustainable Urban Development Delft: IIUE

Deelstra, T. et al. eds. 1999. Developing the Economy from Within. Striking the balance between global and local development. Delft: IIUE

Deelstra, T. et al. 2000. Urbanisation, Health and Environment. Report for UNEP's Global Environmental Outlook, commissioned by the Netherlands Institute for Health and Environment RIVM. Delft: IIUE

Douglas, I. 1983. The Urban Environment. London: Edward Arnold

Downton, P. F. & Munn, D. 1996. Urban Ecology Annotated Bibliography, 2nd edition. Adelaide: Centre for Urban Ecology

Expert Group on the Urban Environment. 1996. European Sustainable Cities. Report. Brussels: European Commission

Forde, C.D. 1934. Habitat, Economy and Society. London: Methuen

Giedion, S. 1941. Space, Time and Architecture. Cambridge, Mass.: Harvard University Press

Gutschow, N. & Sieverts, T. eds. 1978. Urban Space and Ritual. Darmstadt : Technische Hochschule, Fachgruppe Stadt

Herzberger, H. 1991. Lessons for Students in Architecture. Rotterdam: 010 Publishers

Jacobs, J. 1984. Cities and the Wealth of Nations: Principles of Economic Life. New York: Random House

Kennedy, M. & Kennedy, D. eds. 1997. Designing Ecological Settlements. Ecological Planning and Building; Experiences in New Housing and in the Renewal of Existing Housing Quarters in European Countries. Berlin: Reimer

Kostof, S. 1991. The City Shaped: Urban Patterns and Meanings Through History. London: Thames & Hudson

Leitman, J. 1999. Sustaining Cities. Environmental Planning and Management in Urban Design. New York: MacGraw-Hill

Lynch, K. 1972. What Time is this Place? Cambridge, Mass.: MIT Press

Lynch, K. 1991. A Theory of Good City Form. Cambridge, Mass.: MIT Press

MacDonald, F. with Delft, Y. van, eds. 1997. The Ecological Footprint of Cities. Delft: IIUE

McHarg, I. L. 1969. Design with Nature. Garden City, NY: The Natural History Press

Perks, W. & Van Vliet, D. 1993. Assessment of Built Projects for Sustainable Communities. Ottawa: Canada Mortgage and Housing Corporation

Rajarajeswari P. 1986. Environmental impacts of food and energy production in India. The United Nations University Food Energy Nexus Program. UNU: Paris

Rapoport, A. 1969. House Form and Culture. New York: Prentice Hall

Rees, W. E. & Wackernagel, M. 1995 Our Ecological Footprint: reducing human impact on the earth. Gabriola Island BC: New Society Publishers

Rykwert, J. 1976. The Idea of a Town. The Anthropology of Urban Form in Rome, Italy and the Ancient World. New Jersey: Princeton University Press

Sassen, S. 1991. The Global City; New York, London, Tokyo. London, New York, Tokyo: Princeton University Press

Spiegel, R. & Meadows, D. 1999. Green Building Materials. A Guide to Product Selection and Specification. New York, etc.: John Wiley

Spirn, A. W. 1984. The Granite Garden: Urban Nature and Human Design. New York: Basic Books

Steward, J. H. 1955. Theory of Culture Change. Urbana: University of Illinois Press

The International Institute for the Urban Environment 1996. Local Scenario Workshops in the LEC Network, Final report. Delft: IIUE

Thomas, W. L. Jr., ed. 1956. Man's Role in Changing the Face of the Earth. Chicago: The University of Chicago Press

United Nations Population Fund. 1999. 6 Billion: A Time for Choices. World Population Report 1999. New York: UNFP

Van Eyck, A. 1999. Works. Compilation by Vincent Ligtelijn. Basel, Boston, Berlin; Birkhäuser Verlag

Van der Ryn, S. & Calthorpe P. eds. 1991. Sustainable Communities. A New Design Synthesis for Cities, Suburbs and Towns. San Francisco: Sierra Club

Wilkinson, R.G. 1973. Poverty and Progress. An Ecological Model of Economic Development. London: Methuen

Williams, K. et al. eds. 2000. Achieving Sustainable Urban Form. London: E & FN Spon

World Health Organisation 1998. The World Health Report 1998: Life in the 21st century, a vision for all. Geneva: WHO

World Commission on Environment and Development 1987. Our Common Future. Oxford University Press: Oxford, New York

Zeiher, L. C. 1996. The Ecology of Architecture. A Complete Guide to Creating Environmentally Conscious Building. New York: Whitney Library of Design

Urban Lifestyles: Spaces · Places · People, Benson & Roe (eds)
© *2000 Balkema, Rotterdam, ISBN 90 5809 169 4*

Hype, hyperbole, and health: Therapeutic site design

J. M. Westphal
Michigan State University, Landscape Architecture Program, East Lansing, Mich., USA

ABSTRACT: This paper presents an overview of therapeutic site design from the viewpoint of a medical practitioner. Its purpose is to provide realistic goals for design professionals in creating environments that support different patient groups in managed care settings. It begins with a brief overview of historic garden areas in hospital settings, discusses the concept of therapeutic site design, and provides a series of contemporary examples where therapeutic site design has been attempted in the United States. Because an extraordinary amount of hype and hyperbole has surrounded many modern "therapeutic", "restorative", and/or "healing" gardens, the author seeks to use the case studies to strip the topic to its bare essentials—i.e., patients, disease process, standard treatment protocols, and therapeutic outcomes. By encouraging designers to work within this medical framework, she is confident that optimal benefits for patients will be derived from site design. The paper concludes with recommendations for design professionals that would advance the art and science of therapeutic site design.

1 INTRODUCTION

In recent years, interest in therapeutic site design in the United States, especially in managed care settings, has created widespread discourse on its medical benefits. Nationally syndicated newspapers (Raver, 1994; San Francisco Chronicle, 1998) and popular as well as professional magazines (LAM, 1995; Ulrich, 1986) have cited instances where garden areas have had notable positive effects on patient groups. Likewise, numerous books and proceedings, including standard medical references (PDR, 1998), have been printed on the subject (Swerdlow, 2000; Cooper-Marcus & Barnes, 1999; Gerlach-Spriggs *et al*, 1997; Brawley, 1997; Tyson, 1996; Mintner, 1994; Francis *et al*, 1994). These tangible examples are evidence of the enthusiasm that has marked this movement in American society. Titled "therapeutic", "restorative", and/or "healing" gardens, these designed spaces are intended to function as an adjuvant therapy within conventional western medicine protocols. A critical review of this literature, however, shows that much more hype[i] and hyperbole[ii] accompanies many of these designed spaces than health[iii]. The purpose of this paper is to discuss these deficiencies in an effort to improve the end products of the design process.

If one examines the materials carefully, three critical points of omission are prominent. First, while many garden areas do generate remarkable responses from individual patients, research on consistent overall benefits to groups of patients with similar illnesses is absent completely. From a research stand point, case studies without scientifically reliable and valid research designs severely limit our predictive capacity in establishing likely therapeutic outcomes for certain patient populations. Another omission in most articles is insight as to which diseases are most appropriately addressed through design. A corollary to this is what specific design components lead to the creation of an environment that supports improved health conditions in certain patient populations. Finally, the articles fail to address how healing gardens interface with the traditional roles, responsibilities, and limitations of key players in health care delivery today, and more importantly, how they actually serve as adjuvant therapies within conventional medical protocols.

Therefore, the field of design, with the cooperation of medical practitioners, needs to address some very important issues if garden design is to provide the therapeutic, healing, or restorative qualities for which it is being created. For purposes of this paper, I would like to frame these issues by providing a context by which designers and medical practitioners can go forward in producing meaningful garden spaces within health care today. To do this, I will focus on three questions: 1) what is therapeutic site design and what is its historical roots; 2) what is the present-day art and science of therapeutic site design; and 3) where can we go from here in terms of establishing the actual merits of therapeutic site design to different patient populations?

2 HISTORICAL ROOTS OF THERAPEUTIC SITE DESIGN

A number of books include information on the history of restorative or healing gardens (Cooper-Marcus & Barnes, 1999; Gerlach-Spriggs, 1997). However, one of the most thorough and interesting sources of information can be found in a book on hospital design—i.e., *The Hospital: A Social and Architectural History* (Thompson & Goldin, 1975). According to this book and numerous references that are cited in the work, therapeutic garden design can trace its roots in Europe to early Greek asklepieia (around 500 BC). Asklepieia were constructed with the long axis of the patient ward oriented in an east to west fashion along the north wall of the complex. The southern elevation of the ward was open to the sun and an enclosed courtyard. Oftentimes, a temple, official residence of the emperor, a stadium, library, and other buildings occupied a part of the courtyard. The main patient ward was designed to facilitate "dreaming", for the Greeks believed that the therapeutic regimen for curing a malady lay in the subconscious of the patient. Each asklepieion was managed by priests who attended to patient needs through inpatient services like diet, exercise, medication, baths, treatments, etc. If an individual were too ill to travel to an asklepieion, a trusted family member or friend would go to dream instead. According to Rosen (1968), this often led to treatment protocols that produced interesting contrasts to the medical conventions of the time. An excellent example of an Asklepieion can be found in Boehringer (1959).

The Romans were the first to construct military hospitals to facilitate recovery; these structures, called *valetudinarium*, were designed for Roman soldiers who were injured in the field. Similar types of valetudinarium were provided by the state for gladiators and slaves— "individuals who had no homes to go to but were thought to be too valuable to be cast out to die" (Thompson & Goldin, 1975). One of the best examples of a valetudinarium can be found at Vindonissa, 1st century, AD. A series of concentric rectangular wards constituted the hospital design with enlisted men placed in the outer ward and officers in the center ward. A courtyard was a central feature of the hospital design and it was placed immediately adjacent to the officers rooms (Tabanelli, 1960). The Romans believed that fresh air and ambulation were central to the recovery process.

It is thought that the term "hospital" was derived from the term "hospice", a concept that evolved in the Middle Ages. As early at 300 AD, hospices were created for pilgrims (Thompson & Goldin, 1975) as a part of Christian monasticism. During this period, pilgrimages to holy sites were undertaken in an effort to cleanse oneself spiritually. Because many believed that physical illness and/or disease were manifestations of spiritual illness, many pilgrims undertook long arduous journeys to seek repentance. Early Christians believed that "works of mercy" could be embodied in charitable institutions that extended hospitality to the traveler. Therefore, monasteries and convents opened their doors to the infirm, the weary, and the indigent. In exchange for shelter and food, pilgrims were expected to work in garden areas or vineyards. Thus, they were able to perform one form of service for another. Pilgrims of nobler means were given finer accommodations and services in exchange for alms; thus, the first distinction in socio-economic status is seen in hospital settings. The plan of St. Gall monastery, Switzerland, about 820 AD (Horn, 1962) is a good example of a hospice.

As Europe moved into the Dark Ages, monasteries and cloisters were among the few refuges where plant breeding, botanical medicine, animal husbandry, and health care continued to advance. With the Renaissance, hospital design was dominated less by religious orders, and more by lay groups. Public hospitals of two to three stories with central courtyard areas were the standard of the times. The courtyards, however, moved away from their former subsistence function and were used almost exclusively for ambulation, exercise, and fresh air. Eloquent plantings and promenades often were a part of the design. Excellent examples of this type of hospital design in the first half of the eighteenth century can be found in Allegemeines Krankenhaus, Vienna, (Erna Lesky, date unknown) and St. Thomas's Hospital, London (Toms, date unknown).

Even modern hospital design in the United States continued to incorporate interior courtyard areas until the late 1800's. The floor plan and site design for Johns Hopkins Teaching Hospital in Baltimore, Maryland, shows extensive open space areas adjacent to hospital wards in 1876 (Ochsner & Sturm, 1907). At about the same time, shifting theories relating to the transmission of disease, along with technological advances, caused a major shift in hospital design (both interior and exteriorly) during this period. The end result was a movement away from natural fiber materials in hospitals in favor of easily sterilized surfaces, and the grounds of hospitals were sacrificed for improved building infrastructure. At Johns Hopkins the shift was embraced quickly, and it produced very dramatic effects. A later drawing by the architect shows the actual building, as constructed, just a few years later; it failed to carry out the extensive landscaping scheme as originally proposed (Billings, 1890). Today, parking lots and mechanical engineering needs of the facility occupy the proposed open spaces surrounding the hospital.

With the advent of 20th century technology (e.g., x-rays, pathology laboratories, etc.) and specialty fields of medicine, hospital design shifted even more in its three-dimensional form. Escalating urban land values also contributed to this shift. Architecturally, hospital design went up instead of out, and interior courtyards became interior laboratory areas for hospital staff. Thompson & Goldin (1975) call this period the "age of skyscraper possibilities" in hospital design.

With this brief overview of hospital design, one can see that the role of gardens and open space has evolved as the concept of hospitals has evolved. Depending on the particular period, garden areas served to facilitate patients in dreams, ambulation, and repayment of debt; they also served as important sources of food, fiber, and medicine. Only in the late 19th century, did hospitals experience the loss of garden and open space areas. Today, landscaping around hospital complexes in the United States is often relegated to a small green space area at the main entrance of a hospital.

3 CONTEMPORY DEFINITION OF THERAPEUTIC SITE DESIGN

Tight budgets in managed care today require that a strong justification for expenditures relating to hospital infrastructure amenities (like garden areas) be established. Therefore, considerations of benefit-costs must be incorporated into any hospital design. For purposes of this paper, the following definition of therapeutic site design will be used as a yardstick in measuring the effectiveness of a design concept in a managed care settings.

"Therapeutic site design is the creation of three-dimensional spaces (interior and exterior) to facilitate standard treatment protocols and thereby, improve specific therapeutic outcomes for a given patient population. In cases where the projected patient group has a terminal illness, then the provision of space for meaningful activities, including reconciliation and/or reflection, may be the most appropriate design solution" (Westphal, 1997).

This definition works because it fits within the framework of managed care today. Because it considers specific patient groups and "standards of practice" (which is the basis of accountability in medicine today), it allows designers to work within the legal and institutional framework of contemporary medical practice. It also sets "end-points" or goals in terms of patient outcomes. This type of conceptual framework allows designers to creatively develop site solutions that are more effective and meaningful for given patient populations.

4 PRESENT DAY ART & SCIENCE OF THERAPEUTIC SITE DESIGN

4.1 *The Art of Therapeutic Site Design*

What is the art of therapeutic site design today? If we use several case studies from the special issue of *Landscape Architecture Magazine* entitled "Healing Gardens" (LAM, 1995), we will see that a broad range of concepts exist among designers as to what is therapeutic. However, if we hold their designs to the standards set in the above definition, we will see that certain design concepts quickly fall out of the therapeutic realm.

4.2 *Case Study #1: The Mending Wall.*

This garden design was constructed at the San Diego Children's Hospital in an interior court-yard space surrounded by several floors of patient rooms. The written description for the concept called for the construction of a brightly colored mosaic tiled wall with at least five types of brass fixtures with which children were encouraged to interact. The purpose of the wall was to distract young patients from the maladies and/or treatment regimes that they were experiencing. Features in the design include a courtyard and mending wall which are handicap accessible. Numerous tables and chairs occupy hardened areas surrounding the elevated grassy area adjacent to the mending wall, but their dimensions and weight suggest they are scaled for adult use. An inverted cone shaped glass atrium allows natural light into a reception area, which is immediately below the courtyard on the ground floor of the hospital. A topiary of a rooster occupies one small planter box in a corner of the courtyard. It is unclear from the article whether programmed recreation activities were scheduled for the courtyard area.

Field examination of the site at mid-day, mid-week, on a comfortable day in January (Westphal, 1999) approximately four years after constructions reveals that it is completely devoid of children. Nursing staff has placed a pre-fabricated Fisher-Price basketball backstop and children's scaled picnic table adjacent to the mending wall, obscuring access to several brass play areas. One brass play piece has been broken (the telephone) and the receiver has not been replaced. The patina of the brass play pieces suggests that they have been used. However, an examination of other areas of the courtyard shows little wear or tear on grassy areas or other minor architectural elements (e.g., tables or chairs). The painted handrails on the ramp to the mending wall or stairs to the grassy knoll are not worn, suggesting low use. The topiary planter is marked by cigarette butts and litter suggesting an outdoor smoking lounge around the feature. The back-side of the mending wall adjacent to the ramp which provides access to the wall is gray, poured concrete; it suggests an industrial site, not access to a play area. This design concept fails by the author's therapeutic site design standards. It lacks a well-defined patient population; therefore, its features designed for everyone, serve no one specifically. As a result alternative site use begins to appear. The concept that the wall will serve as a distraction to children who are ill or awaiting surgery, fails in its understanding of children's attention spans as well as types of activities that children identify with in play environments. The site, while identified as a children's play area, is scaled to adult use in the size and weights of moveable items like chairs and tables and permanent fixtures like 6 inch risers on stairs. Topiary, while attractive, is not intended for interactive play with children. Therefore, it serves as the unintended ashtray and litter barrel. With the exception of providing fresh air, some sunlight, and limited ambulation, the site fails miserably in meeting standards that fit within well-defined treatment protocols and clear therapeutic outcomes for targeted patient populations. It clearly qualifies for the hype and hyperbole side of therapeutic site design.

4.3 *Case Study #2: The Patricia Neal Rehabilitation Garden.*

This site was located between two hospital wings of the Patricia Neal Rehabilitation Hospital. Described by the designers as two long narrow canyons between multi-storied brick facades, it creates a small oasis of green space and plant materials. The concept underlying the design is that the site should facilitate victims of traumatic head injury, stroke, or heart attack in regaining lost function of limbs or cognitive abilities (characteristic consequences in all three patient groups). The layout of the site permits group as well as individual activities based on the amount of space dedicated to certain activities. Large enough open space is provided for hand-eye skill-based activities like baseball, while still providing universal accessibility. Other design features reinforce privacy through the creation of enclosure and the placement of seating elements that accommodate wheel chairs. Surface materials, slope, and elevation change on a serpentine trail configuration fits within standard treatment protocols of rehabilitation medicine; these treatment protocols call for the negotiation of different surface materials in preparation for discharge to a home environment. Programmed recreation activities are integrated into the site design. It is the author's view that this site fits within the working definition of therapeutic site design. It clearly understands the types of patients that it will serve (based on patient limitations and desired therapeutic outcomes), and it complements standard treatment protocols by providing for activities commonly found in physical and occupational therapy. This site displays more health than hype or hyperbole in its design concept.

4.4 Case Study #3: Fast Forward Reverse.

In this case study, designer Robert Hoover was asked to develop therapeutic garden areas in a nursing home for Alzheimer-type dementia patients. Because the facility consisted of three wings with patients in one of three stages of Alzheimer-type dementia, the garden areas adjacent to each wing could be designed with levels of patient cognitive ability in mind. Because the designer took time to learn about Alzheimer-type dementia as a disease process and the characteristics that it elicits in patients as it progresses, he was able to go beyond the physical constraints of site and offer a conceptual justification for the proposed development of each garden area. This conceptual basis visualized the impairment as a reversal of child development phenomena. As an Alzheimer's patient progresses in the disease, short term memory and abilities to work through complex abstract thought processes deteriorate; therefore, the designer established an argument to create environments that ranged in simplicity of layout and selection of activities as well as plant materials. Garden design for the advanced stage of Alzheimer's patients was the most simplistic in circulation routes and the most enclosing; this was to improve wayfinding and security while reinforcing the nurturing ambience of the site. The earliest stage of Alzheimer's patients were given garden areas where more complex tasks like hanging wash or playing basketball were a part of the programmed recreation. Here the designer's concern for security was significantly reduced; therefore, fencing and other features of the design responded to this reduced concern.

This case study embraces some of the best conceptual work by the design profession in terms of therapeutic site design. It respects patient limitations, understand the disease process and its progression, and provides meaningful opportunities for recreation in an outdoor garden activity. Because Alzheimer-type dementia is an irreversible disease process, the designer does not focus on healing dimensions, but rather on aspects of health care that improves with meaningful outdoor activities. He conceptualizes the design solution as a plausible set of reverse phenomena to normal child development (an observation that is generally held by nursing staffs that serve this type of patient group).

4.5 The Science of Therapeutic Site Design

This leads us to the scientific aspects of therapeutic site design. If one were to highlight the milestones in advancing the science of therapeutic site design, the number of scientifically rigorous research activities have been markedly small. Roger Ulrich (1984) published the most influential of all work in *Science* magazine. Entitled "View through a window may influence recovery from surgery," the article reviewed the benefits derived by "post-gallbladder" patients who had rooms either adjacent to a natural landscape or adjacent to a brick facade and rooftop of the hospital. After matching patients for medical history, attendant surgeon, and other factors, Ulrich found that those patients adjacent to the natural area had statistically significant fewer nursing complaints, lower requested amounts of analgesics, lower blood pressure readings, and fewer days to discharge than patients in rooms without views to nature.

Other research articles have focused on reduced patient anxiety, reduced pain or need for analgesics, lower blood pressure, respiration, or heart rates; however, in most instances this work has focused on buildings rather than garden design. One of the best surveys of research on this subject has been completed by Ruben *et al* (1997). Compiled by health researchers at Johns Hopkins Hospital, it reviews nearly 70 scientific or experimental studies that examine the relationship between healthcare design and medical outcomes. Unfortunately, most of the articles in this review pay little attention to natural areas or designed garden areas adjacent to or within hospital settings.

5 FUTURE WORK

This leads us to the final point of this paper. How can we advance the art and science of therapeutic site design as professionals?

5.1 *Multi-disciplinary Approach*

One of the most important lessons that we can learn from this emerging specialty area in design is that it entails a true multi-disciplinary approach to site design. Designers cannot simply design in a vacuum when it comes to site design that affects patient populations. An effort must be made to understand the disease process involved. This means developing an appreciation for the physical, psychological (and at times, spiritual) imbalances that are created by a disease. Knowing the likely prognosis (end result) of a disease and any temporal changes or stages that mark the progression of a disease is invaluable as well. This type of information can determine whether a design concept is appropriate or not for a given patient population.

One of the best sources of information on a patient group will be the nursing staff. Because nursing staff oversee the daily operations of most managed care facilities, their concerns for the safety and welfare of their patients will always be foremost in their minds. However, because they have closer contact with most patients than even the doctors, they tend to be "tuned in" to the peculiarities that a disease process may elicit. Another important source of information on patients with certain diseases is support groups. Many communities have support groups or networks composed of caregivers who manage individuals with similar diseases. These support groups are an excellent source of information on the disease, its impact on a patient, and even more importantly, its impact on the caregivers who manage the patient. Most support groups are listed in the telephone book or on the Internet.

Finally, all therapeutic garden design should enlist the expertise of a horticulturist, particularly one trained in horticultural therapy. Poisonous plant materials can prove deadly in a therapeutic garden designed for late stage Alzheimer-type dementia patients as well as for other patient groups where cognitive function is incapacitated or under-developed. Therefore, the horticulturist can offer advice on keeping plants--and patients—alive in therapeutic garden areas. If he/she has training in horticultural therapy, additional advice on appropriate types of activities and three-dimensional space needs often is available.

5.2 *Alternative Medicine and Design Tools*

A second point in advancing the art and science of therapeutic site design is the availability of "alternative forms of medicine" in site design. Among the types of therapy that a designer can program and create space for in a garden are pet therapy, light therapy, aromatherapy, herbal therapy, music therapy, and art therapy. These alternative forms of therapy can complement traditional types of therapy prescribed for most patient populations—i.e., physical therapy, occupational therapy, and recreational therapy. Innovative site design can accommodate all of these types of therapy, without hype, without hyperbole, but with plenty of healthy options for those concerned.

5.3 Post-construction Evaluation and Reporting

In addition to the creative use of alternative therapies, design professionals must begin documenting the post construction effects of their designs on receiving patient populations. This does not have to be a highly sophisticated, statistically complex research effort. Rather it can rely on normal nursing records and pre- and post- construction differences in patient performance/behavior. For example, for dementia patients one may compare nursing records concerning blood pressure, eating behavior, aggressiveness, wakefulness at night, sundowning phenomenon (type and degree), and affect (mood). For stroke patients, one might compare improvements in muscle strength, balance, range of motion, affect, abilities to carry on activities of daily living (e.g., bathing, eating, toileting, dressing, etc.), and days to discharge. Simple observation of the constructed site will often lead to recommendations for change that will improve the existing design as well as future design efforts. These recommendations are invaluable in advancing the art of therapeutic site design, and reduces the need to speculate on the end results of a design (a contributing factor to the hype phenomena). Reporting one's findings at professional meetings or in professional journals furthers the field of therapeutic site design, by allowing hypotheses to be drawn from case study experiences. Thus, the science of design is advanced as well.

6 CONCLUSION

Advances in the specialty field of therapeutic site design is almost assured as we move into the new millennium...if designers are willing to move toward a more scientific framework in conceptualizing and evaluating their site designs. Unlike other fields of design where relatively healthy functioning human beings occupy designed sites for leisure or work purposes, in therapeutic site design the patient population (and oftentimes their caregivers) literally are a captive audience in the site. Therefore, greater sensitivity to the intended outcomes of the design is almost mandated. Because standard treatment protocols exist in the practice of medicine, designers must be aware of the peculiarities that mark a particular disease process. They also must have a sense of how those peculiarities can affect the therapeutic outcome that is being sought in a managed care setting. These are new areas of knowledge that a designer must secure if he/she is to be effective in a site design prescription for a specific patient population. Without this information, designers will be tempted to exaggerate on the actual benefits that a site design can afford. This hype or hyperbole can be more detrimental to the health of this infant field than any other factor of site design. Building the basis of a specialty field in design takes discipline and retrospective evaluation. The framework for accomplishing this is in place in the medical field in the form of treatment protocols and therapeutic outcomes. It behooves design professionals to integrate this framework into their design concepts and to use the knowledge from other professional groups to insure the success of a therapeutic garden.

REFERENCES

Billings J. S. 1890. *Description of the Johns Hopkins Hospital*. Baltimore: Johns Hopkins Hospital, pl. 2.
Boehringer, E. 1959. "Pergamon". *Neue Detsche Ausgrabungen im Mittelmeergebiet und im Vordenen Orient*. Berlin: Gebr. Mann, p. 156.
Brawley, E.C. 1997. *Designing for Alzheimer's Disease*. New York: John Wiley & Sons, Inc.
Cooper-Marcus, C. & Barnes, M. 1999. *Healing Gardens: Therapeutic Benefits and Design Recommendations*. New York: John Wiley & Sons, Inc.
Francis, M., Lindsay, P. & Rice, J. [eds] 1994. *The Healing Dimensions of People-Plant Relations: Conference Proceedings*. Davis, CA: Center for Design Research, University of California.
Gerlach-Spriggs, N., Kaufman, R. & Warner, S. Jr. 1997. *Restorative Gardens: The Healing Landscape*. New Haven, CT: Yale University Press.
Gruenwald, J., Brendler, T. & Jaenicke, C. 1998. *PRD for Herbal Medicines*. Montvale, NJ: Medical Economics Company, Inc.
Horn, W. 1962. "On the Author of the Plan of St. Gall and the Relation of the Plan to the Monastic Reform Movement." In: *Studien zum St. Galler Klosterplan*, ed. Johannes Duff, pp.103-27.

Landscape Architecture Magazine 1995. Special issues, "Healing Gardens". *Landscape Architecture Magazine* 85(1): 56-79.

Mintner, S. 1994. *The Healing Garden*. London: Headline Book Publishing.

Ochsner, A.J. & Sturm, M.J. 1907. *The Organization, Construction and Management of Hospitals*. Chicago: Cleveland press.

Physicians Desk Reference. 1998. *PDR for Herbal Medicines*. Montvale, NJ: MedicalEconomics Company, Inc.

Raver, A. 1994. "Patients discover the power of gardens." New York: *New York Times*, Living Arts Section, December 29, 1994.

Rosen, G. 1968. *Madness in Society: Chapters in the Historical Society of Mental Illness*. Chicago, IL; University of Chicago Press, pp. 116-117.

Ruben, H., A. Owens, and G. Golden. 1997. "Status report: an investigation to determine whether the built environment affects patients' medical outcomes." Martinez CA: The Center for Health Design.

San Francisco Chronicle. 1998. "Alternative healers gain lead on doctors." San Francisco, CA: *San Francisco Chronicle*, November 11, 1998.

Swerdlow, J.L. 2000. *Nature's Medicine: Plants That Heal*. Washington, DC: National Geography Society.

Tabanelli, M. 1960. "Gli ospedale delle legioni Romane, lungo 'Limes" Germanico ed Orientale," *Atti del primo Congresso di Storia Ospitaliera*. Reggio Emilia, p.1264.

Toms, W.H. (artist 1717-1750). Date unkinown. Engraving by artist of St. Thomas Hospital, London. London: Library of the Wellcome Institute for the History of Medicine. Courtesy of the Wellcome Trustees.

Thompson, J.D. and G. Goldin. 1975. *The Hospital: A Social and Architectural History*. New Haven and London: Yale University Press.

Tyson, M. 1998. *The Healing Landscape: Therapeutic Outdoor Environments*. New York: Mc-Graw-Hill.

Ulrich, R. 1984. "View through a window may influence recovery from surgery." *Science* 224: 420-421.

Ulrich, R. 1986. "Human responses to vegetation and landscapes." *Landscape and Planning* 13: 29-44.

Westphal, J.M. 1997. "Therapeutic Garden Design". Presentation. E. Lansing, MI: Michigan Horticulture Therapy Association, Annual Meeting, March 1997.

Westphal, J.M. 1999. "Mending Wall". Post-construction, in-field evaluation, unpublished report. San Diego, CA: San Diego Children's Hospital.

---

[i] Hype is defined as an exaggerated promotion.

[ii] Hyperbole is defined as an exaggerated or extravagant statement often made for effect.

[iii] Health is defined by the author as a state of homeostasis or internal balancing of an orgar ism's antomical, physiological, and psychological systems to perform optimal work tasks.

Spaces, places, people

Urban Lifestyles: Spaces · Places · People, Benson & Roe (eds)
© *2000 Balkema, Rotterdam, ISBN 90 5809 169 4*

Urban regeneration through cultural masterplanning

T. Farrell
Terry Farrell and Partners, London, UK

ABSTRACT: 'If (as the philosophers maintain) the city is like some large house, and the house is in turn like some small city, cannot the various parts of the house – atria, dining rooms, porticoes, and so on – be considered miniature buildings?'

Leon Battista Alberti, *On the Art of Building in Ten Books*

Alberti's observation prompts us to think about an infinity of possibilities relating to domesticity, the dynamics of the public realm and the wonder of scale. Seeing the city as a large house provides a clue of how to understand and appreciate the often illusive patterns of order and disorder within urbanity and architecture. The essence of the clue is to uncover and rejoice in these layers of richness and diversity.

1 INTRODUCTION

In writing this paper, I will be going on a journey, connecting many different threads. Rather than conveying the silence of architecture, the idea is to evoke the music of real life. I will start at the house of nineteenth-century architect Sir John Soane – who created the ultimate experience of the city (or even a world) within a house – and will travel, back and forth through time and through scale, from a family home in Maida Vale to a vast cultural complex in China's ancient city of Beijing. Rather than logic and order, it is a journey that will revel in maximum choice and variety and a love of creating a shared experience for all to enjoy.

I think it's interesting at the turn of the century to glance back to the great inspiration of Robert Venturi and the postmodernist movement of the 1980s that challenged mainstream modern architecture. The words of Venturi's book *Complexity and Contradiction in Architecture* are astonishingly beautiful and well put: 'I like complexity and contradiction in architecture. I do not like the incoherence or arbitrariness of incompetent architecture', 'I welcome the problems and exploit the uncertainties', 'I prefer "both and" to "either-or"' and so on. The belief in modernism and the lavishness of high tech has led to an understanding that 'less is more'. Instead, I like the advice of Shelley to Keats to 'load every rift with ore'. Another saying that struck me recently is the quotation by Hugo Young on the intellectual idleness of journalists that 'the truth is too complicated'. Architects suffer from simplification by the need to get the message across conflicting and demanding media internationally, as well as locally. Over-simplification is part of modern communication, but it is a kind of lie, a denial of conflicts and all the contradictions in life today. The complexity of life today is extreme and one has to face up to this as an artist and architect. Every aspect of our lives is overburdened with information and new possibilities and in this way, the city has become a different place. I will be exploring this variety and difference by what I see as the city's five components: the domestic realm; the public building; the urban quarter; the cultural quarter; and, transcending the above, new scales, dimensions and mindsets.

2 THE DOMESTIC SCALE

I see all scales as being comprised of patterns. The patterns that come to make up the domestic scale are comprised of the house, its various rooms, and the garden. A comparison can be made between the seeming order of a minimalist house by, say, Claudio Silvestrin, and the rich patterns forming the house of one of the great duets of the 20th century, Charles and Ray Eames. The Eames house is extraordinarily diverse and complicated. Wonderful collectors of things, they had an eclecticism in everything they touched and, rather than retreating from life, were fascinated by its richness. In my view, the minimalist house shows a catatonic architecture where the emotional experience of the world forces a sleep-like state on those who can't cope – in Silvestrin's words, 'Good architecture makes us silent'. But paradoxically, I think this adds to the richness of our experience today: without minimalism we wouldn't understand maximalism. I withdraw from the minimum and prefer variety and diversity, richness of colour and exuberance of form. I am with Shelley, Keats and Venturi: this is the music of real life.

Charles and Ray Eames embody an intensively creative world. In their cluttered studio, it isn't that order is lacking, but that there are to be found patterns of disorder and patterns of order. On a larger scale, I enjoy urban design because I look at the apparent chaos of cities, look at the layered work of many hands and I try to understand why a particular city is the way it is. I try to understand the patterns not the order. This helps us to understand the complexity of what's there instead of trying to subtract or oversimplify and this I see as being the work of the modern urbanist. The hidden and secret patterns are central to life today. Charles and Ray Eames were great collectors by association, almost as the surrealists would do, by juxtaposition. They put together many different kinds of collections. They revelled in the richness and diversity of these things, but also the hidden patterns of connectedness behind the complexity and variety.

I particularly love the way the Eames played – Charles Eames' solar 'do-nothing machine' sums up this form of experimentation. I think meaninglessness is very important today because it aids the search for meaning and order. Their film 'Powers of Ten' is inspirational for many architects and designers. 'Powers of Ten' is a journey from the furthest edge of the universe ten-million light years away to an atom inside a sleeping figure on a picnic blanket. The message of the film is the closeness of scale: that the molecules and atoms resemble whole universes. It is a wonderful way of saying that there is a connectedness of all the scales of our universe.

In a similar vein, I love Alberti's statement that the house is a small city and the city is a large house. The traditional city has its living rooms (public spaces), bedrooms (apartments), dining rooms (restaurants), storage houses and chapels. The concept of the city as a large house and vice versa is a clue of how to understand patterns of urbanity and architecture as we have understood them so far in our history. The ultimate experience of the city in a house is the complete world of John Soane in Lincoln's Inn. Here, ancient Rome, Greece, the London of Hogarth and Soane's personal experience of life are captured in a wonderful labyrinth that was museum and house all in one.

In my own house, in which I've lived for 25 years, the layers of experience encapsulate a personal environment. Rather than 'architecture', it is a place for living and enjoying. The house is part of the Metroland vision based on the building of the Bakerloo line in the 1920s. When the line was built the excavated soil was left to settle in a field in the middle of Maida Vale and the land lay unoccupied for 20–30 years. The 20-year gap between the existing mansion blocks and the new houses resulted in living styles changing and the evolution of the cottage style, which resulted in our garden-city-style house sitting in a sea of mansion blocks. When the recession of 1975 hit, I split the house into three separate flats. By revealing the lower floor, we opened up the coal cellar and made it into an underground play area. When the tenants moved out, we occupied the whole house. I put a crow's nest sleeping bed up there and I could actually say that I'd bought a two storey three-up two-down and within two years had a five-storey block of flats – but from the outside nothing had changed. I then began to extend the house out to the garden and I placed plants on axis in the front garden that go right through to the back garden so you have a vista that runs 100 foot long from front to back.

As I travelled the Far East I began to bring back bird cages and we bought furniture and designed rugs and tiles, and this eventually became part of our experience of living and it can be explained in many different ways: by way of the children; how my wife and I interacted creatively; and by the ups and downs of the architectural profession. All the booms and recessions are writ large within this house. It's a house that represents layers of enjoyment in things that have accumulated over time.

I have been involved with two houses that cross the boundaries between culture and living. One is the house on which I collaborated with Charles Jencks and the other is the house of collector John Scott. These houses show the owners transgressing the remit of the house in order to become a collection. John Scott's vision grew from the house into the city: he promoted the Piers Gough-designed lavatory in Westbourne Grove and is involved in improving the Notting Hill Gate area. His efforts are now part of a shared experience among many people.

3 THE PUBLIC BUILDING

The public building, patterned with great rooms, halls, corridors, staircases and parkland, takes the Alberti analogy to a larger scale. Our Dean Art Gallery in Edinburgh represents the public 'house'. The National Galleries of Scotland obtained the Dean – a former orphanage – for their headquarters as well as to house a permanent collection of dada and surrealist art works and a bequest from sculptor Eduardo Paolozzi. Next to the Dean was a great cemetery and a picturesque walk around the river of Leith, so as well as gallery design, the job comprised landscaping, town planning and restoration.

I found the collection truly inspirational: I loved delving into surrealism and am fascinated by juxtaposition. You put one object next to another that seems to have no association and let each speak to one another. These artists were fascinated by Freud and the way objects could be unveiled and stripped back to give a different story. Freudian 'free association' works as a visual equivalent of streams of consciousness and interpretation of dreams. This alternative story of art is particularly appealing: against the modernists' desire, there was a subplot of those that didn't believe in the modern order of things and placed their faith in a darker, deeper side that was revealed by psychoanalysis and recognised by tribal and ancient cultures. I was also interested in how the surrealists' idea of assemblage was picked up by the pop artists of the 1960s, such as Paolozzi or Peter Blake, as though making a joke of the whole art thing. One shouldn't be frightened of a new interpretation of a gallery that exposes layers of complexity. If an artist can make order or patterns that are pleasing, an architect should be able to do the same.

I began to look at the form and shape of the Dean and found it a wonderfully powerful thing. Hamilton, the original architect, had taken all the chimneys and diverted them to go up to flues that sat above the main staircases. This no longer seemed classical order. Hamilton also put oculi or windows above every fireplace so that the flues vanished. On the exterior of the building, however, the chimneys dominated the whole facade. Another extraordinary thing was the building's grandeur on the outside but sensory deprivation on the inside. Here was an opportunity to respond to the outside without the fear that one's spoiling something architecturally wonderful on the inside. Hamilton's great work became, to me, as surreal as a Magritte painting.

I was concerned that the circulation wasn't just efficient but was also highly stimulating. We made sure the visitor has the full experience of all the staircases. The ground floor houses the permanent collection and the top floor houses the temporary exhibition galleries. I concentrated on looking at extraordinary opportunities for spatial interconnectiveness. I made oculi that look down to the entrance, and placed vitrines that went down to the basement so that people in the storage areas can see up to the displays on the first floor. I put display areas in oculi in the floors themselves and I put in light chimneys – the main contribution of the new architecture was a manipulation of the old chimneys. We also took out one floor on the axis with the entrance hall and Paolozzi was commissioned to do a sculpture that fitted into this double-height space.

The Dean café contains a Paolozzi plaster cast based on Blake's watercolour of Isaac Newton. Blake remonstrated against Newton and the age of reason. The twin stories of the 20th century are the darker side of dada and surrealism versus conventional establishment art. Blake's interpretation of Newton catches a complex eighteenth-century interpretation of the world by meeting Newton from an opposite direction but converging on his viewpoint. Paolozzi's studio is recreated in the Dean. Again, it appears to be chaos: is it disorder or is it order? The answer is an order of a kind, a pattern or way of working: one person's chaos is another's order. It is the pattern of a sculptor's working method.

4 THE URBAN QUARTER

Moving on from the domestic scale and public building, I am now going up to a third level in scale, using Alberti's metaphor of looking at the city as a great house. I'll now examine the 'cultural district', which has become quite a phenomenon. These are large complexes of culture, urban pieces of the city that become cultural districts. Cultural districts comprise patterns formed by the square and public spaces, streets and public routes, and the hierarchy set up between public and private buildings. The Forbidden City in Beijing is a great piece of city-making, as Edmund Bacon says in his *Design of Cities*, it is 'possibly the greatest single work of man on the face of the earth'. Just outside the gates we were asked to build a cultural complex containing an opera house, concert hall, main theatre and performance space in what is going to be the world's biggest cultural complex as only the Chinese would want to do.

The competition was an extraordinary experience: we were told three times that we'd won and then told three times then we hadn't, and then eventually we didn't. We put in a first scheme that we said was non-architecture. If it was to be a twenty-first-century centre of culture, I thought we should look to the Chinese, who had emphasised the role of local and global, past and future. I was fascinated by the main auditorium which created an experience where you could see the performance inside happening outside. I also designed enormous foyers because we were dealing with a big scale: 10,000 people could be in the building at any one time. China *is* a big scale and we wanted to respond to this. We also felt China should express its connectedness on a large world stage, as the world's largest country, in a very positive way that expressed the nature of 'openness'. This approach fascinated the Chinese and we got shortlisted. But we were then asked again and again during subsequent trips to make the design more Chinese: we went on this journey making it more and more Chinese and the French, who came in with a very Chinese-looking scheme, went the other way and won it with a radical scheme, which is a lesson of some kind!

We were interested in promoting the idea of the building interacting globally, going beyond Alberti's statement to connect with, for example, a show at La Scala, which could be shown in the grand foyer. And what was performing in Beijing could be shown back in London, for example, through the internet. But we were also interested in interaction within the complex: we had 16 venues on the site that could work one with the other. As I said though, the French changed the game. The brief had been recognisable as being space-positive – as shown in Colin Rowe's diagrams in *Collage City* – with spaces that the town planners were encouraging us to enclose, so that eventually a whole series of great spaces would exist outside the gates. But the French went much more grandiose, recalling Napoleonic scales. They came back with an oval building that was building-positive. This wasn't enclosing space, but sat as an object, as does the centre of Paris at the Place de la Concorde, or the centre of Washington DC.

The Beijing experience is one of the building as icon rather than the cultural building as part of an urban complex. Of course in the case of Sydney or Bilbao whole cities were regenerated around iconic buildings so these were positive symbols of the total regeneration. The Louvre pyramid is particularly successful because the icon does seize the focus and the Louvre plan is all about this connectedness – the best of both worlds. So there is a role for the icon but it comes with dangers such as the Beijing example, where only the icon mattered in the end.

One of the problems I had in the 1980s was that so many felt that urban problems were solved through architecture. Urban planning hadn't been fully understood at that time: for my work on the South Bank, I was forced to put in a detailed planning application. Today we'd expect urban design to take precedence. Part of our masterplan for the South Bank was incremental growth with many different uses and many architects.

As each masterplan evolves, even if different hands implement it, or different masterplanners come along, there is learnt, inherited experience. My particular argument at the time was that the South Bank had seven front doors: at the equivalent space in the West End around Shaftesbury Avenue there were 350 front doors. I felt that made a statement about urbanity. Many elements of our scheme have begun to happen. Very early on we had the Imax cinema and the double-sided pedestrian bridge. These cultural complexes are about people movement. A few years ago we were one of the participants in the competition for Albertopolis. Exhibition Road is the great urban design concept of Prince Albert and it is our *grande projet*. The French may have brand new *grandes projets* but we have them already and should be investing in these. As I wrote in the *Independent* in 1991:

'The museum-land of South Kensington… has the potential to be a stunning expanse of city with its peerless Victorian museums, but at the moment it is, collectively, a thing of rags and patches, lacking the cafes and the vitality its exuberant architecture seems to promise. Making Kensington's museum-land better than the sum of its parts would be the right sort of grand project for London and far more meaningful than the construction of a single and hugely expensive building like the Gare D'Orsay Museum or the Pompidou Centre in Paris.'

5 THE CITY AND CULTURE

We now move to the final scale, which is the city and its regeneration through culture. The patterns that characterise this sphere comprise public infrastructure, as well as the equally tangible spirit and uniqueness of a place. This is what the millennium and lottery projects are setting out to do in Great Britain and there is a group of them that are very interesting indeed. The millennium projects are more noticeable in smaller cities such as Sheffield, where the town hall building of the 1970s will be demolished and the existing group of buildings – the Crucible, Lyceum, library and gallery – are being connected with a new town plan with a square and through-route. There is also the Centre for Popular Music and the V&A of the North. These are part of a rejuvenation of Sheffield city centre and it's culture that's driving the regeneration.

The city I know well is Newcastle and at both the east and west ends are two urban regeneration projects that are going to revolutionise the city. At the east end is the renewal of the east quayside, housing offices, hotels and residential space, which we masterplanned. One of the great things about urban regeneration is the knock-on effect: Chris Wilkinson's bridge is now being built across to Gateshead, there is Norman Foster's music centre and Dominic Williams' Baltic Mills arts centre on the Gateshead side. Our International Centre for Life is rejuvenating Newcastle's west end.

The Centre for Life is about the origins of life and DNA. The complex has a new square in its centre, on the line of the old Scotswood Road; it has a research building, linked with the university; a visitor attraction and many layers of interesting town planning history. An infirmary was built on this site; the hospital became a teaching hospital; the teaching hospital became a college; and the college became the university. Now the history has come back to the site with the genetics department of the university. But every piece of urban life, every piece of urban artefact, has a rich story and ICL is a many-layered, many coded building that picks up on and relates to its history. ICL tells a story of another world. Going back to Charles and Ray Eames, it is a world of ten to the power of 1 going inwards. It is a world of DNA and molecules, things that under a microscope are clearly of great beauty.

The other scheme of large-scale impact is the regeneration of Hull through a millennium project with another visitor attraction complex. In this case the building is an aquarium celebrating marine life. The site also contains a business and research centre, and we've done a plan for regenerating this part of the Hull river, and the catalyst is this millennium project again. We are also working on an oceanographic centre in Seattle and I have become fascinated with the world of fish and their habitat within the flora and fauna and the geology of the earth. The deliberate survival technique of diversity in nature has great interest for us culturally: cultural diversity in a world of increasing communications' pollution is as important as the biological diversity of the species. World cultures have evolved that are now just as endangered as biological species.

6 CONCLUSION: NEW SCALES, NEW ORDERS, NEW MINDSETS

As we learn more about our world we discover just how extraordinarily difficult it is to understand. The orders that may have been set by religion or science are no longer applicable and yet our world unveils more mystery at which to wonder. Nature is the real world of maximalism, maximum choice and maximum variety. This is the architecture of nature. The final images show a DNA molecule – one end of the power of ten – and a spiral galaxy, the other end of the power of ten. To conclude, this has not been an explanation of logic and order, but an exploration about preference and feelings, and a love of variety, diversity, richness of colour and exuberance of form. I have not been writing about the silence of architecture but about the music of real life.

Urban Lifestyles: Spaces · Places · People, Benson & Roe (eds)
© *2000 Balkema, Rotterdam, ISBN 90 5809 169 4*

Towards sociable cities

G. Bell
Town and Country Planning Association, London, UK

ABSTRACT: A century ago, the industrialized nations experienced major trends in urbanization. Towns and cities grew in leaps and bounds with people leaving the land to work in the
sweat shops of manufactories. Life for a few was luxurious. For many however, it was hell on
Earth – disease, poverty, malnutrition and slum housing taking its toll. Social reformers of the
period pointed to a new way forward with garden suburbs and new settlements, some of which
were developed and are now home to millions worldwide. As we begin the 21st century, we
have a sense of déjà vu. Urbanization continues, with the pace of growth in developing countries now far outstripping the environmental capacity to accommodate them. So, we should re-
discover models of spatial planning exemplified by our predecessors and show how they can be
reinterpreted in the modern idiom, delivered through public/private partnerships. All this can
lead to the development of more *sociable* cities around the world.

1 OUR COMMON INHERITANCE

This Paper is about people.

There are now 6 billion people living on this Earth. The rise in population, particularly in the
developing countries as primary health care improves, is exponential. If this growth was evenly
spread across the land masses, if people chose to follow self-sufficient lifestyles, if communities
elected to pursue policies to remain within their ecological footprint, then we could view the 21st
Century with equanimity – even optimism.

Regrettably, trends are taking the world in a different direction. A century ago less than 15%
of the world population lived in cities, now it is more than half. As disasters strike, whether it
be floods in Bangladesh or drought in Ethiopia, the people re-settle in cities. As the media
penetrates the furthest corners of the world, so young people in particular are drawn to the images of prosperity and affluence. The city streets may not be paved with gold, but they offer the
promise of change and opportunity.

Rural life, so often portrayed as the country idyll, can more often be grinding poverty and
subsistence. A never-changing (and if you are lucky) never-ending routine of farming the earth
and fishing the oceans for a living. Religion and traditions can be a very valuable means of glu-
ing together people in a community life, but exposure to outside influences leads to tensions and
break-up of the old ways. It is this which drives people to abandon the countryside in preference for life in the *barrios* and slums of cities around the world.

This is a bleak prospect. And not a situation in which anyone on Earth can remain immune. Even those living within the gated communities at Beverley Hills or Knightsbridge have to breath the same air as the rest of us in downtown LA or London (unless of course they transfer between the air conditioned limos and home wearing a gas-mask!). It is the city dweller in many countries who may run out of drinking water more frequently than those living a less sophisticated low-impact existence out in the sticks.

It is against this background that world leaders and government Environment Ministers met in Rio de Janeiro in 1992 at the first World Earth Summit. The concept of sustainable development outlined by the United Nations Environment Programme was confirmed as a goal for achievement through a far-reaching Agenda 21. Conserving and replenishing the World's natural resources became a policy cornerstone. Ratified in succeeding years and fleshed out in further inter-governmental conferences such as Kyoto, where reductions in pollutant emissions to the atmosphere were agreed, one nevertheless instinctively feels that the gap between rhetoric and reality is widening, or at the very least, is not closing.

Whether it be at the macro, global scale of greenhouse gas emissions or the local routine of the short school run, the overriding impression is of business as usual. This is because where people can make a choice, they often prefer the unsustainable solution. And in the democracies of the world, governments find it difficult to persuade voters to go where they don't want to be.

The failure of Communism and the strengthening of the free market, private enterprise culture has fostered the notion that progress is in the gift of the individual. At its extreme is the self-centred, selfish and grasping profligacy of those that have no thought for any save themselves. At its best, is the development of enterprise that provides jobs, sustainable economic growth, the internalisation of environmental costs and the sharing of wealth across communities.

Most often, this social enterprise is the consequence of public/private partnerships where each plays to strengths. Assisted by visionary processes such as Local Agenda 21, communities are able to articulate their ideas of how they want their community to look ten or twenty years hence. Quite often the process identifies actions that individuals and groups may take to live more sustainable lives. The difficulty often rests at the macro scale, where strategic decisions and major investments need to be implemented, in order that people can be better able to take the steps necessary to lead more economically secure, environmentally friendly and sociable lives. In order to find a solution to close this strategic gap I now turn to history. In this case it is a model for the development of sociable cities, developed a century ago, re-interpreted for the 21st Century, in which all people can live a good life in an honest place.

2   EBENEZER HOWARD-A PEACEFUL PATH TO REAL REFORM

The first industrial revolution in the world took place in Britain. In the period from 1800 to 1900, the population of Britain increased from 15 million to 40 million. These people moved from grinding rural poverty to the new centres of manufacturing and commerce – London, Manchester, Birmingham and elsewhere. Cities were born at a pace which mirrors the current rapid growth of cities in developing countries. Much of the growth was speculative, unplanned, highly profitable to a few and exploitative of the many. In a perverse way, some would say it was more sustainable than present patterns of growth, because in 1900 it was public transport led. Before private motor cars swamped the scene, it was the railways that connected the cities both within and to each other. Trains and, later, buses provided the means for all to travel.

Within the city, life but for a few people, was short and brutish. Low wages, long hours, insanitary conditions and bad housing spawned a generation of social reformers from the Webbs to General Booth. Amongst these was Ebenezer Howard, a most unlikely hero. Born in 1850 the son of a confectioner, he lived in Suffolk and Hertfordshire before moving briefly to the USA in 1876. He returned to Britain five years later to start work as an official reporter, working in the Houses of Parliament.

In 1899, Howard wrote his book "Tomorrow: A Peaceful Path to Real Reform" offered his vision of garden cities as a model for relieving pressure on the bulgir heaving metropolis and regenerating the surrounding countryside. In the proces cities would create attractive places for all, in particular the urban poor, to live a f

Howard's energy, persistence and persuasive powers were such that by 1903, after his book was published (and incidentally the year the Garden Cities Assc_ the Town and County Planning Association was established) the first garden city in the woriu was founded at Letchworth in Hertfordshire.

Now a garden city of some 40,000 people, Letchworth still retains elements of the structure of the original diagram – a central avenue, civic centre, commercial district and housing areas with a mix of house types – large and small, public and private. Even the farmland of the rural estate remains intact. However, public transport is a shadow of the service at its peak in the 1950's as train lines have been closed and bus services withdrawn. Nevertheless, it is still possible to see the model which Howard proposed of a settlement which combines the best of town and country, with a social mix and character which appeals a century on. Howard was clearly influenced by the designs and housing layouts of Bedford Park and Hampstead Garden Suburb in London.

Howard never saw Letchworth as being a garden city in isolation. His vision was for a 'group' of "slumless smokeless cities". Connected by an inter-municipal railway and an inter-municipal canal – to move people and goods efficiently, the 'social city' would be a grouping of towns, each with a population of about 30,000, around a central city with a population twice that size. Each of the individual settlements would be of sufficient critical mass to support not only essential services, but also a reasonable range of specialist services. All of this within a compact, not a crammed, settlement. A town big enough to offer variety of opportunity, but small enough that one could walk easily from the suburbs to the centre – or to the countryside.

In recognizing that garden cities should have limits to population growth, Howard was responding to his perception that people wanted a place to which they could feel a sense of belonging. Even within a metropolis, the settlement breaks down into neighbourhoods (or urban villages), which offer a sense of community. He also anticipated that people would want to move for choice, or additional opportunity, just as increasingly they do today. So one lives in one place, works in another, shops in yet another and visits the nearby countryside for yet different reasons.

The model of mixed use and reducing the need to travel is not rejected, but embraced. And the model recognizes that people will want to travel, but that the key to environmental sustainability is good public transport links. These are settlements in which it is possible to feel pride and identity, small enough to see the hills of the surrounding countryside from the town centre, large enough to support large retail stores. In the central city and spread amongst the satellite garden cities, there would be a theatre, art gallery, specialist suppliers and a university that each, individually could not support. This is the truly Sociable City.

3 FUNDING AND OWNERSHIP

A key element in the development of the Garden City was the issue of land purchase and what Howard termed "rate-rent". He recognised that unless the project was profitable, it would not be financed by the market.. However, he wanted to contrive a different way in which backers would receive their return, guaranteed, but over a longer period. This would be secured by debentures in the company that bought the land and would develop the town.

Having bought the land at a premium (but not excessively so) above agricultural land value, the Company had the cost of construction to consider, everything from sewers and roads to the houses and schools. The Company also bore the risk that the garden city might fail – that no-one would come to live there.

The rate-rent concept was applied to tenants of everything from homes to farms. Tenants would pay part of their rent to the Company to redeem the debentures, part into a sinking fund to pay for infrastructure and the future development of the town. Howard calculated that, in time, the Company would be able to redeem the debt from the original backers as land values rose and that having passed that point, the Company would become increasingly profitable.

The normal market model would be for the backers to continue to rake in profits, but Howard saw his Company in a more philanthropic light, dedicated to using profits in later years to provide pensions and social care for residents. By including individuals and groups representing residents' interests on the garden city administration, this was to be secured. People take a much greater interest in affairs in which they have a financial stake, particularly a land owning position.

Howard saw the value of enabling people to borrow money from the Company to build their own homes, on plots offered to them. This added to the pioneering spirit of those who came to the first garden city, to make it a success.

The development of Letchworth Garden City once started, Howard found himself increasingly isolated from control of the Company's affairs and in consequence, he decided to repeat the whole exercise by purchasing a large estate some 20 miles south of Letchworth, that was to be Welwyn Garden City. At Welwyn, Howard would keep a closer control of events.

Howard brought with him some of those from Letchworth who supported his ideals and together they progressed the new development. Welwyn Garden City, now expanded to over 50,000 people, was to be the second in the cluster of settlements, that would together make up the Social City.

4   THE UK NEW TOWNS AND EXPANDED TOWNS PROGRAMME

Following the second World War, two imperatives drove the development of the UK new towns and expanded towns programme. Firstly, the strategic decision to disperse industrial development out of cities where it had proved vulnerable to enemy bombing. Secondly, the urgent need to build thousands of homes to replace those lost in the blitz. People needed housing and it was a hot political issue.

The Town and Country Planning Association (TCPA) led a campaign throughout the period to seek a solution to these problems by developing clusters of garden cities around the main conurbations. The Association was hugely successful, with Government deciding to establish over 40 new towns and expanded towns in the thirty years after the war. Now over 2 million people in Britain – one in 25 of the total population, live in new or expanded towns.

Howard's concept of social mix, of houses to buy and to rent, large and small all grouped together, was largely lost. Large monoculture public or private housing estates were built which led to social exclusion and friction between communities.

The new towns and expanded towns also switched from having public transport as a key framework, to reliance on the private motor car. Indeed, some of the developments were styled as "designed for the motor age". The images that people were attracted to and the lifestyle choice offered was one of bright, new, freedom of choice and liberation from the congestion and pollution of the cities.

5 THE 21ST CENTURY MODEL-THE SUSTAINABLE CITY

In survey after survey, people indicate their dissatisfaction with the condition of towns and cities and the direction that present trends are seemingly inexorably taking. However, a model for the regeneration of existing urban areas, future development of towns and cities both in the UK and abroad can very usefully be informed by our experience of Howard and his ideas.

Where Howard based his scheme on a cluster of settlements, interdependent and linked by public transport, so we can see the viability of polycentric urban developments, connected by cable, light rail, guided busways and trams. Where Howard saw a grand design with civic spaces and public buildings at the heart of the new communities, so we too can recognize the importance of the public realm to civic pride and the commercial success of our towns.

Where Howard promoted a mix of house types to suit single people and large families, so we now recognize the value of mixed communities, of places where young and old, well-off and less well-off people may be neighbours. Where Howard saw jobs being provided locally, within walking, cycling or a short distance by bus away from homes, so a new settlement or a garden suburb can bring the more modern, cleaner industries and commercial companies into locations accessible to where people live.

Howard's views on finance, administration and management can also be re-interpreted in the modern idiom. It is unrealistic to expect the public sector to meet the cost of infrastructure of a town in the 21st century. Likewise, it is unlikely that the private sector would choose to shoulder the total burden. More likely is a public/private partnership with each sector playing to strengths. The public sector assisting with land assembly, possibly using reserve compulsory purchase powers and the private sector, within the envelope of certainty offered by the State, taking a risk on the return of capital for the development as a whole.

A new model of a Development Trust could be created to bring both sectors together, alongside community representatives. The Trust, which would closely resemble Howard's model of administration, would ensure that the community had a strong voice in the development and management of the new settlement. Sometimes there is a dislocation between public aspirations and executive action. By including public representation on the Trust, then such a schism may be avoided. It would make the reality of a truly sociable city all the more likely.

6 THE PORTFOLIO OF SOLUTIONS

Some may argue that to develop satellites away from the main conurbation will sap the city of energy; that it will unnecessarily concrete over the countryside while sites within the city will remain undeveloped; that densities in the city will be lower than necessary to sustain public transport systems and that investment in the conurbation should have first call on resources.

The TCPA rejects the notion that it is an either-or. Rather a portfolio of solutions is required where conurbations are regenerated alongside the extension of urban areas and the creation of new settlements in a polycentric formation around existing towns. The opportunity needs to be taken to regenerate conurbations not just by redeveloping vacant sites and redundant buildings, but by greening cities with richer and more ecologically sound treatment of open spaces. If we are to retain the people who currently desert urban ares for country living (or indeed tempt people back who have already moved), then the conditions have to be sufficiently attractive to achieve that. We could do much worse than re-create the garden suburbs in a new form. Denser, but with lots of green space and a mix of land uses and housing types.

Following the sequence, extensions to urban areas would come next. Rather like garden cities in their own right – edge cities would capture the investment that trends of counter-urbanisation would otherwise dissipate to the wider countryside. Then, the cluster of garden cities themselves, probably based on existing small towns or villages, located on public transport routes and sufficiently accessible from each other that they can operate independently on sustainable transport principles. The beauty of such an arrangement is that both the original cities are re-generated and the countryside is protected from urban sprawl.

This is a planned solution, a green solution, a solution which puts people back at the heart of planning, a solution worthy of the 21st Century. It is taking an idea that was developed against a background of intense urbanization in the UK a century ago, a trend that is now experienced by countries the world over. It is taking a solution that has been tested and applied – not a theoretical model – and shown to work successfully. Millions of people both in the UK and abroad live in garden suburbs, garden cities, new towns and settlements that owe their origins to the thinking of Howard and his pioneers. The time is ripe to consider how we may use this knowledge to extend community-led and truly shared sustainable developments, which offer the promise of a full life and a better life for all.

Urban Lifestyles: Spaces · Places · People, Benson & Roe (eds)
© 2000 Balkema, Rotterdam, ISBN 90 5809 169 4

The politics and poetics of place: What do we mean by the public realm in contemporary urban policy?

K. Worpole
London, UK

ABSTRACT: This paper looks at the current interest in the design of the public realm in urban place-making, but argues that the public realm is, in addition to being a physical realm, also a symbolic (and political) sphere, as well as a relational and emotional sphere. It draws on research undertaken by the author and colleagues associated with Comedia and Demos over the past decade, into the quality of public life in British towns and cities, and cites a number of reports published in this period resulting from this research.

1 THE PUBLIC REALM

The concern over the quality of the public realm in British towns and cities has been growing for some time, and finds clear expression in the Urban Task Force report (1999), where arguments are made for developing a 'public realm strategy' through the creation of a network of public spaces. It is also evident in projects such as London's 'World Squares for All' initiative, in the success of Birmingham's city centre refurbishment, in the continuing interest in town centre management, and also in urban design as a new, and distinct, set of professional practices. Architects, planners, retailers and businesses are once again becoming interested in the spaces in between buildings, the connective and permeable tissue of the modern urban form - and its safety, management and funding. Similar concerns and practices are evident in cities throughout the world, particularly historic or ex-industrial cities which are having to adapt to new economies and lifestyles. One thinks of the extensive work in the pedestrianization of Copenhagen, charted by Jan Gehl and Lars Gemzøe (1996), or of the new parks in Barcelona and Paris (Rowe 1997), or of New York's Battery Park now extending along the west waterfront of Manhattan. There are many other examples of new such urban place-making.

Yet the public realm is more than a physical infrastructure. It is also a symbolic and political realm (where it connects to related concepts such as 'the public sphere' and even 'the public service ethos' in broadcasting, each with its traditions of universality and enlightenment procedures); and furthermore it is a relational and poetic sphere (the setting in which people learn to trust each other and behave appropriately in different kinds of public meeting places, or find themselves a convivial home in the city).

'Public service in culture and communications had two dimensions. One was an ethos of selfless service, rationality and an elevated and rather abstract idea of the public good involving a concern for the national identity And detachment from vested interests. The second was a set of principles about provision: geographical and social universality and provision for minorities as well as majorities.

What was missing from these definitions was any sense of public control or direct democratic accountability. Instead control rested with managers and specialists, intellectuals, librarians and engineers: the ethos and rules of professions.'
(Mulgan, 1993)

One cannot address the physical aspects of 'the public realm' without acknowledging the two dimensions identified here, preferably addressing simultaneously in integrated ways.

So, for example, streets cannot be made safer exclusively through good design. People also need to have a sense of who is taking care of their maintenance, management and security, demonstrating a clear symbolic ownership and sense of proprietorial care.

'The declining quality of Britain's urban parks and open spaces is now a matter of extensive public concern, and is part of a wider fear that we can no longer manage safety and well-being in public spaces. Is the 'keeper-less park', along with the unstaffed railway station, the poorly-lit underground car park, the unsupervised playground, and the deserted town centre at night, going to become another ghost zone of modern Britain?'
(Greenhalgh & Worpole, 1995)

Likewise people expect to trust other users to abide by certain conventions of behaviour and 'rules of engagement' which adhere to the use of public places. This trinitarian approach to the public realm may in the longer term be a more robust way of addressing current concerns than simply though physical programmes of urban regeneration and renewal.

2 THE PHYSICAL PUBLIC REALM

Obviously decline in the public realm is most graphically illustrated through its physical manifestations: boarded up and vandalized suburban railway stations, run-down parks with burnt-out pavilions, broken pavements, unattended and uncompleted street excavations, pot-holed and poorly-maintained roads, graffiti-scrawled walls, shops with iron grilles and shutters, poorly maintained municipal libraries and sports facilities, and so on. Physical dereliction is not simply an eyesore: it produces in vulnerable groups, particularly women, a sense of insecurity and danger. Therefore in a positive sense, repair of the physical fabric is a pre-condition of the repair of the social and civic fabric too. But physical regeneration is only a part of the solution to urban decline.

'After 6 o'clock in the evening many towns offer little to women on their own or in groups except feelings of insecurity and male suspicion. The pub, often the only available refreshment and waiting place after the cafes have closed and before the restaurants open, is effectively out of bounds to single women. Women have particular difficulties with the isolation and darkness of multi-storey car parks, of waiting at bus stops or on station platforms where they are often shouted at or pestered, or of walking past gangs of young men.
The 'Woolwich for Women' survey by Wendy Davies and Dr Bridget Leach noted that simply having more people around improves a sense of safety, but not if they are all groups of young men; that lack of traffic in pedestrianised streets was a cause for alarm in the evenings; that improved lighting and policing was the most frequent response to reduce fear. They also found that older women were more worried about a 'nameless fear' that could not be directly related to any one particular street, park or venue, but reflected a general apprehension about modern urban life. In the Manchester study we found that older women were particularly offended by rubbish, graffiti and poor environmental conditions.'
(Greenhalgh et al., 1991)

Even so, there is still a political mindset which regards expenditure on the physical public realm as economically unproductive, and therefore way down towards the bottom of the list of urban priorities. Often cheap-rate, quick-fix solutions are gaining preference over long term investment. This is both shortsighted and palpably wrong. Much public landscaping in the UK relies on standardized materials and street furniture, and assumes standardized concepts of human need. It rarely responds to the specificities - and histories - of particular places and communities.

Yet we know that a well-maintained park can raise property values in an area and encourage inward migration to urban areas and inward investment too. However we need a way of measuring and capturing this added-value and turning it into revenue funds for maintenance. Certainly the city council in Paris has learned this lesson, and has used large-scale investment in parks such as Parc Villette, Parc André-Citroën and Parc Bercy to stimulate urban regeneration. In Britain it is still more common to develop a new housing estate or industrial site first, and then grass any land left over and call it a park as an afterthought.

3 THE SYMBOLIC REALM

The American architect, Christopher Alexander (1997), wrote that, 'Without common land no social system can survive.' Public space is the essential physical setting for a civil democracy, and therefore it has great symbolic political as well as practical value. The right to free assembly, to walk the streets in safety, without undue interference by authority, have been hard-won freedoms.

> 'Street life is essentially about short journeys. The more interesting the activities in the street the longer the journey will take and the less it will become 'traffic movement', as the planners might call it. Yet as Mayer Hillman and Anne Whalley have suggested, it is an accepted view that long journeys are always more important than short journeys. Why? Surely the escorting of children to school, the daily shopping trip and morning coffee with friends that many pensioners make, the window shopping, the business transaction conducted in the street are all as socially and even economically important as the motorway commuter journey?'
> (Worpole, 1992)

Totalitarian regimes have attempted to destroy the haphazard and often intimate forms of public space by the ruthless engineering of monumental architecture and street layouts, with boulevards and squares monumental enough to dwarf and intimidate the individual citizen. More recently newer kinds of appropriation of traditional public realm spaces, such as can be seen in large, gated shopping malls, or corporate spaces, have re-introduced elements of surveillance and judgementalism that is at odds with the historic freedom of the streets. As Marc Augé (1995) has recently noted, 'the user of a non-place is always required to prove his innocence.'

So public space is human-scale, and owes as much to the historic forms of private and religious architecture - cathedral squares, church grounds, town houses, courtyards, lanes, inns, commercial buildings - as it does to civic architecture and planning. Today, however, local authorities are principally responsible for the adoption and maintenance of the public highways, pedestrian streets, town squares and so on, and therefore are the stewards and guardians of the physical public realm. In the high years of Victorian and early 20th century municipalism - the years of Joseph Chamberlain's espousal of 'the civic gospel' - the municipal coat of arms or badge was often used to imprint this sense of guardianship upon the public realm, whether on lamp-posts, waste bins, street signs, benches, park rules and regulations, and elsewhere, a tradition now maintained fairly weakly, with the possible exception of the Corporation of London which still asserts its patrician sovereignty at every turn. Today the imprint on street furniture is more likely to be that of a global fast food company exerting its sovereignty over the urban terrain.

> 'What is at issue here is the gradual erosion of public space, of the 'civic realm' as it has often been called: that geographical and historical space in our towns and cities that properly belongs to the residents as a community, in the form of town squares, public gardens. street markets and meeting places. Today the building of new, enclosed shopping malls has literally taken that space away. What used to be public thoroughfares

and streets and alleys have now been built upon by large shopping centres, which are closed at night and locked up.'
(Bianchini *et al.*, 1988)

Public space does not necessarily have to be publicly-owned however: there are many squares, gardens, churchyards, courtyards, footpaths, towpaths, and even building interiors which are in private or institutional hands which are nevertheless used by the public as *de facto* parts of the public realm. A recent architectural study of public space in Amsterdam (Kloos, 1993) intriguingly listed a number of department store restaurants, bars, record stores and other, often indoor, spaces, which have become part of the 'public realm' of the city - places which Amsterdam residents regard as belonging to them as much as to their legal owners. So, flexibility of definition is needed, and public practices and attitudes are as much an ingredient of the notion of 'publicness' as institutional or legal attribution.

4 THE RELATIONAL REALM

The public realm is also a realm where different kinds of social relations develop, separate from the family or from institutional life. Strangers talk to each other on park benches, ask for directions, enjoy being one of the crowd, and assume for the most part the goodwill and trust of others. The kindness of strangers is a phrase that is coming to haunt modern political discourses, as we appreciate just how much society is maintained and carried on by the invisible webs of public trust which bind people together and which if broken down - through ethnic or religious enmity and suspicion, or forms of communitarian distrust and even violence - can have catastrophic results. Cities are historically the settings where trust between strangers has become a vital ingredient of their success.

'Lost in a strange city, we ask strangers for directions, assuming that they will come to our aid. If we couldn't in principle trust strangers to be helpful and truthful, then everyday life would quickly grind to a halt. As Durkheim pointed out, most people feel obliged to tell the truth in the same way that they feel obliged to act morally. Modern life, then, is underwritten by working and social relationships based on the assumption that people will seek to do good rather than to do harm, and that the negligent doctor, the dishonest shop worker, the abusive child-care worker, the selfish neighbour or the disloyal friend, is the exception rather than the rule. Yet the question as to what makes up this 'social glue' which holds societies together continues to intrigue us.

Despite the fact that most societies manage to avoid degenerating into a war of all against all, it is often said that modern societies increasingly exhibit greater selfishness and a lack of concern for others, and that within those societies there are now places - particularly parts of cities - where most trust relationships have broken down irrevocably, requiring the enforcement of social control by widespread electronic surveillance, punitive policing and the use of the criminal justice system to remove more and more people from their community in the interests of others.'
(Worpole, 1998)

Yet these trust relations are often rule-governed, or at least codified by conventions. Historians of the public realm such as Jurgen Habermas and Richard Sennett have emphasized the formal, even theatrical, nature of social etiquette and public behaviour in the setting of the coffee house, the street, the theatre, the debating society, and many other public social settings. The creation of a significant and still influential set of public institutions in Victorian Society - the art gallery, the public library, the public park - were all heavily rule-governed and assumed and policed forms of appropriate and inappropriate behaviour through local by-laws and other forms of regulation. In a more formal sense, cities are where we produce citizens.

'The (third) defining principle behind the expansion of public space is the physical experience of democracy. Ideas of democracy are shifting, and electronic media like E-

Mail and the Net bring new opportunities for chance meetings, and a sense of public membership. But they are no substitute for the bodily experience of democracy. This bodily experience of the random goodwill of the majority, unmediated by hardware, is as fundamental to the experience of humanity as the loving touch of the parent.'
(Shonfield, 1998)

The 'rules of engagement' of public life are still mostly adhered to by most people; indeed they are occasionally changed by legislation and new rules quickly fall into place and become accepted as 'natural': no smoking in cinemas or on public transport, no drinking and driving, no mis-treating of animals. Environmentalism is itself slowly establishing new rules of conduct, emphasizing that one individual's environmental pollution affects everybody, and this is becoming an interesting new area of public discourse and form of citizenship.

'Freedom is indivisible' is a fine-sounding abstraction, but it is quite wrong. The moment people live together, they begin to bend each other's freedoms. The tighter we are packed, the more our `externalities' hit others. One loud hi-fi can deprive hundreds of sleep; a small group of anti-social residents can make a whole neighbourhood afraid. So we each turn our hi-fis down so all can sleep; we each pay our share of policing costs through taxes; we refrain from vandalizing the bus stops and trees that add to everyone's amenity.

The city is the classical site of achievement of private desires through provision of public goods, and of a clear recognition of the limits to private decisions and the need to place these within a broader framework of planning for the public good. The city is the home of the social contract. No city can function without it.'
(Christie & Levett, 1999)

Perhaps in the end it is the relational aspects of the public sphere which are the key to long-term urban sustainability, though they in turn are strongly inter-related with the physical and symbolic forms of stewardship and regulation.

5 CONCLUSIONS

The renewed architectural and civic interest in public space is to be welcomed, but it will require a cross-disciplinary and multi-professional approach to design and management if it is to be successful. It will also require a firm philosophical and political underpinning. For there is a struggle going on in cities between 'public-civic' and 'global-commercial' imperatives to gain sovereignty of the urban terrain. Environmentalism, with its requirements for urban design and place-making which respect natural elements, together with forms of waste management and recycling which require a revolution in social attitudes towards the material world, poses a challenge to develop a more benign notion of urban life and the public realm.

REFERENCES

Alexander, C. 1977. A Pattern Language, Oxford: Oxford University Press.
Augé, M. 1995. Non-Places: introduction to an anthropology of supermodernity, London: Verso.
Bianchini, F. Fisher, M., Montgomery, J. & Worpole, K. 1988. City Centres, City Cultures, Manchester: Centre for Local Economic Strategies.
Christie, I. & Levett, R. 1999. Towards the Ecopolis: sustainable development and urban governance, London: Comedia & Demos.
Gehl, J. & Gemzøe, L. 1996. Public Spaces, Public Life, Copenhagen: The Danish Architectural Press.
Greenhalgh, L., Landry, C., Montgomery, J. & Worpole, K. 1991. Out of Hours: A study of economic, social and cultural life in twelve town centres in the UK, London: Comedia.
Greenhalgh, L. & Worpole, K. 1995. Park Life: Urban Parks and Social Renewal, London: Comedia & Demos.

Kloos, M. 1993. Public Interiors: Architecture and Public Life inside Amsterdam, Amsterdam: Architectura & Natura Press.

Mulgan, G. 1993. The Public Service Ethos and Public Libraries, London: Comedia.

Rowe, C. 1997. Civic Realism, Cambridge MA: MIT Press.

Shonfield, K. 1998. At Home with Strangers: public space and the new urbanity, London: Comedia & Demos.

Urban Task Force. 1999. Towards an Urban Renaissance, London: E & F Spon.

Worpole, K. 1998. Nothing to Fear? Trust and respect in urban communities, London: Comedia & Demos.

Worpole, K. 1992. Towns for People, Milton Keynes: Open University Press.

Theoretical approaches to transforming spaces and places

Urban Lifestyles: Spaces · Places · People, Benson & Roe (eds)
© 2000 Balkema, Rotterdam, ISBN 90 5809 169 4

Experiental landscape: Place, neighbourhood and community in landscape architecture

K.Thwaites
Leeds Metropolitan University, UK

ABSTRACT: There is evidence in professional and academic journals of concern about limitations in landscape architecture which bias technical and aesthetic considerations over experiential dimensions important to achieving human fulfilment. This is particularly significant in residential environments. In response, with particular reference to Norberg-Schulz's existential space schemata, environmental psychology research by Kaplan, Kaplan and Ryan and participative practices developed by Christopher Alexander, this paper seeks to integrate spatial and experiential dimensions into a new conceptual structure. It argues that this provides a basis from which to develop an understanding of neighbourhoods as mosaics of experiential landscape places and of communities as living entities which embody the expressions imbued into them through socially inclusive and participative landscape design processes.

1 INTRODUCTION

This paper is about research, which seeks to combine spatial and experiential dimensions in a new approach to place perception in neighbourhood settings. The research has been motivated by a growing awareness that landscape architecture's emphasis on the spatial configuration of residential environments may not always be sufficient to ensure that residents experience them as fulfilling and life enriching places. The research takes as its theoretical foundations the idea, promoted by Merleau-Ponty (1962), Norberg-Schulz (1971), and Alexander (1979) in particular, that routine human experience is intimately related to space and that a good correspondence between space and experience is an essential component in achieving a good quality of human life. The overall aim is to develop from these theoretical foundations a conceptual model and methodology which will enable the locally specific place perceptions of individuals and groups in communities to be accessed, defined and mapped to provide a plan of experiential landscape places which collectively make up neighbourhood perceptions. In the longer term it is envisaged that such maps will provide a basis from which to evaluate neighbourhood quality and to propose design strategies for improvement. This paper's principal purpose is to present key elements of the theoretical foundations of experiential landscape and to show how they contribute to the development of a conceptual model called experiential landscape place.

2 LIMITATIONS IN LANDSCAPE ARCHITECTURE

That patterns of human life have particular spatial implications has been well consolidated in environmental psychology research since the early 1970's. Related disciplines too, including social anthropology, structural geography and aspects of the natural and social sciences concerned with the human-environment relationship, underpin a growing understanding that a close bond of association between what people do and where they do it is crucial to establishing and maintaining a fulfilled life. Making outdoor places fulfilling experiences which add to the quality of human life is central to landscape architecture also and there are well established contributions to theory, mainly from the architectural and urban planning arenas, which lay the foundations for socially responsive approaches (Lynch, 1960; Alexander *et al.*, 1977; Bentley *et al.*, 1985). But, there is growing consciousness in landscape architecture that the importance of human psychological and emotional experiences to the design of landscape places may not yet have penetrated sufficiently deeply into the professional ethos. This is central to the motivation behind Kaplan, Kaplan and Ryan's publication *With People in Mind* in which they say, "There has not been an easy way to access the research literature and translate it into usable recommendations. This book is an effort to address that gap." (Kaplan, Kaplan & Ryan, 1998, p.ix).

The Kaplan's concern is the accessibility of research findings, but there are, I believe, other reasons, related to the mind-set of landscape architecture, to explain why an experiential dimension has yet to become consolidated into landscape architecture. Consider, for example, Ken Worpole's comment in the Guardian newspaper in response to the publication of eight photographs in Landscape Design of the award winning Royal Albert Dock piazza: not one including a single person. "...human needs are sacrificed on the altar of design and aestheticism in many British towns...People tend to go missing in the pristine imagery of architecture and design where life's untidiness is regarded as an aesthetic intrusion." (Worpole, 1998, p.4). This reflects a wider critical debate, ongoing in landscape architecture and particularly evident in the USA *Landscape Journal*, that human meaning in contemporary landscapes is frequently sterilised by over-emphasis on the production of landscapes as expressions of professional excellence, demonstrating technical proficiency and aesthetic value whilst remaining socially irrelevant (Koh, 1982; Lyle, 1985; Howett, 1998). Landscapes arranged to be merely used or merely contemplated for their beauty, it is argued, are incomplete in ways crucial to human life quality (Corner, 1991). This approach overlooks that what is important to human fulfillment is largely experiential, related to understanding, and not simply use of the environment; to freedom of choice to interpret freely and modify the surroundings according to personal assessments of need, desire and aspiration; to be able to experience a measure of autonomy and self-determination. This indicates a deficit in landscape architecture's capability to deliver landscapes which are fulfilling experiences, beneficial to human life quality.

Nowhere, perhaps, is this more important than in residential neighbourhoods where territorial impulses are often intensified and where private needs and personal preferences have to be reconciled with communal interests and shared use of local space. I want to argue for a different kind of mental orientation toward residential landscape, not as product, but as an experiential entity which draws together existential, experiential and participatory approaches to understanding people-space relations into a new conceptual structure called experiential landscape. Much is owed, philosophically and intellectually, to the environmental conceptions of Christian Norberg-Schulz and Christopher Alexander. Their thinking, along with that of others, helps develop an understanding of residential neighbourhoods as interwoven mosaics of places, defined in both spatial and experiential terms, in which the creative engagement of people with them is an important element in the achievement of individual fulfilment and community cohesion.

3 PHILOSOPHICAL AND THEORETICAL UNDERPINNING OF EXPERIENTIAL LANDSCAPE

Understanding landscapes as experiential entities has philosophical and theoretical implications for landscape architecture. It requires a conception of the human-environment relationship that is mutually creative: as people shape their environment, through acts of making and use, so too does the environment shape people. "You cannot divorce man and space. Space is neither an external object nor an internal experience. We don't have man and space besides..." (Heidegger, 1954, p.31). A similar perspective on the human-environment relationship is to be found in Isaiah Berlin's interpretation of the philosophy of Herder (Berlin, 1965). Berlin argues that the shaping of environment by individuals and groups can be understood as a form of expression: not simply the production of an objective product in the form of landscape or building, but a communication, a voice by means of which people express to others something about them-

50

selves, their values, aspirations, needs and desires. "Men, according to Herder, only in congenial circumstances, that is, where the group to which they belong ʰ fruitful relationship with the environment by which it is shaped and which in tʰ (Berlin, 1965, p.65). These ideas present a conception of landscape which has seⁱ expressions of lives being lived. Because the achievement of fulfillment is relat expressive potential in their social and environmental context, something fundaʳ them when they are solely recipients of new landscapes rather than creative and active pₐ... pants.

Mayer Spivak was possibly one of the first to consider the implications of an integrated relationship of human psychological functioning and space for environmental design in 1973. "...what people do in these settings constitutes the "meaning" in our environment. It is what makes a *place* out of a space." (Spivak, 1973, p.46). Spivak postulated a finite range of thirteen behaviourally defined archetypal places, for example; shelter, route, and territory (ibid,p.43), asserting that there is a range of fundamental human behaviour, variable according to age, which has direct spatial implications. Spivak's work not only links psychological health with place, defined as a fusion of behavioural functioning and where it happens, but also with the routine experience of a diversity of places. People who do not experience an appropriate correspondence between what they do and where they do it, and who are unable to access sufficient diversity of place experience may suffer detrimental effects from setting deprivation according to Spivak (ibid, p.44). The wider development of place theory is generally attributed to David Canter (1977) who sought to unite behaviour, subjective impulses and the material world in a phenomenological conception of place. This is strengthened and given a dialectical orientation by Tuan (1980) who says the sense of place is sustained by processes of communication and can be understood as an expression of community cohesion: a demonstration of creative participation rather than simply a process of manufacture. Place is therefore important to the development of processes of individual and community identity just as much as to the development of new material surroundings.

Drawn together these writers present a conception of environment and people, integrated as place, which is important to the achievement of human psychological health. Place is not simply location, but also expression: a means of communicating and sharing values and aspirations with others and, through the participative and creative activity of place making, a means of generating and sustaining community cohesion. The following material aims to bring this conception of the human-environment relationship more closely to landscape design by describing the key components of a conceptual model to combine ideas of place, neighbourhood and community.

4 EXPERIENTIAL LANDSCAPE: THE DEVELOPMENT OF A SPATIAL DIMENSION

Central to this aim is the existential space schemata developed by Christian Norberg-Schulz (1971) in which he defines space as the concretisation of man's existential space. "In a certain sense, any man who chooses a place in his environment to settle and live, is a creator of expressive space. He makes his environment meaningful by assimilating it to his purposes at the same time as he accommodates the conditions it offers." (Norberg-Schulz, 1971, p.11). This spatial concept also recognizes the importance of creative participation in the realization of one's own existential space image. Because it includes aspects of a personal and subjective nature, individuals cannot, entirely satisfactorily, be only recipients of spaces, they must instead have some measure of creative engagement which allows for personal expressions to be realized.

The concept of existential space has three constituent elements, which can be developed as an organizational framework for understanding the spatial and experiential anatomy of neighbourhoods. These elements are: centres or places (proximity); directions or paths (continuity); areas or domains (enclosure). Centres, or places, are the basic elements of existential space and are understood as subjectively centred locations; an awareness of a sense of hereness or inside which is distinguishable from the rest of the surrounding environment. Since existential space comprises many places it is understood as a composite entity; a network, or mosaic, of places. It also has direction, or continuity, as a linear succession. Direction, or path, is the element of existential space which links together distinguishable places. It too has its subjective dimension in that progression is made in the direction of personally significant goals and by means of personally chosen routes. It is experienced as having a distinguishable character of its own, given by perceptions and events that happen along the way and so is more than simply a functional element allowing mobility from point A to point B. Finally, places and paths exist in areas, or domains, which are defined as the relatively unstructured ground on which places and paths appear as more pronounced figures. Domain has a unifying function as a recognizable region within which places, as personally significant centres, and paths, as personally significant directions, can be discerned.

Existential space provides an organizational structure for understanding space as existence, rather than simply as a geometric or physical entity. It is a composite comprising of places as basic elements connected by the concept of direction or path. Places and paths are distinguishable by individuals as existing within a wider and more general domain. It is limited, however, in that actual human experiences in space are not dealt with except at a very rudimentary level. We have to turn to other sources to add experiential elements to the spatial elements described above.

5 EXPERIENTIAL LANDSCAPE: THE DEVELOPMENT OF AN EXPERIENTIAL DIMENSION

In their recent publication, *With People in Mind*, Kaplan, Kaplan & Ryan (1998) highlight four themes which, in their experience, are frequently associated with negative human characteristics. They suggest that people tend to be difficult or problematic when:

- The environment hinders or blocks their *understanding*;
- The environment lacks opportunities for *exploration*;
- The environment fails to foster experiences that are *restful and enjoyable*;
- People feel that their *participation* is not welcome (Kaplan, Kaplan & Ryan, 1998, p.149).

Being able to understand the surroundings, to be able to explore, rest and enjoy, and to feel involved are, according to these authors, fundamental experiences which are directly related to people's attitudes towards each other and to the environment they inhabit. Similar themes also resonate through the work of others and together provide for a more detailed appreciation of human experiences in relation to environmental contact.

Understanding: The need for people to be able to make sense of the surroundings is well established as necessary for orientation. Without this "...the sense of anxiety and even terror that accompanies it reveals to us how closely it is linked to our sense of balance and well-being." (Lynch, 1960, p.4). A perception that particular regions can be distinguished from one another and the presence of distinctive elements as orienting devices are frequently cited as necessary environmental attributes in this respect (Lynch, 1960; Lozano, 1974; Carr *et al*, 1992). The establishment of orienting features in the context of neighbourhoods can be related particularly to the experience of variety and diversity. Lozano (1974) differentiates between the two in visual terms indicating that variety refers to subtle variations within an otherwise co-ordinated set, whilst diversity refers to a range of different sets and implies a greater degree of differentiation. This implies that it is important for people to be able to understand their surroundings at least two levels. One in which there is the experience of a sense of overall cohesion beyond detailed variations, and one in which that particular sense of overall cohesion can be distinguished from others. At the neighbourhood level this implies a need for a diversity of neighbourhoods within a locality or region, so that it is possible to distinguish one's own ground from someone else's, and for each neighbourhood to exhibit its own variations whilst remaining a discernibly cohesive entity.

Exploration: Understanding the surroundings is primarily related to establishing a sense of familiarity, an awareness of where one is, and perhaps where one belongs, in relation to what is around. People also need to experience what lies beyond the familiar from time to time, both physically, to seek out new places for example, and psychologically, in relation to considering options, wondering and imagining, experiencing a sense of mystery and the possibility of discovery (Cullen, 1966). Kaplan, Kaplan & Ryan (1998) consider that exploration is encouraged in settings which are not too explicit, where they contain hints of something yet to be revealed, or where they invite reflective contemplation by engaging the imagination. This strengthens the need for environments to hold a sense of mystery and ambiguity, to be open to interpretation and personalization, so that features and spaces can be used for different purposes by different people on different occasions (Carr, 1992).

Rest and Enjoyment: There is fundamental need for people to be able to retreat from stimulation to relax and recuperate implying two environmental requirements: one is the establishment of the homeground, one's own place of escape from unwanted distractions; second is the ability to access places of retreat in the wider public environment. The first has a clear territorial tone relating to the need for places, which offer the possibility of complete withdrawal. There is, however, an important distinction to be drawn between different levels of withdrawal (Carr, 1992). There is the need, usually associated with one's own private space, for a high degree of personal security and tranquility providing experience of deep relaxation and sleep. But private spaces should not always be so abruptly detached from the surrounding area that they prohibit the possibility for watching and monitoring. Seeing without necessarily being seen is, according to research by Kaplan & Kaplan (1989) and Carr (1992), an enjoyable pursuit, important to the achievement of personal satisfactions. Neighbourhood environments can be structured to accommodate varying levels of withdrawal according to Martin's (1997) evaluation of back-alleys as community landscapes, by balancing revealingness and hiddenness: the extent to which social interactions can be encouraged or discouraged by whether boundary features, such as fences and walls are open or closed to visual penetration.

Participation: The concept of participation is, to some extent, the most important of all in this context. Without this, even though new places may be planned to be as responsive as possible to the kinds of experiences outlined above, people are always recipients. A significant experience is denied them under these circumstances: that of their creative involvement in the design and management of their nearby world. The achievement of personal expressions in the environment has much to do with the level of participation people can experience in planning and design processes. Usually, however, the environments people live in and use are prescribed for them by professionals. Opportunities for personal expressions may be substantially constrained, at least beyond the boundaries of what is perceived to be private territory. Extending beyond this implies a much closer association between people and design and making processes than conventional approaches often allow. Lozano (1974), for example, has argued for planning abstentions in certain circumstances to encourage personal expressions as a positive feature of the fabric of towns. Something similar is also advocated by Alexander who argues that good environmental form is intimately associated with the creative empowerment of people throughout every stage of design and fabrication processes (Alexander *et al*, 1977, 1979, 1985).

6 EXPERIENTIAL LANDSCAPE: PLACE, NEIGHBOURHOOD AND COMMUNITY

I want now to show how the spatial and experiential dimensions can be related as experiential landscape and how they contribute to an understanding of the relationship between place, neighbourhood and community. The building blocks of this conception are experiential landscape places. In the context of residential neighbourhoods, Norberg-Schulz's existential space schemata can be interpreted to mean that neighbourhoods consist of places, distinguishable from one another as focal points of human existence, but linked together by paths, or direction. Places and their associated direction are intrinsically personal entities: different people occupying the same spatial location may not necessarily perceive the same places, since place perception involves a significant subjective component.

Although Norberg-Schulz defines place in terms of human existence, specifically in terms of the sense of centred-ness and direction, the human existential dimension goes little further in his concept. But, drawing from material considered earlier, it is possible to give this conception of place and neighbourhood a more detailed experiential dimension. For example, rest and enjoyment is primarily related to the establishment of the homeground and the need to experience retreat from stimulation. These imply experiences closely associated with subjectively centred locations, or the awareness of proximity, at the heart of Norberg-Schulz's definition of place. Furthermore, Norberg-Schulz's place also includes direction: the sense that places are connected and that it is possible to experience progression in the direction of personally significant goals by means of personally chosen routes. This is close to the concept of exploration suggesting that the existential awareness of direction in Norberg-Schulz's schemata also carries a richer experiential implication to do with engaging the imagination through a sense of mystery and ambiguity and the promise of fulfillment by realizing future possibilities. Experiential landscape places can, then, be defined in terms of the spatial dimensions of place and direction, and associated experiential dimensions, of rest and enjoyment and exploration. Following this conception, neighbourhood, then, equates with Norberg-Schulz's concept of domain, or area, against which places and paths (experiential landscape places) appear as more pronounced figures relating to personal perceptions. It too has an experiential dimension in the category of understanding which emphasizes the experience of orientation through identifying landmark features and the experience of being able to distinguish between the characteristics of one's own neighbourhood and that of others.

Finally I want to turn to the concept of community and its relationship to place and neighbourhood. I have suggested that sets of experiential landscape places are personally significant and can be considered as collectives, or mosaics, which make up neighbourhoods. Because experiential landscape places are defined experientially as well as spatially, it follows that a neighbourhood is not simply a receptacle for people, but is itself a living entity defined, at least in part, by the human activity which takes place there. Similarly, communities are not simply defined as aggregations of people in a common location. For there truly to be community there must be sharing of common interests between people: strong communities tend to be those with a diversity of things they share and care about. Sharing is essentially a process of communication and so if people can find ways to communicate with one another they have the foundations from which communities are built. Alexander (1979) in particular believes that design and building are processes of communication through which people share their values, desires and personal idiosyncrasies in the common aim of making places which will not simply accommodate them as communities, but will embody the values which have been imbued into them through their collective creative effort. The experiential dimension participation defines, then, the means by which places and neighbourhoods go beyond being empty receptacles for living and become living communities where life experiences are not simply contained within landscape and building but are actually expressed through them. This kind of building, essentially emotion in built form, is given the name "pathetecture" by Walter (1988, p.143).

In Alexander's work, the processes by which individuals and communities can design and build residential settings that are "the concrete expression of their place in the world, the concrete expression of themselves." (Alexander *et al*, 1985, p.16) involves setting up a creative process in which user groups participate at every stage. This begins with identifying what the existing environment means to them and how they wish it to support the patterns of their lives as individuals, families and as a community. It is an approach to design and making which attempts to marry together the spatial and physical features of a site with the experiences and uses local people associate with them and want to get from them. There are, of course, many questions about the applicability of these processes to a British system. Indeed, Alexander is quite explicit about the need for significant changes to the social and political contexts of house building if his ideas are to have any widespread relevance. Nevertheless, my own view is that certain features can be identified in Alexander's work which are relevant to the concept of experiential landscape and provide a basis from which to develop strategies for socially inclusive and participatory approaches to the landscape design of certain neighbourhood environments, and which have the potential to foster a sense of community as well as make changes to the physical fabric of the setting. These include: experiencing the act of making in which the purpose is to ensure that the creativity, including intuitive impulses, of all participants are included as positive features; and an emphasis on the accumulative impact of small scale tasks which aim to stress the quality of the work experience rather than merely the manufacture of predetermined end products.

7 CONCLUSIONS

In this paper I have argued that there is a deficiency in landscape architecture which impedes its capability to make places beneficial to human fulfillment and community cohesion, and that this has particular significance for neighbourhood landscapes. The nature of this deficit is the lack of an active experiential dimension in the way the relationship between people and outdoor space is understood and that this results in practices which seek mainly to prescribe and impose solutions onto recipient communities rather than engage their participation. By developing Norberg-Schulz's existential space schemata I have tried to show that it is possible to conceptualize landscape as an entity defined in terms of an experiential dimension as well as a spatial dimension.

I am now developing a methodology to enable experiential landscape places to be mapped. Interpreted locally, the experiential dimension of the concept provides a basis for an evaluatory framework against which to measure the health of neighbourhoods in relation to the perceptions of those who live in them. By this means people in residential environments are empowered to identify their personally significant realm and to understand its quality in terms of their own perceptions of need and desire. It is intended that localized mapping and evaluation of experiential landscape places will inform democratic creative decision making about what improvements are necessary and how they are to be carried out.

REFERENCES

Alexander, C. 1979. *The Timeless Way of Building.* New York: Oxford University Press.
Alexander, C., Davis, H., Martinez,.J. & Corner, D. 1985. *The Production of Houses.* New York: Oxford University Press.
Alexander, C., Ishikawa, S., Silverstein, M., Jacobson, M., Fiksdahl-King, I. & Angel, .S. 1977. *A Pattern Language.* New York: Oxford University Press.
Bentley, I., Alcock, A., Martin, P., McGlynn, S. & Smith, G. 1985. *Responsive Environments.* London: The Architectural Press.
Berlin, I. 1965. *Herder and the Enlightenment.* In E.R. Wasserman, Aspects of the Eighteenth Century. Baltimore: The John Hopkins Press.
Canter, D. 1977. *The Psychology of Place.* London: The Architectural Press.
Carr, S., Francis, M., Rivlin, L.G. & Stone, A.M. 1992. *Public Space.* Cambridge: Cambridge University Press.
Corner, J. 1991. *A Discourse on Theory II: Three Tyrannies of Contemporary Theory and the Alternative of Hermeneutics.* Landscape Journal vol10, Fall 1991, pp. 115-133.
Cullen, G. 1971. *The Concise Townscape.* Oxford: Architectural Press.
Heidegger, M. quote from Norberg-Schulz.C. 1971. *Existence, Space, and Architecture.* New York: Praeger.
Howett, C. 1998. *Ecological Values in Twentieth-Century Landscape Design: History and Hermeneutics.* Landscape Journal, Special Issue, pp. 80-98.
Kaplan, R., & Kaplan, S. 1989. *The Experience of Nature: A Psychological Perspective.* New York: Cambridge University Press.
Kaplan, R., Kaplan, S. & Ryan, R.L. 1998. *With People in Mind: Design and Management of Everyday Nature.* Washington: Island Press.
Koh, J. 1982. *Ecological Design: A Post-Modern Paradigm of Holistic Philosophy and Evolutionary Ethic.* Landscape Journal 1:76-84.
Lozano, E.E. 1974. *Visual Needs in Urban Environments and Physical Planning.* Town Planning Review, 45: 351-374.
Lyle, J.T. 1985. *The Alternating Current of Design Process.* Landscape Journal 4:7-13.
Lynch, K. 1960. *The Image of the City.* Cambridge: MIT Press.
Martin, M. 1997. *Back-alley as Community Landscape.* Landscape Journal, Spring:138-153.
Merleau-Ponty, M. 1962. *Phenomenology of Perception.* London: Routledge and Kegan Paul.
Norberg-Schulz, C. 1971. *Existence, Space, and Architecture.* New York: Praeger.
Spivak, M. 1973. *Archetypal Place.* Architectural Forum. October:44-49.
Tuan, Y.F. 1980. Rootedness versus sense of place. *Landscape,* 24: 3-8.
Walter, E.V. 1988. *Placeways: A Theory of the Human Environment.* North Carolina: University of North Carolina Press.
Worpole, K. 1998. *People Before Beauty.* The Guardian Newspaper, 14 January. Society,p.4

Urban Lifestyles: Spaces · Places · People, Benson & Roe (eds)
© 2000 Balkema, Rotterdam, ISBN 90 5809 169 4

Using and conceiving public space influenced by urban transformation

M. Bassand & M. Zepf
Institute for Research on the Built Environment, Lausanne, Switzerland

ABSTRACT: The staging of urban life is mainly through urban public spaces. At the beginning of the 'sixties, the issues related to public spaces became a "space for thought" embracing questions of a social, spatial and politico-administrative nature. These questions concern the urban context in general. For this reason the ensemble of issues should be studied in relation to the way a city works, its present-day role, and the deep-seated changes (industrialisation, growth of the third sector, urban spread) which affect the city. Three contemporary phenomena relative to the dimensions of the study have been revealed. The analyses of these phenomena will lead to a more precise definition of social, spatial and political-administrative urbanity.

1 INTRODUCTION

The Institute for Research on the Built Environment (IREC) of the Department of Architecture at the Swiss Federal Institute of Technology - Lausanne (EPFL) has been developing research on public spaces for several years. Firstly work on the moderation of traffic (Bonanomi, 1990), then on the sound quality of public spaces (Amphoux, 1995), on the parks and gardens of Lausanne (Amphoux & Jaccoud 1992-1994), then on atmospheres (Amphoux, 1998), and finally the thesis of Marcus Zepf (1999) on four public squares in Lausanne. In this context, two IREC researchers (Bassand & Joye) are beginning research on three public squares in Geneva. It should be added that three IREC researchers have just published a report on public spaces in Lausanne (Jaccoud, Zepf, Leresche, 1999). It is in this research context that for several years Michel Bassand (sociologist), Pascal Amphoux (architect and geographer), Kaj Noschis (psychologist) and Yves Pedrazzini (sociologist) have been directing in the Department of Architecture at the EPFL a teaching unit on public spaces and their users; this gave rise to a whole series of exploratory and interdisciplinary monographs written by architecture students on Lausanne public spaces.

It should be recalled first of all that the concept of a public space has two meanings in social sciences. One meaning affirms the public space as immaterial, the other as material.

The first, the immaterial, is an idea established by Habermas (1978); he defines the public space as a debate within a community, a society or between the two, for example a debate on family and motherhood, on foreigners etc. Actors in the political arena or elsewhere discuss and confront ideas, values, public policy propositions; in so doing, they constitute a public space lasting a given length of time. A newspaper, a magazine, a TV, a political event can generate public spaces on the widest variety of themes. Actors in the social sphere can participate in these in various ways. The political life of a society is thus made up of an important grouping of public spaces, some which are the object of a political decision; for example, in Switzerland, the issue of foreigners recurs ceaselessly despite many decisions which should have settled it.

According to the second meaning the public space is material; it implies a concrete territory whether located in an urban community or not (Sennet, 1979; Joseph, 1992; *Plan urbain*, 1998), for example, a square, a street, etc. As a first step, two criteria are used to define this territory:

1. It is free of constrictions, thus it has not been appropriated by one player alone;
2. It is regulated by public law.

These two criteria, more or less interdependent, mean that an urban public space is open to all city-dwellers.

There is a link between these two meanings of the public space. In this article, we position ourselves with regard to the second. At this stage, we should not forget to mention a very important movement in research which studies territorialized public spaces (Goffmann, 1973). However, it often happens that research which positions itself within this movement omits the interaction between social practices and their material context. We will not follow this tendency, which is in fact a-territorial.

These choices make it necessary to define the term *urban*. Why? Because public spaces are one of the important elements in staging urban life. More than this, they are one of the elements that constitute the urban. The urban is in the process of being radically transformed. We refer to Choay, who has announced that the city is dead and that the urban now reigns. This neologism defines a constricted environment which no longer has anything to do with the city of former times but which nonetheless continues to be of the highest importance in the dynamic of contemporary societies (Bassand, 1997). The city can be characterised by five points:

1. concentration, density, compactness of activities and populations, which implies for both these last a highly advantageous proximity;
2. diversity of populations and activities, which constitutes an enrichment;
3. urban culture – or urbanity – which gives the city-dweller a lifestyle, an identity;
4. city-countryside relations which, because of the advantages the city possesses, always makes the city dominant in relation to the countryside;
5. more or less democratic urban government.

These five points enable us to define the urban, which has assumed its shape as of the fifties. We will do the same within five parameters:

- An urban spread in terms of sub-urbanisation, peri-urbanisation and the urbanisation of the countryside, which gives rise to a new entity: the urban agglomeration. Some are gigantic: in the area of a million inhabitants or more, these are metropolises; they dominate the organisation of territories.
- This urban spread or metropolisation is associated with globalisation. According to the United Nations, in 1999 there are about 400 metropolises in the world, which are laid out in a network of squares across the planet. Thanks to this framework, each metropolis enjoys, to varying degrees of course, world centrality. This is the essential characteristic of metropolises.
- Each metropolis witnesses the breaking up of its space in terms of areas of specialisation and segregation. This raises the threat of social fragmentation. To preserve a certain cohesion, each metropolis attempts to link the socio-spatial fragments (neighbourhoods and zones in particular) by networks of transport, public spaces, telecommunication, water, energy etc. Mobility of people and goods becomes essential.
- The metropolises' survival depends upon their capacity to take advantage of the globalisation of which they are a part, while guaranteeing internal cohesion, but also cohesion at the level of the neighbourhoods, zones, communities that they include. Social science has come up with the neologism "glocal" to designate this necessary dialectic between the global and the local. It is a very important characteristic of the urban and, thus, of the metropolises.
- The urban government of former times is over. A multitude of actors in the private and public arenas (community, national etc.) participate without democratic rules in managing these

macrocosms which are metropolises, as well as urban agglomerations. This partnership of various actors, where the strongest wins, is what is called governing.

What becomes of public spaces in the midst of the city's metamorphosis into urban-metropolis? They are laid out in networks and are, as such, one of the backbones of the city.

2 THE PACE OF URBAN LIFE IS ACCELERATING

Urban phenomena such as the Zurich "Street-Parade", the Lausanne "Rollerblade Contest", the "Wrapped Reichstag" in Berlin and the "scenic illumination" of public spaces in Lyon are witness to the accelerating pulsebeat of urban spaces. This change of pace affects both the real and the imaginary relationships of those who discover and "practise" the city but also, and especially, of those who think and construct it. Thus, the ideas and representations which, in the past, guided the accomplishment of large-scale urban projects are no longer able to respond to today's entangled and complex urban reality.

Thus, the image of future public spaces must strike a chord by dividing space in a manner more suited to the changing pace of urban life. The quest for new points of reference in the domain of the urban which would allow such spaces to be designed requires, therefore, an in-depth analysis of the processes by which these spaces are used, produced and shaped.

First of all, the issues around these public spaces are :
♦ understanding how the representation and designs of "producers" (public space management professionals, administrators and politicians) are constituted;
♦ understanding how the social practices of users (residents, citizens and visitors) are organized;
♦ understanding how spatial parameters (geographical sites, architectural characteristics, compositions of urban furnishings) are formalized.

In the second place, certain contemporary phenomena must be expressed which contribute to highlighting the socio-spatial realities observable today. Phenomena of "theatricalisation", "festivalisation" and "commercialization" appear particularly evocative and authorize a better definition of the recurring idea of discourse on the urban: *urbanity*.

Today, we are witnessing, according to Genestier (1997) the "progressive development of a mentality characterized by a multifaceted process: individuation; the mediatisation and intellectualization of the relation to the real; a demographic rise among the solvent inactive members of society, and an aristocratisation of lifestyle." (Genestier, 1997, p. 44). These social phenomena are witness to a deep-rooted transformation in urban society as regards the use of public spaces. Until now, the main function of most public spaces has been to manage traffic flow, even if certain public squares present a greater diversity of uses (market places, meeting centres, etc.) because of their enriched architectural context. The changes in social practices which have appeared with the "leisure society" have placed the issue of public spaces in the centre of the debate around urban development. More and more urban spaces are becoming strategic in staging the urban because they are supposed to satisfy a growing number of users who wish to consume what is "public".

According to certain authors who are preoccupied by the problem of urban public space production, "mixedness" appears as the main element of attractive public spaces. This mixedness contains an optimum diversity in terms of function and allocation, user groups and users. The result is a great variety of perceivable urban situations.

Moreover, these transformations call into question the integrating organization of the city and give rise among a certain number of authors to a debate on the defining idea of the city. Beck (1993) suggests two models, which form the basis of the urban social structure. The first model applies to a fragmented vision of the city and corresponds to an urban reality where neighbourhoods present more or less exclusive functions and uses. What Beck calls "die Stadt des 'entweder oder'" (the either/or city") refers to the nineteenth-century city (social separation in the interests of domination, security and control).

The second model "Die Stadt des 'und'" (the both/and city) introduces the idea of the city integrating functions and uses which are at first sight conflicting or paradoxical. This idea recovers the diversity, difference, unenclosed totality and the acceptance of ambivalence and irony.

"A tendency in architecture in the fifties was to favour individual life and space. The functions of this individual space were retreat, self-control and the intention of getting rid of external and internal constraints. This individual space however produces no social identity, not even a personal identity. Identity is produced in intermediate spaces, between the public domain and the private domain. The question of social identity becomes more and more important with the emergence of individualization. If the distinction is taken into consideration between good residence in underprivileged neighbourhoods and average residences in privileged neighbourhoods, the former are sought after, the latter avoided." (Beck, 1996, p. 363).

In this regard Augé (1992) can be quoted: "If past experience has taught us to de-centre our gaze, we must take advantage of this experience. The world of super-modernity cannot be exactly measured by the one we believe we are living in, because we live in a world we have not yet learned to look at. We have to re-learn how to think space." (p. 49)

A fundamental aspect of the initiatives to revitalize urban centres that have degenerated is often, therefore, the intention to construct the "both/and" city. In this city, spaces are not separated according to their functions. That is, there should be no political-administrative priority relating to specific spaces (representative, commercial, consumer spaces, etc.) as this type of concentration can contribute to the degeneration of other urban sectors (council flats, wasteland, etc.).

"Die Stadt des 'und'" would continue the struggle against social control, against a system of exclusive difference and for a culture and architecture of "space" (that is living space, daily space, culture space, etc.). This allows what first of all appears incompatible to be brought together: anonymity and community. The issue is to replace tendencies towards exclusion and national pomp by renewal and encouragement of urban democracy. The self-reflexive architecture of the "both/and city" takes into account the place in which it is located. It analyses the specificity of spaces as well as the forces which create identity and which make intermediate spaces (spaces of transition between the public sphere and the private sphere) public and authentic.

Since the beginning of the eighties, professionals of space management have attempted to respond to urban reality by installing interdisciplinary planning processes, which are supposed to take account of the complexity of contemporary urban phenomena in a more integral way. Most often, the organization of a real "space for public negotiation" should contribute to the integration of the various categories of players affected by the urban issue (households, associations, local businesses, county administration, etc.). Moreover, representatives of the county political-administrative network seem to be more and more aware of the problems around dialogue and integration faced by internal and external experts in the context of urban planning procedures. The objective is to increase the transparency of political decision-making processes and, following that, to reinforce the legitimization of public spending.

The growing individualization and emancipation of city-dwellers in relation to traditional society hierarchy has contributed to affirming their demand to be informed and associated with decision-making concerning their urban environment. Today, moreover, spending related to planning and realizing urban projects, whether large-scale or small-scale, is submitted to severer public legitimization, given the budget crisis urban governments are experiencing.

3 THREE CONTEMPORARY PHENOMENA RELATIVE TO PUBLIC SQUARES

For some time, it has been possible to note an increase in the use of the public square, in opposition to the time when Jakobs (1963) concluded that urban life was dead. The popularity of tourism of European squares (even world squares) and the ambitious events held in the public spaces (various markets, festivals, parties, shows, etc.) are witness to an increased demand on the part of users for public squares.

To designate this phenomenon of popularity, Aminde (1996, p.2010) uses the term "new desire for the public square" which is shown in users who are present in the square by "the desire to observe, to participate, to savour, to be present, etc.". According to Aminde, this is a question of "urban publicity" (Stadtöffentlichkeit), young, festive and idle (which sometimes manifests itself in an extravagant and hedonistic manner).

The principle of urbanity lies above all in a paradoxical reasoning which attempts to reconcile opposing elements. The social dimension of the dialectic thus opposes: private sphere and public sphere, density and diversity, security and animation, conflict and tolerance. In the socio-spatial dimension, it is the dialectic between: spatial limits and the availability of space, coherent architecture and a sense of spaciousness (fullness and emptiness), vegetable nature and mineral nature. As for the political-administrative dimension, the dialectic between the following can be noted: potential and real operational capacity of space, urban entity and urban discontinuities, the aspect of permanent residence and the aspect of passing through, order and disorder, preservation of history and the influence of the "Zeitgeist".

The interdependencies between the local and global levels seem moreover to influence the role of the public urban square. Finally, this debate around the current role of the city square has enabled us to bring out certain basic tendencies linked to the social practices which mark the current uses to which the city square is put. It is interesting to bring to light three contemporary phenomena which constitute a sort of guiding line in our quest for urbanity.

3.1 The "theatralisation" of public squares

The phenomenon of the individualization of urban society is shown more strongly in urban public spaces. The fact that these places provide the possibility of free access (in general), of access as an individual differentiated socially and culturally, of accommodating all types of social behaviour and of being present to the eyes of spectators, creates a space which is above all a public stage. The square's furnishings are thus the wings for a play without a written script. This place favours the "*danse macabre*" of its players and so constitutes the place where secret identities are created, through the "masks" presented by the city-dwellers (Flusser, 1995).

According to Joseph (1992-1993, p.213), the professionals are thus directors, "those whose business it is to frame a perspective and a scene of action, articulate a plot or the tale of an ordinary or exceptional use of a public square, analyze the dramatic resources of an urban site, the qualities of a location, the order of places and positions".

The "scenic" layout of the public square refers therefore to the tendency towards a sort of "dramatization" of current usage, which goes against the "banalisation" of the usage of the "modern and rational" period of the middle of this century.

3.2 The "festivalisation" of public squares

The public squares of Europe accommodate more and more shows of all sorts. The example of the Zurich "Street Parade" (which has taken place each year since 1996) is an extreme example of the new festive role of public space. Around 350,000 participants unite in a gigantic, gaudy show in the streets and squares of Switzerland's economic capital. To the rhythm of "techno" (a kind of music which favours dancing without a direct partner within a crowd), there is room for a considerable diversity of disguises and individual appropriations.

Another sort of festivalisation, more religious, but nonetheless related to the Street Parade phenomenon, is the gathering of nearly a million pilgrims for the organization of the World Youth Day in Paris.

But these two examples are only "prototypes" of a wider phenomenon of festivalisation. Those in charge in the county of managing public squares organize or are increasingly encouraging the organization of all types of parties, festivals or events which can contribute to animating this space (for example in Lausanne: the Beer Festival, fashion shows, rollerblading events, etc.).

3.3 The "commercialization" of public squares

The urban public square is the object of a growing economic attraction. The producers of urban squares (politicians, urban managers, administrators, urbanists, etc.) have embarked upon a course of urban marketing, a promotion of the city in order to attract groups of clienteles who are seeking to consume the attraction of a specific public atmosphere. All sorts of players, representing a certain type of media image (young dynamic athletes, serious businessmen, family with children, etc.), are invited to participate in the show. The quality and quantity of the elements which figure in most urban public squares are placed there with the goal of being used for public consumption. Playful objects, for example, are among the most important elements in the design of a square.

Moreover, certain authors like Genestier (1997) ask whether urban space is not undergoing conformity "to standards dictated by contemporary and universal morphology, landscape, aesthetics and cultural heritage, that is to say, to the norms of western tourist mercantilism." This author thus notes that a "plastic homogenization" and a "reduction of social relations are spreading over the public squares." (p. 43).

There is thus a strongly ambiguous tendency and potential which, on the one hand, take into consideration the contemporary city-dweller's demand for more stimulating animation and which, on the other hand, lead to an increased segregation. This is seen above all among those groups of users who are not in conformity with the image of the "gentrification" of the public square.

4 THREE DIFFERENT SORTS OF URBANITY

The idea of the "both/and" city, the reconquest of the particular spirit and ambience of the place, the variety of urban situations created with the help of an operational mixedness, are the factors which have been named in order to mark out the stakes in the changing paradigm of the urban. This new paradigm concerns social, architectural, urbanistic and political-administrative dimensions. However, to think that it is enough to tune only one instrument in the orchestra, like for example being concerned with only a harmonious architectural composition, would be to bring an incomplete answer to the issue of urban complexity. Instead it must be accepted that a great concert integrates various instruments, so it is indispensable to orchestrate the group of instruments, here the architectural and urbanistic composition, social structure, political-administrative process, to be in harmony with the new urban rhythm of public spaces.

4.1 Social urbanity

This is a group of social factors based on the *heterogeneity and density* of social groups, on the image of a *sense of security* based on a sort of informal social control; on a dialectic between private sphere and public sphere which makes *behaviour codes* favouring meeting and communication appear. However, urbanity is also built around conflicts of usage and status which mark the social emancipation of the individual in relation to social control.

The phenomenon of festivalisation constitutes an emblematic example, which brings out the importance of the public space as a space of renewed socialization within a society of individuals increasingly uprooted from their traditional family unit.

4.2 *Spatial urbanity*

This group of spatial elements is first of all linked to high readability of the urban structure at the level of the units that make up the stitches in the constructed cloth, that is to say the neighbourhoods. It is above all the ability to perceive the dialectic between *the full* (constructed spaces) and *the empty* (free spaces).

A certain number of more tangible elements refer to the phenomena of the *spirit and ambience of the place* and the *site's attractiveness*, which come under the category of the topographical specificity, or the topological or toponymic history of an urban area. In this regard, the link between spatial and social configuration can also be evoked, that is to say, a socio-spatial awareness which designates agreement between social actions and the constructed environment. Urbanity is moreover subject to the effects of temporality which pace the cycles of use and disuse of an urban space.

4.3 *Political-administrative urbanity*

One of the stakes in *planning* and *managing* urbanity consists in evaluating the possibilities and the realities of urbanity which an urban space presents. Spatial discontinuities and territorial paradoxes, noted by urbanists and conceptualized through new urbanistic models, constitute moreover theoretical elements at the basis of modern urbanity.

Urbanity is also and above all a concept which integrates historical elements of the city. The presence of elements which refer to the urban collective memory thus constitutes indispensable data. However, the presence of urban contradictions must be noted; these also are inseparable from the concept of urbanity. This is an issue of a general antagonism which can be felt at every level of the urban (social, spatial, political and economic).

5 CONCLUSION

One of the steps in the staging of urban life is the creation and furnishing of public spaces. It is through them that city-dwellers become aware of their coexistence and their place in the world. Such is the importance of public spaces.

The urbanistic and architectural form of public spaces gives the urban meaning, but from our point of view, still more is at stake in the matter of public spaces because they imply mobility, public usage, sociability, identity.

Space management professionals are convinced that it is firstly by acting upon the morphology of public spaces that they influence these stakes. Without denying the validity of this point of view, it is however not the only way the urban is influenced. The cultural, economic, political and social components of the urban dynamic are essential. In short, we are arguing that thought and action on the issue of urban public spaces should be interdisciplinary. On the one hand, the staging of urban life is interdisciplinary, and on the other, it should be accomplished together with its users.

We would like to use this conclusion to respond rapidly to another group of problems and issues. Would metropolisation not sound the death-knell for public spaces, which would then become non-places? Indeed, computer-culture societies, programmed and metropolised, would fatally transform the city-dweller into a user confined to his computer, in short they would create neo-recluses. With telecommunications, no more need for metropolitan public spaces! This threat should not be underestimated, but it should also be emphasised that telecommunications certainly trivialise what can be brought into the scope of the media, but give added worth to what escapes them: atmospheres, sociability, unplanned meetings, parties, the immediately present exchange.

The urban public space enables these two spheres to be articulated: that of place and that of the game. Public spaces are thus multidimensional and, because of this, cannot be accessible to telecommunications.

REFERENCES

Aminde H.-J. 1996. *Stadtplätze*, Deutsches Architektenblatt 2010-2012:12. München
Amphoux, P. 1995. *Aux écoutes de la ville*. Lausanne: IREC-EPFL
Amphoux, P. 1992-1994. *Parcs et promenades pour habiter*. Lausanne: IREC-EPFL
Amphoux, P. 1998. *La notion d'ambiance*. Lausanne: IREC-EPFL
Augé M. 1992. *Non-Lieux*. Paris: Seuil
Bassand, M. 1997. *Métropolisation et inégalités sociales, Lausanne*: IREC-EPFL
Beck, U. 1993. Vom Verschwinden der Solidarität. *Süddeutsche Zeitung* 14. München
Beck, U. 1996. Die offene Stadt. *Deutsches Architektenblatt* 363-364: 3. München
Bonanomi L. 1990. *Le temps des rues, Lausanne*: IREC-EPFL
Flusser, V. 1995. *Der Flusser -Reader zu Kommunikation, Medien und Design*. Mannheim: Bollmann
Genestier, P. 1997. Ville culturelle et espace touristique: sur quelques logiques et réification à l'oeuvre dans l'économie post-industrielle. In: Ecole d'Architecture Languedoc-Roussillon, *L'espace public dans la ville méditerranéenne*: 43-56. Montpellier: Editions de l'Esperou,
Goffmann, E. 1973. *La mise en scène de la vie quotidienne*, Paris: Minuit
Habermas, J. 1978. *L'espace public*, Paris: Payot
Jacobs, J. 1963. *Tod und Leben großer amerikanischer Städte*, Frankfurt am Main/Berlin: Ulstein
Joseph, I. 1992. L'espace public comme lieu d'action. *Les Annales de la Recherche Urbaine* 57-58: 211-217. Paris
Plan urbain. 1988. *Espaces Publics*. Paris: La Documentation Françaises
Sennett, R. 1979. *Les tyranies de l'intimité*. Paris: Seuil

Urban Lifestyles: Spaces · Places · People, Benson & Roe (eds)
© *2000 Balkema, Rotterdam, ISBN 90 5809 169 4*

Monuments of tomorrow: Industrial ruins at century's end

J. Dickinson
Rider University, Lawrenceville, N.J., USA

ABSTRACT: In this paper I explore how new meanings and values are negotiated for recently obsolete, derelict, and abandoned industrial structures. To begin, I discuss how European modernists appreciated industrial structures, particularly those erected in the United States, as elementary forms of a modern aesthetic. I then review ideas about entropy and architecture put forward by Alois Riegl, especially his understanding of historical change as a process in which structures undergo continual decay and thus become the ruins and monuments of each successive age. Finally I apply Riegl's theory of monuments, identifying several possible fates for today's large-scale remnants of the industrial age. I suggest industrial structures of the immediate past are the last great source of ruins and monuments for future epochs.

1 THE "SILO DREAMS" OF ERICH MENDELSOHN

A new class of structures is appearing in the landscapes of the United States, Europe, and elsewhere: abandoned and derelict factories, warehouses, steel mills, refineries, office buildings, railway stations, and dock facilities, as well as unused prisons, workhouses, asylums, and housing projects. What is the fate of these remnants of the industrial age? Can these giant relics of the immediate past become the monuments of tomorrow, authentic rivals to the royal tombs, medieval castles, and Gothic cathedrals of other civilizations and earlier times?

Industrial buildings have always possessed value and meaning beyond the merely commercial and functional. In the first decades of the twentieth century European modernists were attracted to large-scale industrial structures, particularly those in the United States, because they thought these utilitarian buildings supplied the vocabulary of pure architectural forms necessary for developing an appropriately modern, up-to-date aesthetic (Cohen, 1995). Walter Gropius compared the monumentality of American industrial buildings to the "work of the ancient Egyptians" (Banham, 1986). Le Corbusier celebrated the inherent monumentalism of the grain silo and the reinforced concrete factory in his famous book, *Towards a New Architecture.*

Erich Mendelsohn was one of the first European modernists to travel to the United States to see at first hand the wonders of American industrial construction. After visiting Buffalo, New York, he enthusiastically proclaimed: "Mountainous silos, incredibly space-conscious but creating space. A random confusion amidst the chaos of loading and unloading of corn ships, of railways and bridges, crane monsters with live gestures, hordes of silo cells in concrete, stone and glazed brick. Then suddenly a silo with administrative buildings, closed horizontal fronts against the stupendous verticals of fifty to a hundred cylinders....(E)verything else so far seemed to have been shaped interim to my silo dreams" (quoted Banham, 1986).

In *Amerika Bilderbuch eines Architekten* (1926), his book of photographs of the industrial and commercial wonders of New York, Detroit, Chicago, and Buffalo, Mendelsohn (1993) claimed to "perceive in the midst of this magma the first solid foundations of a new era." He described the grain elevators he had seen as "(c)hildhood forms, clumsy, full of primeval power, dedicated to purely practical ends...a preliminary stage in a future world that is just beginning to achieve order." With the appearance of these new, uncompromising structures, Mendelsohn announced, "a bare practical form becomes an abstract beauty."

What impressed the modernists was that industrial builders were now utilizing precisely the same geometrical solids of cube, cone, cylinder, sphere, and pyramid as had been employed to great effect in antiquity--for example, by Egyptian funereal architects and Greek temple builders. Subscribing to a Platonic idealism, the modernists accepted such architectural forms as "always beautiful in their very nature." Consequently these forms made architecture, in Le Corbusier's memorable definition, "the masterly, correct and magnificent play of masses brought together in light." When this dialogue was established between European modernists and American industrial building, "[t]he stage was set for the legitimization, so to speak, of industrial forms as the basic vocabulary of modernism" (Banham, 1986).

As a result of deindustrialization, many buildings celebrated by these eager modernists have been cruelly deprived of the meaning and value that originally sustained them. Formerly prosperous--even imposing--manufacturing and industrial districts in older cities in Europe and the United States have become vast areas of dereliction and decay. Signaling the passing from one historical epoch to another, these remaining industrial structures face a varied, uncertain future.

2 RIEGL'S THEORY OF MONUMENTS

The appearance of a new class of ruins comprising the detritus of the industrial age has revived interest in the ideas of Austrian philosopher and art historian Alois Riegl (1858-1905). In *The Cult of Modern Monument* Riegl identified three principal ways structures from the past are incorporated into the present. First is what Riegl (1982) calls the "*intentional monument*," a surviving structure that "recall(s) a specific moment or complex of moments from the past," which largely retains the same meaning for the present generation as established by its original builder or creator. Indeed, every epoch produces intentional monuments that recall important events or persons. These are familiar to us as war memorials and tombs or as commemorative structures such as the Lincoln, Jefferson, or Franklin D. Roosevelt memorials in Washington, D.C., the Eiffel Tower in Paris, or the monument to the Great Fire in London. As long as factory, mill, and office are home to activities for which they were originally conceived and constructed, the buildings that house these activities, as unchanged survivals, might be considered intentional monuments of the industrial age.

Second, when the specific moment from the past that a structure commemorates "is left to our subjective preference," the result is an *historical monument*. According to Riegl each generation scans the past and selects certain surviving artifacts as monuments on the basis of how that generation conceives of, values, and interprets the past. In such cases, the meaning assigned to a structure may deviate significantly from that originally intended. The Great Wall of China, the Liberty Bell and Independence Hall in Philadelphia, Ellis Island, Stonehenge, and Alcatraz are historical monuments. As cities and regions seek to remake themselves as essential destinations in the landscape of consumption, structures associated with the industrial era can be a rich source of future historical monuments.

Historical monuments are often "unintentional" monuments in that they emerge as such when new value and meaning replace the meaning or utility that sustained their earlier existence. In such a change, a structure is typically transformed through a process of ruination, rediscovery, and preservation. Often the new meaning is supplied by cultural movements such as romanticism or by science or historical scholarship. When industrial buildings find new uses for which they were not originally intended--educational and tourist sites, art galleries, museums, restaurants, sports bars, or condos--they become contemporary forms of the historical or unintentional monument.

Finally, survivals from the past may be appreciated for the way their surface patina and eroded structure record earlier stages in the life of the artifact; Riegl calls these monuments with *"age value."* Age value derives less from scholarly knowledge or historical education (as in the case of the historical monument) than from an "appreciation of the time which has elapsed since (the work) was made and which has burdened it with traces of age" (Riegl, 1982). Any kind of decayed or worn structure, whatever its original function or purpose, can become an age value monument under appropriate conditions. Because of their large size, specialized function, and solid construction, many industrial structures are well equipped for a lengthy sojourn in the ru-ination mill. Perhaps in this way, the factory, skyscraper, or prison can survive long enough to acquire new meaning as an age value monument.

3 THE FATES OF INDUSTRIAL STRUCTURES

Since they are subject to the peculiarly modern phenomenon of technological obsolescence, in-dustrial structures may persist physically despite loss of designated function. The idea that ob-jects could become "useless economically without reference to any residual physical utility" originated with the industrial revolution. As science and technology came to dominate economic development, "the old artifact (tool, factory, town) began to be regarded as an intolerable restriction upon increased productivity" (Fitch, 1990). Thus plants and equipment were consis-tently junked (often in favor of more wasteful and less efficient technologies) long before they wore out physically. Marx (N.D.) called this process "moral depreciation" of the means of pro-duction; he pointed out that in a commodity-driven economy the machine constantly loses "ex-change-value, either by machines of the same sort being produced cheaper than it, or by better machines entering into competition with it." In this way, "the corpses of machines, tools (and) workshops...are always separate from the products they helped to turn out."

Building on an earlier analysis of change in the built environment (Dickinson, 1996), I iden-tify four possible future scenarios for the "corpses" of the industrial era: (1) destruction or demolition, whereby possibilities for the building or structure as new utility, historical monu-ment, or elegant ruin are canceled by its elimination from the landscape and by the transforma-tion of its site, at best, into a cleared lot for some future development project; (2) adaptive recy-cling of the structure as new utility under whatever commercial or other regime prevails. The structure is inserted into the prevailing landscape of consumption, in which the building's archi-tectural envelope is preserved, if not its original internal program of spaces; (3) transformation of building, structure, or site into an historical monument. This fate favors highly specialized structures that are difficult to recycle directly into commercial use in the new economic regime; and, finally, (4) persistence of the structure in the landscape as an age value monument or ruin, a fragment of some past whole which poignantly recalls a lost universe of activity and meaning.

3.1 *Destruction or demolition.*

Today several factors conspire to remove unused, unwanted, or unoccupied structures from the landscape at an unprecedented rate. Indeed, there may be no point in directing people to indus-trial ruins "because it would be the strangest freak if they lasted until those visitors come" (Har-bison, 1991). Programs of urban renewal actively eviscerate cities; they clear away congested older neighborhoods in the interests of the rational organization of urban space, replicating the massive surgery Baron Haussmann, Mussolini and others earlier thought necessary to save the badly infected urban organism (Kostof, 1982; Woods, 1995). Such *sventramenti*, once again commonplace in Europe and the United States, are aided by several factors.

Demolition technology has now reached the point where virtually no structure exists that cannot be brought down quickly and efficiently. Powerful hydraulic attachments including giant grapples, mobile pulverizers, and "huge, swivelling shears...that can snip steel support beams like scissors cutting cardboard" have transformed excavators into "state of the art wrecking ma-chines," capable of pulling apart most structures (Johnson, 1996). Moreover, modern buildings are generally not as "over-engineered" as those of antiquity, thus succumb more economically to the wrecker's ball. Vandalism and fire also play their part. Fire in particular remains a major fac-tor in the remaking of the urban landscape. In cities like Philadelphia, buildings are torched by persons engaged in domestic disputes, teenagers seeking thrills, and drug dealers protecting their turf. Arson also offers a way for owners to extract value from unmarketable tax-burdened properties--in police jargon "selling them back to the insurance company" (McCoy & Sataline, 1996). The burning of buildings, coupled with municipal policies of demolishing unsafe struc-tures that remain, has become so widespread in places like Detroit and Camden as to hasten the return of the industrial city to the open fields and weed-filled lots described by Camilo Vergara (1995) as the "green ghetto."

The elimination of unwanted industrial structures from the landscape is also encouraged by speculative development. This process is reinforced by municipal authorities' failure to protect historic or other important structures. Typically developers, unenthusiastic about the restrictions that historic district and landmark building designations place on their activities, challenge in court the legal basis of such ordinances, or otherwise subvert them by political manipulation or corruption of local officials. Corporations cynically give vacant properties to underfunded community and nonprofit groups in exchange for tax credits. These structures, too large to be developed successfully by such groups, are later demolished at taxpayers' expense. Local authorities, moreover, often fail to see that vacant or abandoned structures are adequately sealed. Such failure facilitates occupation by addicts, scavengers, and the homeless. As these structures acquire reputations as eyesores and problem buildings, local politicians and the public lobby for their demolition. Thus they encourage that mind-set which favors the wholesale razing of structures--urban clear-cutting to create the vacant land parcels desired by today's giant development corporations. Communities even actively promote the dereliction of empty but otherwise sound local buildings, encouraging vandalism and minor building degradation in the hope that the structure will be condemned as unsafe and demolished (Parmley, 1997).

Demolition of industrial-era structures to make way for new development is now commonplace. In Sheffield, England, virtually every structure in the historic Don Valley steelmaking district has been swept away, creating space for American-style shopping malls, superstores, parking lots, and an airport. The Sheffield Development Corporation (N.D.), the organization charged with facilitating this transformation, sees its mission primarily in terms of "land acquisition and assembly" so as to remove "stagnation in the land market," followed by "land disposal and development" to secure "regeneration."

London's Docklands is another spectacular example of urban clear-cutting. An expression of the aggressive monetarist policies pursued by the Thatcher government in the 1980s, Docklands is the product of the London Docklands Development Corporation (LDDC), an urban development corporation (UDC) controlled by business and property interests directly appointed by the Secretary of State. LDDC can bypass controls and regulations on urban land use and redevelopment traditionally exercised by elected bodies such as local councils. Vested with almost unlimited powers, LDDC has appropriated some 5,000 acres of publicly owned land as well as 55 miles of waterfront property, which it sells off to private developers as cleared parcels (Bird, 1993; Imrie, 1997). In cities where these policies have been put into effect, new landscapes have emerged which are "richly symbolic of the social cleavages engendered by neo-liberalism." Typically they are marked by social and economic division, privatization of public space, and a mentality favoring fortress architecture: razor wire, walled estates, and bunkerlike buildings (Davis, 1990).

3.2 *Adaptive recycling.*

Obsolete and abandoned industrial structures may be recycled or reinvented for new uses, and thus survive to become a functioning part of the new economic regime. Harbors, docks and shipbuilding sites are turned into marinas, aquariums, waterfront parks, casinos, and sports bars; warehouses and factories become offices, condominiums, or artists' studios; banking halls become restaurants; railway stations are reborn as shopping malls. Numerous smaller, less glamorous transformations occur daily: A store becomes a church; the neighborhood bank becomes a photo-processing lab or a pizza parlor; an old workshop becomes a methadone clinic. Older industrial cities in the United States and Europe, desperate to reinvent themselves for the new symbolic economy, often devise a "plan" aimed at redeveloping and reworking existing assets into centers of leisure and mass tourism. Examples of this process include London's Covent Garden, Baltimore's Inner Harbor, New York's South Street Seaport, Liverpool's Albert Dock, and Wigan's National Heritage Center. In this way, the old "landscape of production" is converted into a new "landscape of consumption" (Zukin, 1991, 1995).

Adaptive recycling is not always a benign process that produces glittering centerpieces for the official redevelopment plan. Appropriation and conversion of abandoned structures by squatters, drug dealers, and unlicensed businesses produce problems that become simply another reason for communities to pursue a policy of urban clear-cutting. Moreover, state and local authorities may recycle older structures into the shelters for the homeless, the halfway houses for delinquents and the mentally ill, and the drug rehabilitation clinics needed to contain and warehouse the redundant and increasingly recalcitrant population that has no place in the new economy (Vergara, 1995). A particularly striking example of institutional recycling is found in Johannesburg, South Africa, where the once-prestigious 54-story Conde skyscraper is about to become the world's tallest prison.

Adaptive reuse is a function of the relationship between a building's architectural envelope (its outer structure) and its internal program (the layout of rooms and spaces); this relationship must be flexible and dynamic if reuse is to occur (Koolhaas, 1986). Indeed, the reuse of many warehouses, factories and workshops--including the concrete-and-steel wonders so greatly admired by European modernists--reflects the fact that many of these structures originally were designed and built as "universal spaces" able to accommodate a variety of activities and processes. For this reason, office buildings and skyscrapers, less usually regarded as victims of deindustrialization and globalization, also can be converted into condos and hotels.

In general, because particularities of the manufacturing process often dictate a less flexible, more rigid relation between a structure's envelope and its programme, it is often more difficult to recycle the buildings of the industrial city than the office towers of the world's administrative and financial capitals. Gradually the physicality of the city, its built environment, becomes divorced from prevailing systems of meaning; structures exist but have no use; abandonment and dereliction ensue. However, some specialized industrial structures do find commercial viability or reuse within the ascendant regime. Indeed, a grain elevator adjacent to downtown Philadelphia has been converted into fine urban residences. Nuclear missile bunkers in the American Midwest have been recycled as family dwellings, mushroom farms, or storage facilities. A silo in Illinois has been turned into a corporate swimming pool; another, in Texas, into a scuba diving school (Brooke, 1997). Again, Bankside Power Station in London, a massive industrial building "so powerful as a symbol that no one can bear the thought of its being demolished" (Harbison 1991), is now transformed into (temporarily) the world's largest modern art museum.

3.3 *Transformation into historical monuments.*

Monuments, intentional or otherwise, are structures whose meaning transcends, to some degree, the strictly commercial and functional. The industrial age might be regarded as antithetical, or at least indifferent, to monuments, to symbolic and non-utilitarian architecture. After all, many modernists, enamored of the spirit of strict functionalism, were committed to producing a timeless architecture in which buildings, devoid of historical and symbolic ornamentation, were conceived of as "machines" (Frampton, 1997). However, today the heritage movement aims to satisfy the popular desire for symbolic structures, converting obsolete industrial structures into historical monuments: sites and buildings that are visited for their alleged cultural or educational value or for the new meanings (often related to their original, distinctive function) that private and public advocates can negotiate and establish for them (Lowenthal, 1985). Indeed, extravagant size, peculiar architecture, and expressed function are precisely the attributes that attracted commentators to industrial structures in the past (Nye, 1995) and now excite advocates seeking new meaning and value to sustain them into the future.

Enthusiasm for technology often underlies efforts to convert obsolete industrial sites into museums and historic places. In Pennsylvania, for example, the Lackawanna Coal Mine attracts 70,000 visitors a year, and the $66 million federally funded Steamtown Museum in Scranton promises bliss for devotees of nostalgia and the mechanical sublime. Plans also exist to convert part of the defunct Bethlehem Steel works in the Lehigh Valley into a museum of the Smithsonian Institution (Infield, 1997). A more Disneyesque remaking of the Mesabi Iron Range, once the largest open-pit iron mine in the world, is now under way in Minnesota (Goin & Raymond, 1999). Among more recently constructed sites, Cape Canaveral already anticipates its own future as a monument of the Space Age. In Europe, the transformation of industrial sites into historical monuments is well advanced. Coal mines and steel mills are now museums and tourist attractions. The entire Ironbridge Gorge district in Shropshire, England, center of the Industrial Revolution, is now a United Nations World Heritage Site, a multisite museum complex requiring days for a comprehensive visit.

Institutional structures such as prisons, workhouses, and company towns associated with the large-scale management, control, and processing of people are often good candidates not only for adaptive recycling, but also for transformation into historical monuments. In the United States, Ellis Island National Monument, Alcatraz prison in San Francisco Bay, and Philadelphia's Eastern State Penitentiary are popular tourist attractions. In England, a nineteenth century workhouse in Nottinghamshire is about to become "the only fully restored demonstration of the Poor Law system which cast a shadow of terror over the poor well into this century" (Kennedy, 1997).

3.4 *Persistence as ruins*

Ruins occur when a structure survives long enough to pass from one system of meaning, one cultural valuation, to another (Zucker, 1968; Simmel, 1965). Because of their large size and superior construction, their specialized function, which precludes easy recycling into the new economy, and their occupation of sites often without significant redevelopment value, newly obsolete industrial structures can persist in the landscape for decades, even centuries. Thus they gradually acquire the worn patina and fragmented, eroded structure that give familiar survivals from the past, such as castles, temples, and pyramids, their distinctive allure (Tenner, 1997).

Once they fall into disuse, industrial buildings enter a period of abandonment and decay. Succumbing to the ravages of vernacular use, they are stripped of all usable materials. In the absence of maintenance, exposure to the elements increases. Eventually the roof collapses; walls crumble; vines and bushes take over. The resulting ruins thus "lie upon the land like so much detritus," fragments appreciated for their ability to recall lost worlds of action and meaning (Harbison, 1991).

Modern buildings are particularly susceptible to rapid deterioration and hence to ruination. Far from constituting a "timeless white architecture" they "have not withstood the test of time particularly well" (Frampton, 1997). Premature deterioration stems from recent developments in construction technology. For example, modern architects held that good construction was synonymous with a strict economy of materials. Buildings were conceived of as fine-tuned machines constructed of precisely the right amount of the latest materials; as strict expressions of function, buildings needed constant maintenance, something rarely supplied. More fundamentally, the rise of steel-frame construction has effectively replaced the traditional load-bearing wall with the curtain wall, and thus permits buildings to be enclosed with panels of glass or other nonstructural materials. This movement "away from the solid and monolithic wall toward the layered and the veneered," coupled with the need for increasingly sophisticated environmental systems, makes "far greater demands on the building envelope than has traditionally been the case." With the decline of the load-bearing wall come many of the problems associated with modern buildings: water leaks, gasket failures, and especially deterioration of the exterior panels, leading among other things to periodic "showers of bricks" as buildings catastrophically lose portions of their facades (Ford, 1997).

Industrial ruins are ominous reminders of lost civilizations of antiquity. As Camilo Vergara (1999) points out, while the early modernists described American cities as "unbridled, mad, frenetic, lusting for life," today, although still a leader in science and technology, the United States "now leads the world in the number, size and degradation of its abandoned structures." His suggestion that the abandoned skyscraper ruins of downtown Detroit be turned into an American Acropolis anticipates one possible future for the shards of the industrial city. Michael Frank (1997) has imagined the death of Manhattan and its rebirth as a ruin: "Time and wind and water have ravaged the natural and man-made alike, and the city's familiar face has eroded in some places to the skeleton underneath. Manhattan strikes the observer the way ancient Athens or ancient Rome strikes us now--as fragmentary, enigmatic, a *memento mori* at once powerful and poignant."

4 THE NEW FUTURISM

We live in a New Futurism, an age where once again "speed and cybernetic disposability are advanced as the order of the day" (Frampton, 1997). As cycles of economic activity accelerate and intensify, societies are organized increasingly around abstract systems of knowledge and information. Jack Burnham (1968) presciently observed: "We are now in transition from an object-oriented to a systems-oriented culture," a culture less concerned to invent solid artifacts with fixed, static qualities than with the "matter-energy-information exchanges" that organize relationships between people and their environment. Thus the real, lasting, palpable, finite, static and inert world of objects is replaced by an ephemeral, provisional, perishable, mobile, and disposable world dedicated to abstract information and communication. Exchange value prevails over use value, the portable computer reduces the need for office and factory, and the Internet may make much of the transportation industries obsolete. The "non-places" of supermodernity displace history-encrusted real places (Auge, 1995). In this future, aesthetics will be miniaturized and privatized, no longer centered on the architecture of grand structures but on the micro-architecture of the chip, the design of computer program icons, the decoration of the body.

The industrial era is the last culture producing gigantic structures able to run the course from utility to ruin. Indeed, the industrial ruins of today, produced in abundance in the "factory" of entropic change, are likely the last existing class of structures whose massive scale, specialized function, and solid construction make them suitable candidates for survival in the landscape and thus for evolution into the monuments of tomorrow. In the future, this era's power stations, steel mills, floating exploration platforms, oil refineries, cracking towers, tank farms, automobile factories, freeway interchanges, and shopping malls will appear as fantastic and as worthy of preservation as do step pyramids, Greek temples, and Gothic cathedrals today.

REFERENCES

Auge, M. 1995. *Non-Places: Introduction to an anthropology of supermodernity*. London: Verso.
Banham, R. 1986. *A concrete Atlantis*. Cambridge, MA: MIT Press.
Bird, J. 1993. Dystopia on the Thames. In J. Bird, B. Curtis, G. Robertson & L. Tickner (eds), *Mapping the futures: local cultures, global changes*. London: Routledge..
Brooke, J. 1997. *Sleeping below plains, missiles stay on the alert*. New York Times, 15 December.
Burnham, J. 1968. *Beyond modern sculpture*. New York: Braziller.
Cohen, J. –L. 1996. *Narratives and spaces: European architecture and the American challenge*. Montreal: Canadian Center for Architecture.
Davis, M. 1990. *City of quartz*. London: Vintage.
Dickinson, J. 1996. Entropic zones: Buildings and structures of the contemporary city. Capitalism, Nature, *Socialism*, 7(3): 81-95.
Fitch, J. M. 1990. *Historic preservation: Curatorial management of the built world*. London: University Press of Virginia.
Ford, E. 1997. The theory and practice of impermanence. *Harvard Design Magazine*. Fall: 12-18.
Frampton, K. 1997. Intimations of durability. *Harvard Design Magazine*. Fall: 23-28.
Frank, M. 1997. *New York skyscrapers as ancient temples*. New York Times, 4 July.
Goin, P. & Raymond, E. 1999. Recycled landscapes: Mining's legacy in the Mesabi Iron Range. In D. Nye (ed), *Technologies of landscape*. Amherst, MA: University of Massachusetts Press.
Harbison, R. 1991. *The built, the unbuilt and the unbuildable*. Cambridge, MA: MIT Press.
Imrie, R. 1997. National economic policy in the United Kingdom. In Michael Pacione (ed), *Britain's cities: Geographies of division in urban Britain*. London: Routledge.
Infield, T. 1997. *In Pennsylvania, industrial giants are now history*. Philadelphia Inquirer, 16 March.
Johnson, T. 1996. *Razing Philadelphia*, Philadelphia Inquirer, 13 October.
Kennedy, M. 1997. *Old workhouse to stand again*. The Guardian (London), 24 July.
Koolhaas, R. 1986. Response to questionnaire. *Zone* 1/2: 448.
Kostof, S. 1982. His Majesty the pick: The aesthetics of demolition. *Design Quarterly*, 118-119: 33-4
Lowenthal, D. 1985. *The past is a foreign country*. Cambridge: Cambridge University Press
Marx, K. no date. Capital. Moscow: Progress Publishers.
Mendelsohn, E. 1993. *Erich Mendelsohn's "Amerika."* New York: Dover Publications.
McCoy, C. & Sataline, S. 1996. *Who's burning Philadelphia*, Philadelphia Inquirer, 13 October..
Nye, D. 1994. *American technological sublime*. Cambridge, MA: MIT Press.
Parmley, S. 1997. *A crumbling brewery raises ire in East Falls*. Philadelphia Inquirer, 11 August.
Riegl, Alois 1982. The cult of modern monuments: Its character and its origin. *Oppositions* 25.
Sheffield Development Corporation N.D 1998-99. *Annual Report and Financial Statement*. Sheffield, UK: Sheffield Development Corporation.

Simmel, G. 1965. The Ruin. In Kurt Wolff (ed), *Georg Simmel: Essays on sociology, philosophy and aesthetics*. New York: Harper Row.

Tenner, E. 1997. Aging gracefully. *Metropolis* September: 76-79.

Vergara, C. 1995. *The New American Ghetto*. New Brunswick, NJ: Rutgers University Press.

Vergara, C. 1999. *American ruins*. New York: Monacelli Press.

Woods, L. 1995. Everyday war. In Peter Lang (ed), *Mortal City*. New York: Princeton Architectural Press.

Zukin, S. 1991. *Landscapes of power: From Detroit to DisneyWorld*. Berkeley, CA: University of California Press.

Zukin, S. 1995. *The Cultures of cities*. Cambridge, MA: Blackwell.

Changes of space use as a function of lifestyle and space characteristics (the Iranian context)

M. Abbaszadegan
Iran University of Science and Technology, Tehran, Iran

ABSTRACT: How can the intervention of urban designers affect users' pattern of behaviour in urban space? To deal with this issue it is essential to explore the relationship of physical changes of environment and lifestyle. In this study, the behavioural patterns and spatial qualities of a traditional and a modern city in Iran are compared. The spatial qualities of the two cases have been analyzed using space syntax techniques and their spatial features were matched with the users' behaviour. The study in the traditional city indicates that the pattern of use by all groups has been changed based on historical reports. Regardless of similar features of the spaces, lifestyles in the two communities causes different behaviour, although traces of physical effect on behaviour have also been detected. The research concludes that the man-made environment is not the determinant of behaviour, but according to probabilistic theory of behaviour the environment has provided the opportunity for some behaviour to happen more often than others.

1 INTRODUCTION

Three primary types of activities that occur in urban open spaces have been recognized by Gehl (1996) these are: 'necessary activities', 'optional activities' and 'social activities (resultant activities)'. He explains that 'When the quality of outdoor areas are good, optional activities occur with increasing frequency. Furthermore, as levels of optional activity rise, the number of social activities usually increases substantially.' It is essential to explain that because of lifestyle and socio-cultural constraints, people do not necessarily use an urban open space even space when it is pleasant for use and for social engagements.

Lang (1987) discusses that environment does not determine specific behaviour but it makes the opportunities for some behaviour in space. He calls it a 'probabilities approach'. Rapoport (1987) states that "activity in any given setting is primarily culturally based in that it is the result of unwritten rules, customs, traditions, habits, and the prevailing lifestyle and definition of activities appropriate to that setting". Fisher *et al* (1996) explain theories of the relationship of space with the behaviour of users. They explain three views about this relationship, architectural determinism, environmental possiblism and environmental probabilism.

Architectural determinism indicates that the physical environment directly shapes the behaviour of people within it; in other words it assumes that the physical environment is the only or at least the primary cause of behaviour. According to the theory of environmental possiblism, the physical environment provides opportunities as well as limits the activity of people. Fisher *et al* (1996) explain that, according to environmental possiblism people's behaviour is jointly determined by the environment and the choice they make. In other words, according to this theory, people are able to make choices and these are facilitated by the environment. Therefore in this view the environment is determined rather than vice versa (Krupat, 1985).

The third view about the relationship of people with the environment has been called 'dynamic interchange' (Ittelson *et al*, 1974) and later called 'probabilism' (Porteous, 1977;

Rapoport, 1977). Fisher *et al* (1996) explain that, environmental probablism assumes that while an organism may choose a variety of responses in any environmental situation, there are probabilities associated with specific instances of design and behaviour. These probabilities reflect the influence of both non-architectural factors and design variables on behaviour.

The above scholars are pointing to the behaviour in space as the function of lifestyle and space characteristics. One of the characteristics of space that is not covered is the spatial configuration characteristics that have been defined by Hillier and his colleagues (1983, 1986). The findings of much research shows that space configuration creates the opportunities for people to be in a space or segregates the space, thus only local people know about the place and as a result few people use the space.

The spatial configuration theory proposes that based on the way spaces are arranged in the city people may find the opportunities to be present in some spaces more than others. Then the users may decide to come to that space to involve in necessary or optional activity and may engage in social activity. According to probablist view some type of behaviour is more likely to occur in a particular space, therefore the relationship of behaviour and space is a complex task that involves many factors.

To study the relationship between a user's behaviour in urban open spaces and the spaces, two Iranian cities were selected; The two cases were the Old Quarter of the city of Yazd as a prototype of traditional Iranian city and the District of Narmak in the city of Tehran as a prototype of a modern Iranian city. The Old Quarter of Yazd has an organic and traditional Iranian - Islamic structure while Narmak is a pre-planned modern development.

To investigate the relationship of the spatial configuration of the two cases with space use a careful observation of the two cases was conducted. To cover the observation of all types of existing spaces within the two cases, continuous paths were selected in each so as to include quiet and busy spaces and paths. To analyse the spatial structure of the two cases the space syntax technique was employed.

2 SPATIAL CONFIGURATION ANALYSIS

Space syntax theory and technique is an effective tool for the configuration analysis of spaces in buildings and urban areas. It analysis all parts of the system in relation to all other parts. Space syntax has formed the basis for a new generation of software programs through which computer modelling has become both interactive and dynamic.

Space syntax is able to analyse the abstract shape of settlements through an abstract model. This abstract model is called an axial map. It consists of a network of axial lines that represent how far observers can have an uninterrupted impression of visibility and permeability as they move about towns and look from a distance in various directions.

The computer analysis of the axial map produces two kinds of outputs; first numerical data in the form of line numbers with spatial parameters assigned to each and second graphic data in the form of maps in which lines are coloured up according to their value on the various parameters.

The core concept of the space syntax analysis is integration. The concept of integration comes from the concept of depth. By depth is meant the number of lines and changes of direction that need to be taken to go from that space to the destination. The integration of space in a settlement is the mean number of lines and changes of direction that need to be taken to go from that space to all other spaces in the settlement system. Extensive studies in different parts of the world showed that the higher the value of integration the space has the higher density of activity - specially movement. As the integration value decreases the density of movement also decreases. Therefore the graphic presentation of this software allows the designers to acknowledge the heart of the city and roles of various parts of it.

Any intervention within the city would effect all parts of the city. Space syntax enables us to visualise each subtle change. For the purpose of this research three stages of development of the Old Quarter of Yazd and the district of Narmak have been analysed using the space syntax method. Figure 1, 2 and 3 show the integration analysis of the development stages of the Old Quarter of Yazd. The darker lines show the most integrated parts of the town and the lighter shades show the most segregated parts.

As the spatial configuration analysis of the walled city (Figure 1) of Yazd shows, the most integrated parts of the city at this stage were the thoroughfares, which lay between gates. They facilitated access to important places within the city such as the Grand Mosque. The thoroughfares had the highest pedestrian traffic within the city.

The second stage of the historical development of the city consisted of development beyond the defensive wall and development of the Grand Bazaar in the south of the city. The configuration analysis of this stage of development of Yazd (Figure 2), shows that the integration line simply moved to the south of the town where the new Grand Bazaar developed, so the busiest parts of the city became the most integrated part of the town (red lines). After the expansion of the city beyond the defensive wall, the thoroughfares lost some of their past importance.

Imposition of new streets on the winding alleys and the Bazaar occurred in the third stage of development (Figure 3). The configurational analysis of this stage of development shows that the most integrated lines in the old structure, including the Grand Bazaar and thoroughfares as the central core of the city, become less important than the new streets. These modern streets draw integration of the Old Quarter of Yazd to themselves. As a result, most activities draw from the historic part to the new part, and have caused physical and economical dilapidation of the traditional elements within the city.

Figure 4 shows the spatial configuration analysis of the district of Narmak. It is a pre-planned area which is famous for its green neighbourhood squares. The spaces become more segregated as the roads are interrupted by the squares. The spatial integration cores of the district are the main streets and the main square.

To examine the relationship between the spatial properties of the two cases and the way people use these spaces, an extensive observation of the use was conducted and by using statistical calculation these relationships were examined.

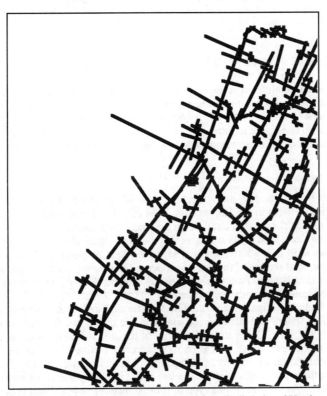

Figure 1. Spatial configuration analysis of the Walled city of Yazd

75

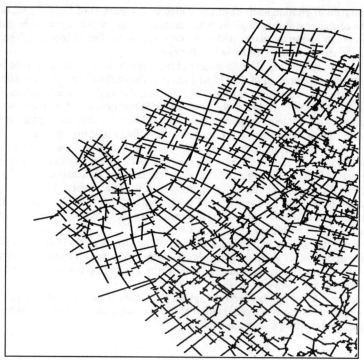

Figure 2. Spatial analysis of Yazd development beyond its defensive wall

3 RELATIONSHIP OF SPATIAL DEPTH FROM MAGNETS AND TYPE OF USE

The effect of spatial depth from urban magnets such as the main streets, the main square of the city and Bazaarches (small traditional shopping centers) creates a specific relationship with the behaviour of users of spaces in the city.   Spatial depth is the number of change of directions taken to reach from one space to other spaces. For the purpose of this study the relationship of spatial depth from some of these magnets and the behaviour of users has been examined.

3.1 *The main streets*

The level of depth from the two main streets of the Old Quarter of Yazd and their relationship with the activities of users in the Bazaar have been calculated, using regression analysis. This analysis shows that as the level of depth from the main street increases, the flow of pedestrians in the Bazaar area decreases. This indicates that the imposition of new streets in the Old Quarter of Yazd draws most of the activity with a negative effect on the level of use of the Bazaar.

To examine the relationship of the spatial properties of the two cases and the way people use these spaces an extensive observation of the use has been conducted and by using statistical calculation these relationships are then examined.

The modern spatial configuration of the Old Quarter of Yazd created uneven concentrations of activity in a few spaces and left deserted spaces inside the fabric. Two of the modern streets of the Old Quarter absorb 23.4% of total activity of the area, while the total of 192 spaces absorb 34.15% of the total activity. To have a more accurate picture of this uneven occupation of spaces, the concentration of activity is compared. The concentration of activity in the new streets is 11.1 persons per length of street (meter) and it is 1.62 persons per meter in the spaces of the inner fabric. As a result of this type of transformation, physical and economic dilapidation of the Bazaar has occurred during the last half century in many Iranian cities (Ministry of Housing and Urban Design 1991).

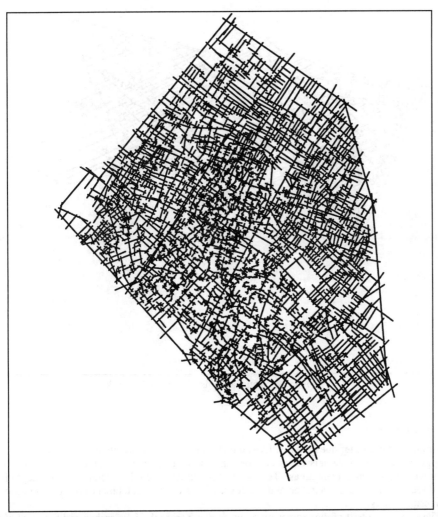

Figure 3. The spatial configuration analysis of the district of Narmak.

3.2 *The main square:*

The depth from the main squares of the district of Narmak shows that this square is able to regulate about half of the users' movement in its catchment area. Spatial depth from the square has a strong negative correlation with the level of movement in the catchment area. As spatial depth from the square increases the level of movement in its catchment area decreases. Numerous shops in the square and its role as a transportation terminal in the district of Narmak, make the square a very strong magnet that absorbs residents as well as strangers.

Bazaarches are small traditional shopping centres that serve individual neighbourhoods. They are usually covered alleys. Bazaarches are scattered within the Old Quarter of Yazd at a reasonable distance from each other and they are usually located in the heart of the neighbourhood. In the indigenous planning and design process of the Old Quarter, the Bazaarches were developed and evolved as effective magnets in the centre of the neighbourhood. They could regulate most of the pedestrian movement within their catchment area. Before the imposition of the new street on the fabric of the Old Quarter, the Bazaarches were in the heart of the neighbourhood which enabled them to serve the majority of the population of the neighborhood with equity.

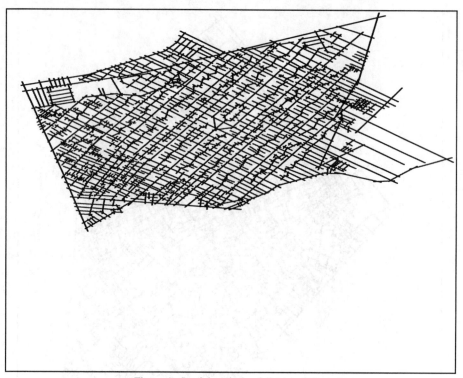

Figure 4. Spatial analysis of district of Narmak

3.3 *Bazaarches*

An important planning questions is, have the Bazaarches preserved their role as neighborhood shopping centres? If the answer is positive, they should be able to regulate part of the movement within their catchment areas. To answer this question the relationship between depth from the three well-known Bazaarches and the level of use of their catchment area is studied using regression analysis.

The goodness of fit of the regression between depth from the Bazaarches and the level of use of spaces in the catchment areas is very low and insignificant. These 'non-relationships' are very important signs of the spatial structure of contemporary Yazd. These signs indicate that the Bazaarches have lost their traditional roles as the shopping centres of the neighborhoods, thus they have also lost their influence on regulating movement in their catchment areas. This is because of the spatial alteration of the Quarter. The Bazaarches are no longer at a spatially integrated core of the neighbourhoods, they are simply alleys in the layout of the contemporary city and their influence as a place on the route of natural movement has been lost. The study of depth from influential elements in Old Quarter of Yazd shows that any intervention in cities can have consequences on the role that each part of the city plays.

4 SPATIAL CULTURE

Various user groups respond differently to spaces. The different response to various layout configurations is called 'spatial culture' by Hillier (1996). The question is: are there any traces of spatial culture in the Old Quarter of Yazd and the district of Narmak? To address this question the co-presence of moving and static men and women in the spaces of the two cases was compared. It is usually assumed that when various groups of people use a space differently it is as a result of various lifestyle and cultural constraints.

But the question here is how much of the variation of activity of men and women can be interpreted by the variation in the spatial configuration? An examination of the response of men and women to local spaces helps to explore this query because the social values can regulate coexistence of different groups of people in local spaces much more strongly than in the spaces that function at the city level.

It should be noted that the co-presence of user groups in a space is the function of many factors, but the spatial configuration factor is the basis for all user presence in the open space of cities. That is because, spatial configuration creates an opportunity for most people to be present or in absent from a space. All other factors, such as size, shops, micro design features and territory are the secondary factors that can add or change the probability of presence in a space or eliminate them. It should be noted that these secondary factors do not necessarily have a lesser ability to regulate the activity of a user group in spaces than the lifestyle and cultural factors.

The observation of users behaviour in the space of the Old Quarter of Yazd shows that response of men and women in the local spaces is very similar while in those which can be classified as city spaces the response of men and women is very different.

In contrast to the Old Quarter of Yazd, in the district of Narmak the response of men and women in spaces with local and global spatial property is very similar. The differences result from differences in lifestyle, culture and in the property of spaces of modern and traditional Iranian urban open spaces.

There is a sharp difference between the Old Quarter of Yazd's spaces and those of the district of Narmak. The local spaces of the Old Quarter are spatially much deeper and therefore, women feel them to be more exclusive and hence intimate. As a result, their responses to these areas are very similar to those of men. In contrast women in the district of Narmak have different responses to local spaces than men, since these spaces are not very deep from the main integrators of its layout.

This implies that men and women have equal opportunities to use spaces at the local level in the inner fabric of the Old Quarter of Yazd. In general, the integration of spaces is better able to regulate the movement of adults than their more static activities.

5 CONCLUSIONS

The built environment has a defined spatial logic that regulates all aspects of a city. Spatial logic is the organiser of the layout of settlements and from it a well organised city regulates its facilities, magnets, densities of buildings with spatial configuration of the city. Therefore, it is vital for developers and urban designers to understand the spatial configuration role of each space within the city and work within its framework. Any intervention which interrupts the previous logic should substitute a completely new concept of space that can fulfil the objectives of the users. On the other hand, it is essential to understand the cultural and lifestyle preferences of the potential users of the space and facilitate them to achieve their requirements.

REFRENCES

Churchman, A. & Ginsberg Y. 1984. The use of behavioural science research in physical planning. *Journal of Architecture and Planning*. 1:57-66.
Fisher, J. D. & Bell, P. A. 1996. *Environmental psychology*, 2nd ed., New York: London; Holt, Rinehart and Winston.
Gehl, J. 1996. *Life between building using public space*, translated by Koch, J., 3rd ed., Copenhagen: Arkitetens Forlag.
Hillier, B., Hanson. J., Peponis, J., Hudson, J. & Burdett, R. 1983. Space syntax: A different urban perspective. *The Architecture Journal*. 178(48):47-67.
Hillier, B. 1996. *Space is the machine*. Cambridge: Cambridge University Press.
Ittelson, W., Rivlin, L., Proshansky, H., Rivlin. L. G. & Winkel, G. H. 1974. *An introduction to environmental psychology*. New York, London: Holt, Rinehart and Winston.
Kubat, A. S. 1997. The morphological of Anatolian fortified towns. *Environment and Planning B: Planning and Design..* 24:95-123.

Lang, J. 1987. *Creating architectural theory: The role of the behavioural sciences in environmental design*. New York, Wordingham: Van Nostrand Reinhold, London: Phaidon, 1965, (Columbia University . Studies in art, history and archaeology: no.2).

Peponis, J., Hadjinikolaou, E., Livieratos, C., & Fatouros, D.A. 1989. The spatial core of urban culture. *Ekistics*. 334,335: 43-55

Porteous, J. 1977. *Environment and behaviour*. Reading, Mass.: Addison - Wesley.

Rapoport, A. 1997. *Human aspect of urban form*. New York: Pergamon

Techno-trends: Urban design implications of the electronic age

R. Durack
Urban Design Center of Northeast Ohio, Cleveland, Ohio, USA

ABSTRACT: The revolution in data processing and telecommunications has radically transformed the production and delivery of goods and services, affecting the nature of work and the
physical and organizational structures of the workplace. Contrary to the assumption that these
changes will accelerate decentralization and ultimately, render the city obsolete, there is emerging evidence that the electronic workplace is supporting a resurgence of urban values in the locational choices of businesses and individuals. To exploit the opportunities that the electronic
revolution is offering for more compact, urban forms of development, planning and urban design practice will have to adopt some significant changes.

To say that advances in data processing and telecommunications have revolutionized the way
we live and work is little more than a cliché. To claim that we understand the scope and impact
of this revolution, however, is simply naive –or at best, generously optimistic. Analysts like
Tom Forester (1987), Manuel Castells (1989), Bill Mitchell (1995) and Christine Boyer (1996)
have been writing about the nature of the Information Age since the 1980s, but for all this elegant theorizing, the disciplines of planning and urban design have done little to incorporate either the current circumstances or emerging trends of this technological revolution, in professional practice or education.

There seem to be two reasons for this failure to embrace the fact of such swift and dramatic
change. The first is that we have never been particularly good at recognizing structural change
when it is actually occurring. In the last great revolution, industrialization had been underway
for a hundred years before we acknowledged its impacts on social and functional systems, or re-
acted to its environmental consequences. It was only when the nineteenth century city had become intolerable, in both physical and social dimensions, that the profession of planning
emerged as an agent for controlling development patterns and minimizing land use conflicts.
Our inability to recognize on-going structural change is similarly apparent in 60 years of highway construction that only now is starting to be questioned –in the light of uncontrolled sprawl
and growing congestion.

The second reason that planning has been slow to respond to the digital age is that the effects
of this revolution are constantly surprising us. Even the most astute predictors are routinely being proven wrong about the outcomes of technological change, or severely miscalculating its
magnitude and speed. In 1978, for example, Bill Gates, who is one of the richest men in the
world because he has been so successful at predicting the direction of computing technology, is
reputed to have said that "640 kilobytes is plenty enough memory for anyone". By 1998, the ordinary home desktop computer came fitted with a standard hard drive of at least 13 gigabytes,
proving that even Bill Gates has been guilty of underestimating the digital demand –and underestimating it by a factor of more than 20,000 in just 20 years.

But as well as miscalculating the speed of technological change, we have made many more
spectacular misjudgments about its effects. About 15 years ago, for example, there was a lot of
talk about the "paperless society" which was going to result from digital information storage and

electronic messaging. The American Forest and Paper Association, however, reports (on the Internet) that paper consumption rose 15% from 1990 to 1998. Instead of reducing reliance on printed material, increasing access to computers, printers and photocopiers has proven to be a stimulus to paper consumption. And despite instant news access on the Internet, the Newspaper Association of America reports that morning newspaper circulation rose 12% from 1997 to 1998; and e-mail notwithstanding, the U.S. Postal Service claims a 20% increase in mail volume between 1992 and 1998.

In the early 1980s, an issue of major concern throughout the United States was the massive unemployment, and under-employment, that was expected to result from the increased efficiencies of computer use. Some planning schools even began to talk about an impending "leisure crisis", and the inevitable stresses that all this additional leisure time was going to place on existing recreation facilities. Twenty years later, according to the U.S. Census Bureau, the United States is enjoying the lowest unemployment rates it has seen in over a decade, despite a 10% increase in the size of the civilian labor force. With respect to under-employment, Rones et al (1997) found that there has been little change in the average number of hours worked each week since the mid-1970s, but the number of people working very long workweeks is rising dramatically: from 1985 to 1993, the number of people in the work force working 49 hours or more rose by over 30%. The anticipated leisure crisis has turned out to be an issue of executive burn-out rather than exploding demands on recreational facilities.

Similarly, we assumed that video rental stores and cable television were going to destroy the place of the neighborhood cinema. Due in part to the multi-plex phenomenon, but also to a heightened interest in film created by ready access to VCRs, DVDs and cable television, there has been a cinematic boom around the world. Statistics provided by the Golden Village Corporation claim that over the last decade, cinema attendance in the United Kingdom has doubled; in Australia it has risen by 80%; and in the United States it has been rising by just under 6% a year since 1993. In the same way, access to artworks and art reviews on the Internet has boosted attendance at museums and art galleries across the globe rather than decreasing the number of visitors viewing the original works. And the travel industry, which shuddered prematurely at predictions of the armchair tourist and video-conferencing, has barely been able to handle the recent explosion in business and leisure travel.

Admittedly, these kinds of impacts may be trivial in the grand arena of planning, but the point is that over and over again, the effects of the computer age are proving to be counterintuitive. The importance of these little surprises is that they hint at the possibility of an urban future that is entirely different from the one we have been expecting. The prevailing wisdom is that advanced digital communications and data transfer capabilities will inevitably accelerate the trend towards decentralization. If business can be conducted from anywhere, so the scenario goes, and if the Internet continues to play an increasing role in education and entertainment, individuals and family units will retreat to semi-isolation in the single-family castle that they will never have to leave –even to shop, now that we have on-line grocery services and the book sellers Amazon.com. According to the technological nightmare, the city will become obsolete, and development will continue to destroy farmland and the fragile, remaining wilderness; while the poor, lacking the resources to escape, will be concentrated in the ruins of the city, eking out a bare existence between the crumbling walls of derelict warehouses and obsolete office buildings.

But, like so many predictions about the effects of computers, this vision of the end of urbanism seems to be similarly unfounded, as evidenced by the recent wave of renewed interest in inner-city living in cities across the United States. To understand why this is happening, at the very moment when technology has conquered geography, we need to look at how the new technologies are changing the nature of the workplace and the processes of industrial production, which is the facet of this revolution that will have the most dramatic effect on the future of cities.

Data processing capabilities and telecommunications have radically transformed the way goods and services are produced and the organizational structure of the businesses that produce and distribute them. In heavy manufacturing, for example, gone are the days of the great industrial giants who manufactured complicated products, like heavy machinery, automobiles or ships, from raw materials to finished product in a vast, multi-functional plant. Today, all the different components of such complex products are made by smaller, more specialized firms that, because of their focus on a specific product, can do the job better, faster and cheaper than the generalist manufacturer. Because of sophisticated tele-connections to their manufacturing partners, these specialist firms can be located anywhere in the world, wherever access to the requisite materials, technical skills and distribution systems is available, at lowest cost.

In the manufacture of a car, for example, the engine block might be cast in Germany, the body paneled in Brazil, the electronic system produced in Hong Kong, and the ball bearings supplied by a specialist firm in Ohio. This new kind of global production system is only possible because of sophisticated electronic processes like CAD/CAM (computer aided design and manufacturing), MVS (machine visioning systems) and VRS (virtual reality simulators) which allow precision design and manufacture of inter-connected parts in distant locations. Because of spectacular increases in the capacity and speed of data transmission from point-to-point around the globe, spatially separated activities can respond immediately to production orders and requested changes in product features.

Obviously, all this has important land use and site development implications. As a simplified illustration, the Port of Philadelphia is working on developing an inter-modal Fast-Ship terminal which will link double-stack, trans-continental rail service with a new kind of semi-hydrofoil shipping technology that travels up to ten times faster than traditional cargo ships. When this distribution network is in place, the new car buyer in California will tell his local Volvo dealer what color and options he wants on Monday; and as they talk, the dealer will be transmitting the order to Sweden by modem, where the specific car will be assembled, whisked across the Atlantic in a Fast Ship, loaded directly onto a waiting train, and the happy customer will drive it home on Friday.

So called "just-in-time" manufacturing and delivery has already been in operation for some time, but its impact on land use and site requirements is not yet obvious, partly because of missing links in distribution networks, existing property commitments, and the reluctance of some industries to adopt the available technologies. But it is only a matter of time –and quite likely a short time– until the site requirements for various commonplace activities will be dramatically revised. The local car dealer, for example, will no longer need to keep a large inventory of in-stock cars, nor will he need the typical 6-acre site to store it. To be competitive, all he is going to need is access to an international network of suppliers, a powerful computer and a high-speed modem, all of which takes up about as much space as a television set.

Or, as Bill Mitchell (1999) points out, perhaps even individual automobile ownership will become a thing of the past, as electronically operated car rental and distribution services replace the inefficiencies of owning a car that sits idle in parking lots and garages for most of its useful life. With electronic fleet management and position-sensing devices to supply the right size and type of vehicle whenever it is needed, the demand for parking will be sensationally reduced, along with a host of other less predictable impacts like the effects on street operations, auto service and repair businesses, the insurance industry, and of course, the loss of public revenue generated by parking violations.

Futuristic speculations aside, however, we are already presented with one of the most dramatic effects of the electronic revolution which is a general re-ordering of the structure of business. To survive in an increasingly competitive, global marketplace, businesses of all kinds and sizes have instituted numerous organizational rearrangements to increase productivity and efficiency. This "reengineering" reflects a general shift from vertically managed, multi-functional businesses to more horizontally organized collaborations of specialized process teams. As for the manufacture of complex products, the business trend is towards flexible networks of small, specialist firms that come together for particular projects and reform according to the specific demands of the task in hand.

The recent wave of mergers and acquisitions in the travel, communications and entertainment industries appears to contradict this trend, but even the corporate giants are internally restructuring to operate like a collection of small, specialized businesses or independent profit centers, located in different parts of the country or around the world, with electronic connections to each other, the head office, and external business partners. In addition, the definition of traditional business hours is breaking down through automated information services and the time differences involved in operating in a global marketplace. We are doing business in a much broader geographic and temporal arena than we ever have before, but the new data processing and telecommunications capabilities are allowing us to do it from a much smaller and more localized base of operations.

This small-unit form of organization, together with the availability of more and more sophisticated computer capabilities at constantly reducing cost, has made office hotelling, telecommuting and the home office a practical reality. Location and size no longer govern access to information or the ability to communicate with colleagues and partner businesses. The effective businessman no longer needs to be physically proximate to his secretary, support equipment or business records. He does, however, need to be developing wider networks of association with other specialist groups, and to be immediately available to service existing partnerships.

The smaller and more specialized the business units, the greater their inter-dependence, and the greater their reliance on networks of communication and social relationships between complimentary enterprises. Nurturing and expanding these relationships have become the central demands of the new business structure. Despite the availability of real-time electronic communications and video-conferencing –or perhaps even because of them– productive business relationships are still most effectively cultivated through local interaction and face-to-face contact. Or, as the prescient Ameritech slogan says: "In a world of technology, people make the difference."

As business continues to break down into smaller, more specialized units, the tendency will be to concentrate in clusters of interdependent functions, rather than to disperse in greater isolation. Contrary to the assumption that tele-commuting and electronic data transfer will promote the physical separation of business activities, there is growing evidence that precisely the opposite is happening, producing dramatic opportunities for the development of higher density, more vibrant, mixed-use communities.

To understand this counter-intuitive trend, we need to consider the effects of technology and the new structure of business on the daily life of the typical worker. The most important consequence of the digital age –at least for white collar workers– is that work is becoming more integrated into the continuum of life. The typical professional no longer operates from a fixed location, on a regular 9:00am to 5:00pm schedule. His days are often spread between various offices and he may not see his secretary for a week or more, although they stay in close touch via e-mail and mobile phone. He works at home on days without scheduled meetings, because after all, everything he needs is on the laptop in his briefcase. He occasionally begins his day at 5:00am to connect with colleagues in London on trans-Atlantic time. He drops off last night's financial analysis at an associate's house on Saturday morning, on the way to the local market or health club. He takes a break over a cappuccino at the nearby Starbucks coffee shop while a large file is downloading, or drops off the dry-cleaning, takes the dog for a walk, picks up little Johnny from day-care, or any number of other household chores or entertainment activities, according to the opportunities locally available.

Technology, thus, is creating a much more seamless kind of lifestyle, where work is structured to fit around daily chores, family obligations and other commitments. Laptops, cell phones and modems are all making the office more mobile, which helps to erase the separation between work and home. These devices, along with the general restructuring of business activities, are turning us into "techno-craftsmen" whose work is simply an invisible extension of life –not unlike the independent artisans of the pre-industrial era who plied their trade from home or a nearby workshop or studio, surrounded by all the services and suppliers on which their businesses depended and the necessities and conveniences of everyday life.

This is precisely the kind of life that creates a demand for the integrated, live/work environment which provides a rich mix of services and entertainments within walking distance of home and workplace –the kind of mixed-use neighborhoods that planning and urban design have been struggling so hard to achieve in cities everywhere for the last thirty years.

Rather than destroying the compact, urban neighborhood, high-tech capabilities are actually providing a stimulus for density and integration. But while this effect is becoming apparent in a growing number of places, like San Francisco's Media Gulch, Rittenhouse Square in Center City Philadelphia, even the Historic Gateway District in downtown Cleveland, progress remains generally slow, and few cities are actively responding to the development possibilities of expanding data processing and communications technologies. The question is, what do we need to do to exploit this technological opportunity? What kinds of changes in approach do we need to adopt to promote the unexpected advantages of the electronic workplace? And how can we speed up the adoption of the new techno-lifestyle as an answer to the continuing decline of inner city neighborhoods?

There at least five types of changes that are necessary. The first is a reduction in our reliance on land use as a planning tool –or perhaps the elimination of land use altogether as a relevant factor in the landscape of the new high-tech neighborhood. Technological sophistications are breaking down the traditional definitions of land uses, to the point where they are no longer accurate or useful descriptors of function. Land use, after all, is only a convenient short-hand for describing the cluster of functional characteristics typically associated with various activities. "Industry", for example, is short-hand for "production activities that involve machines and special equipment; often produce dangerous effluents, noise and other noxious impacts; frequently generate heavy truck traffic in material delivery and product distribution; and usually need large, single-story, shed-type buildings with open surrounding areas for truck manoevring and raw materials storage." In the landscape of the new technology, however, "industry" is just as likely to mean a couple of engineers at a computer terminal transmitting new product designs or machining adjustment instructions to a fabricator in Mexico, with none of the associated functional characteristics of the traditional idea of industry. Or in the case of the high-tech car dealer who has replaced his sprawling auto lot for a visual simulator and modem connections to Sweden and Germany: is his operation "retail"? or "auto service"? or "distribution"? or "office"? And does it even matter?

By maintaining these limited categories of function, we are continuing to support the segregation of business and residential activities, and continuing to limit the possibilities for new, unpredictable combinations and reconfigurations of these activities as the technological future unfolds. Many localities are attempting to achieve live/work environments by establishing "mixed-use" zones but this usually only means a complicated system of approvals for use applications and protracted battles with existing landowners over what it might mean to live next to an industrial or commercial activity whose use classification bears little relationship to the actual operation. A better approach to mixed-use might be to forget about use altogether, and approve or disapprove an activity based on its operational impacts with respect to issues such as air quality and noise, traffic generation, parking needs and so on. This is a return to the idea of Performance Zoning, proposed by Lane Kendig some decades ago.

The second kind of change is a challenge to the architectural profession to develop more flexible building types, capable of customized occupation and cost effective adaptation to unpredictable future needs. It is no accident that the most successful inner-city, mixed-use neighborhoods tend to be developing in historic warehouse districts where the building type lends itself to reuse by a wide variety of functions and where business and residential activities can coexist in changeable and often invisible combinations. The "loft", with its ability to accommodate home, office, studio, workshop, showroom, gallery, and any combination of these uses, is perhaps the most effective type of development unit for the electronic neighborhood. This kind of flexibility, however, needs to find successful expression in new construction as well as historic renovation projects.

Thirdly, we need to expand our repertoire of development incentives to more directly support the operational demands of the electronic neighborhood. Providing the latest in telecommunications infrastructure and wiring streets and buildings with the appropriate fiber optic connections is an obvious first step, but there may be other, more creative incentives worth considering. For example, networking all the buildings to central "super-servers" that provide affordable, state-of-the-art computing capabilities and services; or developing shared access "techno-stations" in one or more locations around the district where small companies, or service professionals and researchers working from home, can use video-conferencing facilities on an occasional basis, hook up to burstable ISDN connections when they need to, access virtual reality simulators, machine visioning systems, and all the other kinds of ultra-sophisticated data processing capabilities that competitive small enterprise needs occasionally, but can not afford to acquire individually. Similarly, access to specialized information webs and properly maintained networks of global contacts and local services could be an important incentive to location in a particular neighborhood.

The fourth requirement is the development of a quality public realm, where public life can flourish and public space becomes an invaluable extension of the private domain. This is obviously the challenge that faces urban design in every location, but it assumes an even higher priority in the electronic neighborhood where a satisfactory synthesis of public and private activities is central to the integrated live/work environment. The design of successful public spaces for these neighborhoods demands a more creative multi-disciplinary approach, in which planning, engineering, landscape and architecture provoke each other to see beyond the present paradigm and together, unlock the design opportunities of a future that embraces technology and all it has to offer.

And finally, we need a more determined commitment to cooperation, not only amongst the design professions, as noted above, but also between traditionally independent actors like private property owners and tenants, as well as between historically competitive groups such as adjacent neighborhoods and suburban communities. The strength of the live/work environment rests on a carefully constructed and constantly maintained web of relationships between interdependent functions and related activities, not all of which are located within the geographic boundaries of the neighborhood, or under its direct control. Cooperation between private property owners on issues such as shared parking, tenant services and maintenance of the public realm, will strengthen the network of local business and social relationships. Cooperation between municipalities, on issues such as infrastructure planning, transportation and transit, public services and revenue sharing, will help to extend this critical network to a regional scale, producing mutual benefits from the broader social, economic and cultural inter-dependencies that emerge.

With these five adjustments to current planning and urban design practice, we will have taken at least a step towards achieving the more compact, integrated forms of development that the new information technologies support. The electronic revolution has created the conditions for an urban revival; our challenge is to find ways to exploit this unexpected opportunity.

REFERENCES

Boyer, M.C. 1996. *Cyber Cities*. New York: Princeton Architectural Press.
Castells, M. 1989. *The Informational City*. Oxford: Blackwell
Forester, T. 1987. *High-Tech Society*. Cambridge: MIT Press
Mitchell, W. J. 1995. City of Bits. Cambridge: MIT Press
Mitchell, W. J. 1999. e-topia. Cambridge: MIT Press
Rones, P. L., Ilg, R. E. & Gardner, J. M. 1997. Trends in hours of work since the mid-1970s. *Monthly Labor Review* April 1977: 3-14

The practice of restoring spaces and places

Urban Lifestyles: Spaces · Places · People, Benson & Roe (eds)
© 2000 Balkema, Rotterdam, ISBN 90 5809 169 4

The Holyrood Project, Edinburgh: Urban regeneration within a World Heritage site

S.W. Filor
Edinburgh College of Art, UK

ABSTRACT: The evolving design for the Scottish Parliament building has stimulated much professional and lay discussion. It is, however, a late arrival to the Holyrood Project, a joint public/private venture which aims to regenerate the run down northeastern edge of the Old Town. This setting, between the Royal Mile, the Palace of Holyrood and the Salisbury Crags, gives the site a context which is full of stimulation and constraints. The bold landform of the Holyrood Park, the organic patterns of the Old Town compromised by industry and public housing and the needs of Tourist Edinburgh are only a few of the factors impacting on the master plan and the urban design proposals.

This paper describes, discusses and reviews plans, proposals and realized projects within the Holyrood Project. It falls into five sections.
    1 Introduction to the aims and objectives of the Project.
    2 Short description of the site.
    3 Discussion of master planning and design principles.
    4 Description and evaluation of key completed projects.
    5 Summary.

1 INTRODUCTION TO THE HOLYROOD PROJECT

As landscape architects we are all too aware that our urban regeneration projects are constantly addressing the dynamics of change. We are trying to aim at at series of moving targets as ownerships, funding initiatives, user asperations and functions all evolve and transmute over and beyond the lifetime of any particular project. The timescale is never finite, as these impacts continue beyond the contract period. These factors are very pertinent when discussing the Holyrood Project, much of which is still under construction. It is difficult even to decide where to start because there is no clear cut beginning. For the purposes of this paper, however, the early 1990's mark the beginning of developer interest in the area.

The major landowner, Scottish and Newcastle Breweries (S&N), were concentrating their brewing activities at Fountainbridge, west of the city centre. Their redundant Holyrood sites now offered obvious redevelopment potential. In early discussions with the then Regional Planning authority, they expressed their desire to use the profits from any land sales to fund a new building, similar in scale and public benefit to two previous buildings donated by brewers, the Usher and McEwan Halls. Initally dubbed The Youngers Universe, this was finally realised as Dynamic Earth, a major new visitor attraction focussing on the natural sciences. S&N, in partnership with the Lothians and Edinburgh Enterprise Company (LEEL) and Scottish Gas, launched a competition in 1992 (Figure 1). This was in two parts. The North Site, between The Royal Mile and Holyrood Road; and The South Site, for the former gasometor yard. S&N also held a right to purchase the Queensbury House hospital, a listed building. This, together with the S&N office buildings to the east, were excluded from the brief.

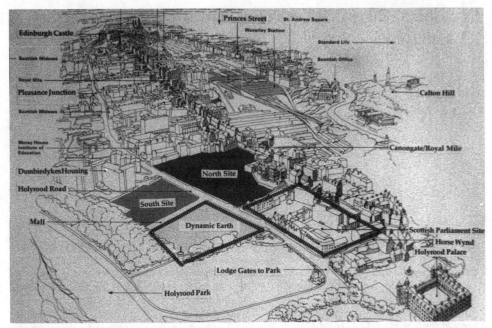

Figure 1. Holyrood Project : sites in urban context

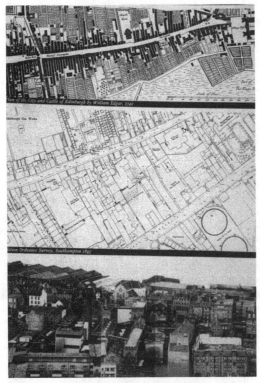

Figure 2. Changing Patterns :   Top 1742
Middle 1895
Bottom 1992, from Salisbury Crags

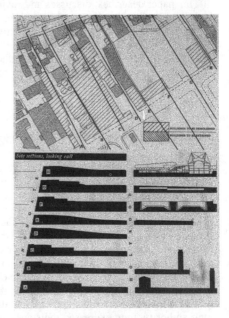

Figure 3.   Sections across North Site
Royal Mile to Park
Note east-west retaining wall
and buildings to be
retained/demolished.

90

This brief, with professional input by Michael Hopkins, architect for Dynamic Earth, and Paul Hogarth, a local landscape company, looked for two very different approaches to the sites. The North Site aims were to positively contribute to local community life, ensure a mix of residential and commercial developments, with improved shopping for Dumbiedykes, retain and convert as many existing buildings as possible, and to retain existing and exploit blocked off closes and courts. In contrast the South Site was promoted as a large scale, single use building, to respect the "landscape setting and historic location adjacent to the Palace of Holyroodhouse" (The Holyrood Project Development Brief 1992). The income from the sale of land to developers was to be made to the Youngers Universe Charitable Trust, reponsible for constructing and operating Dynamic Earth.

To compliment these developer driven projects, the Paul Hogarth Company were commissioned by LEEL to produce two studies, Grassmarket to Holyrood Palace (April 1993) and The Holyrood Area (May 1995). These were to cover the road corridor adjoining and linking the various development sites.

As mentioned earlier, S&N retained the eastern site, between Queensbury House hospital and the Palace. When the Lothian Health Board closed the hospital, S&N acquired this site, and prepared plans for a hotel. Then, for reasons that have never been publicly clarified, the site was selected for the new Scottish Parliament. The Catalan architect, Enric Miralles, in partnership with the Edinburgh office of RMJM, won the limited design competition (Feb 1998). This was for a building of 16,000 sq. metres. The subsequent detailed brief has expanded this to some 31,000 sq. metres, the major reason for cost escalation and design changes.

The South Site was sold to The Scotsman newspaper, who have constructed new headquarters (Comprehensive Design, architects), leaving part of the site for later development. Dynamic Earth (Michael Hopkins, architect; Paul Hogarth, landscape architect) on the adjacent site was opened in July 1999. It aims to be a national visitor attraction, complimenting the historic attractions of the Castle and Palace.

The North Site competition was won by Development Services Partnership (DSP) of Edinburgh. The master plan was by the Edinburgh architect, John Hope, with Ian White and Associates as landscape consultant. The paper will now concentrate on the North Site and on elements of the Paul Hogarth Holyrood Road Area proposals.

2 SITE DESCRIPTION

The Old Town of Edinburgh developed on the crest of a glacial crag and tail feature, running from the defensive crag on the west to the Abbey (now the Royal Palace) at the tip of the tail in the east. The Medieval street pattern of narrow closes running at right angles to the to the spine of the Royal Mile has been likened to a fish skeleton. Buildings fronted the spine, with backlands at right angles along the bones. Within the city walls these garden areas were quickly built over, but in the Canongate/Holyrood area, they remained largely undeveloped until built into by breweries in the 19th century. These largely squeezed out dwellings and smaller crafts and industries. Single use development was exacerbated post War by the Moray House campus and Dumbiedyke public housing to the west. By the mid 1980's, when S&N began to close down their breweries, the site had two contrasting characters, the tight Medieval Royal Mile/Canongate frontage on the north, and the hodge podge of industry and tenements fronting Holyrood Road (Figure 2). Holyrood Road was a rat run for cars, with no concessions to the needs of pedestrians or residents. To the south, adjacent to Holyrood Park, was an unrelated combination of 1960's housing and redundant gas holders and brewery buildings.

The setting, with framed views up and down the Royal Mile contrasting with glimpsed views through closes which fall away towards Salisbury Crags, is a stimulating mix of urban and quasi-rural. The Crags provide a strong background to the large scale buildings along the south side of Holyrood Road.

"There is an irregular line of a retaining wall running east-west which tends to dissect the site into an upper area off the Canongate, and southern sites driven into the hillside level with Holyrood Road" (John Hope, 1993) (See Figure 3). Latent potential existed in the lost closes, blocked by industrial buildings, the generally southerly aspect of the site, and the opportunity to

Figure 4. Model North Site master plan : John Hope

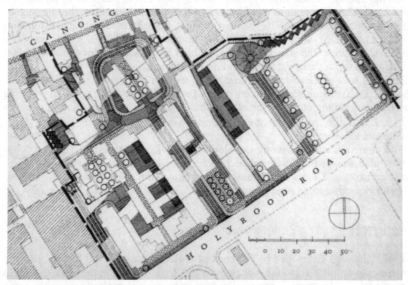

Figure 5. North Site master plan : public realm open space : Ian White

Figure 6. Holyrood Road, looking east, May 2000. North Site on left, Dumbiedyke and Scotsman on right.

mix new development with restoration and return to something like the Medieval fishbone pattern.

3   MASTER PLAN AND DESIGN PRINCIPLES

There are three current projects driving the Holyrood proposals - the North Site; the Holyrood Road; and the new Parliament. At the time of writing, the only tangible planning impact of the Parliament is their decision to terminate Holyrood Road at the entrance, diverting all other traffic through the Mall. The pedestrian connections from here to the Palace, and the spatial and visual relationship to Holyrood Park await final resolution by the Miralles/RMJM design team. The design potential in this hinge point between Dynamic Earth, Palace and Parliament is immense. It is hoped that the quality of the solution responds to these rich opportunities.

The North Site master plan, by John Hope, shows a sensitivity to the site, and an understanding of many of the principles of good urban design. One key factor is that the developer, DSP, are not typical property developers. Their role here is to market the separate small development sites to a range of owners, taking a percentage of the land price as their fee. Each site sale is normally the result of a limited architect/developer competition, with John Hope allowed to select some of the competing architects, not leaving this choice solely to the developers. Hope is also on the judging panels, and, by agreement with the City planners, he must also approve all detailed planning applications. This process has ensured both good design quality and an interestig mix of architectural approaches.

Hope's master plan increased the development density proposed in the competition brief. This was "to reinstate a recognisable Old Town urban pattern" (Hope, 1993) (Figure 5). The level differences across the site are exploited to give the majority of vehicular access and parking at Holyrood Road. The Canongate level, above the existing retaining wall, has minimal parking. Four public routes, using existing and reopened closes, cross the site from north to south. These are generally shared vehicular and pedestrian routes, but vehicles cannot cross the site, due to the retaining wall. The Highways department accepted the existing 1:8 gradients on vehicular routes. This enlightened decision means that the traditional close widths are respected, more existing buildings can be restored, and the tight urban grain is not coarsened. The urban form aims to consolidate the Canongate/Royal Mile frontage. Fingers of buildings then run parallel to the closes, connecting across the site to Holyrood Road. This gives a contrasting street frontage of gables, and allows sunlight to penetrate the site. The gradient is also used to provide basement car parking, although there are also several areas of surface parking.

The development is split into 19 different development sites, with a variety of uses - residential, hotels, commercial, retail and parking garages (Figure 5). The public realm open spaces, by Ian White, "are an integral part of the setting, and.....reflect the spacial qualities of old Edinburgh's ....closes" (Hope, 1993). Natural stone is used throughout the public spaces, Caithness slabs for the principal pedestrian routes and setts for shared spaces.

Planting is largely restricted to private courts, with limited tree planting at special focal points, such as the Clock Tower. White also proposed street trees along the southern pavement of Holyrood Road, but Paul Hogarth disagreed, and omitted trees from here in his Holyrood Road proposals.

To compliment the master plan, Hope also produced four worked examples, showing how different architects might respond to the master planning principles in designing specific development sites. Architects from London and Edinburgh contributed. Subsequently all these sites have been or are being developed, although not always with the same architect, or with the same forms.

The Holyrood Road proposals, by the Paul Hogarth Company, set out seven aims, including improving the environment for residents and visitors, defining the interface between the Park and the city, traffic calming, and dovetailing the various new developments with the road. Their proposals included designs to mark the east and west road entrances, to reduce the overall road width to a uniform 7.3 metres, to provide cycle lanes, parking and service bays, and to introduce robust and integrated lighting and street furniture. The carriageway would be asphalt, but pavements and kerbs would be in natural stone.

Figure 7. Looking south from Calton Hill, May 2000.

Figure 8. Looking north from Salisbury Crags, May 2000

The most important role in this road corridor project has been coordinating with the adjacent developments and sorting out onsite discrepancies in levels and pavement crossings. The impact so far is neccessarily piecemeal, but enough construction has occured to give an impression of the final result (Figure 6).

4 COMPLETED PROJECTS

The previous section covered some of the urban design and site planning principles followed by John hope, Ian White and Paul Hogarth in the Holyrood Project. This section looks at some completed areas in slightly more detail. Given the overlapping nature of the phasing of the various contracts, it is difficult, if not impossible, to illustrate completely finished projects. Adjacent construction work invariably intrudes. This is well illustrated in Figures 7 and 8, where tower cranes and site huts compete visually with occupied projects. The closed elevation to the Canongate (Figure 7) masks much of this gapiness, but it is very apparent from the south, accentuated at present by the gable ended built form (Figure 8).

Nonetheless something of the vigour and variety of architectural form encouraged by Hope's master plan is apparent, as is the striking form of Hopkin's Dynamic Earth, set off by the backcloth of Salisbury Crags. The drop in level across the site allows the scale of building to gradually increase from north to south, helping to mitigate the bulk of the Dumbiedykes flats (Figure 8).

New buildings are generally harled and colour washed-in the case of Ungless and Latimer's student housing in bright blues and reds. Both Malcolm Fraser (The Poetry Library) and Richard Murphy have used timber cladding, while Euan and Fiona McLachlan have used brick in their housing scheme, to complement adjacent existing brick buildings. Alan Murray's new Tun building promises a steel and glass structure, while John Hope is using metal cladding on another new development.

So there is a plurality in architectural forms and materials. To unify these, Ian White and Paul Hogarth bring restraint and tradition in both the materials and construction employed in their open space proposals, Caithness slabs, rectangular whin setts and square granite setts carpet the closes and public courts of the North Site. (Fig. 9).Public planting is minimal, at present restricted to a single lime tree, to avoid conflicts with pedestrian or vechicle movement. The design calls for the private and semi-private courts to contribute the planting; trees to reach over

Figure 9. Public realm paving, on a day of showers,Bakehouse Close, Ian White and Associates

95

walls, climbers to tumble over parapets and down surfaces. All this will take time to achieve, but already something of the expected quality can be experienced.

Paul Hogarth's scheme along the north side of Holyrood Road has begun to knit seamlessly into the North Site paving, by using similar materials and details (Figure 6). Across the road, their new frontage to the Dumbiedykes housing is complete. Previously, prairies of grass were demarcated along the roadside by timber knee rails, giving no privacy, sense of place or security to the flat dwellers. Now the site is enclosed by a metal railing set on a sandstone wall. Entrances are secured by metal gates, hung on sandstone pillars. Trees (fastigiate oak) are placed behind the railings, contributing to both the housing open space and the street.

The road proposals include a central strip of setts down the centre of the asphalt road surface, to visually narrow the carriageways and so decrease speed. This has yet to be constructed, but the new dark blue lampposts are in place (Figure 6).

Hogarth's were also responsible for the planting at the Mall, where they have used double lines of lime trees; and at Dynamic Earth, where the yew hedging compliments the sandstone stairs and ramps, ascending around the amphitheatre to the raised entrance platform.

5 SUMMARY

The dynamics of the Holyrood Project are such that parts of it will reseamble a building site for several years yet. In addition to the Parliament building, the Newcastle architects, Falconer and Brown, are remodelling the Moray Institute Gymnasium. The Institute is now an integral part of the University of Edinburgh, and the gym will conveniently link to the University indoor recreation complex on the Pleseance. The rest of the Institute campus is being reassessed by John Hope. So although the core of the Project may be nearing completion, both the eastern and western approaches are in a state of flux.

This core, however, is already bringing a diverse range of social, commercial and retail activitiy and life into the area. The increase in residential and commercial accommodation is attracting a variety of shops, pubs and restaurants. Two cultural organizations, the Royal Fine Arts Commission (Richard Murphy, architect) and the Poetry Library (Malcolm Fraser, architect) have also relocated their premises here.

Although details like the Mall seem inappropriate in scale, traffic impact on the Park and in character, on the whole the urban density, grain and pattern are fitting to both site and function. In general, the Holyrood Project is a good example of the dynamics of urban design. The role of the public realm open space in giving a coherence and stability to these effervescent processes is extremely significant. In this case traditional materials and contemporary street furniture are being skillfully used to create a suitably scaled and detailed setting for a varied and evolving built form. The project, though still largely under construction, indicates that the end product will be sufficently robust to ensure a high quality environment appropriate to the needs of this increasingly important location.

REFERENCES

Hogarth Company, P. 1993, *Grassmarket to Holyrood Palace: road corridor study.*Edinburgh : Hogarth.
Hogarth Company, P. 1995, *Holyrood Area Study : traffic calming and environmental impovements.* Edinburgh : Hogarth.
Hope, J. 1993, *The Holyrood Project : Development Services Partnership Proposals.* Edinburgh : Combined Arts.
McEvoy V. 1993.*The Holyrood Project Development Brief.* Edinburgh : McEvoy Vigers.

Urban Lifestyles: Spaces · Places · People, Benson & Roe (eds)
© *2000 Balkema, Rotterdam, ISBN 90 5809 169 4*

Sharing the Civic Realm: Pedestrian adaptation in the post modern city

R. F. Abrams
Department of Architecture, Texas A&M University, College Station, Tex., USA

T. R. Ozdil
Department of Landscape Architecture, Texas A&M University, College Station, Tex., USA

ABSTRACT: Achieving a balance between pedestrians and cars will be the greatest challenge facing urban designers in the post modern age. In the United States, this translates into making new places of quality for pedestrians, and gently easing cars, in certain districts and streets, into a secondary role. Cities around the world have experienced success in this regard through a variety of innovative and creative strategies for sharing the public realm. Three "pedestrian tales", from a collection of case studies currently being prepared, are presented in this paper.

1 SHIFTING GEARS

In the fall of 1999, the largest ever community-based trial of methods for the prevention of heart disease definitively demonstrated that "targeting individual behavior was ineffective in reducing the prevalence of cardiovascular disease and obesity." (Williamson, 1999) These findings led to a search for innovative public health interventions, emphasizing environmental change. In an editorial in the *New England Journal of Medicine,* Dr. David Williamson called for a dialogue between "hitherto unrecognized partners", including transportation agencies, urban planners, and real-estate developers, who play key roles in shaping environmental policies that affect the level of activity of Americans in their daily lives. This study was also reported in a front page article in the *New York Times,* which called for the redesign of American cities to promote walking as a primary means of movement. Since the release of the heart disease study, additional studies have been published linking mental health, particularly among the elderly, to the ability of citizens to freely and safely walk within their communities.

Most Americans have experienced at least one of the following situations: being stuck in a traffic jam while driving to a fitness class; attempting to walk or bicycle to a local shop and realizing it is impossible, and in some cases illegal; seeing someone walking alongside a roadway or waiting for a bus, and pitying them for not being in a car. Traffic congestion is growing exponentially in America, particularly in the rapid growth cities of the South, Southwest and West. This is partially due to an explosion of car ownership amongst teenagers. With dual income families, neither parent is able to serve as family chauffeur – thus children drive themselves to school, to after school activities, and to meet with friends. In families with more than one teenager, this often means four cars per household. The low cost of running a car in America serves further to encourage this tendency. (A recent news item showed a government official protesting increases in fuel costs, stating that "the current price of gas is too high for Americans.") Another factor contributing to urban congestion is the rapid pace with which we lead our lives. "Time" should lead the list of rare and endangered natural resources in America, with dual- and triple tasking among all family members eliminating the efficacy of any mode of travel other than motorized.

The central focus of modern city planning in America has been facilitating and accommodating travel by automobile. Since the 1970s, however, there has been a growing acknowledge-

97

ment that this had led to the death of city centers, in no small part due to the discouragement of pedestrian traffic. Now there is also the added pressure to create "healthy cities" that are more conducive to bicycle and pedestrian traffic. Consequently, many cities are struggling to imagine how to "shift gears", and, if not elevate the needs of pedestrians to equal status with vehicular movement, at least provide ways to share the public realm. The desire to pedestrianize parts of American cities represents a significant change in cultural values, and for practitioners of urban design, perhaps the most significant challenge of the post modern age.

Historically and currently, the role of the urban designer in the development and redevelopment of American cities is quite small, if it exists at all. The real challenge behind creating places for pedestrians in American cities is capturing the imagination of those whose investments, policies, and permitting processes actually affect the design of the city. For too long, these forces have conspired to create an attitude of antipathy towards those who walk. Judging from the amount of city staff time and resources devoted to the efficient circulation and storage of vehicles, it would appear that vehicular movement is the primary function of cities. In recent years, the Planning Department in Austin, which prides itself on being the most progressive city in Texas, proposed hiring a "pedestrian coordinator", to serve as an advocate for pedestrian concerns in the face of city actions. The city has at least forty transportation planners and traffic engineers in long range planning, short range planning, transit planning, development permitting, and public works, looking out for the interests of cars. Yet the proposal to hire a single pedestrian planner was made to appear a frivolous concept in the local newspaper, and was quickly laid to rest by the city council. While working with city staff on an historic district master plan in Austin, a traffic engineer stated that, in a "perfect world", the city would remove the last building from every downtown block in order to improve sight lines up and down the cross streets – to allow traffic to move faster without risking knocking down pedestrians.

There has been a prevailing attitude among Americans that the time spent moving between one's vehicle and one's destination should be as short and as uneventful as possible. When it opened in the 1970s, the John Hancock Tower in Chicago was praised for enabling occupants to drive in to its internal garage, shop for clothes and groceries, eat at fine restaurants, lease an office, rent an apartment, and even take a helicopter to the airport, without ever setting foot in the city. This extends to modern day attitudes, as well. A Lexus ad currently running in the *New York Times* shows a well-dressed man walking through an urban park, and being accidentally squirted by mustard from a hot dog vendor. The message conveyed is clear: genteel people should not be subjected to the indignities of walking in the city. They should be cocooned within a soundproofed, air conditioned, luxury vehicle.

In the early 1990s, we were hired to re-design the pedestrian environment around the Galleria District in Houston, Texas. This area is one of the original "edge cities", located just outside Houston's innermost ring road (I-610). At the beginning of the project, we were told that there were two objectives behind making the improvements: 1) to provide sidewalks for blue collar workers within the district to walk from bus stops to their jobs, encouraging them to use transit so white collar workers would have more spaces available in parking garages; and 2) to improve the "look" of the district from the perspective of drivers. At a public meeting with landowners, having presented the schematic design for pedestrian improvements, we were told by a landowner, "You must be thinking of some future generation – we don't walk in Houston." When pressed to explain why not, the landowner said it was just too hot. Further questioning got him to admit that he regularly walked in Washington, DC, and in New Orleans, which are each hotter and more humid than Houston.

Within the last few years, we have begun to sense a sea-change in attitudes towards pedestrians in American cities. Not surprisingly, much of the impetus behind this is economic: there have been enough examples of economic success in revitalized main street districts to attract the attention of developers and politicians. It is an undeniable fact that most Americans never walk around in their cities, and most urban planners and developers have never designed facilities for pedestrians. As the demand for pedestrian-oriented spaces in cities begins to grow, there will be a concomitant demand for demonstration projects that show innovative ways to share space between cars and people. The intent of our research project is not to provide formulae for pedes-

98

trian designs, but rather to show a range of creative solutions where planners have managed to adopt a pro-pedestrian orientation.

2 PEDESTRIAN TALES

The shortage of high quality pedestrian districts within American cities has not been for lack of excellent design resources, which date from the earliest years of post modernism (c.f. Appleyard, Lynch, Moudon, Cooper Marcus, Rapoport, et al), and even from the midst of civic modernism (Sitte). At the same time, conscientious practitioners of urban design know that textbook solutions cannot be applied to complex urban settings in the same way they might be in a more technical setting, such as a medical facility (and even in these settings the design ethos is changing). There is a certain fragility to the life of a pedestrian district, and its design has to be custom made to fit the circumstances of the place, time, and people. It has been pointed out by several environmental design researchers (c.f. Cooper Marcus, Yin, Francis) that the design of human environments is better served by more naturalistic forms of inquiry, such as post occupancy evaluations and case studies, which present real life situations. Design guidelines work best when the designer understands the need for adaptation of the guidelines in light of highly specific local conditions.

In the course of many attempts to assist American cities in becoming more pedestrian-friendly, we have begun a collection of case studies illustrating innovative and interesting ways of balancing the needs of cars and pedestrians. It is in the spirit of sharing stories and telling tales, as opposed to proscribing guidelines, that we offer the in-progress observations below.

2.1 Learning from Lucca

The medieval walls of the original city of Lucca, Italy, are completely intact, creating an ambiance of sheltered space within. Because of the compressed value of land within the walls, the city streets are narrow, the buildings tall, creating the network of interlinked vertical spaces that Rapoport believes is essential to quality pedestrian environments. Within the city walls, one catches constant glimpses of smaller enclosing walls, behind which are the hidden private gardens of Lucca.

The city center of Lucca is closed to motorized vehicles, creating a network of *area pedonales* that weave throughout the town. Places like Lucca provide the chance to experience a real, inhabited city free of cars (unlike the less real-seeming streets of Venice – somehow made familiar to us through Disney). The narrow width of the streets, the comparatively tall height of the buildings, the small scale of shops, the sequence of tight streets and open spaces, the variety of textures and materials, all create a highly sensory pedestrian environment. Within an *area peduncle*, one can experience the exquisite phenomenon of quietude and clean air in the midst of a bustling city. You can hear your own footsteps, and you can hear the sounds of life spilling from adjacent buildings. Bicycles have bloomed like wildflowers throughout the city, parked outside nearly every door. One can wander for hours, seemingly lost, but always sensing the gentle containment of the walls. Lucca is a life-sized laboratory of townscape that perfectly demonstrate how to design spaces for pedestrians.

There are lessons to be learned in Lucca about the importance of mystery, human scale, irregularity, glimpses of greenery; many small opportunities for food and drink, in unexpected places; the provision of contrast: tight spaces and open space/ retail juxtaposed with residential uses/ civic space against private back alley space; and the use of landmarks to give identity to neighborhoods. Perhaps the two greatest lessons Lucca presents are a) the value in integrating pedestrianism into the everyday life of the city, as opposed to limiting it to tourist or entertainment-oriented districts; and 2) the ability of modern urban residents to adapt to, and in fact embrace living in a car-free zone. It is easy to assume that Lucca has always been a pedestrian city and always will be. In truth, it is an unstable situation, with constant pressure from local merchants to open the streets back up. The citizens of Lucca are content with the way it is, and have thus far managed to resist.

In addition to the network of pedestrian streets within the walls, the city has built a wide, tree-lined promenade that runs along the top of the city walls. Here, in a scene somewhat rare in Italy, one can observe residents of all ages vigorously exercising – jogging, fast walking, roller-blading. This raises speculation about the cause and effect relationship between Lucca's pedestrian network and the devotion of the citizens to keeping fit, and appears to support the hypothesis of the American medical study linking public health to a city's walkability.

2.2 *Main Street, Texas*

Many small towns in Texas exist not because of a river running through them, but because a state highway does, or a railroad, or both. Access to transportation determined their success, as they became points of collection for agricultural products such as corn, cotton and cattle. As the political economy in Texas has shifted from rural to urban, and from railroads to interstate highways, many of these towns have suffered economic decline. In case after case, the death of their Main Street districts was accelerated by the construction of a Wal-Mart at the outskirts of town.

The Texas Historical Commission has an excellent Main Street program, which is devoted to the revitalization of historic town centers. Main Street's central belief is that small town centers must learn to operate in much the same manner as shopping malls to compete for custom. While providing extensive technical assistance to building owners and shopkeepers regarding the value and careful restoration of historic buildings, advertising, promotion, and merchant organizations, program leaders emphasize the relationship between happy pedestrians and healthy retail economies. While the program is sometimes accused of creating a generic "Main Street" look to these districts (brick paved sidewalks, barrels of flowers, an overabundance of festivals...), it has had some remarkable successes with revitalization, always with a strong emphasis upon rebuilding the pedestrian environment.

Opposition to improvements in many of these districts has come from a surprising source: the Texas Department of Transportation (TxDOT). While the towns struggle to create pedestrian districts around their main streets, TxDOT is often intent on moving traffic through, with as little obstruction as possible. TxDOT has opposed center medians, pedestrian refuges, narrowing of lanes, additional stoplights, planting of street trees, retention of on-street parking, -- traffic calming, so vital to the health of these retail districts, is antithetical to TxDOT's mission. One small town, College Station, is the home of one of the state's largest universities.

In the City of Weslaco, in the Lower Rio Grande Valley, nearly every shop on Main Street has closed – there are several "big box" stores newly built at the edge of town. Many of the retailers who have remained downtown have opted to enlarge their stores, and try to make them appear to be large outlets by covering the facades with aluminum sheathing, covering most of the windows. Adjacent buildings have been razed to create surface car parks like the big box stores. There is no life left in the district, and little reason to go there. The city is at a loss as to how to reclaim it as a vital part of the town. Yet, if one follows Main Street twenty miles south to the Rio Grande, and crosses into Mexico, there is Weslaco's sister city, Progresso Nuevo, with a booming, bustling Main Street. This is a situation eerily reminiscent of William Whyte's observations about downtown Los Angeles vs. Disneyland. Much of what Weslaco's planners need to know about designing a lively pedestrian district is on display in Progresso – much the same list as can be found in Lucca.

In recent years, the Texas Department of Transportation has begun to express some interest in the concept of streetscape design, but very hesitatingly. It is as if they expect a dam to burst, releasing a flood of requests for street upgrades in these small towns. This is likely to happen. As part of our consulting practice, we are assisting TxDOT in developing a palette of interventions that mediate between a totally car-oriented view on the street, and one that is open to sharing space with pedestrians. This is a primary reason we found our third case study so intriguing.

2.3 Newbury Street, Boston

Newbury Street is a major commuter street leading into the Back Bay area of Central Boston. Newbury presents an excellent case study in pedestrian adaptation because it is a street that has a dual identity. Most of the time it serves as a key one-way collector, an important part of the downtown circulation grid. But on special occasions, the street is closed, and it capably serves as one of Boston's most significant pedestrian districts.

According to Appleyard, and the authors' experience, one-way streets can have a destructive impact on life in the adjacent buildings, particularly if they are residential. Transportation engineers tend to look upon them as rivers of traffic, and attempt to remove any evidence of human occupation that endanger or inhibit the flow. It is significant to note that waterway engineers now realize that removing all restrictions to flow causes more serious problems downstream, and have begun to build back into floodways obstructions such as rip-rap and gabions. Unfortunately, the same cannot be said of transportation engineers and traffic calming measures. Nevertheless, a kind of peaceful truce has been reached on Newbury Street

An interesting symbiosis has evolved between the buildings that frame the street and the use of the street. When Newbury was converted to one-way traffic, the large brownstone homes adjacent were slowly converted to apartments (as Appleyard found in his case studies). Eventually some of the ground floors were converted to shops. These began to coagulate into clusters of interesting shops and cafes, which led to experimental street closures. Now that the street has matured as a pedestrian district, the buildings are being opened up even more to the life of the street via split level shop fronts and sidewalk cafes, and the upper floor apartments have once again become very desirable places to live.

Of particular interest is Newbury Street's ability to function well in two opposing roles: as a major traffic collector, and as a high quality pedestrian district. Site surveys on Newbury Street are currently underway, but preliminary findings have indicated that the dimensions of the street corridor correspond exactly to Camillo Sitte's design guideline - that the width of a high quality public space should be between 1/2 and 2 times the height of the adjacent structures. At the heart of the Newbury Street district, the street corridor is approximately 30 meters in width, and the adjacent brownstones are around 20 meters in height. The continuity of buildings edging the street help define the corridor and provide a backdrop of continuous architectural character, texture, and color. The space between the buildings and the street, framed by deciduous street trees planted in the 1980s, has become an idyllic setting for sidewalk cafes.

Despite Newbury Street's important role in the traffic grid of downtown Boston, rerouting traffic when the street is closed does not cause gridlock to occur in the surrounding area. Somehow the adjacent streets are able to absorb the overage. The threat of gridlock is often behind traffic engineers' objections to closing or narrowing downtown streets to accommodate increases in pedestrian traffic. The best way to prove otherwise is by documenting cases like Newbury Street. It seems a small feat within the context of Boston, but is actually a significant and bold concept worthy of the attention of other American cities.

Another critically important aspect of Newbury Street is the formation of a volunteer merchant organization that provides proactive management for the district. Pedestrian districts do not spontaneously occur, they happen by design and through the persistent will and vision of a group of advocates. But they can quickly deteriorate into zones of neglect without a continuous approach to maintenance. It takes far-sighted merchants to see their neighbors not as competitors, but as co-creators of a whole that is greater than the parts.

3 RECREATING STREETLIFE IN AMERICA

Particularly in the United States, the design and management of the spaces between buildings is neglected. As long as people are buffered from this within cars, it can be tolerated, but in pedestrian areas it cannot. If indeed American cities are going to become more walkable, there will need to be a concerted effort to redesign a significant number of street environments to make pedestrianism even marginally enjoyable. Each city and every climate will provide unique challenges; a single formula won't provide the means for resolving the unhealthy lifestyles of American city dwellers. Experiencing a range of creative approaches is the intent of our pedestrian stories. We are hopeful that by learning about Lucca, city planners and developers in places like Weslaco can move their Main Streets closer to Newbury Street.

Figures
Left: A view of the complexity that is Lucca
Right Above: A view of the sparcity that is Weslaco
Right Below: The synthesis: Newbury Street

REFERENCES

Anderson, S. (ed.) 1986. *On streets*. Cambridge, MA: MIT.

Appleyard, D. 1981. *Livable streets*. Berkeley: University of California, Berkeley Press.

Beatley, T. 2000. *Green urbanism: Learning from European cities*. Washington, DC: Island.

Ben-Joseph, E. 1995. Changing the residential street scene: Adapting the shared street concept to the suburban environment. *Journal of the American Planning Association,*, 61(4): 504-515.

Francis, M. 1999. *A case study method for landscape architecture*. Washington, DC: Landscape Architecture Foundation.

Jacobs, A. 1994. *Great streets*. Cambridge, MA: MIT.

Lynch, K. 1960. *The image of the city*. Cambridge, MA: MIT.

Moudon, A. (ed.) 1987. *Public streets for public use*. New York: Van Nostrand Reinhold.

Peponis, J. 1989. "Space, urban culture and urban design in Late Modernism and after." *Ekistics* 334. 43: January-February.

Polus, A., & Craus, J. 1988. "Planning considerations and evaluation methodology for shared streets." *Transportation Quarterly* 42(4): 587.

Rapoport, A. 1990. Case study: Pedestrian streets. In *History and precedent in environmental design*. New York: Plenum.

Rogers, R. 1997. *Cities for a small planet*. London: Faber and Faber.

Safdie, M. 1997. *The city after the automobile: An architect's vision.* Toronto: Stoddart.
Sitte, C. 1945. *The art of building cities,* trans. By C. Stuart. Westport, CT: Hyperion.
Stake, R. 1995. *The art of case study research.* Thousand Oaks, CA.: Sage.
Untermann, R. 1984. *Accommodating the pedestrian: Adapting towns and neighborhoods for walking and bicycling.* New York: Van Nostrand Reinhold.
Unterman, R. & Moudon, A. 1990. "Designing pedestrian-friendly commercial streets." *Urban Design and Preservation Quarterly* 13(3): 7.
Williamson, D. 1999. Editorial. *The New England journal of medicine.* October.
Yin, R. 1993. *Applications of case study research.* Thousand Oaks, CA.: Sage.

Urban Lifestyles: Spaces · Places · People, Benson & Roe (eds)
© 2000 Balkema, Rotterdam, ISBN 90 5809 169 4

Cultural continuity of Istanbul through urban promenades

S.E.Soygenis
School of Architecture, Beykent University, Istanbul, Turkey

ABSTRACT: Istanbul; with its history of housing Roman, Byzantine, Ottoman and Turkish cultures, possesses and reflects multi cultural quality in its urban fabric. This paper will focus on neighbourhoods of Istanbul which possess monuments of Byzantine, Ottoman period and characteristic urban fabric of Istanbul in history. While these monuments are frequently visited areas of the city, their urban fabric is often neglected. This paper aims to integrate these monuments with their surrounding urban fabric as promenades, reflecting the culture they once possessed and as places of the city rich with spatial characteristics, an excerpt from the past in making today's cities livable. Promenade of Kariye-Ayvansaray, promenade of Eminonu-Nuruosmaniye Mosque are selected for this study. On site observations and analysis of the spatial fabric in sequence, analysis of social and physical development of these neigbourhoods in history are the methods used for this research.

1 INTRODUCTION

There are cities which are in the boundaries of one country yet with their heritage, they can be considered a'world city'. Istanbul can be considered one, with its monuments and urban fabric of multi cultural characteristics. After housing the capital of three empires, Istanbul is full of monuments of Roman, Byzantine and Ottoman culture which are areas of attraction by local and international people. This paper will concentrate on regenerating those 'places' in the historic Peninsula of Istanbul which possess monuments of the Byzantine and Ottoman Istanbul together with the urban fabric of the past as a whole. Promenade of Kariye Museum-Ayvansaray houses important examples of Byzantine period, and is of residential character and promenade of Eminonu-Nuruosmaniye Mosque, houses examples of Ottoman period beside its Byzantine elements and is of a commercial character. Historical linkage of the past to the present can be achieved on the fabric of the cities as promenades that connect different elements of the city in the history to the present city. Cities in the next millennium need 'places' of different character as a sequence to be experienced to emphasize the continuity of the city culture.

2 HISTORY OF AYVANSARY

Ayvansaray is located on the northwest of Historic Peninsula facing Golden Horn. This neighbourhood, in Byzantine period was a small town outside the boundaries of Byzantine Empire and was surrounded by city walls. In the 5th century it was taken into the boundaries of the city walls as a neighbourhood of the city. Old city walls do not exist today. After 11th century, the Byzantine emperor left his palace in Sultanahmet (the old palace) and started to live in the palace of Blacharnai in this neighbourhood which did not survive to today. Ruins of Tekfur Palace which was constructed after Blacharnai Palace survive until today. Kariye Museum , a Byzantine church is located in the neighbourhood. This building is famous for its frescos. The church was converted into a mosque in the 1500 s. Since 1948 it is used as a museum. After the conquest of the city by the Ottomans, Ayvansaray developed as an Ottoman neighbourhood. In 18th century the shore of Ayvansaray was full of houses and yalıs of the well to do. There was a small palace at the shore, belonging to one of the daughters of the Sultan. Christian and Jewish neighbourhoods of Balat and Fener of the Ottoman period are located along the Golden Horn next to Ayvansaray with an Ottoman character. Being close to Fener and Balat, there are orthodox churches in the area. This neighbourhood lost its character especially after 1950's due to people migrating to Istanbul from Anatolia. It is one of the poor neighbourhoods of the city today (Istanbul Encyclopedia, 1994).

3 HISTORY OF EMINONU

Eminonu is one of the oldest commercial districts of Istanbul. There were neighbourhoods in the area such as Balıkhane dating back to Byzantine period which was demolished by 1980's because of the clearance project of Golden Horn. In the Ottoman period it was the only commercial center in the city. There were Ottoman Jewish people living in that area till 17th century. After the construction of Yeni Mosque they moved out . During the Ottoman reign, a lot of monuments were constructed in Eminonu. Due to its pier function, Eminonu developed as a commercial zone with a lot of khans and shopping arcades. Streets with specialized commercial function of the past survive until today. In 1960's it was still an important zone for commercial development. It is still today with changes taking place. Eminonu kept its eastern picturesque look until the construction of the Galata bridge. Construction of Sirkeci train station, post office, Vakıf Khan influenced this change. The most dramatic change came with the clearing of the buildings at the shore which opens up the area in front of Yeni Mosque facing the sea.(Kuban, 1998) Social fabric of the Eminonu area continues to be of similar character due to its commercial function all through its history.

These selected neighbourhoods are two different excerpts from the old city which experienced evolution and transformation socially, culturally and physically. After an analysis of these neighbourhoods, it is possible to see traces of its cultural and architectural heritage. The physical spatial characteristics of these neighbourhoods in relation to the existing monuments of historical and architectural value as a whole can be good examples of reflection of the city, its multi-cultural quality for various disciplines. It is possible to understand cities through perception of the urban spaces and the buildings that form these exterior spaces. In defining the city, Rossi points out the importance of the existence of monuments and housing together. (Rossi,1984) It is with their complex integration that cities are formed. Streets and open public squares are means of transfer in cities. This transportation can be by any means of vehicle or by pedestrian movement. Rapoport emphasizes the importance of the speed of the movement in perception of space and points out that at lower speeds, ability to perceive increases (Rapoport, 1991). According to Clay, streets beside their function as routes of transportation, carry a great deal of information for democratic societies in all phases of life starting from chilhood continuing onwards to elderly age (Clay, 1991). In realization of the value of streets as something more than a mean of transportation, 'Town Trail ' concept was developed in United Kingdom in 1970's as an environmental education movement where defined pathways were used to explore social, cultural, artistic, visual, economic and architectural characteristics of the city (More, 1991). This approach was used in United States as an inexpensive approach to appreciate cities (Francis, 1991). Lynch's definition of the city includes the space that is to be perceived in time. Influence of the past experiences, relation with the surroundings and sequential events are key factors in perception of the environment. He emphasizes the importance of the sensory cues in the cities for the perception and classifies the elements of the city as path, landmark, edge, node and district (Lynch, 1984). Cullen's emphasis is on the 'art of relationship' in the perception of the city. This relationship makes the experience of the city a dramatic event where the sequence of vision changes with the movement of the pedestrian (Cullen, 1998). In relation to the physical spatial characteristics of the cities, Norberg-Schulz talks about the 'genuis loci' of the space as an important element that makes the distinction. He emphasizes the importance of phenomenological characteristics of the space integrated with the architectural- spatial characteristics which makes the difference between the space and the place (Norberg-Schulz, 1984). In the light of this discussion, the spatial characteristics of the selected promenades will be analyzed to show the importance of their existence in the fabric of the city as good examples of continuation of culture, cultural diversity, pathways of education of the history/ architectural heritage of the city and as distinct places in Istanbul that is going to take the city with all its dynamism to the next millennium.

The promenades chosen for this paper that possess typical characteristics are classified under four groups. Common denominator for each case is the presence of 'starting point' , 'the development' and 'the end point' of the promenade. Typological groupings are; Monuments and squares that are linked by routes of traditional housing fabric, monuments and squares that are linked by traditional commercial fabric, promenades that possess strong cultural and physical fabric of the city, promenades with strong city vistas that are in close relation with the sea. Selected promenades will be evaluated with their spatial characteristics as 'places' in the history of the city. Sequential visions of the exterior, semi-exterior and interior space as an integrated whole is the key issue in the continuity of the promenades historically, culturally and spatially.

4 PROMENADE OF KARIYE MUSEUM-AYVANSARAY

Promenade of Kariye-Ayvansaray (Figure 1) which is located at Golden Horn has close contact with the sea and is of residential character. This promenade starts at Kariye Square in front of Kariye Museum which houses rich examples of frescos from Byzantine period. This museum is one of the frequently visited monuments of the city. After exploration of the interior of the museum, the square as an urban space is a place for exploration of the environment. This square which slopes in level is surrounded by Kariye Museum and 2-3 story buildings of traditional character. From this urban enclosure passing through Kariye Turbesi Street via Kugulu Bahce Street with houses surrounded by gardens, one reaches Hoca Sakir Street where view of the Walls of Theodosius II is perceived. This section of the promenade, with the monumental character of Kariye and city walls connected in between by the housing fabric is a typical example of Ottoman urban fabric where monuments dominate and housing fabric is organic and small in scale. Leading down towards the sea, at Sishane Street, directional character of the street continues until Tekfur Palace where space opens up and Tekfur Palace- an example from Byzantine period- meets the pedestrian. This is a stopping point spatially and at the same time it is a place to stop and experience the architecture of the Byzantine palace. Leaving Tekfur Palace and going down hill towards the sea on a curving street, sequential visions of this route of directional character lined by houses of few stories and glimpse of sea view at Golden Horn are perceived. Catching the view of the sea is a reminder of the character of Istanbul in history in strong ties with the sea. Moving along the housing fabric, contact with the city walls is provided at Egrikapi. Change of the scale and change of time in history are the cues at this location. Going out of the city walls at this point, scale of the street changes and view of the Golden Horn is perceived. At this location, it is possible to differentiate historic Istanbul from Istanbul today. Coming back to inside of the city walls, the route curves down towards the sea at Derviszade Street, with 3-4 story traditional houses, leading down to Ayvansaray Kuyu Street where the terrain becomes flat. The route widens up in front of the church at this point then leading towards the sea again, opening up at the shore to the view of Golden Horn to conclude the promenade. Following are the sequential visions of this promenade.

1. Vision:View of Kariye Museum.Feeling of enclosure is created by the wooden houses on both sides and the masonry wall of Kariye Museum. Kariye Museum with its architecture, is a flashback to Byzantine period, wooden houses to Ottoman Istanbul which are together, a typical example for the urban fabric of Ottoman Istanbul. Texture of the materials define planes.
2. Vision: An Ottoman fountain in the square in relation with the museum. There is anticipation for further visions created by the building at the back.
3. Vision: 'Here and there' effect is created by the layering of planes.Light and shade emphasize this effect. An intimate space is created with the enclosure elements.

Figure 1.Map of Promenade of Kariye Museum-Ayvansaray
A.Kariye Square, B.Kariye Turbe Road, C.Kugulu Bahce Road, D.Hocasakir Street, E.Sisehane
Street, F.Egri Kapi Street, G.Derviszade Street, H.Ayvansaray Kuyu Road, I.Ayvansaray Street,
J.Tekfur Palace, K. Cıty walls.

4. Vision: Sequence of spaces is further emphasized by the trees. With the location of wooden houses, there is anticipation for further visions.
5. Vision:View from Kuyulu Bahce Road. Trees behind garden walls foreshadow new spaces to discover, while minaret is a sign for direction.
6. Vision: View from Hoca Sakir Road. Sense of infinity is created by the existence of the Byzantine city wall.
7-8.Vision:View of Tekfur Palace from Byzantine period.
9. Vision:Leaving Tekfur Palace and heading towards the sea, sense of continuity is created by the buildings lining the street. With the curvature of the street, further visions are expected.
10.Vision:Arched way on the city walls is a reminder of Byzantine Istanbul which create a feeling of double space, one on this side of the wall, one on the other side.
11-12-13.Vision:View from Derviszade Street. Feeling of continuity is created with articulated facades of the wooden houses, with the masonry garden walls at various instances.
14.Vision:View of the church at Ayvansaray Kuyu Road, a flashback to Ottoman Istanbul.
15.Vision:Opening to Golden Horn at Ayvansaray Kuyu Road , View of the Golden Horn and the sea, a reminder of the city living close contact with the sea.

5 PROMENADE OF EMINONU-NURUOSMANIYE MOSQUE

Promenade of Eminonu-Nuruosmaniye (Figure 2) is of a typology where there is a strong relationship with the sea. Looking at its fabric, it is a typology where monuments and squares are connected by commercial character. It starts from the square in front of Yeni Mosque where there is a vista of Galata Tower and its surroundings. This is a starting point of the promenade where pedestrians can gather together to catch various visions surrounding this square. After the perception of the space around this square, one can proceed to the interior of Yeni Mosque an example of Ottoman architecture, later followed by the interior of Mısır Carsısı which is an arcade of row of stores. Spatially, this place is an example of commercial life of Ottoman Istanbul. This is a reminder of typical Ottoman commecial fabric at the same time emphasizing the continuity of history related to this neighbourhood. Leaving behind Mısır Carsısı, Bankacılar street with 5-6 storey buildings follows with sequential visions of path character. Looking back the silhouette of Yeni Mosque can be captured. Walking on this street, Turbe and medrese of Abdulhamit lines the street on the right and Vakıf Han on the left. Interior of this Khan, an example of an architecture of Republican period, is an experience to be perceived on this promenade. After the exploration of the interior, one continues on Ankara street. Looking back on this street, relationship with the sea which was out of vision after entering Mısır Çarşısı once again comes into vision. Ankara street is a directional route lined by 5-6 storey buildings. At some point on this street, continuous row of buildings is broken by the presence of City Hall where greenery is also introduced. On Ankara Street after the consulate of Iran the promenade continues at the right to Nuruosmaniye Street. At this point the route narrows and poses a pedestrian character. Lined by commercial shops at first level, this densely landscaped route ends with the arched entrance of Nuruosmaniye Mosque and the mosque itself at the back. Entering through the arched doorway Nuruosmaniye Mosque- an important example of baroque architecture in Istanbul- can be perceived. Interior of the mosque followed by the octagonal shaped atrium are the following spaces to be explored. From this point on towards the door of Kapalıcarsi passing through the narrow and dense street of Kılıccılar, one reaches to Mahmutpasa street. This street of commercial character shows variety of perception depending on the weekly and weekend activity it carries. On weekdays the social activity and the people are the point of interest and are reflection of the social character of the society. On weekends spatial characteristics become dominant elements of the promenade. Khans located on this street with the richness of their interiors contribute a lot the spatial quality of this route and are the semi interior/exterior extensions of the exterior space. This street continuing down the hill provides variety of sequential visions of directional and square character. Commercial activity loses its connection with the street on Asirefendi street. Passing by Buyuk Postane on to Ankara Street, a glimpse of sea view is again perceived. Passing by Vakif Han, one reaches the square in front of

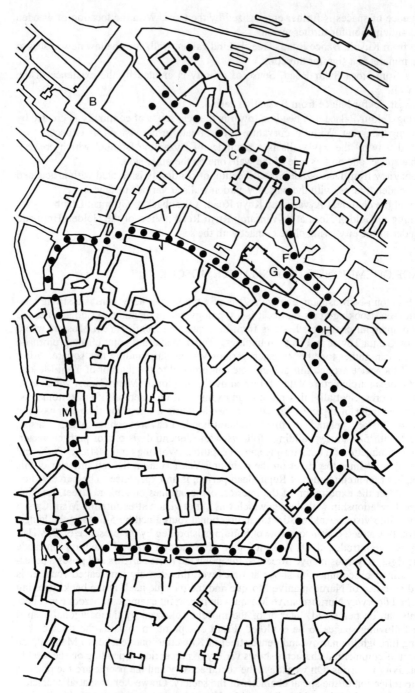

Figure 2. Map of Promenade of Eminonu-Nuruosmaniye Mosque
A.Yeni Mosque, B.Misir Bazaar, C.Bankacilar Street, D.Hamidiye Street, E.Vakif Khan,
F.Mimar Vedat Tek Street, G.Buyuk Post office, H.Ankara Street, I.Babiali Street, J.
Nuruosmaniye Street, K.Nuruosmaniye Mosque, L.Kiliccilar Road, M.Mahmutpasa Road, N.
Asirefendi Street.

Yeni Mosque where promenade ends and views of Galata tower and sea connection is strongly perceived. Following are the sequential visions of this promenade.

1. Vision:View of Yeni Mosque, example of Ottoman architecture.
2. Vision:View of Misir Bazaar, reminder of the continuity of commercial activity in the area.
3. Vision:View from Bankacilar Street towards Yeni Mosque among the street vendors, typical character of the area from the past.
4. Vision:Continuity breaks with the intrusion of a different structure on the right side, an example for incident.
5. Vision:Feeling of enclosure is created at Hamidiye Street. Building at the end with its location foreshadows new routes to explore. With its domed structure at the corner, this building acts as a focal point.
6. Vision:Post Office building from the republican period creates a feeling of enclosure, at the same time leads to further visions.
7. Vision:At Ankara street, looking back, view of the sea is the reminder of close relationship with the sea. Feeling of continuity is emphasized by the view of the sea and the other side of the Golden Horn.
8-9.Vision:Scale of the commercial fabric is evident with the height of the buildings and the width of the street.
10.Vision:View on Nuruosmaniye Street. Trees create a feeling of depth, at the same time an enclosure.
11-12.Vision:Looking towards Divanyolu, this street is a typical example of Ottoman shopping strip.Trees help to strengthen the effect of enclosure.
13.Vision:Entrance to Nuruosmaniye Mosque and Grand Bazaar. Arched entrance create an effect of double space.

6 CONCLUSION

Istanbul is in threat of losing its social, cultural , architectural and urban characteristics that is inherited from Roman, Byzantine, Ottoman cultures especially after 1950's till today. Cities are cultures that have to be transferred to the generations to come. They are places of education for a variety of disciplines especially for architects. They are places to be experienced by the children and the elderly. Integration of the places in the city with the people, integration of elements of the city as a whole, are ways to ensure continuity of city culture and living. This is especially valid for societies where transformations are rapid. There are long and short term practices that will help to keep this continuity. Preservation practices are long term means. Short term practices which seem to be vital for the case of Istanbul include signage/information systems in the selected neighbourhoods to provide orientation and necessary information about the historical, cultural, architectural and spatial characteristics of these promenades. Control on vehicle traffic, street furniture, services can be short term means of regenerating these places in the city for their survival as examples of cultural continuity of the city of Istanbul. They make up good examples of space, architecture, history and culture of Istanbul and are places to be integrated to the city as linkages of the past to present and to the future.

REFERENCES

Clay, G. 1991. The Street as Teacher. In A.V. Moudan (ed.), *Public Streets for Public Use* : 95-109. New York, NY: Columbia University Press.
Cullen, G. 1998. *The Concise Townscape*. Oxford: Architectural Press.
Dunden Bugune Istanbul Ansiklopedisi (Istanbul Encyclopedia). 1994. Istanbul: Kultur Bakanligi / Tarih Vakfi Yayini.
Francis, M. 1991. The Making of Democratic Streets. In A.V. Moudan (ed.), *Public Streets for Public Use* : 23-39. New York, NY: Columbia University Press.

Kuban, D. 1998. *Kent ve Mimarlik Uzerine Istanbul Yazilari (Istanbul Writings on City and Architecture)*. Istanbul: YemYayinlari.

Lynch, K.1984. *The Image of the City*. Cambridge, MA: The MIT Press.

More, R.C. 1991. Streets as Playgrounds. In A.V. Moudan (ed.), *Public Streets for Public Use* : 45-62. New York, NY: Columbia University Press.

Norberg-Schulz, C. 1984. *Genius Loci – Towards a Phenomenology of Architecture*. New York, NY: Rizzoli.

Rapoport, A. 1991. Pedestrian Street Use: Culture and Perception. In A.V. Moudan (ed.), *Public Streets for Public Use*: 80-91. New York, NY: Columbia University Press.

Rossi, A. 1984. *The Architecture of the City*. Cambridge, MA: The MIT Press.

Urban Lifestyles: Spaces · Places · People, Benson & Roe (eds)
© *2000 Balkema, Rotterdam, ISBN 90 5809 169 4*

Urban landscapes could make a brownfield site green

M. Juvara, C. Barrett & I. Carradice
Ove Arup and Partners, London, UK

ABSTRACT: This paper aims at the promotion of quality urban amenity landscapes on previously developed land because we believe that landscape is a fundamental element of the urban renaissance. We look at plants and their needs to try to minimize waste production and find ways to create the necessary conditions for plant development *directly* into the brown soil. In fact, if the appropriate conditions for planting were established without the traditional capping layer and new fill system, the creation of quality urban amenity landscape would become far more environmentally and financially sustainable. The last section of the paper outlines a strategy for the implementation of the proposals.

1 THE BROWNFIELD SITE DEVELOPMENT TRAP

It is the UK government policy that a large proportion of new urban development occurs on brownfield sites (previously developed land). This means that, in the future, development will have to deal more and more with site reclamation, disposal of waste, man-made soils and contamination. As a consequence, most new parks, green squares and street planting, so essential to the quality of urban living, will occur on non-natural soils. This trend is not unique to the UK: many other Western countries are moving towards similar policies, with the aim of controlling urban sprawl and encouraging the reuse of industrial land.

At the same time, new environmental policies insist on reduction of waste and correction of practices that are not environmentally responsible. Designing out waste is an imperative for the construction industry, which is one of the largest producers of tipping materials.

1.1 *Stale remediation practices*

An assessment of brownfield redevelopment schemes carried out by Arup in recent years shows how low cost and environmentally responsive solutions depend on the close match between early remediation strategy and development master plan (see Figure 1). Yet very often a one-fits-all remediation solution is adopted, embracing invariably generic targets for clean up that turn out to be unnecessary and detrimental to the environment as a whole.

The creation of amenity landscape associated with brownfield development is an example where common site practices are expensive and not necessarily well suited to the environment and to the viability of the projects involved. The stripping or capping of existing ground and import of new fill and topsoil from elsewhere, for example, entail the production of vast quantities of contaminated waste and the generation of a large number of lorry movements in and off site. Furthermore, this system is sometimes employed prior to the sale of the land for redevelopment despite being unsuitable as an advanced remediation technique as Figure 1 shows.

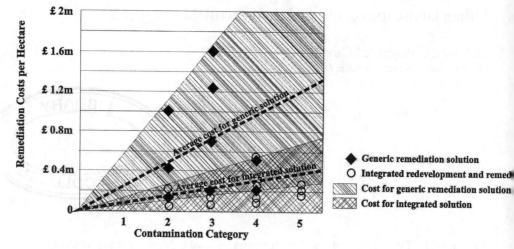

Figure 1.

1.2 *The result is poor for landscape*

Remediated brownfield sites all too often display an environment with no trees, patchy lawns and cheap materials and a geography of engineered plateaus and geometric mounds. This is the consequence of the engineering-led remediation approach that builds up the landform as a way to contain the export of waste material and demands unnecessary works. In some cases this approach ends up in small budgets for the external works and dictates the final landscape by making it impossible to plant trees in the shallow depths of soil on top of the capillary break.

2 OUR PROPOSAL FOR THE FUTURE

Our proposal is to promote urban regeneration and make brownfield sites green with lush open spaces and imaginative landscape designs: the redevelopment of brownfield sites should not be a synonym of poor environment. Trees should be planted in the new streets. Hardly grassed waste mounds should become a thing of the past. Mud fields and stockpiles of rubble should disappear from the back of our partially redeveloped sites. Truckloads of waste and topsoil could stop going up and down redevelopment sites.

By changing the most common approach to soil remediation, it is possible to design better landscape schemes, cut the budget for decontamination and reduce the impacts on the environment.

2.1 *The proposal*

We propose to look at plants and their needs to try to minimize waste production and find ways to create the necessary conditions for plant development *directly* into the brown soil. In fact, if the appropriate conditions for planting were established without the traditional capping layer and new fill system, the creation of quality urban amenity landscape would become far more environmentally and financially sustainable. And once the enormous costs of site remediation are reduced, funds could be released for higher landscape specifications.

We made the following observations:

1. Generally plants have good resistance to contamination. In some cases they do not only thrive but also have a positive effect on site conditions. Lack of nutrients or deficient moisture are generally the principal causes of poor landscape development in an urban situation, and these can be easily overcome by appropriate landscape maintenance.

114

2. Not all brownfield sites are extremely contaminated and phytotoxic: cleared urban neighborhoods or local industries do not generally present such high contamination as to radically prevent vegetation. The spontaneous green cover that normally develops on ex-industrial sites is a visible proof. Landfill or radioactive sites, which give rise to very complex remediation problems, do not constitute the majority of urban redevelopment sites by any means.

3. Legislation and guidelines establish the principles of risk assessment to define contamination (a source of hazard, a pathway and a potential receptor) and of fitness for purpose. They suggest that soil used for urban amenity landscape should be safe, but not necessarily free from pollutants.

3 LANDSCAPE DEVELOPMENT AND BROWFIELD LAND

This section illustrates the technical and scientific information that backs up the proposal: the effects of contamination on vegetation, plant tolerance and the characteristics of soils that are suitable for plant growth. In the last section of this paper we offer a strategy and decision tree for action.

3.1 Plants, soil and contaminants

The relationship between plants and soil is very complex, but in very simple terms a soil supports vegetal life depending on a few main factors: the availability of nutrients, oxygen and water.

Nutrients can be subdivided in macro-nutrients, such as nitrogen (N), phosphorus (P) and potassium (K), and micro-nutrients, such as zinc, iron, manganese, molybdenum, copper, sulphur and boron. Nutrients can be of organic or mineral origin: organic nitrogen from decomposition for example is particularly important because of its long-term availability, while mineral nitrogen is easily lost as a gas or washed away by water. Water is essential for plants to take up nutrients in solution through their roots, and oxygen is necessary for root growth. Plants will grow unless:

- The soil is deficient in nutrients: a very common problem in the revegetation of brownfield land, where the percentage level of organic matter can be particularly low.
- Nutrients are made unavailable to plants, by the soil acidity or alkalinity (pH below 3.5 or above 8.5) or by the excessive presence of metal ions: iron or aluminum for example immobilize phosphorus.
- There is excessive supply of nutrients, leading to toxicity: a problem more common in over-fertilised agricultural land; not so common in urban brownfield sites.
- Moisture is lacking, compromising both the capacity to absorb nutrients and the cell structure of plants. The aptitude of a soil to retain moisture depends by the presence of fibrous organic matter, soil texture (the relative percentage of sand, silt and clay components of the soil) and soil porosity. Lack of moisture retention is a very common occurrence in brownfield sites and it is typically caused by lack of organic matter, the coarse texture of made grounds (sands and rubble) or low porosity due to compaction by heavy structures or vehicles.
- Roots fail to develop, which is generally caused by nutrient deficiency, compacted or waterlogged soils (lacking oxygen), or extremely alkaline soils with pH above 10.

The presence of chemical contaminants such as heavy metals, salts, herbicides, oils and tars affects vegetation in three principal ways:

- Contaminants make nutrients unavailable to the plant roots by making nutrient elements insoluble. This in turn is dependent of soil pH: chemical reactions between metals and nutrients are possible only in acid soils.
- Contaminants are absorbed into the roots or other plant tissue and cause toxic effects, such as changes in the permeability of cell membranes, occupation of cell sites and replacement of essential nutrients, inhibition of enzymatic system, etc. This phenomenon (phytotoxicity) manifests itself with poor germination, death of seedlings, death of rapidly growing succulent tissue, stunted or delayed plant development, misshapen plants or leaves, chlorosis, russeting of leaves or fruit, yellowing of parts of the leaves.

- Substances hazardous to animal health are absorbed and stored in roots or leaves without toxic effects to the plant. This phenomenon constitutes a problem only if the plant material has a chance of entering the food chain and affecting natural ecosystems. This is not normally an occurrence in amenity landscape in urban redevelopment sites, while it constitutes a critical factor affecting the construction of private gardens.

3.2 *Plants tolerate contamination*

Field observation suggests that a sufficiently wide variety of spontaneous or planted species grow on contaminated sites. It may be unwise to generalise and assume that some plants may grow in any situation. However it must be noted that London Planes, Whitebeams, Horse Chestnuts and Italian Alders were growing to mature proportions at the ammunition research and production site of the Royal Arsenal in Woolwich even prior to remediation. And Maples, Alders, Elms, Ashes, Poplars, Red Oaks were spontaneously growing at the ex gas work site of Westergasfabriek, near Amsterdam.

Plant life is in fact less sensitive to contamination than animal or human life. Generally pollutants are more likely to affect microbial and invertebrate organisms than to kill plants. Often, in heavily contaminated sites, it is not the direct presence of contaminants to limit plant growth but the slow decomposition of organic litter which causes poor nutrition and blighted growth. This was for example the case of the coal mine site of Gelsenkirchen in the Ruhr region, where birches planted directly on the coal shale where growing at a very slow rate. Fertilization and maintenance could easily mitigate this problem.

Little scientific research studied the precise correlation between pollutants and decorative planting, making it difficult to define exactly above which level of contamination it may necessary to carry out more conventional remediation. Research, particularly in the U.S., actually privileges the study of crops and the ingress of harmful substances into the food chain rather than amenity planting in the urban environment. Scientific studies, however, show that toxicity in plants is relatively limited compared to animals and humans and that some species are very tolerant even to high levels of contamination.

There is a clear need for research involving field trials of woodland and amenity species if we want to nurture the urban renaissance. The UK Environment Agency and Forestry Commission pilot project on establishing woodland on contaminated land (CLAIRE, due to start in 1999) has unfortunately been suspended.

Various species and cultivars in fact respond to adverse factors in very different ways. For example, a waterlogged soil could be the limiting factor for the healthy growth of some species, while for others the presence of even moderate levels of zinc would be a key problem. Choosing plants that tolerate contaminants and the poor soil conditions typical of brownfield sites is an essential part of the strategy for reducing the production of waste and the cost of remedial works.

We collated and organised information from site experience, field observation, ecological and agricultural research and internationally sponsored field trials and we came to a first list of plants that research and experience indicate as tolerant. The list already shows sufficient variety of choices for the landscape architect and is obviously open to expansion as research continues.

3.3 *Phytoremediation: an opportunity*

Phytoremediation is a bio-technique involving the direct use of living plants for the in situ remediation of contaminated soils or wetlands through contaminant removal, degradation or containment. It is currently explored in pilot projects and lab research, particularly in the U.S., as a cost effective and environmentally responsible system for improving industrial or agricultural wasteland.

It represents an appropriate technique for minimizing waste arising from urban brownfield sites having shallow contamination with medium to low levels of metals, solvents, oils, polyaromatic hydrocarbons, explosives and landfill leacheates. Because of its moderate costs, it could also be employed as a blanket remediation technique in the lapse of time between site clearance and reuse, thus avoiding the common concrete cap or the mud and rubble appearance of sites awaiting redevelopment.

116

Phytoremediation research, even at these early stages, begins to provide experimental information on plants that will tolerate pollutants and may constitute a successful landscape scheme and improve the soil conditions at the same time. It works through a combination of mechanisms, such as:

- Phytoaccumulation: an approach suitable only to interim vegetation projects because plants are harvested and carefully destroyed once they accumulated a high level of contaminants in their tissues, after a few growing seasons. Sown grasses, for example, proved particularly efficient in the degradation of fuels in test fields at Craney Island Fuel Terminal in Virginia.
- Phytostabilisation: involving the absorption and precipitation of contaminants by plants, thus controlling the pathways to potential receptors. Suitable plants should be resistant to the contaminants, feature high production of root biomass, retention of the contaminants in the roots as opposed to transfer to shoots.
- Phytodegradation and phytovolatilisation: the processes by which plants are able to metabolise and break down pollutants such as ammunition waste, chlorinated solvents, herbicides. Part of the fragments is turned into new plant tissues or released in low concentration to the atmosphere through transpiration. Hybrid poplars proved beneficial in pilot projects of heavy metals, chlorinated solvents and tars.
- Rhizodegradation or plant-assisted bioremediation: it involves the breakdown of contaminants in the soil through microbial activity enhanced by the presence of the rhizosphere, which releases natural substances and nutrients that stimulate the soil micro-organisms and their activity of biodegradation.

3.4 *Alternatives to imported soils*

A sustainable approach to site remediation should avoid as much as possible the export of waste, the creation of tipping mounds and the import of natural soil (topsoil naturally forms at a rate of 0.1 mm per year and cannot therefore be viewed as a renewable resource). It is possible to consider to reuse the existing site material to manufacture a substitute for subsoil and topsoil that replicates the fundamental characteristics of a natural growing medium. Plants in fact are capable of growing on completely mineral materials, providing the material is not phytotoxic and has sufficient water and nutrients. As a matter of fact, many commercial glasshouse crops are grown on sand based artificial soils.

A natural soil, suitable for growing plants, has nutrients, both organic and inorganic; a pH that allows nutrient uptake; good moisture retention capacity, depending on soil texture and organic matter content; good soil aeration to favour root growth and non harmful levels of metals, salts and organic compounds. These characteristics will have to be replicated in the soil substitute. Texture should be similar to that of natural loamy topsoil: this often occurs in brownfield sites without any special action, otherwise the crushing of rubble and the picking of larger elements will have to be evaluated as part of the clearance strategy. An appropriate pH should be comprised between 6.5 and 8 to make residual contamination less harmful, should not be far from the pH of most urban redevelopment sites. Organic matter, essential for texture, water retention and nutrients, will most likely have to be added to the existing substrate in significant quantities. Non-contaminated composts, sewage sludge or manure constitute viable and sustainable options.

The process of manufacturing suitable planting backfill should in itself bring residual contaminants to acceptable levels. Soil washing or other sustainable processes may be considered in addition if necessary. Contamination tolerant species and species with phytoremediation characteristics should be selected to further reduce the need of clean up. However, it is likely that larger planting pits and extra maintenance will be required to sustain successful development on brownfield land. This extra expenditure is generally small when compared to the costs of conventional remediation and of import of natural soil.

3.5 *The importance of maintenance*

Whenever a tree is transplanted, only about 5% of the roots are taken with the tree. Root replacement can take 5 years for a small tree and even 12 years for large trees. Reduced root systems and poorer soil quality on brownfield land will require an appropriate landscape maintenance plan, which should last at least 5 years to ensure the proper establishment of woody species. This compares with the standard 3-year maintenance contract for the average landscape scheme.

Watering may be essential in coarse man-made ground, because the reduced root system means reduced capacity to absorb water. Adequate fertilizing (organic matter plus a slow release mineral fertilizer) will have to be carried out until full establishment and in certain cases for a very long period of time. Fertilizers that push leaf development should be avoided. Stakes may have to be kept for an extra growing season if root and plant development is particularly slow.

In some heavily contaminated sites it may be necessary to test plant material prior to composting as it may contain abnormal levels of contaminants.

4 A SIMPLE DESIGN PROCESS

Our approach to the development of amenity landscape on brownfield land is made of four different steps, to be considered at planning stage of the site redevelopment:

1. Appropriate site investigations to establish the potential for developing vegetation on the site; investigations should assess contaminants, nutrient content and physical soil characteristics that specifically affect plant establishment.
2. A strategy for reclaiming the existing soils for planting in order to minimize waste and import of materials; bio and phytoremediation techniques should be considered as part of the overall strategy and as interim cover.
3. The selection of species that are beneficial or at least tolerant to eventual adverse soil conditions and contamination;
4. A specific maintenance program to ensure the long-term establishment of plants.

4.1 *Action Plan and Decision Tree*

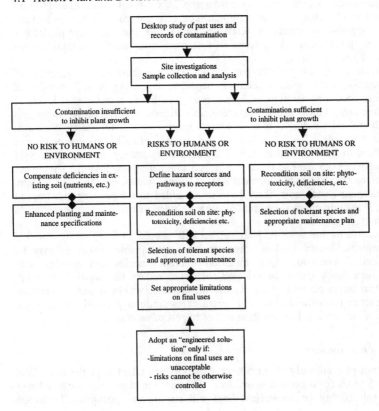

Sustainability

The benefits of this approach are decreased waste production, better landscape schemes and reduced up front remediation costs. The environmental and financial benefits are illustrated in the diagram below:

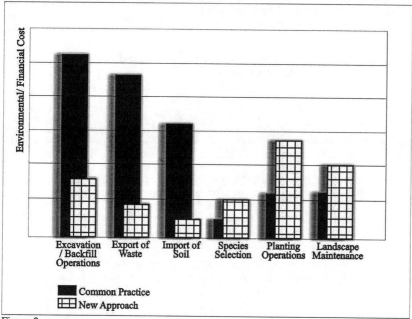

Figure 2.

4.2 *Legislative framework*

Current UK legislation on contaminated land is principally contained in Part IIA of the Environmental Protection Act 1990, which was retrospectively inserted by Section 57 of the Environment Act 1995. This legislation came into force this year when the Government issued Statutory Guidance to Local Authorities.

The legislation and the guidance endorse the principle of *suitable for use*, where remedial action is only required if there are unacceptable risks to health or the environment, taking into account the use of the land and its environmental setting. The very definition of contaminated land embodies the concept of risk assessment in terms of significant pollutant linkages within a source-pathway-receptor model of the site and the existence, or absence, of plausible pathways between the identified hazards and receptors.

The statutory guidance suggests that soil quality guideline values may be used as screening tools, provided that such guidelines are available and are appropriate to the site circumstances. The DETR is expected to issue new technical guidance later this year and, in the meantime, the principal values used in the UK are the Interdepartmental Committee on the Redevelopment of Contaminated Land (ICRCL) Trigger Values of 1987 and the Dutch Intervention Values of 1994. However, the Dutch Intervention Levels do not consider phytotoxicity in the published tables. And the ICRCL Trigger Values include four phyototoxic threshold values above which further professional judgment is required. Concentrations of contaminants exceeding these values do not actually imply that the ground is unsuitable for vegetal life.

The approach of the UK legislation allows flexibility and innovation in the practice of remediation whenever it can be demonstrated that there is no unacceptable risk to human health or the environment.

REFERENCES

Banks, M.K., Schwab, A.P., Govindaraju, R.S. Phytoremediation of Soil Contaminated with Hazarduous Organic Chemicals, *Kansas State University*.

CIRIA. 1999. Designing out Waste, *Royal Academy of Engineering*. 12 October.

CLAIRE (Contaminated Land: Applications in Real Environments)& NATO/CCMS. 1999. Pilot Studies.

DOE. 1994. Guidance on Preliminary Site Inspection of Contaminated Land.

Dutton, R.A. & Bradshow, A.D. 1980. Land Reclamation in Cities.

EPA. 1998. A Citizen's Guide to Phytoremediation.

EPA. www.epa.gov

Phillips, L.E. Jnr. 1993. Urban Trees.

Planning Policy Guidance for England and Wales, PPG 1 (1997), PPG 3 (2000)

Urban Task Force. 1999. Towards an Urban Renaissance

Urban Lifestyles: Spaces · Places · People, Benson & Roe (eds)
© *2000 Balkema, Rotterdam, ISBN 90 5809 169 4*

The restoration of Mowbray Gardens, Sunderland

P.Gowans
Facilities Management (Outdoor Recreation), Sunderland City Council, UK

ABSTRACT: Mowbray Gardens is the jewel in the crown of Sunderland City Centre's extensive redevelopment and regeneration. The £13.3 million project, which will be completed by Spring 2001, is in three connected parts – Mowbray Park, Sunderland Museum & Art Gallery and Sunderland Winter Gardens. The Heritage Lottery Fund has contributed £9.9 million to the development of this internationally important, unique and stunning "one place visitor destination centre". It is integral to the Council's vision for the City Centre both as a viable, competitive shopping and commercial centre and as a vibrant, safe, visually-appealing social and cultural centre. The population was widely consulted and informed via exhibitions, competitions, lectures and extensive media coverage. This process was a major factor in the funding arrangements. Wearsiders are delighted that a cherished part of their cultural heritage is being restored, further developed and presented to them with all the technological trimmings of the 21st century.

1 HISTORICAL BACKGROUND TO MOWBRAY GARDENS

"...a picture of wretchedness, filth and poverty, which, accustomed as he had been from his professional duties to visit the abodes of human misery, he could not have believed to exist in the present age in any part of civilized Europe."

That was the impression that eminent French doctor François Magendie had about the older working class areas of Sunderland in 1831. Properties which lined narrow streets and airless courts were overcrowded and subdivided - living space was only 38sq. yds. per person. Only 670 of the 6,086 houses in the town had a direct water supply, only 7% had privies attached and the poor stored urine in tubs in their houses to sell to dye manufacturers. In October 1831 the nation's first outbreak of cholera started in Sunderland – the town's growing public health problem was one of the factors leading to the establishment of a municipal corporation in 1837. Shipbuilding and coal mining attracted more and more work-hungry poor. Coal exports had grown to 1,500,000 tons by 1847 and one Dr Dibdin wrote: "Houses, windows, walls, pillars, posts and posterns were all more or less veiled in what may be deliberately designated as 'black crepe' ...Even the human countenance seemed to partake of it."

By 1949 concern about housing and urban conditions and their effect on health and morale promoted a Public Heath Inquiry into the town's sanitary condition. Sunderland Corporation concluded that people needed to get out into the open air and that a public park would coax them from their squalid living conditions. Building Hill, at the southern end of what is now Mowbray Park, was suggested as a location. It was to be the green lungs of the town. Widespread concern about urban sanitary conditions prompted the government to offer £10,000 in grant aid for public parks and walkways in larger towns. Sunderland applied, and received, £750 towards the purchase of the land.

The People's Park was opened in 1857 and it was extended again in the 1860s when a lake, terrace and formal planted gardens were added and the two sections linked by a wrought iron footbridge over the railway cutting. Around 17,000 people joined the opening processions. The notion of building a Museum, Library and Winter Gardens on a single site in the Park was first noted in July 1855. A series of objections were registered but in 1876 the Appeal Court in Westminster upheld the Council's proposals for the free facilities. There has never been a charge levied nor will there be when the entire Mowbray Gardens development opens in 2001.

A competition to design the building was undertaken and won by local architects J. and T. Tillman. Sunderland Museum & Art Gallery, situated at the north end of the Park, was the first local authority museum to be opened outside of London. The Winter Gardens were attached to its south side. The elegant glass and iron conservatory, inspired by the Great Exhibition's Crystal Palace, contained exotic tropical plants, ferns, birds and fish. Both opened in 1879. The heavily industrialized town continued to grow as the century turned and the Park, Museum and Winter Gardens continued to find a place in the hearts of the people. The Sunderland Echo reported in February 1929 that no fewer than 10,000 townsfolk descended on the area one snowy Sunday afternoon. However, on April 16, 1941, the Winter Gardens were badly damaged by an exploding parachute mine and were subsequently demolished. (Figure 1). A Museum extension was placed on the site in the 1960s.

Figure 1. Winter Gardens, April 1941 following Parachute Mine Damage

1.1 *The Present Day*

"The Council's long-term vision of Sunderland is of a City which provides an enhanced quality of life for all its citizens, through the enrichment of the economic, social, educational, leisure, health and housing opportunities available to them. This is matched by a concern for the well-being of the City itself, of its physical and environmental character, its systems of communication and its arts and culture." (Sunderland City Council's Vision Statement). The context to this vision is two decades of massive structural changes in Sunderland's economic base. The rapid decline and restructuring of traditional industries, principally mining, shipbuilding and heavy engineering, have brought demanding challenges. The Council has worked hard to regenerate the economy, the physical environment and the communities of the City. Sunderland is now the

UK's fastest growing car manufacturing centre and our economic base continues to flourish. Prestigious companies like Nike, London Electric, One2One and Barclays occupy space on industrial parks. The redevelopment of the City Centre is key to the economic and social prosperity of Sunderland. It is the Council's aim to make it the cultural, sporting, leisure, social and shopping focus of the City. The plans are ambitious and dynamic and they include vital improvements to the infrastructure of the City.

- The Bridges Shopping Centre has recently doubled in size to 47,844 sq. m. The 20 new shops, occupied by top retailers, brings the City Centre total to 100.
- A new three-storey department store and two new car parks offering nearly 1,000 spaces, plus Shop Mobility facilities for the disabled, are included in the redevelopment. There's over £100 million worth of new investment and existing businesses are also investing heavily as the tide of change sweeps across the City.
- Good transport links are vital, hence the new, award-winning £6.5million Park Lane Interchange integrating bus, coach, taxi and (from 2002) Metro train services. The sweeping futuristic designs are further enhanced by cosmopolitan street furniture and lighting. It's the second busiest bus station in the country and has over 263,000 passenger boardings per week.
- The prestigious and historic Empire Theatre has undergone improvements and the Exchange Building, the oldest public building in the City, is being restored as a community venue for arts, dance, music and theatre. Next door the Eagle Tavern is being carefully restored with workshop space for local artists.

There are plans submitted, too, for one or more multi-million leisure and entertainment complexes, luxury hotels and new housing. A major part of the Mowbray Gardens design brief was that the entrance, which can be seen from Sunderland's main street, should be an imaginative and eye-catching link between the two areas.

1.2 *Echoes of the Past*

History has indeed been repeating itself. The Park was created for the well-being and recreation of the residents and the Museum was for "diffusing taste and knowledge amongst our fellow townsmen". There's no film of "black crepe" today, but modern city life brings its own stresses and strains. Mowbray Gardens, nestled in the very heart of the City Centre, broadens opportunities for lifelong learning and offers relaxation, amusement and mental and sensory stimulation. History has repeated itself in the unfolding of the project too. The Council ran a national competition for the design of a predominantly glass building (glass making was established in Sunderland in the 1690s and the City is home to the National Glass Centre). Sixty-six architectural practices submitted concepts and the Newcastle-based Napper Partnership won the Winter Gardens contract. It is interesting to note that the Council sought funding to revitalize the very area which was originally created via government grant. The bid represented a desire to bring the historic development into line with the social and educational aspirations of a new millennium society.

2 THE PROJECT

In 1996 the Council put in a Heritage Lottery Fund (HLF) bid for the £5 million redevelopment of Sunderland Museum & Art Gallery. The City Library had relocated leaving more space for Museum use. The Museum also needed better visitor, storage, conservation and education facilities plus adequate access for people with disabilities. The plans included a new even entrance (the original access was via steps), new toilet facilities, a lift, new café, shop, a purpose-designed education/lecture area. New fire and intruder detection systems were needed plus new heating and ventilation to protect the exhibits. Funding was granted and matched funding from other bodies was also secured.

The City made a further HLF bid for Mowbray Park and the Winter Gardens. The HLF's Urban Parks Initiative and its Historical Buildings Programme gave an "in principle" grant offer but requested a second stage application which brought the three elements together. A national design competition for the Winter Gardens was then launched.

A consultation process with the people of Sunderland also began. There is a strong, historical sense of public ownership in connection with the Park and Museum. They conjure up a kaleidoscope of memories for many Wearsiders. Grandmothers who once perched on the backs of the stone lions near the lake as children, have in turn taken their children and their children's children, to do the same. The tradition, in fact, goes back seven generations. Some of the Museums' exhibits, particularly Wallace the stuffed lion and the walrus which, it was thought, (all but incorrect) inspired Lewis Carroll to write his poem "The Walrus and the Carpenter", have enchanted generations of wide-eyed youngsters. The Council knew it needed to listen to this strong heartbeat of affection and that the people of the City needed to have a say in the decision-making process. The Council mounted exhibitions showing concept drawings and models by four architectural practices and community lectures, talks and meetings went on all over the City. The local and regional media gave excellent coverage. Nearly 6,000 people went to see and comment on the final designs - 84% who signed the comments book were in favour of them. Comments ranged from "very impressive" to "an asset to the City". Eighty-one per cent of those who filled in questionnaires also liked the design. Views from local associations and businesses were also sought.

2.1 *The Winter Gardens*

Sight, smell, sound, taste and touch – these are the five themes which will fascinate and stimulate visitors in an environment which is alive, restful, atmospheric and interactive. The conservatory, which is 14m high and 28m wide, will be a canvas for stunning visual displays with the inclusion of scented plants for the visually impaired. It sits on the eastern side of the Museum. (Figure 2). This striking landmark building takes the City into the 21st century yet reflects the heritage of the original.

Figure 2. Photograph of the scale Architectural Model of the New Winter Gardens

Victorian Wearsiders never saw the exotic flowers which crowned the trees and plants. New millennium visitors, however, can enjoy their appearance and fragrance, thanks to a treetop mesh walkway 8m off the ground. Plants that were rare to the Victorians now sit on supermarket shelves. However, the Council has enlisted a specialist firm to source many exotic trees and plants which will surprise and delight even the well traveled. There will be ground, shrub and tree cover, all kept at exactly the right temperatures, and periodically misted, by computerized systems. Some of the plants, such as the hairy water lettuce, are there to be touched by inquiring hands.

The atmosphere will be further enhanced by background noises of birds and wind and by the sound of water trickling down a large monolith waterfall designed by foremost waterfall artist William Pye. A sweeping curved stairway and a glass bubble passenger lift take visitors up through the planting. Other features include koi carp, reptiles in glass cases, a ravine, stream, plus beautiful views across the lake. The integration of the project meant the ground-floor brasserie was moved from the Museum into the Winter Gardens to provide a unique eating experience. It also has access to North Terrace which will be utilized by the brasserie in summer months. The Winter Gardens is indeed a green and colourful oasis in the heart of the City, an all-year-round sensory adventure.

2.2 *Sunderland Museum & Art Gallery*

The Museum is owned by the City of Sunderland and administered by Tyne & Wear Museums. It is a mix of classical and Roman designs with a French mansard roof. Whilst it is visually attractive, market research showed that 90 per cent of respondents supported the need for improved visitor facilities. Areas highlighted included better disabled and pushchair access, new toilets, a lift, new café, shop, and a purpose-designed education/lecture area. It's thanks to the bringing together of the three projects that the two-story Museum Street exists. This attractive Street links the Museum to the Winter Gardens and is topped by an atrium. It is also central to other areas of the Museum.

The Museum houses collections of regional, national and international importance including a large collection by L.S. Lowry and the largest collection of locally manufactured pottery in the world. It is also home to the only example of a gliding reptile found in Britain – at around 250 million years old it it's the oldest yet to be found in the world. Market research also highlighted the types of display that the people of Sunderland want. The new space means there will be more displays focusing on textiles, pottery, fine art, geology, natural history, archaeology, local history and ship building. Educational use will be greatly enhanced by lecture areas. Since 1991 the Museum has won nine national, regional and local awards for its displays, education programmes and work with groups with disabilities.

2.3 *Mowbray Park*

The Park is one of only nine urban parks on English Heritage's Register of Parks and Gardens of Special Historical Interest in the North East of England. It has an abundance of features and monuments which tell the history of Sunderland and its people. Many of these are of national and international interest. The Victoria Hall Disaster Memorial, for example, is returning to its original home in the Park. The life-size statue shows a grieving mother holding her dead child on her lap. In 1883, 183 children died in a public hall in Sunderland. They were going down a narrow staircase to get free toys when they were crushed against a door which only opened inwards, The disaster led to important new legislation that outward opening exits should be provided in all places of public entertainment.

There is also a statue of local lad Jack Crawford, who climbed the mast of Admiral Duncan's ship when the top of his flag was shot away during the Battle of Camperdown in 1797. Crawford nailed the flag back up with a marlin spike to make sure it was not signaling retreat – his action was crucial to the subsequent victory and he helped save Britain from invasion. Ironically, Crawford died in the outbreak of cholera in Sunderland in 1831. Former features such as a fountain and bandstand have been reintroduced while others have been restored to their former glory. There are some new, sympathetic works of art too and all obtrusive and inappropriate modern features have been removed.

2.4 *Management Philosophy*

Victorian Wearsiders enjoyed "controlled recreation" when they visited the Park. It was a green open space for the health and socialization of the working classes. The Park Keeper was an authoritarian figure and the drinking fountain even had "keep the pavement dry" written on it. The layout was a meandering journey of discovery, punctuated by shaded corners and seats overshadowed by leafy boughs. Personal safety was not the burning issue it is in the 21st century. Today's Park has open vistas and CCTV offers extra security. It is only one of a handful of parks to be run specifically as a tourist attraction. Mowbray Gardens as a whole has to fulfil the public's increased expectations of service. All staff have to be welcoming, friendly, knowledgeable, approachable and able to communicate. It is for this reason that the Council has opted for Park Rangers dressed in casual uniforms – there is no place for the officious, formally uniformed Park Keepers of yesteryear. Gardeners are to cultivate more than just plants – they themselves are part of this unique tourist attraction and they are encouraged to cultivate conversation with inquisitive visitors. A staff training programme is underway. Indeed, in 1929, when 10,000 people descended on the Park and Museum and the snowballing got out of hand, the Museum Director told the Sunderland Echo: "When Sunday opening was introduced nine years ago, the average attendance was 280 – almost entirely of the class of person for whom the facilities were intended." Today social inclusion is high on the Government's agenda. The Council wants Mowbray Gardens to be enjoyed by everyone.

2.5 *People v. Plants*

In the early planning stages of the Winter Gardens late night functions were envisaged complete with refreshments in the brasserie which nosed its way directly into the planting areas. Jungle music, warmth, atmospheric lighting – it would indeed offer a unique social experience. It was thought too, that the south-facing conservatory glass could be treated to prevent the sun's rays from causing discomfort to visitors. However, it soon became apparent that while late-night heating and lighting might benefit people, they would be disastrous for the plants which need to "rest" at night. There was no debate – the plants had to have priority. This led to a series of changes being introduced during the design process. Firstly, the brasserie was screened off by a curved glass wall. The HLF wants the Council to use biological pest controls – predators with an appetite for the bugs which would accompany the plants from their overseas habitats. At times hundreds of ladybirds, parasitic wasp pupae and mites will be released into the planting. Add to the increased insect activity the periodic misting process, and it became obvious that a glass wall was needed. The education/lecture room, which is directly opposite the brasserie, became multi-functional in its design. This allows concerts, poetry readings etc. to take place on an evening and guests can have refreshments in the brasserie where they can still enjoy the atmosphere of the Winter Gardens via the glass wall. The plants need a minimum night temperature of 12°C and a maximum daytime temperature of 26°C. Visitors, especially on very sunny days, may find the building very warm and humid but that, the Council felt, was part of the overall experience. The comfort of the plants has priority. It became apparent, too, that tinting the glass would block UV light which is vital for plant growth. Sensor-controlled blinds will doubtless help the comfort of the visitors but their main purpose is to prevent leaf scorching.

3 BENEFITS TO THE CITY

Mowbray Gardens is a unique heritage one-place visitor destination of national and international importance. It is an intriguing mix of the historic and the contemporary with much to tease and stimulate the mind and senses. It is indeed the glittering jewel in the restructured City Centre crown, a prestigious, stunning symbol of the regeneration of the City. It is also a celebration of the City's heritage and its architectural and technological achievement – just as it was in Victorian times. Even recent history has shown that people in the region appreciate the quality of displays and exhibitions in the Museum. Increased space and better layout can only enhance these perceptions. The Winter Gardens project is primarily for the enjoyment of the people of the City but will inevitably entice people from much further a field. The whole development will bring in extra revenue – it is, after all, only a short stroll away from the main shopping area. The marketing strategy includes key target groups. These are: local communities within ¼ mile of the development; City Centre visitors and shoppers; the 22,000 people working in the City Centre; City visitors; and specific groups such as the elderly, women, parents with young people and the temporary resident student population.

3.1 *The People Factor*

Mowbray Gardens will be a focal centre for cultural activity, events and entertainment. It will also be a great place to simply relax, have some fun and unwind. The fact that entry is free means that people can visit as often as they choose. There is an ongoing programme of events and live music in the Park and space has been designated in the Museum for evening concerts. Parts of the buildings can be hired for private functions. Such initiatives are vital to the Council's aim to encourage people to stay in the City Centre after 6pm. North Terrace will be open on summer evenings so people can enjoy drinks and coffees in a pleasant, safe, open-air environment. Parents can visit with their children in the early evening -the whole development is family-friendly. Holiday and weekend activities, guided walks, quiz sheets, interactive and hands-on exhibitions, behind-the-scenes tours and children's galleries are all possibilities for youngsters to explore. Sophisticated fibre optic lighting will bring a touch of spectacular magic to the development at night. The top of the Winter Gardens' dome will appear to float, like a flying saucer, against the night sky. These are the things that precious childhood memories are made of.

For many it will be a place of remembrance. Even the very publicity about its restoration inspired people to write down their thoughts and feelings. Maureen Woodward wrote to the Sunderland Echo from Scotland and said: "As a child it was a special pleasure to be taken by my father into the original Winter Gardens and talk to Polly the Parrot, enjoy the exotic plants in their vivid colours, the water fountain and the goldfish... Childhood memories are always very precious..."

It will also foster community spirit and civic pride. Sunderland will have a unique development primarily dedicated to the people of the City. The opportunities for lifelong learning are significant. The Museum hosts over 8,000 educational visits a year and every school in the City makes use of its services. There are strong links too with the City's colleges and university and the Museum hosts many adult and general leisure courses. It is anticipated that all of these links will grow even stronger. The majority of visitors, however, will enjoy an informal learning process as they brush with historical and present day developments in a vibrant, safe environment. Features which enthralled and bewitched the people of yesteryear will continue to delight today's and tomorrow's citizens. The past has been preserved and restored with integrity while the present has been expressed with taste and flair, and future generations will be able to peel back layer after layer of rich, social history. It is for them, and for the 300,000 who live in the City today, that the Council has undertaken this exciting yet ambitious project.

Policy, planning and place-making

Urban Lifestyles: Spaces · Places · People, Benson & Roe (eds)
© 2000 Balkema, Rotterdam, ISBN 90 5809 169 4

Towards a healthier environment for London

H.R.Howes
Environment Agency, Thames Region, Camberley, UK

ABSTRACT: Urban regeneration has been built on linking economic issues with land use planning. However, social issues in general and social exclusion in particular have not so far been well integrated into either economic or land use planning. Regeneration has been most successful where local authorities have moved away from their role of service providers and have acted as a catalyst for creating partnerships. The new Greater London Assembly has limited direct powers and its success will depend on how far it is able to develop this catalytic role. The Government is committed to reducing health inequalities (1). However, the gap between the health of rich and poor appears to be widening. The Government's thinking appears to be less than wholly joined up. The Environment, Transport and Regional Affairs Committee recognises that "a damaged environment impairs quality of life and at worst may threaten long-term economic growth" (2). However, the Social Exclusion Unit, looking at the relationships between poverty, health and regeneration, does not recognise the effects of environmental conditions (3).

1 INTRODUCTION

The Environment Agency in its work with the Greater London Assembly has identified a number of crosscutting issues (4). One of them is 'Environmental Awareness, Civic Pride and a Healthy City'. The agency will be promoting this concept with a view to establishing new partnerships. The Agency must take a broad view of environmental regulation, which will include considerations of human health and well-being. The Agency already has responsibilities to evaluate and assess the risks to human health from the wide range of activities which it regulates (5).

London is a world-class city: a world-class financial centre, a world cultural centre, and a world heritage centre. Nevertheless it contains some of the worst concentrations of urban deprivation and unemployment in the country in terms of both extent and intensity. Parts of inner London including the Lea Valley are characterized by above average unemployment rates, high levels of social deprivation, low skills levels, low educational attainment, poverty, poor health prospects, dependence on declining industries and derelict urban fabric (6). There are close correlations between the Under-Privileged Areas index, which ranks health authorities in order of hardship, and basic levels of human health.

However, the Lea Valley has significant assets in terms of transport, proximity to the growing commercial centres of Canary Wharf and Docklands. It also enjoys a number of partnerships for regeneration and multi-agency working arrangements.

Over the last year, The Environment Agency has worked to ensure that London's environment is treated as a critical part of the city's capital which will make a significant contribution to its sustainable development. Many crosscutting themes have emerged.

Sustainable development is seen as including economic and social issues as well as the environment. Significant swathes across London suffer from declining industries, social exclusion and degraded environments.

Poor health and poverty are linked to the quality of the wider environment. Richer people tend to have the ability to avoid or mitigate the impacts of environmental problems. Poorer people tend to live in areas of cheaper housing which are often sited near commercial and industrial sites and are often beside congested and polluted roads. Mortality differentials have increased despite the Governments' commitment 'to improve the health of the worst off at a faster rate.' (1). In short, one's postcode is an indication of everything from one's credit worthiness to one's life expectancy.

The health and well-being of London's citizens is affected by the health of the wider environment. Healthy environments and healthy populations are interdependent and variously related to socio-economic factors. Effective management of health and other environmental risk requires an integrated approach including consideration of interactions and cumulative effects. Improvements to the environment have an important role to play in contributing to the wellbeing of Londoners.

Design and management of the physical environment alongside policies to foster social inclusion and economic success will be crucial in achieving a step change in the quality of life in those parts of London which need regeneration.

2 PLANNING POLICIES

A number of areas of regional significance are identified in the Regional Planning Guidance for the South East (7) as Priority Areas for Environmental Regeneration (PAERs). The criteria for designation include above average unemployment rates, high levels of social deprivation, low skills levels, dependence on declining industries, derelict urban fabric, peripherality and insularity. These areas need tailored regeneration strategies backed up by appropriate resources to address their problems and maximize their contribution to the social and economic well-being of the region.

Regional Planning Guidance seeks to adopt an all-embracing approach to these issues by including the following policies: -

The quality of life in urban areas, including suburban areas, should be raised through significant improvement to the urban environment, making urban areas more attractive places in which to live, work, shop, spend leisure time and invest, thus helping to counter trends to more dispersed patterns of residence and travel. (Q2)

Health, education and other social infrastructure requirements need to be taken into account fully in development planning throughout the Region. (Q6)

In order to address strategic spatial inequalities around the region, particular attention should also be given to actively supporting economic regeneration and renewal in Priority Areas for Economic Regeneration (PAERs). (RE7)

Similarly PPG3(8) states

"The Government intends that everyone should have the opportunities of a decent home. They further intend that there should be greater choice of housing and that housing should not reinforce social distinctions. ......Now housing and residential environments should be well designed and should make a significant contribution to providing urban renaissance and improving the quality of life".

It is clear that the planning policies are comprehensive in their approach to social and health issues but that mechanisms implementing these policies have some way to go.

3 THE ENVIRONMENT AGENCY'S INITIATIVES FOR THE GREATER LONDON AUTHORITY

The Environment Agency has seized the chance to promote environmental interests through the Greater London Authority. It has held conferences and breakfast meetings to identify the issues that are of most concern to Londoners. Air quality, waste disposal, contaminated land and riverside urban form emerged as of prime concern for the Agency (9). Cross cutting themes were then examined. They included 1) Integrated Environmental Management 2) Environmental awareness, Civic Pride and a Healthy City and 3) Ecological Networks and Regeneration. The agency is now explaining to the newly elected Assembly how the Agency can play its part in addressing these issues.

3.1 *Integrated Environmental Management*

The environmental issues for London are inter-linked and affect other areas including regeneration and development, health and social well-being, and extend much more widely than the city itself. An integrated approach is fundamental to progress the sustainable development of London.

3.2 *Environmental Awareness, Civic Pride and a Healthy City*

The Environment Agency has set out its vision for London:

A FIRST CLASS ENVIRONMENT FOR A WORLD CLASS CITY.

Changes in the attitudes of Londoners will be necessary to create the vitality, creativity and diversity that inspires civic pride. Attractive environments will need lifestyle changes to reduce the consumption of natural resources, reduce and reuse waste, and reduce our reliance on the private car. Changes in personal responsibilities need to be encouraged through trust and partnership. The health and well-being of Londoners is affected by the health of the wider environment which includes the quality of air, land and water, transport and accessibility, green and open spaces. Health is wider than freedom from disease and includes quality of life such as freedom from stress and fear of crime. The Agency has duty to educate and inform on environmental matters and it will work with the Mayor and the Boroughs to improve environmental awareness with positive urban living for London.

3.3 *Ecological Networks and Regeneration*

London's waterways offer excellent opportunities to promote regeneration. Their role as a resource for recreation, amenity, nature conservation, sustainable transport and a focus for London's communities presents a wide range of opportunities for environmental enhancement. For example, improvements in water quality can improve the value of developments and encourage attitudes of positive urban living. The increased value of waterside sites is understood but access must be retained for Londoners themselves and, for example, the Agency will object to any development that fails to facilitate the agreed route of the Thames Path. New development proposals must respect and enhance the river and water environment. The Agency will work with the Mayor and the Boroughs to ensure that the many demands on the water environment are integrated and appropriate to their location.

The Lea Valley provides a good example of how these themes can be applied to an area in need of social, economic and environmental regeneration.

3.4   Partnerships

London's Partnerships environment is the responsibility of everyone. The new SDS must take a broad and holistic approach to London's future and the integration of economic development and regeneration, transport, social equity and London's environment will only be achieved through creating new partnerships and making existing ones more effective.

The Institute for Environment and Health report (5) for example found 'an apparent weakness of links between the Agency and the Department of Health. In addition the Agency has very limited representation on statutory committees, expert groups and advisory bodies that deal with health related issues in the environmental context'.

Similarly an investigation by the Health and Safety Executive (12) found differences in their approach to land-use planning by the three areas of the HSE – fixed sites and pipelines, explosives and nuclear installations.

In order to establish a comprehensive overview of this issue the Environment Agency is embarking on a project on "Strategic Risk Assessment" which will develop a methodology for assessing environmental harm using a range of social economic and environmental criteria. This will provide a steer on identifying new partnerships.

4   THE LEA VALLEY, EAST LONDON

4.1   Background

The Lower Lea presents a considerable challenge to Local Authorities, the Environment Agency, Thames Water, British waterways and the Lower Lea Project alike (10). Its southern reaches are a scarred landscape of the formerly industrialised inner London. It does, however, present a major opportunity for improving economic, social and environmental conditions. All parties are actively involved in establishing sustainable environmental improvements as a catalyst for regenerating the heart of East London.

Significant incidences of deprivation and social exclusion are matched by poor water quality, air quality problems, and issues relating to contaminated land.

Until the 1960's the area was a significant manufacturing centre and relatively prosperous. The Lea Valley was home to a profusion of important industries including the design and manufacture of ships, boats, explosives, armaments, porcelain, bricks, perfume, chemicals, plastics, furniture, floor and wall coverings, vehicles and their accessories, rubber commodities, footwear, clothes, alcoholic beverages, musical instruments, office equipment, electronic and electrical goods. Many well known companies disappeared from the Lea Valley. These include: Bryant & Mays, Ediswan Lamps, Belling, Thermos, Thorn EMI, Royal Small Arms, JAP, Lebus Furniture and Gestetner.

The loss of Lea Valley industries in recent years has been influenced by shifts in the manufacturing base. A rapid decline began in the 1970s which resulted in a downturn in the local economy and social deprivation, with an urgent need for regeneration through public/private partnership.

4.2   Regeneration

The whole area enjoys Objective 2 status. This means that European funds have been made available for projects which will initiate the social and economic regeneration of the area.

In recent years a 'halo' effect from regeneration in Docklands and Stratford has taken place. This has been enhanced by the opening of the Jubilee Line extension. House prices in the London Boroughs of Newham and Tower Hamlets are rising rapidly which may prove to be a spur for regeneration.

Local Planning Authorities are promoting regeneration schemes. For example: - The Newham Arc of Opportunity lies between Stratford and Docklands, both of which have enjoyed the benefits of major regeneration schemes.

Similarly on the western side of the River Lea, Tower Hamlets is promoting the Leeside Single Regeneration Budget Scheme. Buildings dating from the 1920's are to be replaced by mixed used development which will take advantage of the riverside location.

The most environmentally significant constraints on regeneration are water quality, air quality and land contamination

4.2.1 *Water quality*

Water is an important element in urban regeneration (11). The multiple sources of pollution of the River Lea demonstrate how complex it is to achieve significant improvements in water quality. They are: effluent from Sewage Treatment Works stagnation, surface water run-off, combined sewer overflows, misconnection of domestic plumbing, discharge of untreated sewage at times of heavy flow and saline incursions at times of high incoming tides when salt water can sometimes flow over the top of Bow Locks.

Urban sewerage systems, through their sheer complexity can give rise to a number of problems, often through ignorance or mismanagement. North London is no exception. A prevalent issue is the misconnection of foul sewage to surface drains often through DIY plumbing. Tracing the sources is not easy because of the large number of cases involved. Conversely there are instances of roof and surface water discharges connected to foul sewers. Where a foul sewer connects to a combined system surcharging can occur and foul sewage is discharged through combined sewer overflows into urban watercourses, with attendant health hazards.

Most of the water in the southern part of the lower Lea is of a quality suitable for coarse fish populations (RE4). There are, however, reaches of poor quality likely to limit such coarse fish populations.

Thames Water has already made a considerable investment in its Abbey Mills Pumping Station. Its function is to pump sewage from the deep level sewers of north London into the Northern Outfall Sewer. The original building housing the pumps is a fine example of Victorian gothic design which is now being restored to its former glory. However, to protect the River Lea against the failure of its ageing equipment, a new £26m pumping station has been constructed. This new station not only deals with existing sewers but also the new North London Flood Relief Sewer which provides 40,000 cubic metres of storage reducing the risk of flooding to approximately 800 dwellings.

The Asset Management Plan process will mitigate one irregular but highly undesirable occurrence. In times of heavy rainfall the Abbey Mills pumping station discharges raw, if dilute, sewage from the Northern Outfall Sewer into the River Lea. In future storage will be provided for the first 3 minutes worth of effluent and all effluent will be screened.

The quality of effluent from Deephams Sewage Treatment works is high but, because it discharges into the static water of the Lea Navigation, a fixed 'bubbler' is to be installed at Edmonton. This will pump oxygen in at times of storm when surface water run-off is at its worst.

Further improvements will depend on:

a. Whether source control measures are included in major development projects.
b. Whether water companies are able to track down misconnections of foul sewage into surface drains.
c. Whether the problems of combined sewer overflows can be addressed
d. The extent to which phosphate removal at STWs upstream will reduce algal growth.
e. How soon British Waterways are able to provide additional gates at Bow Locks to prevent silt and salt water form entering the Lea Navigation and Limehouse.

4.2.1.1 Integrating Water Quality into the Town & Country Planning System

The town & country planning system has traditionally dealt with spatial issues. It has relied on constraints that can be readily shown in a map as its basis for environmental protection. The qualitative spatial aspects of environmental protection have been dealt with under separate legislation of which the Environment Act which set up the Environment Agency is a prime example.

Increased public pressure for addressing a wide range of environmental issues is resulting in an integration of urban physical planning and environmental management

The River Ecosystem Scheme, whilst a useful measure of water quality for the purposes of the Environment Agency does not readily translate into land use planning. A better approach would be to recognize that incremental improvements to water quality do open up significant additional opportunities for land uses and development in general and for activities related to the waterside in particular.

The following progression would provide local planning authorities with specific objectives to be achieved during the lifetime of their development plans.

Threshold	Outcome
1) Very poor water quality	Developers turn their backs on the river and it has no recreational appeal.
2) Activities of volunteer groups in clearing rubbish and planting reeds, stabilising banks and encouraging community projects	A less intimidating environment encourages access and a presumption against depositing litter and waste.
3) Upgrading of water quality so that it does not smell	Developers are prepared to face the river rather than back onto it.
4) Upgrading of water quality to a basic fishery standard	Wildlife returns, as do anglers and basic forms of waterside recreation. A waterside location becomes a significant selling point for properties.
5) Upgrading to good quality fisheries	Developers are prepared to make water a major feature of development. Contact water sports became possible and restaurants, bars and cafes are attracted to the waterside.

The next step will be to draft policies for local planning authorities which will give practical effect to this high level aspiration. This is the culmination of a three year programme of close working between the Environment Agency and SERPLAN.

For example, a local planning authority could aim to move from Stage 2 to 3 within the first five years of a development plan and then from Stage 3 to 4 in the second five years. This will link into a phased programme of urban regeneration.

4.2.2 Air quality

Levels of air pollution in London exceed those recommended for human health from time to time. In the Lea Valley concern has been expressed about the construction of an Olympic standard athletics stadium adjacent to the Edmonton Incinerator which is about to be substantially expanded.

However, the potential impact of the emissions would be insignificant against a background of vehicle emissions. The flue from the new incinerator will result in faster hotter emissions which will rise further before spreading out. The effect will be to reduce levels of air pollution in the immediate surroundings.

Visions of athletics suffering from bronchial problems would therefore appear to be ill founded.

4.2.3 Land contamination

The Governments policy is to encourage the redevelopment of 'brownfield' sites. The Agency wishes to encourage the use of such sites as it can provide a positive contribution towards sustainable development with environmental, economic and social benefit, and the prudent use of a finite resource.

136

However the redevelopment of Royal Small Arms Factory site at Enfield has resulted in health problems for new residents.

The proposed remediation strategy for the site was to construct a clay cap over the whole of the site. Following protracted discussions, this was agreed by the Agency as this alleviated any risk of contamination to ground or surface water.

In assessing the proposed remediation the Agency's comments as a consultee in the planning process are limited to the impact of the work on the aspects of environment for which the Agency has responsibility. Issues of risk to future inhabitants rest with the Environmental Health Department of the local Authority.

Advice is now available (13) to ensure that appropriate advice is taken to deal with existing contamination where it poses unacceptable risks to human health or to the environment. It stresses that even where expert assessment may indicate tolerable levels of risk, community perceptions may be very different.

5 CONCLUSION

Town and Country Planning goes through phases when either it is strictly about land use or when it embraces social and economic considerations as well. The advent of sustainable development appears to have reinforced its wider role and planning policies are now comprehensive in nature. This augurs well for integrating social and health issues into the planning agenda.

In contrast the actual mechanisms for delivery are decidedly uneven. The Agency's work in assessing environmental harm should provide a sound basis for establishing the most effective new working arrangements.

ACKNOWLEDGEMENT

The author is grateful to the Environment Agency for permission to publish this paper. The views are those of the author and do not necessarily reflect the policies of the Environment Agency. The author wishes to acknowledge the help in the preparation of the paper by the staff of several local authorities, water companies and environmental organisations for much of the material used in this paper.

REFERENCES

DETR. 2000. Planning Policy Guidance Note: Housing . March.
Environment Agency. 2000a. *Creating a greenprint for London.*
Environment Agency. 2000b. Linking the Environment Strategies for London.
Government Office for the South East. 2000. Draft Regional Planning Guidance for the South East RPG9.
Health and Safety Laboratory. 1999. *HSE's role in Land Use Planning.* October.
Howes, H. 2000a. *Urban Regeneration – The Water Element.* Water and Environment Manager. May.
Howes, H. 2000b. *Urban Regeneration – The Water Element.* Water and Environment Manager . July.
Institute for the Environment and Health. 2000. *The Role and Delivery of Human Health – Related Guidance for the Environment Agency* – An unpublished report. January.
National strategy for Neighbourhood Renewal: a framework for consultation
Quality and Performance in the WHS: Highland Performance Indicators
Select Committee into the Environment Agency 2000
Shaw, M., Dorling, D., Gorden, D. & Dancy Smith, G. 1999. *The widening gap.* The Policy Press
SNIFFER. 1999. *Communicating Understanding of Contaminated Land Risks*

Spatial aspects of the socio-cultural local context in post-socialist urban planning

E. Dimitrova
University of Architecture, Civil Engineering and Geodesy, Sofia, Bulgaria

ABSTRACT: The paper discusses the effects of the 'transition' period in CEE on the existing social and urban fabric of the settlements. It argues that the degree of applicability of European participatory planning approaches to sustainable development will depend on the development of new communication instruments to provide for the democratization of the planning process. The wholesome shift of the dominant patterns in post-socialist urban planning towards decentralization should incorporate a greater sensitivity for the peculiarities of the local social, cultural and spatial context. Based on the results of current research work, the need for introduction of socio-cultural indicators in appreciating urban sustainability is substantiated.

1 INTRODUCTION

Besides and before being a fashionable catchword used by politicians, business companies and NGOs, sustainable development is a point of a 'rational conscious choice of mankind to survive on the face of Earth' (Bossel, 1998). The post-socialist 'transition' period undergone by Central and Eastern Europe posed to the societies there a lot of challenges - often including that of physical survival as well. In most cases it has little to do with the requirements for a sustainable path of development, yet a period of a societal crisis could be also regarded as a favourable opportunity for needed profound changes in the value framework of society. Thus the concept of sustainable development proves to be of particular importance there at a moment of choices to be made (Sofia Statement, 1998). At the same time one of the important challenges facing the whole of Europe as a result of this same process of transition is to find out 'how to be together in this world' (Higgins, 1999). Should the tendencies of integration be translated into unification of approaches and policies, and could it be expected that the ongoing transformations in CEE will readily follow universal schemes of sustainable spatial development?

2 URBAN CULTURAL IDENTITY AS AN ASPECT OF SPATIAL SUSTAINABILITY

Spatial sustainability, and urban sustainability in particular, is a research and policy issue of importance for two reasons: the continuing urbanization of the contemporary world and the fact that from the very historical birth of the city it has been the stage for all the complex processes of human societal life.

   That is why to investigate the co-relation between the social and urban profile of a community could be an appropriate approach to finding many of the answers concerning sustainability. The dominant scientific approach to sustainable urban development up to the present moment has been technical-rational, as applied research has been trying to provide the necessary instruments to turn sustainability into a definable, measurable - and manageable - object. The considerable variety of key variables, chosen to describe different aspects of urban and environmental systems and their relationships illustrates the complexity of the systems and the difficulties to define their characteristics (Alberti, 1996; OECD, 1997). Research on the sustainability of urban environments at different scales started from environmental issues because information in that field is comparatively abundant and accessible, and the results are more easily incorporated into the decision-making process. The social aspects of sustainable development are stressed by many authors (Marcuse, 1998; Needham, 1999), yet in the process of criteria formulation and indicator choosing, social considerations are most often interpreted as distributional effects. The fact that the wider ethical framework is very often eclipsed is due to belonging to 'genuine' conflicting areas (Carley & Cristie, 1992), and the existence of contradictory interpretations of ethical references (Hewitt, 1995; Owens, 1997; Voogd, 1997; Tate & Mulugetta, 1998). Moreover they are difficult to quantify and measure. The same refers to the cultural aspects of sustainable urban development. Although the culture and values of urban communities are mentioned as important factors with respect to the quality of urban life, they are not directly included within the set of sustainability indicators usually proposed (and focused on environmental quality, human health, efficiency, equity, diversity accessibility, learning). It is obvious that both researchers and politicians know little of how to incorporate the subjective dimension in valuing socio-cultural aspects of urban life. It is clear however that any complete model of urban sustainability must integrate all aspects and 'some measurable performance dimensions should be found that can relate the spatial form of a city to human purposes and values'(Alberti, 1996, p. 388). Considerations with culture are many times dominantly focused on the preservation and enhancing of the existing architectural heritage. Yet, focus on heritage alone brings about the danger of 'nostalgic historicism, which transforms romantic past into dogma' (Pusic, 1999) and the potential threat of substituting cultural pluralism with intolerance to others' culture and uniqueness.

Estimating the city as an 'object of nature and subject of culture' (Levi-Strauss), would give us grounds and a starting point to interpret socio-cultural aspects in a broader sense as they deliver the opportunities of science and technology within a model of society that regards the cultural space as wider than the economic one. That is why the issue of cultural identity is central to urban sustainability.

One of the oldest city charters in Medieval Europe - that of the town of Strasbourg (XII c.) - stated that the main privilege given to everybody living within the city walls is the status of personal freedom. The city was a place to make people free - moreover - it made them citizens, giving birth to civil society. The intrinsic value of the European city as a cultural phenomenon is one of the main arguments for EU policy of preserving and promoting cultural diversity as a prerequisite for sustainable development in space. Economic and urban development which is 'using but not abusing culture' lies in the focus of an international project, incorporating the efforts of European countries at different stage of development and with encouraging results (Fisher, 1999)

Then next comes a set of questions with no easy answer to be offered: How would the strife for economic and political integration at the European level influence the urban development of the Eastern European city and what could be the effects of the transformation of an urban society if the ideas about this 'are derived from environments which do not understand the cultural context of the community'? (Pusic, 1999)

3 THE BULGARIAN CASE. A SPATIAL PLANNING SYSTEM IN TRANSITION

3.1 Structural changes in Bulgarian society during the transition period

The transition period caused a series of interrelated structural transformations in Bulgarian society. The main changes undergone by the economic structure are characterized by privatization of production funds, restitution of land ownership, restructuring of the main branches of economy. The resulting changes in the social structure incorporate negative demographic growth, considerable external economic migration and the destruction of large social strata. The fragmentation of society is to be observed both in the living patterns and value systems and it is expected to go even deeper. Thus the present situation in the country presents all possible symptoms of unsustainability - demographic, economic, social, cultural, etc. (Evrev et al., 1996, p. 17). That was the reason some years ago that led experts to state that the human resource had remained the only reliable one as a result of the period of a prolonged crisis (Genov, 1997). However, the frequently mentioned need for patience and sacrifices is often met with apathy and disbelief. The results of an inquiry published in one of the daily Bulgarian newspapers in May, 2000, states that only 30% of the young people (aged 15-30) would like to live in the country; an equal percent want to leave and there is an optimistic share of 40% who would prefer to go abroad for some years and then come back.

The dominant tendency of the changes in the political structure is decentralization. Local autonomy is increasing, guaranteed through changes in legislation. The local level of governance gains weight, new responsibilities are being transferred to the municipalities, so the lack of both human and technological capacity there to manage them becomes a problem waiting for an urgent solution.

3.2 The spatial dimensions of the crisis

The complex integrity of social, economic and cultural processes is more or less tangibly present behind the image of the contemporary Bulgarian settlements. Actually the tendencies towards an unsustainable path of development are deeply rooted in previous historic periods - after WWI and later on in the period of industrialization (1960s) when the processes of urbanization brought about overcrowding of urban areas and depopulation of the rural ones.

As a result nowadays about 48% of the population is concentrated in 34 cities and towns out of a total number of more than 5300 settlements. Highly urbanised territories comprise about 20% of the whole territory of the country (Evrev et al., 1996). Economic migration and strict functional zoning in large towns have resulted in demolishing the historical set of the integral urban fabric there; the urban peripheries have undergone rather chaotic development of functions and accompanying problems (the formation of mono-functional residential territories with no public spaces, industrial zones lacking energy- and resource-efficiency and a considerable degree of industrial enterprises with polluting and out-of-date technologies; chaotic development of recreational zones with no appropriate transport and technical infrastructure and no consideration for the value of the natural landscape).

Land speculation and practical lack of development control during the recent 10 years of the 'transition' period brought about additional pressure. The dominant changes in urban land-use are mainly connected with the increasing pressure for new commercial and prestigious residential development at the central and some of the peripheral parts of the cities and towns and with the restructuring of industry and the appearance of numerous small and medium size enterprises.

3.3 The changing spatial planning system

Being an instrument of public policy, spatial planning could equally facilitate or hamper its effects. Within a strongly centralized state the democratization of the spatial planning process has never gone beyond the 'decide-announce-defend' scheme. That approach was one of the reasons for an extremely negative reaction to the very process of spatial planning at the very beginning of the transition period.

The next years witnessed how the imaginary 'public interest', up to that moment centrally defended by the socialist state, turned to have split into numerous - and usually contradictory - interests, in a dramatic process of redistribution of social wealth and land speculation. The planning system had to conceptualize the shift from 'radical idealism' to 'common sense' and to adapt to the appearance of new partners and new rules of the game in the development process. The recognition of conflict was a first, and crucial, step, learning to solve conflicts is a next challenge to face.

Major barriers to the process are considered to be the existing conflicting aims and interests, and short-term considerations prevailing in local decision-making. Decisions in spatial planning and management are now strongly influenced by external pressure, considerable corruption, lack of information and instruments to provide it, generally insufficient resources, lack of mechanisms and motivation for the public to join in a 'participative' planning process.

The elaboration of a new Spatial Planning Law, taking into account the restituted private property and private initiative is still in progress and it is expected to provide the needed legal basis for the new public relationships in space. Yet, it will not be enough in order to overcome the main shortcomings of the present spatial planning situation - the lack of societal consensus on ethical values and priorities, and the lack of policy implementation instruments at the local level.

4 SUSTAINABILITY APPRAISAL IN URBAN PLANNING - THE NEED FOR SOCIO-CULTURAL CRITERIA AND INDICATORS

The further development of the spatial planning system in Bulgaria surely needs new policy instruments - democratic information networks and mechanisms providing for effective and efficient public participation, as well as policy testing indicators - easy to apply and estimate - in order to turn sustainable development from a slogan into a definable and attainable object of the spatial planning profession. However, educating greater activity and responsibility in all the groups and individuals involved, and also the formulation and development of a societal consensus on a new value framework and ethical references should be regarded as a priority. That is where the cultural aspects of urban sustainability could be expected to be of particular contribution to constitute a basis for collaboration and partnership in a fragmented society.

Sustainability is a process which requires a major societal decision and a 'partnership ethic' that presupposes no temporal and spatial discounting. That is why it needs a rational and transparent process of decision-making. Indicators are the variables supposed to provide for such a process through characterizing the system, the rate of the occurring changes in it and the way in which it contributes to the achievement of defined objectives. Any selected set of indicators is contextually specific and is supposed to bear information about the system to be managed - its present condition and viability, about the possible ways of interfering and influencing the system's behaviour. Besides, it contains references to the desired outcomes of the system's development. 'Show me your indicator list and I'll tell you what your ethics are.' (Bossel, 1998) draws attention to the ethical connotations contained there and influencing the political choices to be made. The socio-cultural indicators would provide for conceptualizing the present situation from the point of view of the long-term urban development, to bridge the gap between functional considerations, economic competition, political turbulence and the cultural meaning of the historic evolution of an urban community - to guarantee the viability and continuity of the city as a cultural phenomenon.

5 CONTEXTUAL OPPORTUNITIES FOR SUSTAINABLE DEVELOPMENT AT THE LOCAL LEVEL

It is without doubt that spatial planning is a process based on much wider than the local level considerations and real power to materialize large scale spatial development schemes lies at higher strategic levels rather than with local communities (Colenutt, 1997). Anyway, the successful realization of a path to sustainability is guaranteed by the presence of three main factors: institutional ones; relevant attitude and behaviour of the community in terms of way of life; the urban environment characterized by its structure and morphology. Urban planning is a local experience, so both research into its impacts and processes of planning and political campaigning over new directions of spatial development have to look to the locality for evidence, ideas and support for future change.

In order to be able to connect the physical image of the urban 'milieu' with its cultural one, a sustainability appraisal of all planning should be incorporated into the decision-making process at the municipal level. Having in mind that the local level is likely the most competent to provide information about the socio-cultural identity of a community, sets of socio-cultural indicators are to be derived from the local context. Thus the role of the expert would be to provide the framework for control and monitoring of urban development in terms of sustainability without taking the responsibility away from where it actually belongs - the decision makers at relevant political levels.

5.1 A case study

As stated in the National Report of Bulgaria for the Habitat II Conference, the development of the small settlements situated in the field of influence of the larger cities should be considered 'one of the priorities of the regional policy' (Evrev *et al.*, 1996). That was the reason to focus current research work, partially funded by Bulgarian Science fund (project No 712/97), aimed at developing a set of sustainability criteria and indicators for the local level of urban planning and management, on the small settlements at the periphery of Sofia - the largest city (about 1.2 million) and capital of the country (Dimitrova *et al.*, 1999).

The administrative unit (region) of Novi Iskar, chosen for a case study, is one of the 24 'territorial administrative regions' within (Greater) Sofia municipality, situated about 20 km from the city centre to the North of Sofia. In an inquiry carried out for the needs of the new Local Plan (now in process of elaboration) only 5% of the population of the capital declared ready to move out to the region of Novi Iskar. Yet, only 5% of the local population would move out of there if an economic opportunity existed (Genov *et al.*, 1999).

The main research objectives related to the issues of the socio-cultural identity of the population and its co-relation with the urban environment focused on the regard of:

- the physical characteristics of the territory and of places and elements of the urban environment at different scale to the way in which they are used by people (influence on the way of life in the community) and the inhabitants' estimation for their specific role and importance to personal and community life (the estimated value of the urban environment);
- life priorities and the expected life realisation (especially these of the younger generation) to views of the future of the settlement (dynamics in the value system of the community). Two subgroups of the inhabitants were asked to answer the questionnaires - relevant samples of pupils (aged 15 - 18) and of the economically active population (aged 19-70).

5.2 Discussion of the results

The investigation on the inhabitants' self-identification with the place, their way of life and the role of the physical environment proved the existence of co-relations. The analysis of the results obtained demonstrates the viability of the traditional values of urban culture - the most important places were estimated to be the square, the mayoralty, the church, the local cultural centre. At the same time a conclusion was drawn that the respective places and spatial elements often fail to meet the value expectations of the population. The lack of a relevant political culture of the authorities in order to support and develop cultural traditions may come to have a cumulative destructive effect on cultural sustainability.

The investigation on the relationship between the visions on the settlement's future and the personal expectations for life realization demonstrated another missed meeting point between short- and longer-term considerations. Instead of an almost 50 year-long industrial development of the region and an existing large industrial territory (undergoing privatization and conversion) at the very heart of the town, more than 80% of the economically active inhabitants are nowadays partially or fully involved in agricultural activities - a tradition still alive, and in a difficult time of crisis providing a way of survival. Yet, only 30% see the future of the region as a rural one, the others would rather expect it to have a development potential in the field of transport services and processing industries. Meanwhile the preferred life realization of the younger generation lies in the fields of science, education, journalism and law.

An urban structure is a product of the needs and visions of the past and present inhabitants, it is a result of slow and irreversible changes and an important factor to influence the formation of future needs and values of its communities. That is why in order to provide for the continuity and sustainability of development, the process of urban planning should introduce several important criteria and indicators to continually focus the attention of planning authorities on:

- self-identification of the population of the community with specific places of the urban environment;
- the detection of and special attention to the 'strategic points' in the urban structure, defined by their estimation in the community memory and value framework, even when the

existing urban spaces do not meet the requirements of present life, will help to preserve and develop the 'cultural dimension';

- promotion of contact zones between the fragmented parts of the urban fabric, resulting from the application of strict functional zoning of the settlements;
- sensitively reacting to the dynamics in the way of life and the resulting changes in the cultural identity of the communities in the locality.

6 CONCLUSION

Environmental management for sustainability (including natural, built and socio-cultural environment) is an intensely political process, which involves continuous mediation between environmental values and socio-economic and cultural goals. The currently dominant ethical framework of short-term consumerism in society with regard to environmental issues will lead to a mounting environmental as well as cultural crisis. In order to join in the efforts to overcome it, the spatial planning system still has to overcome institutional inertia and introduce the socio-cultural dimension of urban environments in everyday practice.

Local sustainability is a holistic process and not a sum of environment, economy, society and culture. A period of irreversible transformations in the social and cultural meanings of Bulgarian urban space requires a new role of the expert and new instruments for it. To aim at supporting the cultural sustainability of urban communities would mean to define the city through the opportunities it gives people for realization and development.

REFERENCES

Alberti, M. 1996. Measuring Urban Sustainability. In *Environmental Impact Assessment Review,* 16:381-424.

Bossel, H. 1998. *Earth at a Crossroads. Paths to a Sustainable Future.* Cambridge University Press.

Carley, M. & Cristie, 1992. *Managing Sustainable Development.* Earthscan.

Colenutt, B. 1997. Can Town Planning Be for People Rather Than Property? In Blowers, A., B. Evans (eds). *Town Planning into the 21st Century.* London: Routledge:105-119.

Dimitrova, E. *et al.,* 1999. *Sustainable Development Strategy for the Small Settlements of Greater Sofia Municipality.* Sofia, National Science Fund of Bulgaria: Research project No. 712/97 (1997 - continuing). Unpublished report In Bulgarian.

Evrev,P. *et al.,* 1996. *Settlement Development in the Republic of Bulgaria: State, Problems, Opportunities* Report for Habitat II. Sofia: Ministry of Regional Development and Construction, National Centre of Regional Development and Housing Policy. In Bulgarian.

Fisher, H. 1999. *Cultural Innovation and Economic Development, Greece Good Practice in View of Problems of Sustainability.* Athens, National Technical University, Paper, International Conference on Sustainable Development and Spatial Planning in the European Territory:13-16 May.

Genov, N. 1997. Bulgaria In the Global and Regional Contexts. In Genov (ed). *Bulgaria Today and Tomorrow* 19-61. Sofia: Friederich Ebert Foundation.

Genov, N. *et al.,* 1999. *Public Appraisal of the State of the City of Sofia.* Sofia Municipality: Preliminary Investigations for the Development of Sofia's Master Plan: unpublished report on a sociological survey. In Bulgarian.

Hewitt, N. 1995. *European Local Agenda 21 Planning Guide - How to Engage in Long Term Environmental Action Planning Towards Sustainability?,* Brussels: ICLEI publication.

Marcuse, P. 1998. Sustainability is not Enough. In Environment and Urbanisation, 10,(2):103-111.

Needham, B. 1999. Pursuing Spatial Development Which Is Environmentally Sustainable: Who gains and who Loses? Athens, National Technical University: Paper: International Conference on Sustainable Development and Spatial Planning in the European Territory.

OECD. 1997. *Better Understanding Our Cities. The role of Urban Indicators.* ISBN 9264 15454X

Owens, S. 1997. 'Giants in the Path'. Planning, Sustainability and Environmental Values. In Town *Planning Review*, 68 (3):293-302.

Pusic, L. 1999. Sustainable Development and Urban Identity: A Social Context. Athens, 13-16 May: Paper presented to the International Conference on Sustainable Development and Spatial Planning in the European Territory, National Technical University of Athens.

Selman, P. 1998. A Real Local Agenda for the 21st Century? In *Town and Country Planning*: January/February 1998.

Tate, J., Mulugetta, Y. 1998. Sustainability: The Technocentric Challenge. In *Town Planning Review* 69(1):65-74.

Taylor, N. 1998. Mistaken Interests and the Discourse Model of Planning. In *Journal of the American Planning Association*, 64(1):64-75.

The Sofia Statement 1998. *Towards Local Sustainability in Central and Eastern Europe*. Adopted on 14 November 1998 by the participants of the Bulgaria, Sofia: Regional Conference on Sustainable Cities and Towns.

Voogd, H. 1997. Comment in Policy Forum. In *Town Planning Review*, 69(1): 79-82.

Urban Lifestyles: Spaces · Places · People, Benson & Roe (eds)
© 2000 Balkema, Rotterdam, ISBN 90 5809 169 4

Urban parks and green space: Quality of life and LA21

G.L. Evans & J. Bohrer
Centre for Leisure and Tourism Studies, University of North London, UK

ABSTRACT: Urban parks have been in long term decline due to local government rationaliza-
tion of spending and services; the impact from development - buildings, traffic - and a lack of
understanding of either their usage or value in the urban landscape. Their historical significance
as buffers and green lungs has arguably been devalued due to this lack of maintenance and attention. At the same time, parks in cities have come under renewed pressure for animation, as
venues for sporting and cultural events, and for built structures - new and renovated - bringing
conflicts with the core values of open space as passive amenities, rather than as active 'pleasure
gardens' - a role they once had in the eighteenth and nineteenth centuries. This paper draws on
surveys of parks users in London and a review of open space planning standards, in the context
of urban design, lifestyles and Local Agenda 21.

1 INTRODUCTION

Parks and open spaces are perhaps one of the few residual 'public good' recreation services,
alongside libraries and public museums, and it is no coincidence that in all of these areas a decline in their management, maintenance and provision has been experienced at a local level over
the past twenty years. Standards of provision have never been mandatory, or at least enforce-
able, one reason why guidance on standards has produced little response from local authorities
other than a limited reference in borough plans e.g. 'presumption against loss' (Evans, Worpole
et al 1999). To a greater extent, recreation planning standards have been developed for and been
easier to implement in new town and rural areas, rather than in cities. Since the emergence of
post-war leisure planning which saw the growth in new facilities, it is not surprising that leisure
provision has been facility-led. Passive parks and open space provision has therefore fallen between the two stools of sport and recreation including play, and 'green belt', with parks fulfilling their benign role as buffers or green lungs to encroaching urban development and density
i.e. they are perceived in a negative sense as 'not-developed' land. Their position as risky and
unsafe areas also has deep roots for example associated with the London County Council's
'Board of Works' and their cleaning up campaign - ridding parks and open spaces of 'vagrants,
anti-social behaviour and gambling' (still a concern today - below), and the rational recreation
movement that limited the popular pursuits carried out in the Pleasure Gardens and their predecessors, the town fairs. One hundred years on, these invaluable green spaces are under threat:
"Studies show that Londoners perceive parks as places where sex attackers and weirdoes lurk"
(Kossoff 1994), however crime statistics do not bear out this perception of parks as unsafe,
compared with streetlife and homelife where most crimes are committed. Parks nonetheless present an image of risk and danger, especially at night, and of uncontrolled spaces in an otherwise
controlled built environment.

The role assigned to parks and open space is also a secondary one in the view of architects
and urban masterplanners, as Richard Rogers in the Urban Task Force Report claimed (DETR,

1999), "open space is the glue which binds together buildings…" As a building-designer, this perspective is perhaps not surprising, however someone should point out that whilst <u>sniffing glue</u> might take place outdoors, it is the "space' that comes first (and last, as buildings become derelict, fall and are removed). As Sten Görannson of the Department of Landscape Planning at Alnarp University more generously put it: "the green urban elements distinguish and give character; they divide and structuralize, they bind together and create wholenesses; they facilitate orientation; they have a contrasting and a softening effect; they create a human scale; they reflect cultural and natural history; they symbolise and represent (e.g. nature, park, countryside); they show culture, art and architecture and they are important for the visual image and for the public image of the city" (Worpole in Evans, Worpole *et al* 1999).

The historical ('Garden City') and utopian origins of town planning in Britain also provide a clue to the limitations of the consideration of amenity in urban planning, since "amenity is one of the key concepts in British town planning, yet nowhere in the legislation is it defined" (Cullingworth, 1979, p. 157). Whilst its importance had been recognised for example through the civic amenity acts (1967, 1974), this was limited to the preservation and enhancement of special architectural and historic sites and buildings, which led to the designation of conservation areas in Great Britain. Paradoxically, whilst lacking a definition in the legislation, "amenity" is claimed to be one of the most relied upon concepts in British town planning! Amenity in this context has been defined as: "a quality of pleasantness in the physical environment [which] ranges from an essentially negative restriction against nuisances to a notion of visual delight" (HMSO, 1951) and as Foley observed: "one sometimes gets the feeling that the British have quite self-consciously sought to protect themselves against the pragmatic inventiveness of their own designs" (1973, p. 81). The terms 'park', 'open space', 'green space' are also used without any consistent definition and in practice these range from controlled - fenced, 'open and closed' parks - open commons/heaths; heritage sites; town squares and gardens; to allotments; cemeteries; city farms and community gardens - of which there are over 60 (and 150 town squares) in London alone. Community gardens and pocket parks have often been created within dense housing, both private and social, as a neighbourhood resource. Due to their location they are often under threat from expanding development and lack normal local authority maintenance services, and some are tenant/resident managed. In New York for instance 114 city-owned neighbourhood gardens were put up for auction to developers only to be saved at the last minute by a $2m donation by the New York Restoration Project, a park conservation group financed by Bette Midler. Many urban parks share boundaries with a wide range of land uses, not only residential, but commercial and industrial properties, and the encroachment and loss of green space has often occurred where boundaries are not clear. As a resident in the borough of Islington remarked (see below): "Swimming pools and adventure playgrounds are wanted, but they should be done on derelict land, not at the expense of existing parkland" (Bohrer & Curson, 1998).

This situation contrasts with Barcelona, where between 1981 and 1997 over 140 urban space projects were completed, mostly in the form of 'plaza dura': small, hard-surfaced squares and piazzas (Worpole in Evans, Worpole *et al*, 1999). The dominant public space aesthetic in the city 'belongs to the tradition of no trees.' These new squares are designed to be outdoor living rooms, not gardens, 'involving a public architecture of intimacy, one that brings people together in an experience of confidence and trust'. More recently there has been an emphasis on encouraging institutions and private companies to create small parks and gardens in the centre of this densely populated, heavily built-up city. Barcelona was awarded the 1999 RIBA Gold Medal, the first time a city rather than an individual architect had been so honoured "partly to send a message to Britain's politicians". Josep Acebillo architect and former director of urban projects in Barcelona criticised the British reluctance to involve local people in regeneration projects, stating that: "if Margaret Thatcher had been mayor of Barcelona, the city's public realm would be nothing" and citing the fact that crime rates in Barcelona dropped from 25% to 5% in 10 years, whilst London's rose one and a half times ('Building Design' 25.6.99).

In Paris, with an absence of basic planning documents in the late 1970s, the city began to revise its planning procedures, including establishing Regional Development and Ground Use Plans. The latter articulated detailed land-use and densities and the preference for developing new *quartiers* which would more modestly respect the dimensions of surrounding buildings and wherever possible parks, gardens and public amenities would be positioned at the heart of new housing blocks. Despite the fact that these Plans, Ratios, and Mixed Development Zones, are more costly and more space-consuming than previous practice, these are well accepted by inhabitants who "are at last beginning to find a quality of life they have always aspired" (Evans in Evans, Worpole *et al*, 1999).

2 PLEASURE GARDENS

The commons and opens spaces of medieval towns provided the foundation for public gardens and areas for walking and promenading, which were also used for festivals and sporting events. This adaptation of rural popular entertainment was mirrored in the pleasure gardens of London, which drew large numbers of participants to Vauxhall, Ranelagh, Sadlers Wells and Cremorne Gardens - modelled on Tivoli, Copenhagen - to Crystal Palace where a gigantic garden included refreshment rooms, music, paintings, sculpture, tropical trees and architectural models (Best, 1979, p. 234). Mr Sadler had established his fairground and pleasure garden on a natural spring ('clerks well') in Islington in 1683. Whilst visitors took the waters, Sadler added a Musick House. In a song of the day: "sweet gardens and arbours of pleasure" (Senter, 1998).

By the late-1700s most larger cities had commercial pleasure gardens in which concerts, dances and other recreation took place. In 'Don Juan in London' (1836) Thornton observes: "the gardens are beautiful and extensive, and contain a variety of walks, brilliantly illuminated…and terminate with transparent paintings, the whole disposed with so much taste and effect as to produce sensation bordering on enchantment to the visitor". Pleasure gardens tended to draw their crowds on warm dry days and evenings, and as well as the major gardens, countless smaller ones cropped up in and around most cities: "Wherever streets and houses lay thick, it was worth someone's while to set up a vista of Arcadia" (Best, 1979, pp. 234-5). As well as a local pedestrian population, the larger sites relied on public transport such as horse-buses and expanded rail networks, but their prime location also made them exposed to speculative building. Some pleasure gardens actually built halls on site, losing green space but maintaining their clientele in the new saloon theatres. Some of the remaining gardens were later to become urban parks, as a buffer to counter and soften rapid population growth and density, but more a product of rational recreation than popular pleasure pursuit. The fate of the pleasure gardens was to be similar to the fairs - sealed by the appeal of the music hall and 'dream palaces', with their wide variety of entertainment, food and drink, and internal safety, on which the gardens increasingly could neither compete nor satisfy the licensing authorities: "semi-rural places of entertainment were beginning to lose their attraction and were tolerated less and less as the bricks and mortar of the expanding city covered the fields" (Weightman, 1992, p. 10). By 1711 Sadler's Wells audience were described as "vermin trained up to the gallows" and by the Inquisitor as "a nursery of debauchery" (Senter, 1998, p. 6) and in 1851 after many changes of style, management and illegal operation, Dicken's opinion was no better: "as ruffianly an audience as London could shake together, like the worst kind of fair in the worst kind of town, it was a bear garden, resounding with foul language, oaths, catcall shrieks, yells, blasphemy, obscenity" (p.10). By 1876 it was turned into an ice-rink and Winter Garden (sic).

As urban population density and building intensified in the next century, the importance of town squares and gardens and the need for public parks was recognised, although less for active pursuits, but for rest and respite from streetlife. With the popular success of Paxton's pioneer park at Birkenhead on Merseyside, Manchester opened three urban parks in 1847; Bradford opened Peel Park (jointly financed by the mayor and textile industrialist Salt); in Dundee the Baxter (People's) Park; and Bolton Heywood Park in 1866 and several parks were opened by the Metropolitan Board of Works in London: "The public parks and promenades which began to be opened must have made life a little pleasanter…in every town or city of any size, wealth and concentration, the crystallising of a cultural apparatus providing for every level of the community...The leisure patterns of the modern industrial urban mass society now begin to take shape" (Best, 1979, pp. 219-20). Parks hosted regular band concerts which were not engaged by the local council but of course, played with their permission ('licence'), as today. Outdoor city entertainment also suffered once public transport enabled quick and cheap access, with the popular growth of seaside resorts, the piers and promenades, and the establishment of fairs, winter gardens and summer palaces in less threatening and controlled environments than the inner city. From the second quarter of the nineteenth century, whilst city-centre recreation zones survived, although not unchanged, neighbourhood entertainment was not sustainable with the decline in the local music hall, pleasure garden and later, the cinema.

2.1 *Symbolic Heritage and Royal Parks*

As the corollary to local and neighbourhood parks, central and historic parks serve as both the top of a hierarchy of public open space (Evans, Worpole *et al*, 1999), and as locations for built and landscaped 'natural' heritage. The Royal Parks in London, other city parks such as in Madrid, New York and Copenhagen, and palace parks of Versailles, Vienna and Berlin, serve as both symbols and visitor attractions in their own right and are frequently used by tourist promotion bodies and transport operators, e.g. airline in-flight magazines and videos, to depict and frame the heritage images of city tourism destinations. The proximity of parks to palaces and gardens which are often located within their boundaries, reinforces their association with Royalty, past and present, whilst park architectural landscapes and heritage buildings serve as icons for a whole city - for instance Park Guell, Barcelona, one of the city's Gaudi landmarks and world heritage site, which is used as a symbol of the city's unique design image (Guell was termed a 'park' as a opposed to the Spanish parque or Catalan parc due to its reference to and influence from the English tradition of country estates and pleasure gardens).

Historic houses, palaces and attractions located in or adjoining Royal Parks include features such as monuments, landscape and amenities, from galleries, zoos, lakes to recreational facilities for horse riding and pitch sports. Parks, particularly those located in central city zones, are also used for festivals and gatherings, both exploiting their size, transport links and symbolic association over time. This was seen in London with the choice of Hyde Park as host to the national VE day celebrations in 1995 and large scale gatherings, most recently the Countryside Alliance demonstration which brought 250,000 country dwellers and farmers to London. This park has also played host to 6 million visitors to the Crystal Palace at the Great Exhibition in 1851, to the Rolling Stones free concert in the Park in 1969 attended by 500,000 people, and more recently 'Pavarotti in the Park' and other concerts and extravaganzas. Indeed the demand for parks as places for entertainment harks back to their origins as Pleasure Gardens which brought together the rural fair and early urban entertainment (above). The mall which now describes the ubiquitous multi-purpose shopping centre, in fact originated from the Mall of St. James's Park, frequented by the nineteenth century flaneur: "the independent yet pecunious young man, an artist or writer who wanders the streets and cafes, dreaming, desiring, devouring the city with a cynical yearning hunger" (Zukin, 1995, p. 188), and now replaced by the tourist seeking the symbolic heritage experience of the Royal Parks environs (Curson *et al*, 1994-1996).

The significance of city parks as repositories of both symbolic and economic capital is also evident in the case of New York's Central Park which during the 1960s "became a symbolic staging ground for various 'unifying' events, from rock concerts to protest demonstrations" (Zukin, 1996, p. 55). During the 1970s upper Fifth Avenue became another symbolic centre represented by its new name, the 'Museum Mile', as a result of museum expansion (Metropolitan, Guggenheim) and blockbuster exhibitions, encroaching into the public space of the park itself (Rosenzweig & Blackmar, 1992). Central Park, like the Royal Park in Greenwich, is the annual starting point of the popular city marathon. London's Regents Park has for over 25 years hosted a well known summer season of Shakespeare and other open air theatrical productions, as well as Easter Parades, whilst Primrose Hill is used for one of London's most popular fireworks displays exploiting its hill view across London. These spacious parks located in otherwise densely built-up areas not surprisingly influence the values of overlooking and adjoining property, both residential and commercial, and they therefore emulate the historic and museum quarters of these cultural capitals.

3 CORE VALUES OF PARKS

The core function of city parks has therefore developed as 'green lungs' and buffers to encroaching urbanization and industrial life in the nineteenth and early twentieth centuries. The importance of natural and green spaces is still paramount, although the imperatives of urbanization, population growth and manufacturing industry have declined. Pressure for the use of Green Belt land for housing and other developments has, however, placed more emphasis on the retention of urban/fringe parks, as has the loss of playing fields and other recreational land.

The value placed on urban parks was evident from research into users of the nine Royal Parks in London (n=33,000), carried out between 1993 and 1995 in the central London parks of Hyde Park/Kensington Gardens, Regents, St James's and Green Parks to the suburban Parks at Greenwich, Richmond, Bushy and Primrose Hill (Curson & Bohrer). Here their value was reaffirmed according to parks users: 'Open Space', 'Like the Country', 'Beauty' being the most frequently quoted, followed by 'Convenience' and 'Variety of activity/experience'. Again the features parks users particularly liked: 'Large/open space'; 'Flora/fauna', 'Tranquil/relaxing' and 'Landscape' not surprisingly dominated. From a study of the Lee Valley, a linear, urban fringe Regional Park (Evans & Wray, 1996) this sentiment was echoed: "There is so much countryside and such a variety of birdlife right in the middle of our environment"..."Personally I like the peace and quiet, so to me to have any play facilities for children would put me off". This raises the fundamental issue of potential conflict of use with more intensive activities associated with public events, organised sports and entertainments.

This conflict encompasses both the impact on the park landscape and fabric itself, to noise, parking and other intrusion, reducing the amenity for regular parks visitors seeking the traditional peace and quiet. Examples include the banning of rollerblading in Hyde Park (but approval of VE-Day and concerts), and conflicts between festival promoters, locals and the police, with residents tying themselves to trees in Melbourne's Albert Park to block a Grand Prix track, despite an A$100 million aid package for the park. This is more of a problem with single space parks where one such activity precludes other usage and where environmental impacts are felt to be too excessive - one reason for Greenwich Park refusing permission for Millennium celebrations despite its prime location as the 'home of time'. In the Lee Valley Park, policies to expand on existing events, are based on 'perceived demand' and the success of annual events such as the British Waterways Festival, and the income generation potential. On the other hand, their main opposition arises from the car traffic that such events attract, the dominance over existing usage, and the impact on wildlife. Between 1989 and 1994 car usage within the Park increased by 10% to over 1.1 million a year. The traffic dilemma was seen with a proposed leisure complex on a marshland area adjoining Park land, comprising a multiplex, hotel, restaurants and industrial units on a 12-acre site. 'Friends of the Earth', who opposed this planning application, foresaw the equivalent of a 5-mile traffic tailback since the private development is targeted at a car-only user with onsite parking for 1,400 cars. Changing leisure lifestyles have also seen the growth in outdoor pursuits, from gardening, active sports and sunbathing, as one can witness on a sunny weekday and evening in city parks, and which has coincided with the growing incidence of skin cancers and global warming (Evans, 1997, 1998b).

4 LOCAL AGENDA 21 AND URBAN PARKS

From their historic roots and the contemporary scale hierarchies applied to parks and open space, the relationship between Local Agenda 21 (LA21) policies and the role, impact and contribution of parks to urban quality, raises some fundamental issues around the British approach to urbanism and urban society. LA21 as a new development has not yet featured significantly in parks operation and related policy areas, however the differing position of the three scales of park provision: neighbourhood - local - regional, reveals notable divergence and generally the absence of consideration of parks and open spaces in LA21 strategies at local and neighbourhood levels. This is perhaps not surprising given that "the importance and the potential of parks has been ignored, forgotten or undervalued, even though parks are especially relevant in an era concerned with ecology and economic sustainability" (Comedia, 1994). Philosophically this persistence is summed up in the reluctance to celebrate city and urban life, preferring instead to deal with the urban environment as a 'problem'. This again is in contrast with mainland Europe, where: "Europeans appreciate urban life. The towns and how they are adapted to modern needs, funded and managed illustrate a belief that urban life can be rich, varied, complex and fun. People like living close to the centre of Town. Conversely in Britain we appear to distrust urban life, seeing it as often as sinful and dangerous and the countryside as the repository of safety and virtue" (Walton, 1991, p. 9).

The 'problem' of cities also surfaced in the Comedia study of urban parks, as one contributor put it "Cities and parks represent opposite polarities of human nature..I believe the cultural role assigned to cities is greatly exaggerated...modern cities are environmental disaster zones" (Nicholson Lord, 1994, p. 4). This anti-urban sentiment was echoed following the UN Habitat II conference held in 1996, where press coverage was dominated by the disaster zones of both burgeoning third world and resource hungry western cities. This meta-view of cities as either the causes of, or solutions to the problems of urban environmental disaster features highly in late-twentieth century sustainable development agendas, which: "can be viewed as an attempt to extend an ethically, socially and culturally, reformed modern project into the future" (Knutsson, 1998, p. 30). The city-as-solution however, is seen by an unlikely source, the Green Movement: "For inside the city problem of cities lies the solution. The city - always the place of greatest dynamism and creativity - may also present the greatest opportunity for a greener future" (Baird, 1999, p. 8). A new mega-shopping mall, that drive-in, out-of-town phenomenon, 'Bluewater' (sic), has paradoxically created the largest new area of landscape and trees in Kent (Evans, 1998).

4.1 LA21 Case Study - Islington

Islington is located in inner north London, and is one of the most densely populated and least 'green' boroughs in the UK. Like many post-industrial urban areas it is divided between well-heeled private housing (one of the first in London to experience gentrification after the war) and declining council estate areas and in consequence, an extremely polarised socio-economic resident profile. It is significant therefore that parks and open spaces and the relationship between recreational space and air quality in this most densely built-up north London borough, is absent from LA21 strategic policy. This is largely dominated by the control of the negative aspects of pollution, energy, transport and waste. An LA21 'Mental Health' topic suggested an opportunity for environmental and quality of life indicators, even therapeutic values of parks and gardens, however this issue was focused only on residential care and problems with the health system and resources.

The absence of open space in LA21 consideration to date is also a reflection of the corporate and therefore policy and professional separation between environmental planning functions and parks management within leisure services departments. This was mirrored in a national survey of Tourism Officers and LA21 policy which sought to assess the consideration of tourism within Local Agenda 21 initiatives. It was concluded that there had been a 'poor take up' and little development of LA21 by tourism offices and there was little evidence of any interrelationship between LA21 and tourism. Many environmental initiatives have been sector-led and not spatially-based but which might strengthen the links with Local Agenda 21 policy and practice in local areas. Unless LA21 develops a cross-departmental approach therefore, integrated policy development and meeting the overarching Agenda 21 aims, is unlikely to be achieved, let alone sustained. The dominance of environmentalists, special interest groups and professional 'officers' risks marginalizing the LA21 process and in practice excluding the interests and concerns of the resident community and their everyday lives.

General environmental policies on parks and open spaces in this borough did however feature in other statements. In 'The State of the Environment in Islington' (1996) policies were directed at protecting loss of public open space and the creation of new open space where opportunities arise. However this Council document concedes the impossibility of achieving the open space standards seen elsewhere in London. A strategy includes making better use of existing assets like canals and linking spaces ('green chains'), as well as maintaining access to existing parks and open spaces. Here the Council maintains that 100% of metropolitan open land (MOL) in the borough is "accessible to the public" - compared with only 30% of Green Belt and 76% of MOL generally. However, our user and household surveys (n=3,500) of local parks in this borough

152

presents a different picture - or realistically, a more genuine interpretation of 'public access' and barriers to parks usage (Bohrer & Curson 1998). The quotes below represent some of the personal opinions expressed in the survey of householders and parks users. These range from the negative threat and misuse of parks: "...there are problems for residents living next to parks: noise late at night; children climbing in after closure; vandalism of private property; and number of people attracted to parks from outside the area"; "[They're] closed in, dark and unwelcoming"; "The parks in my area of the borough are glorified dog's toilets, probably because there is so little open space in north Islington. ... ; "Stop the wine lay- abouts sleeping on the seats - disgraceful"; to the socio-spatial divide in quality of amenity: "As with every facility in Islington, if you live in the posh bits they're fine (eg. Highbury Fields) and if you live in the working class bits they're crap. ; "Parks in middleclass areas seem to be more well-kept and planted"; "... we quite often visit parks outside the borough"; the inappropriate and conflicts of usage: "I think Highbury Fields is overused by fairs, concerts etc. It is not big enough and the grass ruined too often"; "... in Islington they are gardens not parks"; "I do not think it is right when people say drunks should not be allowed into parks. They have as much right as anyone else in my opinion"; "... over organisation of events and sporting facilities ruin any feeling of wide, open green space..Spend the council tax on rubbish removal and keeping streets clean"; and their protection and regeneration: "Pooles park - shut for 4 years - why? - we could do a voluntary park watch if it meant it could be open"; "There is so little open space it ought to be vigilantly protected"; "It would be good to close a lot of roads, remove most car and lorry traffic, and turn the roads into parkland walks".

The relationship between access, health and open spaces was also one observed by O'Keefe. Based on Norbury Park, Surrey, this case study prompted her to "link the more obvious health issues about access to open space and less obvious ones about the intensification of spatial and social segregation which feeds fear and nimbyism" (1996, p. 5). The divide between car ownership (43% with 2 or more: 17% none) is acute in this area, given that 96% of visitors drive to Norbury Park. In the Lee Valley Park region 55% of the urban residents did not have car access, whilst 75% of the outer/suburban population did (Evans, 1998b). In Norbury, the local newspaper urged local people to travel to the park by rail, however: "the public lavatory in the station has been bricked up and disabled access to the platform is long overgrown and locked...so far only improvements have been making access easier for the already keen largely male mountain bikers for whom paths through the Park have been negotiated" (O'Keefe, 1996).

5 CONCLUSION

Despite the growing attention and research into urban parks (Comedia, 1995, CELTS, DoE, 1996) and the capital funding for heritage and new park creation (Landscape, 1999), calls for a national urban parks body and statutory duty for their protection and management have not been heeded. In London, the new Greater London Authority and Mayor has inherited both a spatial strategy and detailed review of open space demand and provision (Evans, Worpole et al, with W.S.Atkins 2000), so there is no longer a lack of either policy analysis or primary research into the state of urban parks, or knowledge of the problem and comparative solutions. As well as the environmental and physical impacts considered by sustainable development, a section of Agenda 21 relating to social and economic dimensions focuses on strengthening local economies, changing consumption patterns and also on strengthening the role of local communities in their environment and provision of amenities. Reconciling urban living, environmental quality and adequate amenities, including parks and open space, is therefore not an option (any more than a wholesale return to the countryside) and the place of parks in LA21 policies warrants greater consideration than has been evident to date. Local community input to park programmes and development is also needed, however given the absence of parks-based issues in the LA21 and other initiatives studied here, the contribution to urban environmental quality and design (not just the spaces in between buildings and roads) is likely to require both a more integrated policy exchange and planning framework (DCMS, 1999) and wider consultation than the present mechanisms and professional bias allows. Research into parks usage, benefits and conflicts, provides a particular contribution to LA21 policy development and perhaps provides the counter-balance to the 'anti-urban' dialectic, and the predominant concern for the built environment and the environmental excesses of urban communities.

REFERENCES

Baird, V. 1999. Green Cities, *The New Internationalist*, June. London: 7-10.
Best, G. 1985. *Mid-Victorian Britain 1851-75*. London: Fontana Press.
Bohrer, J. & Curson, T. 1998. Survey of User and Households in Islington Parks & Open Spaces, Centre for Leisure & Tourism Studies (CELTS) for Islington Parks and Women's Committees.
Comedia. 1994. *The Future of Urban Parks and Open Spaces* - Working Paper No.4. Comedia: Stroud.
Comedia. 1995. *Parklife: Urban Parks and Social Renewal*. Stroud, Gloucs.
Cullingworth, J.B. & Nadin, V. 1994. *Town and Country Planning in Britain*, London: Routledge.
Curson, A., Evans, G.L. & Bohrer J. 1994 to 1996. *Survey of People Using the Royal Parks: Annual Reports 1994, 1995 and 1996*, CELTS for Royal Parks Agency. UNL Press.
DCMS. 1999. *Guidance for Local Authorities on Local Cultural Strategies*, Consultation Draft. London.
Department of the Environment. 1996. *People, Parks and Cities*, Comedia. London: HMSO.
DETR, 1999. *Towards and Urban Renaissance*, The Report of the Urban Task Force, London.
Evans, G.L. 1997. *Trends in Outdoor Recreation*. London: Health Education Authority.
Evans, G.L. 1998a. Urban Leisure, Edge City and the new Pleasure Periphery. In M. Collins & I. Cooper (eds.), *Free Time and Quality of Life for the 21st Century*. Wallingford: CAB International.
Evans, G.L. 1998b. 'Sun Exposure and Incidence of Skin Cancer in the UK - Implications for Health Education, Leisure Lifestyles and Agenda 21'. *The Environment Papers* 1(3): 5-15.
Evans, G.L. & Wray, D. 1996. *Arts, Culture and Entertainment*. Lee Valley Regional Park, London.
Evans, G.L., Worpole, K. et al & W.S.Atkins. 1999. *Review of Standards for Assessing Demand for Open Space in London*, London Planning Advisory Committee (Final Report to LPAC. 2000).
Foley, D.L. (1973) *British Town Planning: One Ideology or Three?*. In A. Faludi (ed.) *A Reader in Planning Theory*. Oxford: Pergamon Press: 69-94.
HMSO. 1951. *Town and Country Planning, 1943-1951*, Chapter 10 Amenity. London: 138-54.
Kent, C. & Prindle, D. 1993. *Park Guell*. New York: Princeton Architectural Press.
Knutsson, K.E. (ed.) 1998. *Culture and Human Development*. The Royal Academy of Letters, Stockholm
Landscape Institute. 1999. The Work of the Heritage Lottery Fund, *Landscape* #283, September. Surrey
Leslie, D. & Muir, F. 1997. *Local Agenda 21, Local Authorities and Tourism*, Report prepared for Tourism Concern. Glasgow Caledonian University Press.
Nicholson Lord, N. 1994. *Ecology, Parks and Human Need* - Working Paper No.4. Comedia: Stroud.
O'Keefe, E. 1996. Health-promoting designs on darkest Surrey, *Health Promotion*, September: 5-6.
Rosenzweig, R. & Blackmar, E. 1992. *The Park and the People: A History of Central Park*. New York: Cornell University Press.
Islington, L.B. 1996. *State of the Environment in Islington*, Technical & Environmental Services. London.
Islington, L.B. 1997. *Islington Agenda 21 Forum: Strategies for Sustainable Islington*. London.
Senter, A. (1998) *Sadler's Wells A Celebration 1683 -1998*, London: Sadler's Wells Appeal Fund.
Kossoff, K. and McVeigh, K. 1994. 'Green and unpleasant lands', *Time Out*, September 28: 12-13.
Walton, D. 1991. *Past Imperfect, Future Improbable*, Llewelyn-Davies Planning. Royal Town Planning Institute National Planning Conference, 13th June, Newcastle-upon-Tyne.

154

Urban Lifestyles: Spaces · Places · People, Benson & Roe (eds)
© 2000 Balkema, Rotterdam, ISBN 90 5809 169 4

Evidence of the socio-political implications of urban design

L. Kathlene & J. Lynn
University of Nebraska, Lincoln, Nebr., USA

ABSTRACT: Various forms of political participation in the United States and European countries have been steadily declining. Combining theories and empirical findings from political science with critical assessments of modern community planning, we propose that certain built environment features of neighborhoods serve to strengthen or weaken engagement in civic and political behavior. Of particular interest is the homogeneous, single-use, auto-dependent communities, long a familiar style in U.S. suburbs and increasingly infiltrating European cities.

In this pilot phase, two structurally distinct Midwestern U.S. neighborhoods were studied in terms of the built environment features and the residents' neighborhood activities, perceptions of their neighborhood, and evaluations of their city. Upon its completion, the research project will link together the impact of the built environment on the creation of social interactions, civic engagement and political participation.

1 POLITICAL PARTICIPATION AND COMMUNITY DESIGN

For decades, political scientists have debated the implications of low civic engagement on the health and functioning of a constitutional democracy. As the years passed and political participation in the forms of voting, working for a political party, attending political or civic meetings, and attending political rallies or speeches continued its downward spiral (Rosenstone & Hansen ,1993; Putnam, 1995), other longitudinal trends in the form of public opinion polls on government trust (Lipset & Schneider, 1987), social trust (Uslaner, 1995), and democratic governing processes (Hibbing & Theiss-Morse, 1998) followed suit. Such widespread measures of political and civic disconnect suggest that US citizens may best be described as politically alienated, civically disengaged, and highly individualistic. Democratic governing in this age of "uncivic culture" (Bennett, 1998) faces serious challenges ranging from the need for fundamental institutional and process reform (Bennett, 1998; Bickford, 1999; deLeon, 1997; Fischer, 1995; Torgerson, 1986) to a full-fledged legitimation crisis (e.g., Lowi, 1979).

Citizen disengagement has been blamed on a myriad of problems, from institutional structures that limit citizen participation (Rosener, 1978; deLeon, 1992, 1997; Fischer, 1993, 1995; Kathlene & Martin, 1991) to technology that changes our communication patterns and social interactions (Putnam, 1995) to ever heightened levels of individualism leading to "lifestyle" politics (Bennett, 1998). But if we remember de Tocqueville's (1956) insightful early observations of the American experiment with democracy, we must also consider the day to day social environment and cultural norms that make up the American citizenship psyche. Practicing democracy "at home" via town hall meetings in the 1830s or through social organizations in the 1990s builds what Robert Putnam (1995) calls "social capital." And possessing social capital, the "networks, norms, and trust that enable participants to act together effectively to pursue shared objectives" (Putnam, 1995, pp. 664-5), is a necessary precursor to civic engagement which, itself, is a prerequisite for political participation. The simplified causal chain takes the following form:

social capital <---> civic engagement ---> political participation ---> healthy democracy   (1.1)

If Putnam and de Tocqueville are correct, then "change" must focus first on social capital building. To rebuild social capital requires identifying the cause(s) of its dismantling. While Putnam (1995) singles out the television as the main culprit, Norris (1996) demonstrates that it is the content of the television shows, rather than mere viewing hours, that is related to declining levels of group membership and political participation. Bennett (1998) argues our standard measures of political participation are seriously out of synch with actual political participation, redefining the problem as a paradigm shift to an "uncivic culture" rather than a politically disengaged citizenry. The challenge is not how to re-engage citizens in "old" forms of political participation, but rather how to govern effectively and legitimately in the highly individualistic environment of "lifestyle politics." Bennett seems at least partially on the mark in his analysis of the problem and its origin but his "solution" suggests he is too easily swayed by the forces of global capitalism. Must we accept -- more pointedly, can we risk accepting -- a democratic politics that lacks a sense of community, of civic duty, of societal well-being?

It is well known that civic [dis]engagement is not equally distributed across socio-economic classes; yet, Oliver (1999) demonstrates these indicators mask important differences between relative political, civic and social activity. Economically diverse areas have significantly higher levels of local participation than economically homogeneous areas, be they rich or poor. Oliver hypothesizes diverse areas create political activity via multiple perspectives, values, and groups vying for the same political resources. Utilizing insights from Bickford (1999) and Freie (1998), we extend Oliver's findings to argue that it is the socio-political impact of diversity itself -- be it economic, social, or ethnic -- that stimulates political participation. Finally, drawing upon critics of homogeneous modern community planning (Fowler, 1992; Kunstler, 1996), the built environment is linked to diverse activity via the following linkages:

diverse built environment ---> diverse economic environment ---> diverse social activity (1.2)

Although theory and research suggests our present method of development is problematic for social sustainability and civic engagement, the reality is that many people prefer the suburban areas (Dahmann, 1985) and most Americans live or have lived in a suburb (Fowler, 1992). Despite the impact of inefficient resource usage, increasing environmental destruction, and the daily frustrations people experience due to sprawl, people continue to move to the edge of cities Freie (1998) attributes this seemingly antithetical behavior to deliberate marketing ploys of large developers who utilize the discursive symbols of "community" but offer only a counterfeit of it. Overtime more and more people accept the counterfeit community as desirable due to their lack of experiencing a genuine community.

Various theories have been put forth linking the type of neighborhood a resident lives in to the way the resident perceives the city. Jacobs (1961), in describing the multiple layers of a city (neighborhoods, districts, city), states that the city as a whole is in essence only a larger neighborhood. Lynch (1960) discusses how residents use the idea of a neighbourhood, a commercial area or even a specific store type in their daily routines to create images and expectations that allow them to feel comfortable in other neighbourhoods with similar aspects. This suggests neighbourhood structure and function affect people's perceptions of the larger city. The degree to which neighbourhoods foster more or less attachment to surrounding areas and the city as a whole has important political implications.

1.1 *General hypotheses*

While the link between the built environment and civic participation via social capital building is theoretically plausible, empirical evidence has been piecemeal. This project examines the full causal model set out in diagram 1.1. Based on the literature, we hypothesize the follow relationships with respect to the built environment, social interaction, and civic activity:

1. Residents who live in diverse mixed-use neighborhoods will have more day to day interactions with acquaintances in their neighbourhood (Kunstler, 1996), will belong to more social and civic organizations, and will be more engaged in forms of socially-based political

and civic organizations, and will be more engaged in forms of socially-based political participation (Putnam, 1995) than residents who live in homogeneous single-use neighbourhoods.

2. Residents who live in diverse mixed-use neighbourhoods will have higher levels of satisfaction with their city and local government than residents of homogenous neighbourhoods. Higher levels of local satisfaction will be related to higher levels of social trust and trust in government,which is positively correlated with support for policies that enhance the public sphere.

3. Neighbourhood diversity will lead to more political participation, whether that diversity is in terms of the built environment (e.g., mixed use), economic stratification (Oliver, 1999) or the social/ethnic make-up of the neighborhood (Bickford, 1999). Diversity experienced at the neighborhood level will result in higher levels of acceptance for policies that address specific social and economic needs of a variety of groups.

4. Local civic engagement will be positively correlated with accepting and embracing democratic processes, while a lack of civic engagement will be negatively correlated with views of democratic processes (Hibbing & Theiss-Morse, 1998).

1.2 Social aspects of the built environment

To operationalize the causal model in diagram 1.2, we draw upon Jane Jacobs' (1961) research on neighborhood design features and Edmond Fowler's (1992) discussion of the social consequences of neighborhood planning. The following consequences are of particular interest:

1. Stimulation of intelligence. People are drawn to places that are visually interesting, that activate their mind. Monotonous, repetitive scenes dull the senses and hence, lack social activity (Jacobs, 1961). If our neighborhoods lack sufficient visual diversity, few people will choose to engage with the physical environment (e.g., go for walks, use their parks) thereby lessening opportunities to interact with people outside a friendship circle. More privatized social life is theoretically linked to less civic engagement (Putnam 1995).

2. Sense of orientation. Lynch (1961) and Nasar (1998) both found that people who live in cities lacking clear landmarks are (1) unable to remember much about the areas, and (2) have a distorted perception of areas. Most importantly, Lynch found that people who had clear images of their city were happier than people who lacked it. Theoretically, people who live in monotonous neighborhoods, lacking diverse images and landmarks, will be more dissatisfied with their city and more disaffected with [local] politics (Hibbing & Theiss-Morse, 1998).

3. Sense of personal identity. A sense of individuality is lost not only in the limited architectural styles, lot sizes, setbacks from the street of suburban housing developments but further limited by restrictive covenants typical of subdivisions (e.g., exterior decorations). The psychological impact of restricting personal identity found in workplace studies and high rise apartment living include increased neurosis, less life satisfaction, and fewer friends (Fowler, 1992). Residents of more disorderly "messy" urban neighborhoods had more "likes" over "dislikes" than residents of the clean, orderly suburban neighborhoods (Fowler, 1992). To the degree that not expressing one's personal identity publicly becomes "natural" and acceptable, people will find those places and people "not like them" more disagreeable or distasteful. Increased social distance will result in less social and political tolerance of diversity, which, theoretically, will be linked to less tolerance for democratic processes, i.e., pluralistic interests and compromise (Hibbing & Theiss-Morse, 1998).

2 RESEARCH DESIGN

The pilot research results reported here are part of a larger comparative neighborhood research plan that will collect and analyze data on the impact of varying neighborhood design, socioeconomic stratification, and racial/ethnic diversity on political participation. Using multiple data collection instruments (n=4), in a panel design, three distinct neighborhoods in Lincoln, NE, will be assessed. The three neighborhoods are (U) a traditional urban neighborhood that is economically and socially diverse; (S) a suburban neighborhood that is economically and ethni-

157

cally homogeneous (white, middle-class); and (E) a traditional urban neighborhood that is economically homogeneous (lower income) but ethnically diverse. The pilot study examines a traditional urban neighborhood (U: a mixed-use/mixed housing type, grid-style street layout), and a suburban neighborhood (S: a typical suburban residential development with a Planned Unit Development) in terms of its (I) built-environment features and (II) the residents' perceptions of the city and neighborhood.

3 COMPARISON BETWEEN URBAN AND SUBURBAN BUILT ENVIRONMENTS

Built-environment features are important for creating social interaction opportunities. At the neighborhood block level, sidewalks bring together people who do not know each other creating social interaction that would otherwise not occur. Without destinations that are easily accessible or nearby, people will not walk and the intermingling of the public will not occur. The design of houses also has social implications. Front porches, large stoops, and low wide retaining walls on the street side of buildings provide places for people to sit, watch and interact with the on-goings of street life (Freie, 1998; Jacobs, 1961; Kunstler, 1996). Decks and patios off the back of houses and backyards surrounded by privacy fences are the antithesis of neighborhood public social life. The more physical distance placed between people through deep setbacks of buildings or auto-dominating structures (attached garages, garages placed at the front of the house, wide driveways), the less opportunity people have for social interaction.

To assess the built environment features of each neighborhood, an extensive data collection instrument was developed, tested, and revised several times over the course of nine months. The resulting instrument consists of 15 specific data collection sheets ranging from macro secondary data on the neighborhood (e.g., number of housing units, population, etc.) to primary data collection of block level features (e.g., use types, street design, etc.), side by side features of a block (e.g., sidewalks; vegetation; number and types of buildings; set back of buildings; front porches, etc.), and details of specialized features (e.g., parks, schools; round-a-bouts; etc.). Table 1 reports on the built environment features of residential homes for each side of the block.

Table 1. Comparison of built environment features: urban versus suburban blocks containing residential homes

Structure and features of neighborhoods	Urban neighborhood (U)	Suburban neighborhood (S)	Statistical signif. level
# of residential homes per side of block	avg. = 4.7 units	avg. = 6.3 units	.042*
Features of residential homes per side of block:**			
livingroom window faces street	94.7%	86.7%	.158
useable front porches	86.4%	46.7%	.001
facade front porches	15.9%	56.7%	.000
garage dominating front of home	8.0%	86.7%	.000
garage behind home	56.8%	00.0	.000
detached garage	69.3%	00.0%	.000
single car driveway	85.2%	00.0%	.000
double car driveway	26.1%	93.3%	.000
triple car driveway	02.3%	36.7%	.000
driveway extends from street to front of house	38.6%	93.3%	.000
driveway extends street to along side of house	89.8%	03.3%	.000
driveway off alley or side street	52.3%	13.3%	.036
basketball hoop in front of house	27.0%	70.0%	.000
mailboxes on building	93.2%	03.3%	.000
mailboxes centralized on block	00.0%	76.7%	.000
yards open to adjacent lots	75.0%	63.3%	.050
yards closed to adjacent lots	53.4%	76.7%	.023

* ANOVA between groups means; ** Pearson's chi-square

Certain features serve to enhance social interaction opportunities (see italicized features in Table 1). Other features (not italicized) decrease social activity due to physical barriers, large distances between homes, or using publicly accessible space for the automobile. Strikingly, of the ten social enhancing features, eight are disproportionately found in Neighborhood U. In addition, all seven of the social barrier features are primarily located in Neighborhood S. In short, of the seventeen socially-related features, all but one are statistically significant and 88 percent are correctly categorized based upon the expected built environment differences of urban and suburban neighborhoods.

4 NEIGHBORHOOD PERCEPTIONS AND EXPERIENCES SURVEY

The second instrument, the Neighborhood Perceptions Survey, taps into how residents experience their neighborhood and the city. Twenty-four residents (twelve from each neighborhood) participated in the pilot study. The survey contains several different measures including resident-defined neighborhood boundaries, location of business patronage, and resident perceptions of their city as a whole as well as various identifiable segments of the city.

4.1 *Defining neighborhood boundaries*

Neighborhood boundary definitions tap into the structural design impact on residents' cognitive images of place. Theoretically, urban neighborhoods, through their small blocks, grid pattern streets and the mixed uses, offer more structural flexibility in the imaging of neighborhood boundaries. Short blocks laid out in a grid pattern are conceptually logical and provide people with many efficient ways to reach their destination within the neighborhood. When destinations are "close by," people are more likely to go to them and travel by means other than the automobile. Walking or biking creates more opportunities to interact with people in the neighborhood. Reliance upon automobiles to navigate our cities and neighborhoods reduces opportunities to practice civility with strangers. The less civil we become with strangers, the less tolerance we have for those we do not know. The political impact is profound.

Among our respondents, four distinct definitions of "neighborhood" emerged, which included: (1) the automobile neighborhood, (2) the developer's neighborhood, (3) the block size neighborhood, and (4) a variable size idiosyncratic neighborhood. Residents in Neighborhood S produced the first three patterns; Neighborhood U residents created the fourth pattern.

First, the automobile neighborhood created by residents in Neighborhood S was based upon major arterial streets. These large areas were based upon auto travel. Conceptualizing a neighborhood in terms of major street boundaries is not necessarily lacking a social dimension; however, none of these residents provided social interaction spaces or destinations as their reason for selecting the boundaries. Second, some residents in S conceptualized their neighborhood by identifying precisely the street names that bounded the subdivision. Due to limited entrances, signage, and distinct housing styles people are highly cognizant of the developer's neighborhood in which they live. Third, residents in S created block-size neighborhoods with boundaries consisting of the residents' own block or own street. Their neighborhood was based upon friendship patterns developed from living in close proximity to each other. While friendship is one measure of sense of community, it alone is inadequate for creating genuine social and civic community based on place (Fowler, 1992; Jacobs, 1961). A genuine community must contain both private (personal) and public relationships (casual face-to-face interactions) to create "authentic politics" (Fowler, 1992, p. 118) or "communal obligations" (Freie, 1998, p. 107).

Strikingly, Neighborhood U residents did not follow any of the above three patterns. These residents created idiosyncratic boundaries, all of which were larger than the block level, some of which were quite long in one direction while being narrow in another direction. Residents' comments indicate their conceptualization of neighborhood boundaries was based upon social experiences and activity destinations. Their idiosyncratic neighborhood shapes are in distinct contrast to the patterns found in Neighborhood S, all of which can be described as more or less externally and systematically imposed upon the social and psychological neighborhood experience of suburban dwellers. In the same way that suburban developments provide only a few travel routes through the neighborhood, the same built environment features (long blocks, dead ends) and use patterns (separating housing types, separating residential and business) provide only a limited number of ways to experience "neighborhood." In contrast, U's mixed-housing type does not create visual distinctions among the residential stock, the mixed use brings a variety of daily activities close to the home, and the short block, grid system streets create innumerable configurations of movement. The experience of "neighborhood" becomes diversified based upon individual patterns of behavior in a highly "flexible" built environment. Residents of the urban neighborhood have a level of attachment and understanding of their neighborhood that the suburban residents did not display.

4.2 *Business patronage in neighborhoods*

In order for an area to have a continuous social life, it must consist of more than one use. Single use areas not only under-utilize space but attract more crime. Without continuous human activity or "eyes on the street," areas of our city become places to shun. Without old buildings, the only businesses and services that can exist are those that can afford the cost of new construction. Gone will be the neighborhood bar, the corner drug store, the local butcher, the small appliance store, family-owned restaurants, and ethnic businesses. But small neighborhood businesses build community (Freie, 1998). Residents frequenting small neighborhood businesses become familiar with its employees and owners. They cross paths with other residents -- some who are friends, others who are acquaintances, most who are simply familiar faces. Such places provide public social space to sit or loiter. Without them, community lives are reduced to consumer lives -- where the totality of social interactions occur with the salesperson or the cashier.

The two neighborhoods differ in the types, variety, and quality of businesses. Typical of older neighborhoods built prior to modern zoning laws, businesses are located throughout Neighborhood U, in clusters as well as individual storefronts, in the same building or close proximity to the residential housing. Retail is housed in small to moderately sized buildings, which limits the variety of goods offered in a particular store, specialty stores in U are unique, and the stores cater to the needs of moderate and lower income households. Notably lacking in U are clothing stores, children's stores, and bookstores. Access and travel routes to businesses is highly varied via the grid system. Typical of old urban design, many of the front entrances to businesses are located directly off the sidewalk facilitating pedestrian travel and access. In contrast, commercial activities in Neighborhood S tend to be targeted at upper-middle and upper class customers. The neighborhood contains big box and chain stores typical of most suburban areas. The businesses in S and in the surrounding area are all grouped together, along wide four lane arterial roads, and sharply separated from residential areas. There are only a few travel routes for residents to access their neighborhood businesses, all of which are auto-dominating. Street sidewalks are adjacent to the parking lots, not the commercial buildings, with no pedestrian routes leading from the street sidewalk to the stores.

To examine location of business patronage, we asked residents what percentage of their patronage occurred in twelve types of businesses within their neighborhoods. After taking into account the difference in quantity, quality and variety of businesses in the two neighborhoods, it is surprising that only four of the eleven business types are patronized at significantly higher rates in Neighborhood S. Similar patronage occurred with regards to health care, even though U has fewer specialists, dedicated clinics and family practices. However, U does have a hospital and medical building, providing for more of the residents' health care needs than in S. Percent of drug stores and grocery store patronage is almost the same between the two neighborhoods, despite the fact that both the grocery store and drug store in S are much larger and newer then those in Neighborhood U. Service and retail are again almost the same despite the fact that there are far more stores in the suburban neighborhood.

Several observations can be made with respect to these patterns. People want to and do shop and use services in their own neighborhoods, if available. People will use them even if they are not the largest, or do not have the most extensive selections. At a minimum, we can assume people value convenience and their time. When stores and services are nearby and easy to reach (i.e., around the corner is literally that, not through the winding long block streets of the neighborhood), this may be as important a factor in patronage as offering many brands of any given item or having a superstore. In other words, contrary to the big box retail philosophy that dominates our new commercial districts and drives our zoning laws, successful businesses and socially thriving neighborhoods can be interspersed with each other.

4.3 *Perceptions of the city and areas of the city*

Mixed use/mixed type areas are not a form of chaos; rather, they represent complexity. Monotonous, architecturally-limited, single use areas may on the surface represent order but underneath this visual facade is a serious deep psychological disorder: they provide no grounding, no direction, no sense of place (Jacobs, 1961; Lynch, 1960). People living in homogeneous neighborhoods are barred from developing full cognitive maps of their area as it lacks the intricacies found in special places of interest, oddities, and environmental or architectural landmarks. A city of many single use areas creates in its citizens a broader sense of uncomfortableness with the diversity of city life. An inability to visualize one's neighborhood and/or city in intimate ways is linked to lower satisfaction with the city (Lynch, 1960). Lower satisfaction with one's place-based lived experiences will likely translate into lower satisfaction and more disaffection with the political structure and processes of the city.

We developed a measure to look at the resident's perceptions of their present neighborhood, their perceptions of the city as a whole, the downtown, the periphery and the suburbs. This measure was made up of twenty-nine different adjectives and phrases that the residents were asked to rate based on their existence in each area. The adjectives and phrases covered five different features: the built environment and atmosphere (e.g., vegetation, sidewalks, condition of neighborhood, safety, noise level), the social aspects (e.g., level of social interaction, friendly, interesting people), the level of diversity (e.g., ethnically, socially, economically and architecturally), mixed uses (e.g., schools, retail, restaurants, recreation), and civic engagement (e.g., civic mindedness, community pride, political activity). The final adjective list was drawn from concepts in Kunstler (1996), Jacobs (1961), and Lynch (1960).

We found suburban residents rated 83% of the variables higher in their present neighborhood (S) and in the suburbs as a whole (S-like areas). However, the opposite trend occurred with the variables for the periphery of the city, the downtown of the city, and the city as a whole -- that is, those places in the city not like the suburbs. Here the urban residents (U) rated 76% of the variables higher than did the suburban residents (S). The data indicates that residents of the suburbs are less comfortable with areas of the city not similar to their own neighborhood while residents of the urban area have a stronger emotional attachment to the city as a whole. The political implications are profound as suburbanites may be less likely to support public policies and services that benefit the entire city or populations/areas not like themselves.

5 CONCLUSION

The built-environment features of urban and suburban neighborhoods differ dramatically in terms of their social interaction opportunity features. In examining the structural components of residential single family homes, stark differences emerged. Feature after feature of suburban housing serves to isolate and privatize its residents from each other, while the opposite is true of urban homes. With regard to residents' evaluations of different areas of the city, in the levels of neighborhood business patronage and in their self-defined neighborhoods patterns, differences based upon residential area emerged. Suburban residents do not identify with their surrounding areas as much as urban residents. They do not use the businesses within their neighborhoods as much as one would expect given their quality and quantity. And perhaps most important in terms of relating to others and in terms of social cohesion, they display a lower level of comfort with the parts of the city not like their own. How these social perceptions, arising out of the ways cities structure neighborhoods, ultimately impact social capital building, civic engagement and political participation is our ultimate research interest. Based upon our pilot study, we are convinced that there are significant differences in the lived experiences of suburban and urban dwellers, and these experiences profoundly affect the social lives of their inhabitants. If Putnam (1995) is correct, we have every reason to be concerned that the necessary ingredients to creating an engaged citizenry may be seriously compromised as we lose opportunities to have diverse social experiences. To the extent that our built environments function as a barrier or a catalyst to democratic citizenship, we can no longer ignore or passively accept how our cities are changing.

REFERENCES

Appleyard, D 1981. *Livable streets*. Berkeley, California: University of California Press.

Bennett,W.L. 1998. The uncivic culture: communication, identity, and the rise of lifestyle politics. *PS: Political Science & Politics* 31:741-61.

Bickford, S 1999. Reconfiguring pluralism: identity and institutions in the inegalitarian polity. *American Journal of Political Science* 43:86-108.

Dahmann, D.C. 1985. Assessments of neighborhood quality in metropolitan america. *Urban Affairs Quarterly* 20: 511-535.

deLeon, P. 1992. The democratization of the policy sciences. *Public Administration Review* 52:125-29.

deLeon, P. 1997. *Democracy and the policy sciences*. Albany, NY: SUNY Press.

Fischer, F. 1993. Citizen participation and the democratization of policy expertise: from political theory to practical cases. *Policy Sciences* 26:165-87.

Fischer, F. 1995. *Evaluating public policy*. Chicago: Nelson/Hall Publishers.

Fowler, E.D. 1992. *Building cities that work*. Buffalo, NY: McGill-Queen's.

Freie, J.F. 1998. *Counterfeit community: the exploitation of our longings for connectedness*. Boulder, CO: Rowman and Littlefield.

Hibbing, J.R. and E. Theiss-Morse 1998. Process space and american politics: what the people want government to be. Paper presented at the annual meeting of the American Political Science Association, Boston, MA, September 3-6.

Jacobs, J. 1961. *The death and life of great american cities*. New York: Vintage Press.

Kathlene, L. J.A. Martin 1991. Enhancing citizen participation: panel designs, perspectives, and planning. *Journal of Policy Analysis and Management* 10:46-63.

Kunstler, J.H.. 1996. *Home from nowhere*. New York: Simon & Schuster.

Lipset, S.M. and W.Schneider 1987. *The confidence gap*. New York: Free Press.

Lowi, T.J. 1979. *The end of liberalism* (2nd edition). New York: W.W. Norton. & Company.

Lynch, K. 1960. *Image of the city*. Cambridge: MIT Press.

Michelson, W. 1976. *Man and his urban environment: a sociological approach*. Reading, Massachusetts: Addison-Wesley.

Nasar, J.L. 1998. *The evaluative image of the city*. Thousand Oaks, CA: Sage.

Norris, P. 1996. Does television erode social capital? A reply to Putnam. *PS: Political Science & Politics* 29:474-80.

Oliver, J.E. 1999. The effects of metropolitan economic segregation on local civic participation. *American Journal of Political Science* 43:186-212.

Putnam, R.D. 1995. Tuning in, tuning out: the strange disappearance of social capital in America. *PS: Political Science & Politics* 28:664-83

Rosener, J.B. 1978. Matching method to purpose: the challenges of planning citizen-participation activities. In S. Langton (ed), *Citizen Participation in America*. Lexington, MA: Lexington Books.

Rosenstone, S.J. and J.M. Hansen 1993. *Mobilization, participation, and democracy in America*. New York: Macmillan.

Tocqueville, A. 1956. *Democracy in America*. R.D. Heffener (ed). New York: Mentor. Two volumes, originally published in English in 1835 and 1840.

Torgerson, D. 1986. Between knowledge and politics: three faces of policy analysis. *Policy Sciences* 19:33-59.

Uslaner, E. 1995. Faith, hope and charity: social capital, trust and collective action. Paper presented at the annual meeting of the American Political Science Association, Chicago.

Urban Lifestyles: Spaces · Places · People, Benson & Roe (eds)
© 2000 Balkema, Rotterdam, ISBN 90 5809 169 4

Market-based transportation finance reform in the central Puget Sound region

R.Cipriani & M.Kitchen
Puget Sound Regional Council, Seattle, Wash., USA

ABSTRACT: The central Puget Sound region (Seattle) of Washington State has been engaged in an evaluation of transportation pricing finance mechanisms in an effort to better align the supply of infrastructure and increasing personal vehicle travel. Through a full cost accounting framework, and using the principles of benefit-cost analysis, regional policy makers have increased their awareness of the need for substantive transportation finance reform in order to help achieve the region's growth, transportation, and economic objectives. However, significant challenges, in the areas of public education, the development of better analytical tools and methods, and the provision of a broader array of transportation alternatives, remain, making the future of substantive finance reform uncertain.

1 INTRODUCTION

1.1 *Problem Statement*

Metropolitan regions throughout the United States face the converging challenges of providing for the basic mobility needs of their residents while also attempting to manage growth in personal vehicle travel. Limited public financial capacity for transportation infrastructure investment has encouraged transportation professionals and regional policy makers to begin discussing the potential benefits associated with reforming the way we pay for, and finance, transportation.

A combination of scarce public resources, difficulties associated with making large new infrastructure investments within mature urban areas, and environmental and social constraints on building new roadway facilities, require a new approach to improving transportation systems. The ecological, congestion, and public health costs of personal vehicle travel are receiving increased attention in local, national, and international transportation policy discussions, with no sign that these concerns are likely to diminish. The result is existing transportation facilities must first be managed efficiently, then new investments must demonstrate large net benefits to society, and transportation revenues must be sufficient to cover a wide range of mitigation and project costs. These objectives are furthered through a full cost accounting framework for decision-making, and marginal cost pricing of transportation facilities and services.

Today, in the central Puget Sound region (Seattle) of Washington State, the surface transportation system moves more people and more goods, to more places, in a manner that is safer, cleaner, and more convenient than ever before. Yet, considerable regional growth and development during the 1980s and 1990s has contributed to increasing demand for the use of our transportation facilities.

In 1998, citizens, businesses, and public agencies spent over $26 billion for travel on, and improvements to, the surface transportation system. (PSRC, 1996) Over the next 20 years, the region can expect to spend the equivalent of nearly $500 billion on regional mobility. Yet citizens more and more often find that existing roadways and transportation services are inadequate to meet their needs. Many citizens, as well as civic and community leaders, have been asking the question: how can so much money be spent every year, while the region continues to have so many transportation problems? In part, the answer lies in the manner by which we pay for transportation (PSRC 1999).

1.2 *Supply and Demand: Use and Financing Out of Balance*

The way we pay for transportation makes it difficult to meet growing transportation demands. Most of the public revenue sources that help pay for the transportation systems do not increase with increased system use. As the region travels more, public revenues for transportation purposes are not keeping pace with costs, leaving an aging transportation infrastructure system near capacity and with a backlog of unmet transportation needs (PSRC 1999).

The low cost of transportation at the time it is consumed sends out misleading price signals, which encourage people to "drive more," even while roadway capacity is insufficient, and revenues to increase capacity are not forthcoming. As a result, single-occupant vehicle use exceeds the capacity of many miles of roadways for several hours each day, creating current congestion levels (Schrank & Lomax, 1999).

Historically, national and metropolitan transportation policy has been focused around supply side infrastructure investments to meet travel demand (Giuliano & Wachs, 1992). Over the last couple of decades, transportation professionals have begun to question the effectiveness of merely increasing roadway capacity. The low variable costs of auto operation and the added benefit of new, unused capacity combine to attract new users to the previously constrained roadways. New and converging users lead to increased congestion as unpriced capacity is filled once again (Hansen, 1995; Noland, 1999).

Only recently, has demand management become part of the transportation policy and planning toolbox. In application, demand management practices are often used in isolation, without the benefit of supporting policies and programs (Giuliano & Wachs, 1992). When the variable costs of solo automobile travel are comparatively low, transit and ride sharing have difficulty competing. Successes in the area of water and electricity conservation have shown that managing demand requires a comprehensive set of policies that relate to both the price of supply, and satisfying demand through alternative strategies (Hanson *et al.*, 1991; Sheets & Watson, 1994).

Yet, with limited funds available to invest in regional transit services, automobile ownership often represents a necessary and large up-front cost of entering the transportation system. This means that elderly, disabled and economically disadvantaged residents in this region face significant mobility barriers. Even those lower-income members of our communities who do manage to purchase an automobile find themselves spending a higher percentage of their limited income on moving around within the region (Giuliano, 1994).

1.3 *Financing Transportation for the Future*

Market approaches to pricing the use of transportation infrastructure and services are receiving increased attention from Federal, State, and local transportation policy makers. Many states, such as Oregon, California, Florida, and Texas are currently testing the real world application of a number of use-based market financing approaches (U.S.DOT, 1998). Numerous countries, England, the Netherlands, France, Singapore, and Australia, to name a few, are increasingly relying on transportation prices based on the full marginal costs of travel (including congestion) to bring transportation supply and demand into balance (Gomez-Ibanez & Small, 1994).

Market pricing approaches are based on a sound principle that we pay for what we use. In this way market pricing can help improve equity. Pricing policies can reduce congestion on major transportation facilities and reduce vehicle emissions associated with engine starts and fuel consumption. Prices tied to use can ensure that revenues are available for maintenance, preservation, and capacity expansion when and where they are most needed. This helps service providers make rational investment decisions, while at the same time helps consumers to make rational travel decisions (Gillen, 1994). A balanced set of financing and pricing policies, combined with a balanced set of transportation investments, provide additional travel choices for individuals.

Within regions with relatively mature transportation systems, peak period demand drives the need for marginal investments in roadway infrastructure. Often, it is these peak trips that are incorrectly or non-optimally priced, and these price distortions that lead to increased cost to the region in the form of congestion delay and wasted investment resources. The decline in traditional transportation revenues and the public sector's limited ability to provide capacity investments where and when they are most needed are leading regions in the U. S. and abroad to increasingly consider various forms of variable peak period charging.

2 REGIONAL TRANSPORTATION FINANCE

2.1 *The Puget Sound Regional Council and the Metropolitan Transportation Plan*

The Regional Council is the Metropolitan Planning Organization for the central Puget Sound region (King, Kitsap, Pierce and Snohomish counties), and serves as a forum for collaborative policy development and decision-making about growth-management, transportation and economic issues that cross jurisdictional boundaries.

Guided by *VISION 2020*, the regional growth management, economic and transportation strategy, the Regional Council works to promote economic and environmental sustainability and enhance quality of life in the region. *VISION 2020* envisions economically and environmentally healthy and diverse communities framed by open space and connected by a high-quality, multi-modal transportation system. It calls for a greater focus of growth into urban centers and along transportation corridors.

The Regional Council began examining the issue of transportation finance and pricing reform while developing the region's 1995 Metropolitan Transportation Plan. The 1995 plan calls on the region to pursue a more market-based, user-oriented approach to financing the transportation system and to help balance the growth of future travel demand on the region's roadways. As a first step in examining transportation finance and pricing reform, the Regional Council created a Transportation Pricing Task Force in 1995 to contribute to public dialogue, educate and inform, and provide public and elected officials with a framework for discussion and problem solving. The Task Force agreed to prepare a series of three research papers.

The first research report, *The Costs of Transportation: Expenditures on Surface Transportation in the Central Puget Sound Region for 1995*, was published in October 1996 and updated in 1999. The second report, *The Effects of the Current Transportation Finance Structure*, examined the manner in which finance structures contribute to the supply/demand imbalance, as well as add to transportation planning and programming complexities. The third report in the series will summarize the technical analysis of broad strategic options available to help create a more stable, sufficient, and fair transportation financing and pricing structure.

2.2 *The Costs of Transportation*

In 1998, the central Puget Sound region spent over $26 billion on surface transportation (Table 1). This amount represents the total costs for transportation for over three million people living within King, Pierce, Snohomish and Kitsap counties and includes: the purchase, maintenance and operation of private vehicles; public investments in roads, ferries, and transit service; and conservative estimates of the costs of transportation-related pollution and congestion. The $26 billion spent on surface transportation is equal to one-quarter of the region's personal income. In 1998, per capita expenditures on auto ownership and operation were $5,400, and total per capita private expenditures on transportation we choose to pay for (autos, transit fares, bicycles, walking shoes, and freight costs) were over $7,600. Per capita public expenditures totaled $690. The $690 included the costs of transportation purchased from the taxes we pay, including: road building and maintenance, transit service, ferries, school bus service, and other services that support growing needs to get people and goods from place-to-place. Before it was possible to begin a discussion of finance reform, the region needed a better understanding of the full costs of transportation under the current finance structure (Green & Jones, 1994).

Table 1. The 1998 Transportation Price Tag

Expenditure	Billions $$	% of total
Private auto ownership & operation	16.3	62%
Freight (moving goods & services)	6.4	24%
Bikes, bus & ferry fares, etc.	0.2	1%
Roads, transit, ferries & other services provided with the taxes we pay	2.1	8%
Congestion/pollution	1.2	5%
Total		$26.2 billion

2.3 *The Effects of the Current Transportation Finance Structure*

The second paper provided an historical perspective on federal, state and local milestones in the evolution of the current transportation finance structure. The majority of current programs and the institutional environment surrounding transportation finance were created in the early part of this century. The current transportation finance structure no longer serves the region well in terms of either personal or freight mobility. The current structure evolved over decades in an era dedicated to significant highway expansion. The current transportation finance system contains unnecessary complexity, has too much institutional fragmentation, contains too much program rigidity, and works against regional coordination that seeks to target and fund investments where they are most needed.

A tremendous amount is being spent by individuals to gain access to the transportation system through ownership and operation of personal vehicles, but a comparatively small amount is provided to public agencies to maintain, operate and improve the transportation systems upon which vehicle travel depends. The lack of connection between use of the transportation system and the manner by which it is financed results in a considerable amount of unnecessary congestion, energy conservation and environmental costs. In essence, by sending out inappropriate pricing signals to the region's residents, individual travel behavior results in impeding the achievement of the long-term visions people have for their neighborhoods, communities and the region as a whole.

3 CURRENT RESEARCH

3.1 *Evaluation Methodology*

In November of 1999, the Transportation Pricing Task Force approved an evaluation methodology to guide the eventual development of a strategy for introducing market finance mechanisms into the regional transportation planning and financing efforts. To begin with, the evaluation framework established a set of analytical principles consistent with the general philosophy of benefit-cost analysis (Zerbe & Dively, 1994). These principles help to focus the analysis, and allow for a level comparison of policy alternatives. The principles of analysis addressed a number of questions including: (1) simplifying the analysis through minimizing the number of criteria considered; (2) paying careful attention to avoid double counting of benefits and costs; (3) discounting values to present value; (4) established an analytical perspective which considers all costs and benefits; and (5) focusing analysis on marginal changes.

3.2 *Evaluation Criteria*

Five basic criteria were agreed upon by the Task Force to evaluate which pricing approaches might provide the greatest net benefits. (1) *System Efficiency* – the degree to which the pricing alternative improves the well-being of travelers and/or reduce the amount of resources used by the transportation system; factors measured include direct costs of developing and maintaining new improvements, travel time, costs of operation for users and service providers, accident and crime risks. (2) *Secondary Efficiency* – efficiency effects that are manifested outside of the travel activity itself, such as emissions (air, water, and noise) and neighborhood externalities in the form of traffic spillover effects. (3) *Equity* – the fairness of alternatives was evaluated. Our approach was based upon a criteria referred to as the Kaldor-Hicks criteria (Zerbe & Dively, 1994). This criterion considers the effects of subtracting from an alternative's measured benefits, the cost of compensating individuals who lose out under the alternative. (4) *Technical Feasibility* – where there appeared to be serious technical limitations, the cost to overcome these limitations was estimated and included in the analysis. (5) *Public Acceptance/Political Feasibility* – public acceptance was not included in the monetized analysis described here. Rather, it seemed appropriate to evaluate public acceptance separately.

3.3 Preliminary Result of Analysis

The Regional Council's travel demand model was used to simulate the implementation of pricing policies within the region's road and transit networks. Facility-level model output data was then used as input to a benefit/cost model developed by the consulting firm ECONorthwest. The results of the application of the benefit/cost model were intended to guide discussion of the various broad market financing approaches tested: ubiquitous congestion pricing; mileage charges; fuel tax increase; charges on employee parking; and high occupancy toll lanes.

Region-wide congestion pricing yielded the greatest net benefits to society, as tested. Congestion pricing, in the form of optimal tolls on all freeways and arterial streets, resulted in significant travel time and vehicle operating cost savings for all income classes of users. High-income users realized the greatest benefits, but all income classes realized net benefits. Congestion pricing generated in excess of $8 million per average weekday, enough revenue to finance all identified regional transportation needs.

To ensure a level comparison, all other pricing policies were specified to generate equivalent revenues. By holding revenues constant, the magnitude of change for benefits and costs between alternatives could be more easily evaluated. The mileage charge and gas tax increase led to the greatest reduction in vehicle miles traveled and the highest switch from low to high occupancy travel modes for all trips, but did less to manage transportation facilities for efficient vehicle travel. Employee parking charges achieved the greatest shift from low to high-occupancy travel modes for work trips, but the freed roadway capacity was filled by non-work automobile trips. In the long run, employee-parking charges may also result in more diffuse firm locations in selected instances, contrary to regional adopted growth policies. High occupancy tolls lanes help to manage the vehicular capacity of individual facilities, but result in little measurable effect on the performance of the regional transportation system.

The table below (Table 2) shows a comparison of the three system-wide alternatives tested. Employee-parking charges and high occupancy toll lanes are place and/or facility specific, and do not cover the entire regional transportation system. These selected results clearly demonstrate that different pricing options support very different public policy interests, and suggest that reforms to the existing transportation finance system must carefully consider multiple and competing objectives.

Table 2. Selected model output for 3 pricing scenarios in the year 2020

Performance measure	Mileage charge	Gas tax	Peak pricing
	(change from unpriced base scenario)		
Vehicle miles traveled	-5.5%	-5.8%	- 2.4%
Person travel time	-6.3%	-6.7%	-31.4%
Auto operating costs	-5.5%	-5.8%	-19.6%
Transit revenues	8.1%	8.6%	33.4%
Daily net benefits (million $$)	3.4	3.6	20.6

These initial attempts to simulate pricing in the travel demand model provide some insight into the possible performance of individual market financing policies, as well as point out the complexity of conducting this sort of sophisticated technical analysis with existing planning tools.

The mode choice sub-model used in the travel demand modeling suite relinquished only small changes in choice of travel mode when pricing policies were introduced. Significant effort was put into reprogramming the mode choice sub-model to allow for the testing of pricing policies, yet it is possible that this sub-model is not very sensitive to the price of travel. Additional modeling is ongoing.

Use-based financing policies were shown to be a significant source of potential new revenues, sufficient to pay for all planned transportation investments. The generation of sizable revenues for transportation investments relates closely to issues about whether all planned investments are necessary once existing facilities are managed more efficiently. An additional question emerges relating to how revenues, other than those that are dedicated to efficient investments in transportation infrastructure, should be dispensed. Should tolls be reduced, should "excess" revenues off-set other taxes or be returned to residents of the region in some other manner (Small, 1992)?

4 LAND USE IMPLICATIONS

The passage of Washington State's Growth Management Act in 1990 was a response to a decade of unfettered urban (largely suburban) development. The problems, in the form of large-scale loss of agricultural, recreational and resource lands; overcrowded suburban schools, declining water and air quality; etc., were most visible in the rapidly growing counties surrounding Seattle. And yet, the decade that followed the adoption of the GMA brought even greater economic and demographic change than the decade before.

Nearly 10 years since its political leaders passed landmark growth management legislation, Washington State is still riding the crest of a wave of economic expansion that is the envy of a nation. Contrary to some early claims, attempting to better manage and coordinate growth in communities (the new jobs and households that follow opportunity) has not led to the stifling of the region's economic competitiveness. In truth, the current major threats to economic health (insufficient affordable housing; overtaxed transportation systems; school systems of inconsistent quality) are the products of continued rapid growth, not growth management.

Changes in land use, at the regional level, take place over long periods of time. From a transportation perspective, it is typically only the major system-wide investments, such as the Federal Interstate Highway System, or a high-capacity network of regional rail and express bus service, that provide evidence of major changes in land use or development at the regional level.

The perception of "free trips" by automobile further reinforces land uses that accommodate the automobile. As a result, the proliferation of local automobile trips creates a more hostile built environment for pedestrians and for non-automobile related uses. The devotion of parcels of land solely to automobile-related uses is further reinforced by Euclidean zoning principles that are designed to dedicate only a single use to a single parcel of land. Traditional zoning, coupled with traditional pricing mechanisms, does little to contribute to land use changes necessary to better accommodate transit and non-motorized travel.

Efficient transportation pricing, on the other hand, increases the perceived costs of travel at the point when travel decisions are made, and over time may influence the location decisions of firms and households. In total, these decisions may contribute to marginal transformations in regional urban form through the development of more highly differentiated and closely spaced centers of concentrated activity (Lee, 1999).

5 PUBLIC OPINION

In the Fall of 1999, the Puget Sound Regional Council conducted an attitudinal survey of the region to generate information that would aid the development of the 2001 update of the region's Metropolitan Transportation Plan. Areas of particular interest to the development of the 2001 plan update related to public attitudes on the financing and prioritization of transportation investments and programs.

This survey of regional households about attitudes concerning transportation issues revealed that there is a misalignment between the recognition of serious public financial shortfall, common among transportation professionals, and the broader perceptions of the general public. Over 49% of the survey respondents stated they believed that state and local governments have adequate financial resources to meet transportation needs.

A substantial number (72%) of all survey respondents agreed with the statement *"reducing congestion should be the primary goal of transportation plans"*. There appears to be public agreement that congestion is a major concern, which needs to be addressed by transportation plans. Yet a majority of the survey respondents do not agree with the statement *"building more roads will solve the region's congestion problems"*. It is possible that many respondents believe that road building is an important element of congestion reduction, but it appears that few believe that building roads will "solve" congestion.

A sizable percentage of all respondents (27%) completely disagreed with the statement *"the gas tax should be increased for highway improvements"*. Respondents who were most opposed to increasing the gas tax were, either against increasing their taxes to pay for transportation in general, or concerned that the gas tax would lead to significant new roadway investments, as opposed to investments in other types of transportation programs and services.

Less than 15% of all survey respondents agreed with the statement *"the money generated from the gas tax and vehicle licensing fees are effectively used in improving our region's transportation system"*. This response suggests there is a broad and consistent perception that government could use existing funds more efficiently, even if there is little agreement that spending should be prioritized in a manner that emphasizes road building over alternative means of improving the transportation system.

Even when believing that overall *there are adequate financial resources to meet transportation needs,* over 30% of respondents did not agree that the current *"gas tax* (the primary transportation user fee financing mechanism) *is adequate to finance transportation maintenance and improvements"*. Many of these respondents recognized that the existing road network requires continued investment to keep it operable, and for the most part did not agree with the statement *"the roads I use to travel on have already been paid for and I shouldn't have to pay more to use them"*. These responses reveal a sophisticated understanding of transportation finance issues, and yet overall, survey respondents did not agree that the gas tax should be increased for highway improvements.

6 BARRIERS TO FINANCIAL REFORM

The work of the Pricing Task Force has brought to focus a number of significant challenges, faced by transportation professionals in the central Puget Sound, as they attempt to investigate and outline market-based transportation finance reform alternatives. These challenges are not unique to the Seattle metropolitan region and must be considered and addressed by any region undertaking significant finance reform efforts.

There is a scarcity of readily available appropriate tools for conducting technical analysis. Most travel demand models need significant refinement to be useful in analyzing market finance mechanisms. The primary operating characteristic of most functioning markets, prices, are not well factored within travel demand methodologies.

There is no suitable language for addressing market finance issues in the transportation public policy arena. A reoccurring question during the course of the work of the Transportation Pricing Task Force was how analysis of transportation pricing relates to the regional economy. A benefit-cost framework, which considers all resource costs, and the values of benefits, is predominantly interested in broad economic implications. In the public policy environment, however, the term "economy" is often used to refer to a more limited set of concerns, such as freight mobility or the activities of specific high profile industries.

It is extremely difficult to identify transportation facility investments that can be avoided as a result of the more efficient management of existing transportation facilities. Without agreed upon standards for transportation needs assessment, it is likely that there will still be pressure to make inefficient transportation investments. This could negate the service delivery efficiency gains potentially realized from a more rational pricing structure.

The region has scattered land uses, and change is incremental. Greater specialization in the economy has resulted in longer and more diffuse trips. Major imbalances in the location of jobs and housing have placed even greater demands on the regional transportation system. A system of interstate highways, originally intended to link states and regions, has gradually become the primary means to move from home to work within the urban region. Since the 1970s, overall residential densities have dropped 30 percent, resulting in the consumption of land for new development growing at a much faster rate than population growth. During the 1980s, automobile travel grew almost four times as fast as population, while transit use increased only slightly. Since the 1980s, the region's growth has continued to decentralize. This is significant as suburban households make more and longer trips by automobile (PSRC, 1998).

There is no immediate fiscal crisis; things can go on much as they are for some time. The costs of doing nothing to change transportation financial management, such as ecological degradation and declining urban environments occur in the long-term and are spread broadly throughout society. These costs are not immediate or personal and can easily be ignored within a short-term decision-making processes. Often the benefits of reform are not clearly stated or fully discussed and understood.

It takes leadership: if the people will lead, the leaders will follow. Transportation finance and transportation system management are complex subjects, poorly understood by the general public and their elected policy makers. Lack of understanding, however, does not prevent the development of a broad array of strongly held convictions on these issues. Paying more for what one currently receives for less is never a popular idea. New financing strategies must clearly articulate the mobility benefits they will produce in a manner that is simple and appears "fair" to a wide variety of transportation system users. Only then can policy makers embrace reform.

7 MARKET FINANCING IN THE METROPOLITAN TRANSPORTATION PLAN

The work of the Transportation Pricing Task Force has been on a parallel track with the update of the region's Metropolitan Transportation Plan. The market financing research is intended to guide the development of long-range financing strategies that can help balance supply and demand. Given the significant challenges associated with introducing new transportation user-fees into a region unaccustomed to such mechanisms, the plan update is not expected to immediately incorporate a bold new financing direction. The plan will include principles guiding the eventual adoption of market financing, as well as a regional commitment to design and implement a pilot demonstration project to familiarize users with market approaches to paying for transportation infrastructure.

8 CONCLUSION

The work of the Puget Sound Regional Council, and its Pricing Task Force, may incrementally move regional transportation planning toward a more rational evaluation of issues related to transportation supply and demand. Yet, the challenges ahead are substantial, and may prevent major financing reform from occurring in the foreseeable future. Major efforts will need to be made in developing a language for continued discussion of market approaches to providing and managing transportation facilities. This language must capture the complexities of more formal economic analysis while speaking broadly in an understandable and appealing manner. One major step in this direction will be the agreement to continue to evaluate the full costs and benefits from transportation investment and management decisions. A systematic method of full cost accounting is the necessary framework for continued discussions of rational transportation financing, as well as system-wide needs assessment and project level evaluation. In the end, movement toward market financing of transportation investments will depend upon users' willingness to pay directly for valued transportation services, in the face of the public sector's inability to ration its increasingly limited supply of new transportation infrastructure.

REFERENCES

Gillen, D. (TRB). 1994. Peak Pricing Strategies in Transportation, Utilities, and Telecommunications: Lessons for Road Pricing. Washington D.C.: National Academy Press.

Giuliano, G. (TRB) 1994. Equity and Fairness of Congestion Pricing. Washington D.C.: National Academy Press.

Giuliano, G & Wachs, M. 1992. Managing Transportation Demand: Markets Versus Mandates. Los Angeles: Reason Foundation.

Greene, D. L. & Jones, D.W. (David L. Greene, Donald W. Jones & Mark A. Delucchi) 1997. The Full Costs and Benefits of Transportation: Conceptual and Theoretical Issues. Heidelberg: Springer-Verlag Berlin.

Greene, D. L., Donald, W. & Delucchi, M.A. 1997. The Full Costs and Benefits of Transportation: Contributions to Theory, Method and Measurement. Heidelberg: Springer-Verlag Berlin.

Gomez-Ibanez, J.. & Small, K.A. 1994. Road Pricing for Congestion Management: A Survey of International Practice. Washington D.C.: National Academy Press.

Hansen, M. 1995. Do Highways Generate Traffic? Access, no.7. Berkeley: University of California Transportation Center.

Hanson, M., Kidwell, S., Ray, D. & Stevenson, R. 1991. Electric Utility Least-Cost Planning: Making It Work within a Multiattribute Decision-Making Framework. Journal of American Planning Association, 57 (1): 34-43. Winter. Chicago: American Planning Association.

Lee, D. B. 1999. The Efficient City: Impacts of Transportation Pricing on Urban Form. Unpublished manuscript.

Noland, R. B. 1999. Relationships Between Highway Capacity and Induced Vehicle Travel. Washington D.C.: U.S. Environmental Protection Agency.

Puget Sound Regional Council 1996. The Costs of Transportation: Expenditures on Surface Transportation the Central Puget Sound Region for 1995. Seattle: Puget Sound Regional Council.

Puget Sound Regional Council, 1998. Puget Sound Trends, Number T2 (August).

Puget Sound Regional Council 1999. The Effects of the Current Transportation Finance Structure. Seattle: Puget Sound Regional Council.

Schrank, D. & Lomax, T. 1999. The 1999 Annual Mobility Report: Information for Urban America. Texas Transportation Institute & Texas A&M University.

Sheets, E. W. & Watson, R.H. 1994. Least Cost Transportation Planning: Lessons From the Northwest Power Planning Council. Seattle: University of Washington Institute of Public Policy and Management.

Small, K. A. 1992. Using the Revenues From Congestion Pricing: A Southern California Case Study. Los Angeles: Reason Foundation.

Transportation Research Board 1994. Curbing Gridlock: Peak-Period Fees To Relieve Traffic Congestion. Washington D.C.: National Academy Press.

United States Department of Transportation 1998. Reducing Traffic Congestion: Using Market Prices to Enhance Mobility. Washington D.C.: U.S.DOT.

Zerbe, R. O. & Diveley, D.D. 1994. Benefit-Cost Analysis: In Theory and Practice. New York: Harper-Collins.

Design and planning for sustainability

The practice of sustainable landscape design and its relevance to the global urban population

M. Herrmann
Leeds Metropolitan University & Surrey Institute of Art and Design, UK

ABSTRACT: The response of the design professions to the rising profile of sustainability is explored in the context of the global trend towards urbanisation. Particular reference is made to commentators and practitioners of sustainable landscape architecture, and an attempt is made to identify some of the key principles and characteristic features of a sustainable design process, and their relevance to urban populations.

1 THE URBAN CENTURY

We now have indisputable evidence of impending environmental crisis in various guises, such as climate change, loss of biodiversity, and ozone depletion. This is largely a consequence of our industrial activities over the last 200 years. We need to ask ourselves how we as designers are responding. We urgently need to consider issues such as the ways in which designers can involve their public in the decision making process, how the use of land and materials impacts on the processes of the natural world, and the extent to which 'man made' interventions can be organised so as to make a positive contribution to the present and future expectations for all living species. As Robert Thayer points out "Landscape is where the current conflict between technology and nature is most easily sensed; it is also the place where any attempt at resolution of the conflict must be tested and proven." (Thayer 1994).

As representatives of a profession that deals with the design and management of both the built and natural environment in so many ways, at every level, from strategic planning down to detailed design, landscape architects find themselves in a position of great influence. It is, after all, the landscape itself that is the physical entity connecting all activities, groups, and land uses, however diverse their interests and requirements. The significance of landscape as an experience is felt at all levels too; from the performance of practical functions through to deep psychological and spiritual meaning.

On January the first, 2000AD, we entered the 'urban century'. For the first time in history, more than half of the global population now lives in cities and towns. The UN Centre for Human Settlements estimates that within thirty years urban populations will be twice that of rural populations. What does this mean for the experience of these metropolitan inhabitants? What are the problems and opportunities presented? How should the design and planning professions respond?

Many of the 600 million urbanites of the 'developing' world live in poverty, suffering appalling levels of pollution and threats to health from inadequate provision of water, sanitation and drainage (Girardet, 1999). Even in the metropolises of the 'developed' world, quality of life is often poor, and even in the most affluent nations, urban centres continue to contain high proportions of people living in poverty and squalor. The way towards solving such complex and involved problems undoubtedly lies in a multi-disciplinary, multi-tool approach, beyond the remit of any single profession. The landscape architecture profession does however have a degree of influence on such matters, and can also, within its own sphere of influence, tackle specific, vital roles and responsibilities, contributing its own ideas and experience of practice.

2 THE ROLE OF THE DESIGN PROFESSIONS

The professions that are involved with the design, specification, and management of urban space have the responsibility of identifying ways in which we can begin to make urban life more fair, self supporting, energy and resource efficient; but also rewarding and fun. In the words of Herbert Girardet, "The cities of the 21st century are where human destiny will be played out, and where the future of the biosphere will be determined. There will be no sustainable world without sutainable cities" (Girardet, 1999). Richard Rogers reinforces this sentiment when he states that "The benefits to be derived from this approach are so great that environmental sustainability should become the guiding principle of modern urban design" (Rogers, 1997).

Over the last decade the concept of 'sustainable development' has been the touchstone of all dialogue that reflects on our common future. This new paradigm was defined by the World Commission on Environment and Development as "development that meets the needs of the present without compromising the ability of future generation to meet their own needs" (WCED, 1987). As a moral guideline it can offer deeper meaning to the work of designers, and in practice, a sustainable design approach contributes strong principles and structure to the design process. Sustainable design is here defined as 'the intentional shaping of matter to achieve a desired consequence, whilst giving due consideration to ecology, equity, economy, and ethics'. Equity refers to social justice and human rights (including the notion of inter-generational equity), economy refers to market viability and financial security, and ecology refers to the intelligent handling of environmental systems. The relationship between these issues can be represented by the 'sustainability matrix' (Figure 1), where ethical issues are seen to have a bearing on each of the three other realms. The 'target' is the central triangle, where each of the realms is considered in the context of the others. This is sometimes referred to as the 'triple bottom line'. We are thus considering an approach to design that seeks to balance these realms, weighing up the various considerations and implications, recognizing that any such balancing act will inevitably require degrees of compromise, but none the less attempting to optimize the outcome. Sustainable design can therefore be seen as an approach which, whilst driven by lofty ideals and abstract concepts, is actually manifest in pragmatic and practical detail. The degree to which it is successfully implemented must be assessed on the ground, by a range of indicators representa-

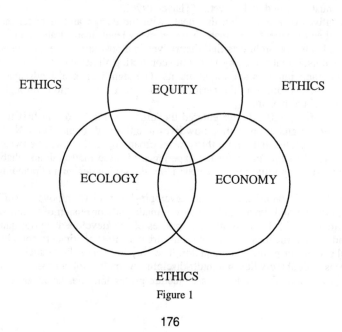

Figure 1

tive of these three spheres of interest. As William McDonough points out, "all sustainability is measured at the local level" (McDonough, 2000).

The results of a design process that operates effectively within all of these realms are likely to vary greatly. The consequential designs will necessarily be 'site specific', responding as they must to particular local conditions and requirements, accommodating negotiation with stakeholders. What then does 'sustainable landscape design' look like? How will we know it when we see it? The answer to these questions is not obvious as many of the measures by which a scheme can be judged are qualitative, and the relative significance attributed to their impact is subjective. How for example does one compare the relative impacts of a locally produced and affordable material, but which uses a non-renewable resource, with an alternative that is renewable, but requires considerable transportation? It is more useful to think of sustainability as a continuum, where absolutes become theoretical poles. This approach thus shifts the emphasis towards appraisal of the degree of sustainability of a project or proposal. This is likely to involve a judgment of relative value, perceived either in relation to other projects of comparable scale and type; or in relation to incremental (or step) improvements made within the design itself. The frequent inability of landscape architects and urban designers to have a significant influence on the social and economic spheres of the sustainability matrix should be considered when assessing the assessment tool that will be of greatest relevance to the design process. Strategic decisions regarding the location, scale, function, infrastructure, and timing of a project may be made by the client, long before the designers are appointed. Likewise, decisions regarding staffing and details of implementation and on-going management may well be beyond the influence of the designer.

3 TOOLS AND TECHNIQUES

Product design increasingly uses life cycle assessment (LCA) tools to focus attention on environmental impacts, providing data on which to base design improvements and to stake environmental claims. The architecture profession is making progress with the refinement of LCA tools such as 'Enviro', developed at the Building Research Establishment in the UK. LCA packages usually take the form of computer software specific to the analysis of embodied energy and impacts associated with design for the built environment, albeit tailored to architectural interventions, engineering, and product design. This approach is likely to become increasingly relevant to landscape architects as they become more aware of the concept of life cycle thinking, embodied energy, and environmental impacts of materials and processes. LCA tools tend to focus attention on environmental impacts, and do not currently allow a holistic approach to the sustainability matrix. For designers with concerns over issues such as the democracy, or on-going economic viability of a design solution, or its continuing relevance over time, the use of checklists and social auditing schemes and guidelines may be useful additions to their armoury. During the design process, the use of sustainability checklists can help steer attention to otherwise overlooked issues. The advantage of LCA tools is that, as they become standardized, comparisons will be possible, and there will be the potential to begin to rate projects according to their LCA performance. The long term implications of a tool that allows fair empirical comparison of the environmental performance of schemes are great, ranging from government controlled, financial incentive/disincentive schemes, through to public accountability and PR issues.

Whilst we urgently need examples of 'best practice' in order to make an apparently nebulous subject real, given the degree to which the variable factors in the sustainability matrix may influence results, the relevance of 'exemplars' of sustainable landscape design must be questioned. As sources of inspiration and as a demonstration of aspects of good and bad practice, case studies are invaluable. However, 'blueprints' for sustainable landscape design they are not. Each case will be necessarily unique, responding to site specific conditions and circumstances, each with a different 'genius loci' (sense of place) and social/cultural context. Moving away from the empirical assessment methods then, how are we to recognize the relative sustainability of a landscape design? Where will we find our 'best practice' models from which to learn? This study seeks to explore some of the characteristics of a sustainable design process. In *Gray World, Green Heart*, Robert Thayer concedes that "For now, sustainable landscape is a promising vision, which, although somewhat fuzzy, is sharpening quickly" (Thayer, 1994). What then are the hallmarks and defining characteristics that distinguish sustainable landscape design from conventional practice?

Many influential and thought provoking theories, methodologies, and tools for the delivery of sustainable design have come from the fields of architecture, product and engineering design. It is estimated that between 80 and 90 per cent of the total life cycle costs (both environmental and economic) associated with a product are committed by the final design stage (Fabricky & Blanchard, 1991; Gattenby & Foo, 1990). As the Design Council point out "Design for environmental sustainability at this point will provide substantial financial and environmental benefits further along the process" (Design Council, 1998). Although landscape architecture is a different field of design to that researched for the above statistic, it seems probable that the significance of decisions made at the design stage of a landscape will be at least as great, if not more so. This is likely given the combination of often high embodied energy, imported (or long distance transported) materials and landscape furniture, coupled with the energy and resource intensive nature of on-going management and maintenance regimes.

4 CHARACTERISTIC FEATURES OF SUSTAINABLE DESIGN

The characteristics of a future sustainable phase of human industrial activity have been defined by the architect, William McDonough and environmental chemist, Dr Michael Braungart (Braungart & McDonough, 1998). McDonough's theory involves moving to a more profound level of life cycle thinking than the 'cradle to grave' approach familiar to product designers. Instead he calls for 'cradle to cradle' thinking which considers of the possibilities for reuse, recycling, reclamation, or remanufacture at the design stage. McDonough and Braungart have thus defined the principles of 'the next industrial revolution':

- Waste equals food: closed loops whereby materials continually circulate at the end of each product life (as in natural systems). Wastes and emissions thus regenerate rather than deplete.
- Use current solar income: do not rely on the fossilized store of solar energy that fossil fuels represent, instead ensure that wherever possible the energy used for manufacture and construction is from a renewable source.
- Respect diversity: designs respect the cultural, regional, and material uniqueness of a place, flexible design, allowing for changes in the needs of people and communities.

Thayer echoes these principles (Thayer 1994), adding that sustainable landscapes will:

- Preserve and serve local human communities rather than change or destroy them
- Incorporate technologies that support the goals of sustainable design. In the sustainable landscape, technology is secondary and subservient, not primary and dominating

Sustainable landscape is defined by Thayer as "a physical place where human communities, resource uses, and the carrying capacities of supporting ecosystems can all be perpetually maintained" (Thayer, 1994). Sim Van der Ryn defines the related field of ecological design as "any form of design that minimises environmentally destructive impacts by integrating itself with living processes" (Van der Ryn, 1996). Five principles of an ecological design process are defined by these authors:

1. Solutions grow from place: designs should respond to local conditions and context
2. Ecological accounting informs design: gathering information for making design decisions in the absence of prices that accurately reflect overall ecologoical costs
3. Design with nature: allowing guidance from natural forms and processes, which are thus integrated within the design. Also, where appropriate, facilitating 'self-design' by natural systems and processes
4. Everyone is a designer: Listen to everyone in the design process, honouring the special knowledge that each person brings

5. Make nature visible: lending coherence and integrity by revealing natural forms and processes within design solutions

Despite arising from different design professions, these authors share a commonality of view. The concept of cyclical flows, as opposed to the traditional, linear movement of materials and information within the design and implementation process is a defining characteristic. Case studies of sustainable landscape design projects demonstrate several more specific requirements and common features of practice (Herrmann et al, 2000). These include:

*   The creation of a sustainability brief to guide the client, designers, suppliers, and contractors. It should be seen as an 'unfinished work' allowing the addition or update of information as new materials arise, also allowing adaptation for projects with specific needs. A sustainability brief ought to incorporate the principles of life cycle thinking, with consideration of re-use or after use of the site, products, and materials.
*   The adoption of quality control certification in environmental management systems, and a clearly defined environmental policy, with targets, ensures that high standards are maintained.
*   Access to the latest independent surveys, reports, 'green' building directories, or specialist ecological advice pertaining to the environmental credentials of materials, products, and processes.
*   Continuity of involvement, and the adoption of 'duty of care' commitments by the designers allow the adaptation and refinement of a design subsequent to implementation. By returning to a project, the designer is able to develop sensitive responses to changing conditions or unanticipated events and uses.
*   Early and effective links with stakeholders. Designers need to explain and justify the ways and means of achieving a sustainable end result to clients, community groups, and potential users. This is particularly vital in relation to the implementation and continuing cost implications. With community based projects, the creation of a sense of common ownership through early dialogue with user groups can prove to be critical to success. The apparent complexity of balancing the diverse aspects of sustainability makes the development of effective communication strategies crucial.
*   Another common feature of sustainable landscape design is the need for effective interdisciplinary and cross-disciplinary working, facilitated by good channels of communication between professions.

One of the fundamental principles of sustainable development involves the notions of self sufficiency and 'local solutions to global problems'. When translated to a model for sustainable urban settlements, this means 'closing the loops', with local production of energy and food, and disposal of 'waste'. Chinese cities still have highly intensive urban agriculture, with many cities self sufficient in food grown on adjacent land (Girardet, 1999). Perhaps it is not too far fetched to suggest that the delivery of sustainable landscape design in the future will include attention to the provision of space for the growing of vegetables and other foodstuffs, as well as for the composting, recycling and remanufacture of 'waste' materials. Energy production can be achieved locally too, with short rotation coppice for local and regional power generation, and solar, and wind energy generation schemes located at, or close by the facility requiring power. Borrowing some of the principles of permaculture, urban designers can demonstrate greater concern for energy flows within the landscape, designing with nature, capitalizing on natural forms and features (Mollison, 1990; Findlay, 1996/7). Dan Epstein, Director of Sustainability at the Earth Centre, UK, describes his experience of sustainable landscape design to be concerned primarily with low energy design, biodiversity, productivity and usability, amenity and health, and play. He believes that the focus for design guidelines should be on the careful and considered use of materials, energy, water, chemicals/pollutants, labour, maintenance, and ecological issues (Pers. Comm., 2000).

The principle of 'flexible design', that allows for adaptation to changing conditions and requirements is another implied feature. Richard Rogers and Renzo Piano referred to this principle in their design for the Pompidou Centre in Paris, "when society demands buildings capable of

179

responding to changing requirements, then we must provide flexibility and search for new forms that express beauty within adaptability" (Rogers, 1997). Kevin Lynch also referred to this issue when he talked of the requirement of public space to be responsive; both manipulable, and to be designed to allow changes to be reversible (Lynch, 1981). Carr *et al* (1992) interpret the former of these requirements to refer to the freedom of present users, whilst the latter refers to the freedom of future users, and go on to call for designers to cater for people's need to test themselves, intellectually and physically, and to allow users the opportunity to physically manipulate elements within the design, such as movable furniture or interactive sculpture (Carr *et al,* 1992). The concept of freedom as a condition of self expression and as a positive incentive to become involved with design also relates to Van der Ryn's notion that everyone is a designer. Michael Laurie (1997) points out that "just as an ecosystem embraces change and adapts according to self-sustaining process, the city must likewise change and adapt to new circumstances to remain viable". Whereas natural systems respond to ecological or physical changes, cities respond to cultural (and physical) changes. Adaptable, modifiable designs will be able to respond to altered contexts without necessitating wholesale redesign and rebuild. This is a principle that is also enshrined in the ethos of sustainable product design, aiming to cater for adaptation, modular development, and upgrade. Within architecture, Brian Edwards (1992) notes the emergence since 1992 of "new key words, health, ecology, flexibility, alongside the old ones of low energy design".

What of issues of access in the sustainability equation? At its broadest, this refers to the need to make urban public spaces relevant to local people by means of their proximity and placement in relation to people's daily lives. Thus in inner city Leeds, a toddler's playground that was located near to a popular bus stop was more often used than one located away from the parents' routine activities. Catering for the public to arrive by a variety of routes and transport types is important, whether it be by foot, horse, bus, car, train, boat, skates, or bicycle. Access issues also include the concept of 'inclusive' or 'universal' design. This means always aiming to cater for all people, whatever their particular needs (related to age, sex, race, handicap etc.), within the main design, and not as a peripheral, perhaps retrospective 'add-on'. Carr *et al* (1992) concur with this sentiment when they define three primary values of public spaces as "responsive, democratic, and meaningful" allowing the "active involvement of users with producers, designers, and managers in the creation of good, durable spaces." By catering for diversity of use, including physical activity of both a formal and informal nature, the designer can ensure that an urban landscape design has greater relevance to the potential users. As well as catering for the need of all ages to exercise, and express themselves physically, by catering for a greater number of 'niche' activities, an urban park will be more populated, and for more of the time. This brings with it a security aspect, as well as simply allowing diverse groups to coexist without friction.

Of great relevance to the swelling urban populations of the world is the role which sustainable landscape design can play through the introduction of nature to harsh city environments, a factor of particular importance for the emotional nourishment and educational experience of children. Contact with nature in the form of trees, grass, water, flowers, insects etc. is well documented for its therapeutic and calming effects (Kaplan & Kaplan, 1990; Ulrich 1979, 1984; Baines, 2000). From their extensive research into the subject, the Kaplans concluded that "When viewed as an amenity, nature may be replaced by some greater technological achievement. Viewed as an essential bond between humans and other living things, the natural environment has no substitutes" (Kaplan & Kaplan, 1989). Research evidence also supports the common sense principle that people are attracted to natural elements within cities: gardens, street trees, and other vegetation are highly valued (Francis, 1987; Spirn, 1984; Ulrich, 1979). The need for 'wilderness' areas within reach of urban centres is felt by some commentators. Tuan (1974) describes the ironic reversal of images, whereby "the wilderness stands for (ecological) order and freedom, whereas the central city is chaotic, a jungle ruled by social outcasts". Marion Shoard (1982) claims that "Wilderness does not even have to be visited for human beings to draw strength from it".

In its potential to remind us of our connection with the natural world, cycles of birth and death, and the inevitability of change, access to vegetated pockets of nature must be seen to provide a positive contribution, one that can lend coherence and order in the midst of so much urban clutter and frenetic activity. Carr *et al* concur with this sentiment when they observe that a "level of biological connection can be found in the natural cycles of life, the daily cycles reflected in the passage of hours, the cycle of seasons, and the progression of birth, aging, and death. While these can be seen directly in nature…they can also be components of public spaces making conscious the biological clock that is part of all life" (Carr *et al*, 1992). Revealing the natural forms and processes that are at work, even in the apparently 'man-made' urban streetscape is a skill of a landscape architect practising sustainable landscape design. As the work of Frank Lloyd Wright and Ian McHarg demonstrates, an urban design need not necessarily look ecological in order to communicate environmental principles to people. Michael Laurie (1997) calls for 'ecological expressionism' to emphasize a sense of place and to reveal natural processes that are at work, or that would have been, had the site not been transformed by urbanization. Mark Johnson goes further when he calls for landscape architects to "create an aesthetic that brings the natural landscape into the conventional notions of beauty in the city" and argues that a new "aesthetic that includes cultural disorder and the 'accidents' of nature can inform the public of the substance of the human condition and the significance of natural processes that modernism excluded" (Johnson, 1997).

As long ago as 1965, James Lovelock's Gaia theory (Lovelock, 1965) advocated an holistic view of the earth, rejecting a reductionist perspective that tended to bring myopic attention to environmental problems, without acknowledging the degree to which natural phenomena influence and depend on each other. Gaia theory recognizes the inter-relatedness of natural processes and systems. This principle is recognized in sustainable landscape design at various levels; Gary Lawrence, former Chief Planner in Seattle, USA, said that "we should embrace complexity" (Girardet, 1999), while Peter Thompson demonstrates a system of mixed and multi-layered planting, where plants compete with each other to create their own communities (Thompson, 1999). The provision for complexity and adaptation by natural systems is a characteristic of ecological design also described by Van der Ryn (1996).

5 LOOKING TO THE FUTURE

Why is it that most landscape architects practising in the UK today do not fully address the sustainability agenda in their everyday work? Is it because it is felt to be a labyrinthine subject of intractable complexity, leading to unavoidably unsatisfactory results? Is it because neither they, nor their clients are terribly interested? Or is it because many practitioners inevitably care for the environment, and hold a strong sense of social justice, hence feeling that they are already 'defending the green battlements'? Perhaps it is simply due to a lack of exposure to the issues, or to the available tools and techniques. It seems likely that there is a grain of truth in each one of these suggestions.

What of the future for sustainable landscape design? It must be hoped that as the concept of sustainability continues to remain on the agenda in all walks of life, landscape architects and others involved with the design, specification, and management of public space will begin to develop a deeper understanding and appreciation of the means and measures of sustainable design. Closer working relationships focused on sustainability issues, between landscape architects, engineers, and architects will play a vital role. The motivation to pursue a design process that is more concerned with achieving sustainable solutions will come from various sources, some pushing the process, others pulling. These include tighter environmental legislative controls and tax incentives, public pressure, as well as the possibility of reduced costs (both of implementation, as well as management and maintenance). Another possible incentive is the deeper sense of meaning to the work of a designer that can be felt by engaging with the issues of equity, ecology, and ethics. As they said in the 1960s, if you're not part of the solution, then you must be part of the problem. Acknowledging the relationship between the activity of design for the built environment, and the manifest environmental problems of the planet is a first step. Once this mental connection is made, the concerned professional can begin to alter their practice, and to influence the actions and intentions of clients, contractors, suppliers, and colleagues. Taking greater care in the identification of materials and products fairly produced, and sourced from sustainably managed renewable sources can be good for the morale of designers and clients alike. In an urban context of frustrated and often disenfranchised open space users, great rewards can be experienced for a design team prepared to engage in dialogue with all stake-holders; and to take positive action as a consequence of this contact. From the first hand experience of a pro-active approach to the sustainability agenda, the designer can derive a sense of deeper purpose and thus greater incentive to continue to develop the skills necessary to balance the sustainability matrix.

The effective delivery of sustainable landscape architecture depends on the successful integration of theory with practice, and the ability of practitioners to understand and prioritise the issues involved. Whilst most landscape architects may feel that they are already considering certain aspects of the sustainability agenda, few take the time and energy needed for the consideration of sustainability in all its guises. If practitioners are familiar with neither the possibilities, nor characteristics of a sustainable design process, expectations are inevitably low.

The quest for the widespread delivery of sustainable landscape design clearly requires practitioners to consider diverse issues. However, landscape architects have always needed to be skilled in the art of analyzing and balancing diverse and often conflicting interests. The challenge then is to take these skills and harness them to incorporate the sustainability agenda into the routine pattern of day to day practice. If the landscape professions are to aspire to the rigorous standards to which the construction industry is proceeding (Building Research Establishment 1998), consideration will need to given to the creation and adoption of a more formal system for assessing and raising standards of environmental performance.

Maybe as the design professions begin to learn from each other's experiences and examples of best practice we will come closer to the aspiration of Ezio Manzini for "a culture that is capable of making products generated by attention to detail, love for the life of things in their relationship with men (and women) and the environment; subtle and profound expressions of human wit, creativity, and even wisdom" (Manzini, 1990). Perhaps the final word though should go to Ian McHarg, the father of ecological design, when he points out that his seminal work, *Design with Nature* was not only an explanation, but also a command (McHarg, 1969).

REFERENCES

Baines, C. 2000. Greening the Streets of Stress City, *Green Futures*. May/June: 36, 38
Braungart, M. & McDonough, W. 1998. The Next Industrial Revolution. *The Atlantic Monthly*. October.
Building Research Establishment. 1998. BREEAM 98 for Offices, CRC
Carr *et al*. 1992. *Public Space*. Cambridge: Cambridge University Press.
Design Council 1998. *More for Less: Design for Environmental Sustainability*. London: Design Council.
Edwards, B. 1999. Eco-cool: the new aesthetic, *Building Design*. May: 12 – 13
Fabricky, W. & Blanchard, B. 1991. Life Cycle Cost and Economic Analysis. Prentice Hall
Findlay, C. 1996/7. Bio-power. *Landscape Design*. 256, December/ January, 41 – 45.
Francis, M. 1987. Some different meanings attached to a public park and community gardens. *Landscape Journal*, 6: 100 – 112.
Gattenby, D. & Foo, G. Design for X: The Key to Competitive and Profitable Markets. AT&T Technical Journal, 69(2).
Girardet, H. 1999. *Creating Sustainable Cities*. Dartington: Green Books.
Herrmann, M., Millard, A., & Royffe, C. 2000. Sustainable Landscape Design in Practice, in J. Benson & M. Roe (eds), *Landscape and Sustainability*. London: E & F.N. Spon (Routledge).
Johnson, M. 1997. Landscape Architecture and the Changing City, in G. Thompson & F. Steiner (eds), *Ecological Design and Planning*. New York: John Wiley & Sons.
Kaplan, R. & Kaplan, S. 1989. *The experience of nature – A psychological perspective*. New York: Cambridge University Press.
Kaplan, R. & Kaplan, S. 1990. Restorative Experience: The Healing Power of Nearby Nature. In M. Francis & R. Hester (eds), *The Meaning of Gardens*, pp. 238 – 243, Cambridge: MIT Press
Laurie, M. 1997. Landscape Architecture and the Changing City, In G. Thompson & F. Steiner (eds), *Ecological Design and Planning*. New York: John Wiley & Sons.
Lovelock, J. 1989. *The Ages of Gaia*. Oxford: Oxford University Press.
Lynch, K. 1981. *A Theory of Good City Form*. Cambridge: MIT Press.
Manzini, E. 1990. The New Frontiers, *Design*. September: 9
McDonough, W, 2000. University of Virginia, Institute for Sustainable Design web site, accessed 10am 15/5/2000, *Sustainability Indicators Toolkit*, http://www.virginia.edu/~sustain/piedmont/mapping.html
McHarg, I. 1969. *Design with Nature*. New York: Natural History Press

Mollison, B. 1990. *Permaculture:A Practical Guide for a Sustainable Future.* Washington D.C.: Island Press.

Rogers, R. 1997. *Cities for a small planet.* London: Faber & Faber.

Shoard, M. 1982. The lure of the moors, In J. Gold & J. Burgess (eds), *Valued Environments.* London: George Allen & Unwin Ltd.

Spirn, A. 1984. *The Granite Garden: Urban Nature and Human Design.* New York: Basic Books.

Thayer, R., Jr. 1994. *Gray world, green heart: technology, nature, and the sustainable landscape.* New York: John Wiley & Sons, Inc.

Thompson, P. 1999. Communal Living. *The Garden.* Journal of the Royal Horticultural Society. 124(1): 46 – 51

Tuan Y. 1974. *Topophilia:A Study of Environmental Perception.* Englewood Cliffs: Prentice Hall.

Ulrich, R. S. 1979. Visual Landscapes and Psychological Well being. *Landscape Research* 4: 17-19.

Ulrich, R. S., 1984. View through a window may influence recovery from surgery, *Science* 224: 420-421.

Van der Ryn, S. 1996. *Ecological Design.* Washington DC: Island Press.

World Commission on Environment and Development. 1987. *Our Common Future.* Oxford: Oxford University Press.

Urban Lifestyles: Spaces · Places · People, Benson & Roe (eds)
© 2000 Balkema, Rotterdam, ISBN 90 5809 169 4

Urban forestry landscapes – Urban lifestyles and urban living

R.W.Coles & S.C.Bussey
Urban and Community Forestry Research Network, School of Landscape, University of Central England, Birmingham, UK

ABSTRACT: We examine the usage patterns and perceptions of the public to an urban forest complex in relation to urban needs and urban lifestyles. Results point towards the high social value of urban woods as an urban support mechanism, capable of relieving the stresses of everyday life and raise some fundamental issues regarding the location, size, and structure of urban woodlands for public use. Key parameters are that woodlands should be 5 to 10 minutes walk from home – be of a suitable size to create a woodland environment – and have an open structure. Species or woodland type were not significant factors, all types of woodlands being enjoyed irrespective of woodland designation. Woodland interaction is highly personal, and is related to personal events, past and recent, where urban woodlands provide a vital release from urban life, despite some being less than 25 years old.

1 INTRODUCTION

The year 1989 saw, in the UK, the development of forestry initiatives which sought to apply forestry ideals, and, in particular, the broad environmental and recreational aspects of forestry, within urban and peri-urban situations (Countryside Commission, 1989a; 1989b; 1989c; Forestry Commission, 1989; 1991), thus realising the benefits that forestry planting and management could bring when developed close to where people live, particularly since it offers a scale of landscape which is able to compete effectively with the scale of the built form (Coles, 1985; Countryside Commission, 1989b). However, the real potential of urban forestry appears to be the way in which the urban forest landscape, and the use of its constituent woodlands, can engage the urban population as part of the process of urban living with a vital social remit. This work investigates this issue by examining the potential contribution of urban forestry to the everyday lifestyles of urban populations in the UK, using the case study area of Redditch, located in the Midlands.

Redditch is particularly suitable for study since it has a highly developed landscape structure which includes over 240 individual woodlands, all in public ownership, scattered over a 3,000ha area, differing in size, shape, location, structure and species, where the public can choose which woodlands they prefer to visit. In particular, these include woodlands which are designated for their high nature conservation value as well as plantations of broadleaves and conifers established in the 1960s. These woodlands combine to form the urban community forest which totals approximately 15% of the urban area. These are made up of three categories, Ancient Semi - Natural Woodlands inherited from Redditch's rural past and now encapsulated by the urban form, plantations established in key locations as part of the landscape development of Redditch (Winter, 1995) and roadside verges, generally narrow, but again established in key locations (Figure 1). It is the public use of the plantations and the Ancient Semi natural Woodlands which are considered in this study.

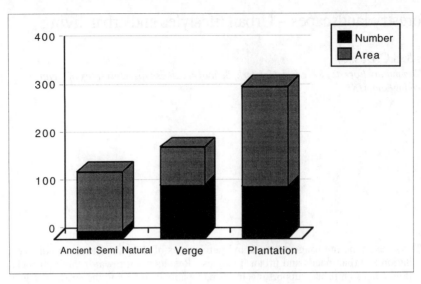

Figure 1. The overall distribution of the woodlands comprising the urban forest estate of Redditch, by area and number.

2 METHODOLOGY

Redditch was established as a case study area in 1993 (Bussey, 1996; Bussey & Coles, 1995; Coles *et al.*, 1995), its importance being that it is possible to establish, in an every day urban situation, how users interact with these woodlands, and thus to assess their significance to the users and their lifestyles. Extensive study was undertaken, initially by Bussey, yielding over 2,800 data sets which were gathered over 5 years, to analyse:

-the structure of the urban woodland estate

-patterns of use, in terms of frequency of visits, length of stay, recreational activities

-the perceptions and emotions of users of the woodlands.

Data on usage patterns, including location and user preference (Figure 2) were obtained through an initial household questionnaire survey involving 592 respondents and representing a random 20% sample of one electoral ward in the Borough, an 83% response rate. These were supplemented by additional household questionnaires of residents living adjacent to woodlands being managed by the Borough Council, a total of 832 households, with 356 forms returned, a 43% response rate. Questionnaire design included multiple choice, open ended and closed questions. and were analysed using a standard SPSS software package (Bussey, 1996).

Specific qualitative data on the woodland experience, including emotions (Figure 3) were obtained from 295 interviews undertaken in 18 selected woodlands which had already been identified from the earlier questionnaires as being popular. Interviews were held in three equal time periods from 10am to 8pm throughout the week (Bussey, 1996; Millward, 1987; Millward & Mostyn, 1989). Quotations from these interviews serve to identify the nature of the woodland experience in terms of individual personal valuations; a selection of these are reproduced to illustrate this aspect.

This information was used to identify the physical parameters and personal valuations that demonstrate the relationship between woodland and user in respect of urban living and urban lifestyles. These were further tested by using two groups consisting, respectively, of -

(a) professional rangers responsible for the woodland management (Brahnam 1995) and

(b) local users. These groups were interviewed firstly in woodlands with high nature conservation value, all being ancient semi-natural woods (Walkwood Coppice: 7.2ha, extended by broadleaved planting of 4.3ha in 1978, total area of 11.5ha, and Pitcheroak Wood: 41.5ha) and secondly, in those with low nature conservation value, all recent plantations (Compartment 2 : 4.5ha, planted in 1967, and Compartment 11: 6.2ha, planted in 1971, consisting primarily of poplars). The reaction of the two groups, professiomal and local user, were compared to obtain a valuation of the woodland structure and its management.

3 RESULTS AND DISCUSSION

3.1 Defining woods by access and location

Figure 2 shows the relationship between the frequency of woodland visits compared to their distance from the home, measured in walking time. The relationship is dramatic and demonstrates the key factor of close location in determining the popularity of a woodland. In fact access serves to set the entire context in relation to urban lifestyles, where we can usefully talk about a preferred 'home range' which can be defined in terms of a walking distance of 100 - 400m, or in terms of walking time of 5 minutes or less from the home, with a stated ideal time of 6 to 8 minutes.

These are similar findings to the results of others. For example Schroeder's (1990) study of urban forestry in Chicago, and Harrison et al (1995) in their review of accessible natural green space, who state that green spaces should be within 280m of the home. In Redditch 75% of the population lives within 275 m of a woodland (Bussey 1996). With children (under 14) the relationship is even more crucial in that 90% spend 5 minutes or less travelling to a wood, findings which support Hillman's and Matthews' studies (1988 and 1987 respectively) which suggest a distance of around 400 metres as being the actual permitted range of this age group. Walking is the most preferred means of travelling to woodlands again confirming other studies, for example, the 1993 Visitor Survey, undertaken by the Countryside Recreation Network, found that 60% of visits to forests were made on foot; in Redditch it is even higher at 83%.

3.2 Woodland Structure and Species

The factor of location, although critical, is qualified by additional factors concerning the value of the woodland walk to the user. Users do not always pick the nearest woodland to their home,

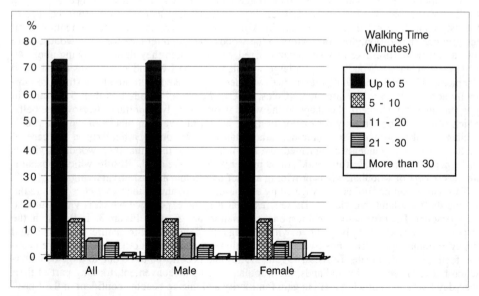

Figure 2. Actual time, in minutes, walking to urban community woods

187

to qualify woodlands need a minimum size and appropriate structure, in fact this simply reflects the quality of the experience where these parameters influence that experience.

As an example, we can look at compartment 2, a linear woodland 300m in length, but only 40m across at its widest point, totalling 4.5ha. The main species are Alder, Alnus glutinosa, Norway maple, Acer platanoides, Larch, Larix decidua, Norway Spruce, Picea abies, Corsican Pine, Pinus nigra, Oak , Quercus robur, and Ash, Fraxinus excelsior, but how does it fare in terms of use? This wood was less frequently used by the general public for recreation than other woods of similar area and level of accessibility, although it is much valued by local residents for its intrinsic value of being there (Bussey, 1996). The reasons for this appear to be that it does not provide sufficient release from urban life: "We hardly ever go for a walk in the wood at the back - its too small. It doesn't feel like a wood because you can always see the houses and hear the traffic noise."

Here is one of the most important aspects of the significance of urban woodlands to urban living, in that the most valuable urban woodlands present a refuge away from urban life and probably human (urban) activity where the woodland must be of sufficient size to ameliorate urban qualities and absorb the user. Similarly, study indicates that any feature that suggests urban activity, or unnecessary human intrusion at the expense of 'natural', dilutes the woodland experience and gives a negative response. These include rubbish, tipping, car dumping and management activities which are felt not to conform to natural, even though they may be highly conventional nature conservation practices, as the following examples demonstrate:

"This is where everyone from this area seems to bring their rubbish......we used to love to come out for a walk when we first came here, we used to constantly go through the woods, we don't now, the actual area itself has really deteriorated" (compartment 11 plantation).

"None of the trash (brash) has been removed and stands several feet high (standard management in this large Ancient Semi Natural Woodland) ....and as a result we are left with an impenetrable layer of bracken and bramble growing through the trash...." (Pitcheroak wood).

So while we can obtain data on what woods are actually used, it is, in fact, the qualitative information, compiled via interviews, that tell us about the perceptions of the user. These are crucial in understanding why they are used, and begins to identify the nature of the user valuation process in the context of urban living.

In terms of actual woodland size, data suggest that an area of around 2.0 hectares is the smallest wood that people wish to visit regularly, a figure that gains support from the recommendations of Harrison et al (1995). At this size, woodlands are attractive for recreation to all age groups. In addition, 46% of visitors to the woods state a preference for large woods, but a substantial proportion like to visit medium sized woods, which they define as being about 40 hectares (Pitcheroak Wood), in fact a large woodland for the UK, and 11 hectares (Walkwood Coppice). 15% of respondents prefer small wooded areas linked by footpaths, a structure eminently achievable in urban situations (Coles, 1992). For small woods less than 5 hectares in area (the majority studied), the shape of the wood is increasingly important. Narrow tree belts, which offer little opportunity for exploration, are less attractive than blocks of woodland of a similar size that allow for a circuitous, rather than a linear route, particularly in the case of adults. Several respondents commented that it is important to them that their woodland visit is an "experience", a "break from work", or "a proper walk for the dog". Results which substantiate the concept of woodland visits providing a relief or antidote against urban living.

This aspect can be further investigated by examining the nature of the experience in more detail via the woodland interviews. These stress that it is the experience which is vital, but also very personal. The broad emotional responses of visitors are given in Figure 3. In Redditch, the response is overwhelmingly positive with feelings of 'being close to nature' - 'relaxed' and 'happy' dominating. Such a positive response is higher than found in other studies where negative feelings can dominate (Burgess, 1995a; 1995b) and is believed to be due to the close interaction between users and woodlands, the woodlands being so convenient, forming part of their everyday lives, and allowing them to gain familiarity and thus to become confident in their use:

"I visit the wood every day. I have done ever since I was a girl. It's part of my life, I'm not afraid of being there on my own. I know all the paths and bolt holes, besides you get to know the regulars and watch out for the strangers". (Pitcheroak Wood).

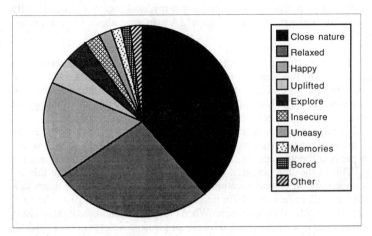

Figure 3. Emotional responses of those visiting urban community woods

In these circumstances users become very personally involved with the woodland and interpret its structure according to a personal ideal which is constructed according to need (Burgess *et al.*, 1988; Millward & Mostyn, 1989; Costa, 1993).

The importance of this experience is evident in the eloquence of the language used to describe the woodland visit. In particular, in the examples given below, notice the use of symbolism, the recalling of memories, the emphasis on the ease of access and convenience, and the contribution to well-being, all key aspects of urban lifestyles.

"I feel so fortunate to have such a wonderful place of natural beauty so close to home ...The wood is so diverse in character - like the different rooms in your house. The part that has the big oaks has the atmosphere of a cathedral. In other parts, where the honeysuckle grows, the air is heavy with its scent on a summer's evening."
(... who lives near Pitcheroak Wood)

"I usually come to the wood three times a day, to walk the dog. But it's more than that. I really love this wood. I get really excited when its time for a walk. It makes me feel wonderful. It's lovely here all the year round. In the winter when the frost is on the branches. In the spring there are bluebells everywhere - you must come back to look in the spring. And then in the autumn the leaves turn colour and fall and I kick through them like I did when I was a child." (A lady in her late forties, interviewed in Walkwood Coppice)

"I like to pop into the wood for 10 minutes or so when I get back from work. It helps me to unwind. Its very relaxing you know. Much better than just going for a walk somewhere. I've got a gate out from the garden straight into the wood, so I can go in anytime. If I don't feel like it, I can just sit in my armchair and watch the trees and birds from my lounge. It's just the job. That's why I bought this house".(Mr. ..... lives next to Walkwood Coppice)

"We really enjoy having a wood so close. We quite often go out for a walk in the evening, especially in the summer. It makes a nice walk to the pub! The wildlife that comes into the garden is great. We get all sorts of different birds and animals. We get hedgehogs come into the garden and we often hear foxes. You wouldn't think that you are in the middle of an estate with factories only a couple of yards away - It's like living in the country but with all the advantages

189

of a town. The footpaths are nice, you can go out even in the winter." (Mr. and Mrs. .... live near compartment 11, a plantation).

"I walk around this wood a lot, sometimes to meet my mates but usually on my own. I can't get a job and I'm fed up. Walking around here helps me to get my head together. I don't really do anything, I just walk around. I like the peace and quiet".(A man aged about 17 years, interviewed in Compartment 11.)

This last quote is particularly interesting; it alludes to the ability of the woodland experience to relieve the stress of modern (urban) life, presenting a completely different environment to that associated with urban development, yet this is a 24 year old mature poplar plantation established as a fast growing screen against industrial buildings, featuring tarmac footpaths and lighting and having no official conservation status, but being a true, highly valued, urban woodland.

These values expressed can appropriately be called social values. They are directly related to personal lifestyles and are constructed from an interaction between woodland and user where the woodland appears to provide the appropriate, non urban, stress releasing, environment, the antidote to urban living. This is the true potential value of urban woods. To achieve this requires specific criteria concerning woodland location, size and quality, and while users talk about 'close to nature' and 'natural', in fact this definition is largely a social construct. Accordingly, this does not require a truly natural environment. When close woodland/user interaction is achieved the woodland experience is also constructed from past pleasurable experiences, including social contact and memories. If we rely purely on conventional woodlands ideals and classifications based on nature conservation, in the context of urban woodlands, the professional definition does not recognise this interaction and is far too limiting.

This is illustrated by a couple who moved from a house near Compartment 11, the 25 year old Poplar plantation already identified, to a house by Walkwood Coppice, an ancient semi natural woodland. They compare the social value of the coppice to compartment 11-"....although its not as pretty as Walkwood, we're used to it (compartment 11) we like to see if there have been any changes....sometimes we bump into old neighbours".

Additionally, we can compare the professional valuation of the plantation adjacent to Walkwood coppice - "They're just plantations, if you ask the locals they will tell you that they are not part of the woods" (focus group woodland rangers) to the reality where this extension to the wood is highly valued by residents for its security and easy access - "I often take Murphy (the family dog) for a walk in the wood at the back of our house even if its getting dark, but there is no way I would go into the main part of the wood on my own even during the day time...you never know who might be there....it isn't safe...I remember when the trees at the back of the changing room were first planted....." (Woman using new plantations adjoining Walkwood Coppice)

Such feelings are expressed across the full range of woodlands irrespective of species or woodland designation, in particular there is no automatic preference for truly natural woodland, but there are broad general requirements regarding structure. Open structured woods or wooded natural areas are preferred by both sexes to woods with a dense canopy cover. Furthermore, those urban woods in Redditch that are little used for recreation at present, all have a very dense canopy cover in excess of 85%, findings that are consistent with those of other studies concerning preferences for woodland types (Lee, 1991; Forestry Commission, 1991; Bell, 1994). Open woodlands give a positive image, whereas, in contrast, dense gloomy woodlands can create negative images, with many places that might hide an attacker or poor sight lines which limit the view ahead and accord with Burgess's (1995a; 1995b) observations that inappropriate woodland structures can induce fear of crime. This is the "preferred structure" where an open woodland offers qualities that are unique to the woodland environment, different to other urban green spaces. Dappled shade, noise, smell, grandeur and a sense of timelessness are qualities that are closely monitored by users, as determinants for the walk and as natural signposts, important for personal confidence. Importantly, as stated, no strong preference is expressed for any particular tree species. Fast growing species, such as Poplar and Alder, are considered to be perfectly acceptable by the woodland users. Where woodland age is the only variable, the relatively young plantations are as popular as ancient semi-natural woodlands.

4 CONCLUSIONS - THE CONTRIBUTION TO URBAN LIFESTYLES

In examining the case study of Redditch, we start to get an insight into the way in which urban forestry, and its constituent urban woodlands, can form an important part of urban living, although there are specific requirements that have to be met in order to achieve a close relationship between user and woodland. Where such a relationship can be achieved then the experience is highly personal, highly valued and is eloquently expressed by users.

We need to understand that it is vital to recognise the value system used by the public, particularly the inclusion of social parameters and descriptors, that actually define woodlands as relevant to urban lifestyles and that new woodlands and existing woodlands will not become valued purely because they are natural or have a certain species mix, but because they have the ability to support social need and a personal image.

The experiences described serve to value the urban woodlands in terms of their remit as part of the urban fabric and is one that serves the various needs and aspirations of individuals as cherished areas with a "Sense of Place" (Tuan, 1977; Bachelard, 1969; Norburg-Schulz, 1979) where its meaning is constructed to conform to a personal requirement, selected and refined, according to the overall experience, upon a complex set of emotions, symbolism and memories, and that this works across a wide range of woodland types even when they are quite recent, such as compartment 11 which is only 24 years old.

There are a range of parameters that need to be fulfilled in order for woodland/user interaction to become close. Woodlands need to be located close to where people live and to have a size and structure that produces an appropriate landscape character. Small woods, less the 2ha in size, appear to suffer from too much intrusion from urban influences to achieve this, and similarly narrow linear woods are less effective. Open woodlands are preferred as creating the right image, dense woodlands are less favoured, particularly where the extent of the canopy is over 85%.

In Redditch woodland users express confidence in their woodland use, with an associated positive emotional response. This is believed to be due to the close interaction that can be obtained where woodlands are local. The positive aspects of woodland use can be easily negated by insecurity, signs of vandalism, neglect or management which does not accord with the user's required image.

Professional understanding of the potential role of urban forestry is generally concentrated on broad nature conservation aspects and tends to ignore the user based social criteria which are thought to be so important to urban lifestyles and urban living. Consequently, there is a need to be aware of professional bias in terms of woodland creation, management and classification. However, we should be confident that we can develop highly valued woodlands in a relatively short period of time, providing that we understand the relationship between urban woodland and user and that such ideals should be incorporated within urban development and redevelopment strategies where they offer a highly significant contribution to the quality of life and urban living.

REFERENCES

Bachelard, G. 1969. The poetics of place. Boston: Beacon Books.
Barnham, R. 1985. Redditch park rangers. In Coles, R.W., Bussey, S. C. & Heslegrave, W. Community Forestry in an Urban Context: 50-55. Urban and Community Forestry Research Group. Birmingham: Univ.Central England.
Bell, S. 1994. Elements of visual design in the landscape. Hants., UK: E & FN Spon Ltd.
Burgess, J. 1995a. The ambiguity of woodland landscapes. In Coles, R.W., Bussey, S. C. & Heslegrave, W. Community forestry in an urban context : 39-43. Urban and Community Forestry Research Group. Birmingham: Univ. Central England.
Burgess, J. 1995b. Growing in confidence, CCP 45. Cheltenham, UK: Countryside Commission.
Burgess, J., Harrison, C.M., & Limb 1988. People, parks and the urban green: A study of popular meanings and values for open spaces in the city. Urban Studies. 25: 455-473.
Bussey, S. C. 1996. Public use, perceptions and preferences for urban woodlands in Redditch: PhD thesis. Birmingham: Univ. Central England.

Bussey, S. C. & Coles, R. W. 1995. Recreation patterns in an urban community forest. Quarterly J. Forestry: 85 (3).

Coles, R. W. 1992. Living in a community forest. In Proc. 10th World Congress on Housing, Birmingham, 21 -25 September.

Coles, R. W. 1995. The forest concept - The forest and woodland resource. In Coles, R.W., Bussey, S. C. & Heslegrave, W. Community forestry in an urban context : 1-11. Urban and Community Forestry Research Group. Birmingham : Univ. Central England.

Coles, R. W., Bussey, S, C. & Heslegrave, W. 1995. Community forestry in an urban context. Urban and Community Forestry Research Group. Birmingham: Univ. Central England.

Countryside Commission. 1989a. A new national forest for the midlands: consultation document. CCP 228. Cheltenham: Countryside Commission.

Countryside Commission. 1989b. Forests for the community. CCP270. Cheltenham: Countryside Commission.

Countryside Commission. 1989c. A new National Forest in the midlands, CCP 278. Cheltenham: Countryside Commission.

Countryside Recreation Network News. 1994. 1993 U.K. day visits survey: vol. 2, no.1. Cardiff: University of Wales, College of Cardiff.

Forestry Commission 1989. The Forestry Commission and urban forestry. Edinburgh, Forestry Commission.

Forestry Commission 1991. Community woodland design. Farnham, Surrey: Forestry Commission Research Station.

Harrison, C., Burgess, J., Millward, A. & Dawe, G. 1995. Accessible natural greenspace in towns and cities: a review of appropriate size and distance criteria. English Nature Report No. 153. Peterborough: English Nature.

Hillman, M. 1988. Foul play for children: a price of mobility. Town and Country Planning. 56 (12).

Lee, T. 1991. Attitudes and preferences for forestry landscapes, unpublished report. Surrey, UK: University of Surrey.

Matthews, M. H. 1987. Gender, home and Environmental cognition. Transactions of the Institute of British Geographers.12: 43-56.

Millward, A 1987. Community involvement in urban nature conservation: case studies of the Urban Wildlife Group 1980 - 85, unpublished PhD thesis. Birmingham: Univ. of Aston.

Millward, A. & Mostyn, B. 1989. People and nature in cities: the social aspects of planning and managing natural parks in urban areas. Urban Wildlife Now No. 2. Peterborough: Nature Conservancy Council.

Norberg -Schulz, C. 1979. Genius loci: towards a phenomenology of architecture. New York: Rizzoli.

Schroeder, H.W. 1990. Perceptions and preferences of urban forest users. J. Arboriculture, 16 (3): 58-61.

Tuan, Yi-Fi. 1974. Space and place: the perspective of experience. London: Edward Arnold Publishers Ltd.

Winter, R. 1995. Forming the forest. In Coles, R. W., Bussey, S, C. & Heslegrave, W. 1995. Community forestry in an urban context: 12-16. Urban and Community Forestry Research Group. Birmingham: Univ.Central England, Birmingham.

Urban Lifestyles: Spaces · Places · People, Benson & Roe (eds)
© *2000 Balkema, Rotterdam, ISBN 90 5809 169 4*

Earth sheltering a positive contribution to help the greening of city environments

D.A.Woods
Witney, UK

ABSTRACT: The Earth Sheltering approach is at last beginning to start to mature in the UK. The potential of its concept is being grasped by clients, designers and forward thinking planning departments(!). The approach to problem solving is constricted by far less fixed preconceptions, the resultant designs do not make excessive demands on high technology or diminishing natural resources. The Earth Sheltering concept naturally helps to create a structure offering:-

Low energy requirements
Low maintenance
Long life
Multiple usage of land
High landscape potential which will mature both physically and visually over time

As a result there are now an increased number of non-domestic projects in the U.K. which include Visitor Centres, Museums, University facilities, Commercial premises and Office headquarters. The domestic field has increased primarily in the self-build area, but interest is actively being shown by small developers and housing associations.

NOTES: THE SITUATION

Before Man arrived or developed on the planet, Nature had developed considerably. Some creations of land failed, or were replaced by greater eruptions but, a temporary balance evolved between water, land and the atmosphere.

As all plant life forms developed, they had to be in sympathy with their local environment or fail.

As all animal life forms developed, they to had to be in sympathy with their local environment or fail.

Much of this 'life condition' still exists, albeit some plants and animals have developed ways in which they can overcome new conditions or extend the time before they face extinction.

Apart from the Barbary Ape and the Japanese Snow Monkey, the only primates ever to escape from the tropics are humans. We have successfully colonised all corners of the world by the 'simple' means of taking a personal 'tropic' with us. By swaddling our bodies with more or less insulation, we can face the worst weather conditions the globe can throw at us, for a limited time at least.

193

The trouble with clothes is that they can be heavy and cumbersome. When they are wet they become more cumbersome and insulate less well. Clothes which protect an active human may not be adequate when needing sleep. The cave became the answer.

They would operate from the mouth of the cave for much of the time but, had the advantage of being able to retreat to the comparative shelter, warmth and protection when necessary.

Leaping forward to modern times and society in the UK: Earth Sheltering has suffered from two historical attitudes, Victorian Cellars and Anderson Shelters. These have helped to create the 3D argument against Earth Sheltering i.e. Dark, Damp and Dingy.

It has taken the past 30 years for those few committed designers in the UK to overcome this standard concept. Spending time with children, students, other designers, planning departments and government representatives, the potential of the concept is at last beginning to be grasped, or at least recognised as a valuable option.

Arguments have incorporated much of the experience and work produced by Malcolm Wells from Cape Cod, U.S.A. For the last 35 years, he has progressively demonstrated the true benefits of regreening development on a significant scale in one of the World's largest land masses. He still feels that society has a long way to go (Wells, 1999).

One of his methods of demonstrating in a simple manner, which has also been a technique used by some of us in the UK, is to turn a model for a standard development scheme on its side so that all those considering a decision, are made aware of the land they are about to obliterate unsympathetically and kill. Following on from this, to do the same with a model of an Earth Sheltered scheme of similar scale needs very little explanation.

By demonstrating just one of the potential benefits of integrating buildings with the landscape, the concept of Earth Sheltering is beginning to be grasped by more designers, clients, developers and some planning developments.

We have stressed we are not trying to encourage urban development to continue its expansion into the rural scene but, that rural landscape should be greatly encouraged to regain its foothold within the urban boundaries.

The resultant designs do not make excessive demands on high technology, or more especially diminishing natural resources. They try to demonstrate how the structure reduces its demand on energy provision and maintenance, whilst at the same time giving long life, multiple use of land which will mature both physically and visually over time.

It should not be forgotten that much of our technology has been developed by understanding Nature more thoroughly but, that does not always mean that the result is the only way to proceed. Sometimes the energy demands and life cycle costings are so great that a more natural method is more appropriate.

Whilst a lot of verbal support is given to international agreements or conformities, e.g. Agenda 21, it is encouraging to find a trading country's government positively encouraging regreening of industrial, commercial and inner cities.

Thankyou Germany! We hope you generate other governments to carry out further action.

Their method is primarily by a form of taxation whereby rebates or lower rates are granted to help support more openly, research into development of regreening methods and practicable solutions.

Berlin, in recent times, has made public that they intend to introduce legislation to tax commercial developments approximately 50 m for every square metre occupied by roof area, concrete, tarmac or any other non-living materials. A tax rebate of up to 50% will be given to planting systems which are integrated as roof gardens. It may also be granted to parking areas with greater planting porous surface structures.

Is the situation finally turning for us here in the UK?

In simple terms it is, by virtue of the government issuing statements about energy conservation, which encourages regional and local authorities to produce paperwork indicating their instructions. In addition, encouragement is growing for redevelopment of inner cities and brown field sites rather than the continued expansion of boundaries for the convenience of car bound super-marketeers. Practically it is very varied in its achievements.

From an Earth Sheltered point of view, yes its acceptance is finally increasing throughout society, without it being contained with a 'sack cloth and sandal' image. More planning applications are being made and more gaining approval. More applications are in less contentious positions and an increasing number of planning officers are understanding more about the potential of Earth Sheltering rather than seeing it as a threat to their controlling power.

This year we have, what probably represents, the busiest in terms of Earth Sheltered work on site in the UK. Two major centres related to nature are close to being completed.

Eden, Nr St. Austel in Cornwall, incorporates a spectacular series of multifaceted domes together with Earth Sheltered perimeter structures. The object of the whole to produce a bio diversity of plant life by copying their required climatic conditions.

Nr. Carmarthen in South Wales. The Botanical Garden of Wales is open at the beginning of a long life internal and external garden research centre. Whilst more conventional than Eden, it does incorporate its own biomass and methane digester.

A further introduction to the construction industry this year, has been made by Corus Building Systems who have combined their KAL-ZIP aluminium standing seam roofing system with the botanical skills of the Blackdown Horticultural Consultants. The combination has produced a 'Nature Roof' system requiring low maintenance and providing a self sustaining plant community.

By so doing, additional benefits should be forthcoming, with particular regard to commercial, industrial, education, office and some housing developments.

It can assist in the removal of carbon dioxide, release of oxygen and water vapour. Locking up particulate pollution.

By moderation of urban air temperatures, they will reduce the extent of the urban 'heat island' effect and thus improve the passage of clean cool air into the city centres.

A reduction of water and speed of rainwater run off the roof by up to 80%, which being retained will be lost gradually by evaporation and plant transpiration.

Finally, the UK has an increasing interest being shown by several Housing Associations or Trusts. The significant advantage of this being that they are concerned with many inner city sites and also looking at the longer term balance or bonus that Earth Sheltering can offer.

A particular Trust is involved in a comparison exercise, where they intend to demolish a significant number of conventional flats/maisonettes. In addition to the previously voiced benefits offered by Earth Sheltering, the visual link given between greater areas of the same sites will offer a further bonus to all residents.

REFERENCES

Carpenter, P. 1994. Sod It. Coventry. Coventry University.
Wells, M. 1999. Recovering America. Singapore. Malcolm Wells.

Urban Lifestyles: Spaces · Places · People, Benson & Roe (eds)
© 2000 Balkema, Rotterdam, ISBN 90 5809 169 4

Greenways and quiet roads – Urban transport choices

J.Turner
AJT Environmental Consultants, Gosforth, Newcastle upon Tyne, UK

ABSTRACT: Greenways and Quiet Roads have been around since mankind began regular migrations and trade. These terms have become more familiar recently and have been promoted by the Countryside Agency to promote wider rural, urban fringe and urban travel choices. This paper outlines some of the work undertaken as part of a ongoing national research project into these parts of the transport network. Is there a Greenway or is this a fast disappearing eddy in the ever widening flood of the motor vehicle?

1 INTRODUCTION

Greenways and Quiet Roads have been around since mankind began regular migrations and trade. These terms have become more familiar recently and have been promoted by the Countryside Agency to promote wider rural, urban fringe and urban travel choices. This paper outlines some of the work undertaken by as part of a ongoing national research project into these parts of the transport network. The work involves network development process, physical characteristics and environmental quality assurance.

2 ANCIENT PROVENANCE

The minor country lane and Greenway (Green Lane) has an ancient provenance. Like the cabbage which developed its dense texture and perfect form by careful selection and breeding, the early country routes were honed and developed by human colonisation into dense networks.

Today these networks are severed from their communities of users by perceptions of fear, real lack of physical connection, poor continuity and by inertia of users.

3 WHO DESIGNED THEM?

G.K. Chesterton had an idea that expresses the form of the network:

> *Before the Roman came to Rye*
> *or out of Severn strode,*
> *the rolling English drunkard*
> *made the rolling English road*

The first parts of the transport network like the Ridgeway or Icknield Way, developed as humans colonised the land as the ice sheets retreated some 10 - 15000 years ago. Defensive positions and other settlements became transport nodes like Uffington Castle or Maiden Castle. The

Romans imposed and integrated their military and civilian networks within this existing network.

Land holding changes and the process of enclosing open fields changed the nature of the network in many areas of the country. In the18th and 19th century canal, tramway, railway and road construction created new nodes and interactions with this ancient network.

4 QUIET ROADS AND GREENWAYS TODAY

The road network is well known today - Motorway, A-Roads, B-Roads, C-Roads. Unclassified rat runs and thousands of kilometres of unclassified roads. These remaining rural and urban fringe networks from a mix of provenances are intact and extensive.

5 WHAT ARE GREENWAYS AND QUIET ROADS?

The minor unclassified road network and public rights of way have been identified by the Countryside Agency within their Greenways and Quiet Roads Initiative as a valuable transport and environmental resource. Our research in over ten Demonstration Areas has investigated whether networks that include these elements can provide increased facilities for walking, cycling and horse riding, sharing the road and enjoying their journey without domination by motor vehicles.

Greenways and Quiet Roads Allow Vulnerable Users and Vehicle Drivers to Identify Attractive networks on which they can Travel with no or Low Volumes of motorised Traffic Travelling At Speeds That Are Not Threatening

Quiet Roads and Greenways are :

5.1 *Distinctive*

Reflecting the date, materials and purpose for which they were first created. A distinctive part of the landscape character.

5.2 *Diverse*

The nature of the rural network is diverse, reflecting the topography, purpose and land uses in and for which they were created.

5.3 *Useful*

Quiet Roads provide access for homes, schools, businesses, local residents and for all manner of other journey purposes.

5.4 *Necessary*

Often this network is the only access to homes, businesses and other destinations.

5.5 *Dense*

The network permeates vast tracts of the countryside, urban areas and urban fringes, linking other transport modes and a wide variety of local journey origins and destinations.

5.6 *Heritage*

Ancient lanes and Greenways are some of the most important historical, ecological, access and landscape features.

There is already use of these networks in places for non-motorised access and there is significant latent demand to utilise it further. Recent studies for the Countryside Agency suggest up to 30% of users would use non- motorised transport on these networks if origins and destinations were better connected and coherent. Busy roads are the usual forms of severance and deterrent.

6 DOES THE MINOR ROAD AND GREENWAY NETWORK REQUIRE ANY SPECIAL MANAGEMENT?

Given that this network has lasted hundreds, and in many areas, thousands of years, is neglect the best form of management? Whilst the network is in places intact current and predicted motorised traffic growth trends, development pressures and rural landuse pattern changes pose significant threats to this national network.

Urban and rural development and motorised traffic growth, larger HGV and farm vehicle access have and will continue to quietly destroy this important and useful heritage. Hedgerow, wall and other boundary erosion and neglect can largely remove the value and quality of this network.

In the Quiet Road pilot in Norfolk, it was discovered through monitoring that these lanes were well used by disabled users. If inclusive access is to be maintained, non motorised use promoted and the heritage and living landscape value of these networks maintained, special management is required.

7 QUIET ROAD AND GREENWAY NATIONAL DEMONSTRATION AREAS

7.1 Design

Current authorised signage and much of the footway conversion work is not acceptable to promote use or as treatment on historic features. It is a bit like the installation of cheap UPVC double glazing in a Grade 1 listed building.

Early work on design, such as Underloughrigg in Ambleside, Cumbria, is more sensitive but still produces an urbanising effect that damages the distinctiveness of the lane and landscape. The National Cycle Network and conversion of the former waggon way network in the North East of England has shown that routes will be well used. However many of the traffic management measures such as Gateway features at villages such as London Colney in Hertfordshire and in West Sussex seem to serve little function and add nothing to the quality of the landscape.

7.2 The Design Process

In order that the heritage and other value of these networks can be enhanced and conserved we have developed a process with the acronym PACE. This is an essential methodology to developing non-motorised networks in England and can be viewed on the Countryside Agency website along with other technical information.

7.3 Design Measures

The whole process for the Countryside Agency National Demonstrations has focussed on public involvement with the understanding and positive influence on attitude and behaviour.

7.3.1 Signage

A new authorised traffic sign has been developed with the DETR which has enabled the pilot networks of Quiet Roads to be identified. Similar signage is being trialed to establish whether it is the best form of network information provision to promote inclusive access.

7.3.2 Entry Treatments to Quiet Road Networks

Subtle entry treatments, such as tree planting and changes in verge management, have been pioneered. In many lanes entry treatments have been considered not to be required.

- Some peripheral traffic calming has been considered to re-connect the lanes directly with settlements.
- A route hierarchy and wider traffic management strategy has to be an integrated part of the development of Quiet Roads.
- Integration to other transport modes is vital.
- A user Code of Conduct "Share With Care" is being developed with the Demonstrations and National User Groups.
- An information plan to handle the press and deliver information on the network to existing and potential non-motorised users is essential.
- Public consultation and developing a process for continued public executive involvement is necessary.

7.4 Actual Design Treatment

On many parts of the network in the National Demonstration Areas the design treatment of Quiet Roads and Greenways should be nil. In other areas new routes and radical legal and physical changes may be necessary. However, a careful management trialing with landowners and the highway authority will be a necessary component to maintain and manage landscape quality and change.

The example of Greensand Ridge in Kent illustrates the sort of change that the management of the Quiet Road network in the national Demonstration pilot areas is trying to achieve. No change. For many parts of the network no change at all is appropriate and for the rest suitable, sensitive enhancement.

8 CONCLUSION

So with apologies to Masefield . . . .

> My Quiet Road and Greenway calls me, lures me
> West, east, south and north.
> Leaving my car still standing
> as my own power leads me forth.

In the effort to conserve our landscape heritage and encourage non-motorised use, developing provision seen in parts of England is highly damaging to non-motorised use and must be in part responsible for the decline in walking, cycling and horse riding.

The Country Lane and Greenway network has an important transport role to continue to play. The Countryside Agency have shown in this vision of a network that provides wide choice of routes harnessed to provide attractive transport links as part of a more sustainable way of living. Before they become the Dodo of the transport network we should realise the value of our rural and urban fringe Quiet Road and Greenway network by re-connecting them to as many origins and destinations as possible to maintain and enhance their transport and landscape contribution.

If we do not do more to develop these networks many potential benefits will be lost resulting in degraded health, urban lifestyles and environmental quality. More a blackway than a green.

Urban Lifestyles: Spaces · Places · People, Benson & Roe (eds)
© *2000 Balkema, Rotterdam, ISBN 90 5809 169 4*

Locating sustainability: Competing visions of urban technology

G. Farmer & S. Guy
University of Newcastle, Newcastle upon Tyne, UK

ABSTRACT: The recently published Final Report of the Urban Task Force, *Towards an Urban Rennaissance* promotes a vision of the sustainable city framed in the largely physical and formal terms of compaction and intensification of urban structures. The report also suggests that to ensure sustainable urban development, the individual buildings that inhabit this urban structure should be designed to be long life, loose fit and energy efficient. This paper, written by an architect and a sociologist explores this overlapping relationship between urban form and technology by linking concerns for the sustainable city at a macro level to diverse debates about appropriate technologies at an individual building level. In doing so the paper problematises a singular vision of the sustainable city and suggests a number of competing pathways towards sustainable design, thereby highlighting a possible diversity of sustainable urban futures.

1 INTRODUCTION

This paper reflects on some of the conceptual challenges for policy makers as they strive to achieve the objective of building a sustainable urban future. Our approach draws upon our involvement in a number of sustainable-cities research projects (Guy & Marvin, 2000) and in particular from research into the development of 'green' or sustainable buildings (Guy & Farmer, 2000, 2001). We do not intend to critique or promote any one model of sustainable building or the sustainable city. Instead, we want to enlarge the concept of the sustainable city by suggesting a more complex and contextual understanding of the development of sustainable buildings. In particular, we begin to acknowledge the heterogeneity of design approaches that often coexist within a single city (Guy & Marvin, 1999). There are three stages to our argument. First is the need to shift from a singular model of urban sustainability towards the recognition of multiple models of what the sustainable city might become. Here, our own research on green buildings has suggested a possible multiplicity of environmental innovations that could each make a quite distinctive contribution towards the development of more sustainable futures. The paper highlights three recently completed commercial office buildings in the North-East region of England each of which embody a contrasting and particular sustainable building design response to three very different urban locations. Second is the rejection of simplistic models of the sustainable city, and the recognition of competing pathways towards sustainability. By adopting an interpretive framework we can begin to view different models not as blueprints for sustainable buildings or cities, but as a lens through which we can begin to understand competing visions of the sustainable city. This approach emphasises the development of a contextual understanding of urban sustainability that links a diversity of appropriate technological pathways to particular local contexts. Third, is the recognition that a wide variety of sustainable urban futures are likely to co-exist within a single city. The challenge here is to examine the tensions and similarities between these pathways; in particular, focusing on the widely differing motivations and competing social commitments of the actors involved in the design and development process.

2 MODELLING THE SUSTAINABILE CITY

Much of the recent sustainable-cities literature appears to be underpinned by the assumption that a single desirable sustainable city can be pre-defined. The dominant emphasis is placed on the achievement of sustainability through one model – compact urban form which is often presented as "today's visionary solution", and is hurriedly adopted by academics and politicians as an "all-embracing panacea of urban ills" (Fulford, 1996). For example, the recently published Final Report of the Urban Task Force 'Towards an Urban Rennaissance' promotes a vision of the sustainable city framed in the largely physical and formal terms of compaction and intensification of urban structures. Here it is claimed that: "Increasing the intensity of activities and people within an area is central to the idea of creating sustainable neighbourhoods" (DETR, 1999). It is assumed that higher densities will inevitably result in "reducing the need for the car" and thereby "contributing to urban sustainablity"(DETR, 1999). In highlighting the individual buildings that might inhabit the compact city the report suggests that they should be designed to be "long life, loose fit, and energy efficient" (DETR, 1999). In the case of building technologies, this is to be achieved through the introduction of new innovations in mass production, renewable energies, passive solar design and district heat and power generation. The environmental benefits of compact settlement patterns are assumed to be the minimisation of energy consumption due to increased building densities, resulting in reduced heat losses and making district power generation feasible. The "big idea" (Breheny, 1996) of compaction and intensification has received such wide support to the extent that it "seems inconceivable that anyone would oppose the current tide of opinion towards promoting greater sustainable development and the compact city in particular" (Smyth, 1996). In this context, it is not surprising that the "move towards the compact city is now entrenched in policy through Europe" (Jenks *et al*, 1996).

However, our research would suggest that maybe too much faith is being placed in the physical powers of land-use planning, building design, conservation and ecology. While we would not discount the importance of physically re-ordering the city in order to achieve environmental benefits, we are concerned that the narrow search for a universal model of sustainable urban form can blind us to the multiplicity of design innovations that could make a contribution towards the development of sustainable urban futures. In our previous work on sustainable buildings we have explored the complex social and technical processes involved in the development of different approaches to environmental innovation. Here we identified multiple models of sustainable building, all embodying quite different assumptions about the form, design and development of future buildings. This work has enabled us to recognise the emergence and coexistence of a variety of environmental logics, each with the potential to reshape cities in a myriad of ways, some overlapping some conflicting. In particular, we can identify a wide range of environmental innovations, or models of appropriate design including; commercially driven smart technologies, community inspired participatory design, through to recycled and autonomous buildings. Each of these models or logics of innovation prioritise differing aspects of the sustainability agenda ranging across ecological, technological, aesthetic, health and community issues. This would suggest that design and development actors do not simply pick up on and implement a pre-defined notion of environmentalism. Instead, the notion of the 'environment' has been broken up and re-interpreted by real estate actors as they pursue new property strategies; "Green real estate development has more than a single face. For one project, the most visible 'green' feature might be energy performance; for another, restoration of eco-systems; for yet another, the fostering of community cohesion and reduced dependence on the automobile"(Wilson, 1998).

Thinking about environmental innovation in this way, we must become sensitive to range of possible logic's of innovation which may surface in new buildings, and locate these design logic's in particular contexts of local, regional and national development. In the next section we explore three alternative models of sustainability by examining three recent building developments in the North-East of England.

3 MULTIPLE MODELS: THREE BUILDING CASE STUDIES

The buildings we have chosen to highlight are; the Groundwork Trust Eco-centre in South Tyneside, the Solar Office at Doxford Business Park, Sunderland and the Central Square development in Newcastle. Before describing the three case studies it is necessary to explain why we have selected these particular examples. First, we have chosen the same building type in the same regional context; each is a commercial office building located in the North-East of England. The buildings do, however, occupy three very different urban locations, sites within the city centre, the city periphery and city edge. Second, each of the buildings embodies a contrasting and particular building design response to these three very different urban locations and each has been, in its own right, portrayed or promoted as an exemplary example of sustainable construction.

3.1 *The Groundwork Eco Centre, South Tyneside (see http://www.projects.co.uk/prop-north)*

Groundwork Trust's 'Eco-Centre' in Jarrow, South Tyneside is conceived both as a demonstration facility and as a working office, providing space for commercial rent. The centre has won the British Royal Institute of Chartered Surveyors (RICS) 1997 'Efficient Building of the Year' and was a finalist in the 1998 Green Building Award competition organized by the British Heating and Ventilating Contractors' Association (HVCA) and the British Independent on Sunday newspaper. The Eco-Centre is located in an urban regeneration area on the south bank of the River Tyne in Hebburn, South Tyneside. It is located on the Viking Business Park, a former industrial area of South Tyneside that has been in decline since the closure of its shipbuilding and heavy engineering activities. It is situated within an urban regeneration area enabling the project to receive funding from the Tyne and Wear Development Corporation. In selecting the site it had to be in South Tyneside for the Managing Director to meet his charitable objectives. Furthermore and most importantly the client and the architect ideally wanted to locate the Centre not more than five minutes walk from the nearest station on the Tyne and Wear Metro rapid transit system and a major bus route (interview).

In the design process both the client and the architect shared a vision of a totally autonomous office building. The aim was to design and construct a building that could generate all its own electricity, provide all its own water and dispose of all its own waste, an exercise in urban autarky. As the architect states: 'the project is about constructing a building whose self-reliance can make a positive contribution to the environment' (interview). The original conception was of a building that did not have to rely on the external infrastructure services - a building that could be totally disconnected from the mains infrastructure networks, thereby not contributing to the sum growth of infrastructure demand. The 1400m^2 two storey building generates it's own power from an on-site 80KW wind turbine, its coastal / riverside site is an exposed location providing the necessary wind speeds for on-site wind power generation. To incorporate the wind turbine the eco-Centre not only had to be located in an area with a good wind regime but it had to be located at least 200 meters from any housing so that noise disturbance to local residents would be minimal (interview). The site enables good borehole access to provide the building with on-site water that is used for the building's non-potable water supply. A heat pump extracts low-grade heat from the groundwater to supply underfloor heating circuits. The open nature of the site means that the building has good solar access with no overshadowing problems allowing a passive solar and daylighting strategy. Energy use is minimised through high levels of insulation and through building form and planning. The context has allowed freedom in both the form and orientation of the building. The triangular form of the building encloses a central atrium, this form optimises daylight from the east and west and helps to reduce unwanted solar gains from the south in summer. The site has few noise or air quality problems and this facilitates the use of a natural ventilation strategy. The ventilation strategy utilises the central atrium to draw air from perimeter opening windows in the office spaces by a combination of convection (the stack effect) and wind pressure differences, made possible by the fairly predictable wind patterns of the site and its exposed nature. Occupants are free to open windows and a training program is established so that all users understand the part they play in making the building work (interview with Director). All this means that the building's energy target is set at 75 kWh/m^2/yr. as compared to 130 kWh/m^2/yr. for typical non-air conditioned offices (Bunn &

Ruyssevelt, 1996). There are similar innovations in the handling of waste. All human sewage is digested on-site via three Clivus composters and a holding tank in the basement of the building. The resulting brew will be used as compost, restoring fertility and helping to recreate land-scaped gardens on the surrounding ground rendered toxic by mine waste. Water demand in the building is also minimized via the use of water saving technologies such as low flush toilets supplied by rainwater collected from the roof, this also houses solar thermal panels to provide hot water. As far as possible, all the materials used in construction are of sound environmental pedigree. For example, the building is constructed using a timber frame clad with second hand bricks; the roof is made of recycled aluminium and all timber is from sustainable sources, there is almost no use of toxic paints, glues or varnishes. The external paving slabs are recycled from Gateshead Metrocentre; the car park is made from recycled road surfacing from the streets of Newcastle; and three defunct railway lines from the local transport system, Tyne and Wear metro, form a central column supporting the roof.

3.2 *The Solar Office, Doxford Park, Sunderland (see http://www.akeker.co.uk)*

The Solar office is a 4600m^2 speculative office development built by Doxford International, an Akeler Group Company, as part of Phase 6 of the 32 hectare Doxford International Business Park Development. The site is located by the A19 on the outskirts of Sunderland and in the heart of Sunderland's Enterprise Zone. Akeler promote themselves as a company that "believes strongly in environmental construction" (Winter, 1998) and all of the buildings for Doxford have achieved either 'excellent' or 'very good' BREEAM ratings, the Solar office has itself been rated 'excellent'. In describing their approach to development, Akeler state that: "Build-ings which are not energy efficient will be increasingly expensive to occupy. In our buildings we use natural resources – the sun, the wind and the earth's constant cool temperature to pro-duce and save energy. We employ ventilation techniques used for hundreds of years in tropical climates, just adding today's technology to make them more efficient and easy to use" (http://www.akeler.co.uk). In describing the building the developer has stated their ambition to create a "forward looking" building (Evans, 1997). The project architects Studio E are a practice with a reputation for low energy design and they became involved in the project when they vis-ited the park as assessors for the Green Building of the Year Award. The building has been widely published as an exemplary example of low energy and sustainable design. According to the architects the Solar Office, through its incorporation of photovoltaics is "making the leap from building-as-consumer to the building as consumer-and provider" (Lloyd Jones, 1998).

The most dominant feature of the three-storey building is its high-tech 66m long south eleva-tion that "boasts Europe's largest integrated photovoltaic façade" (Pearson, 1998). This 532m^2 photovoltaic array is also the first application of the technology to a speculative office building (Evans, 1997). The location of the building within an Enterprise Zone meant that the cost of the low energy features, most notably the photovoltaic installation was provided by a grant of £1.5 million from the European Regional Development Fund. Additional funds of around £150,000 were also provided by the DETR for design development and monitoring studies. The photo-voltaic panels, imported from Germany, provide between a quarter and a third of the building's electricity demand (Evans, 1997). Any surplus energy is exported back to the grid. The photo-voltaic installation placed several constraints on the design, the building needed an unobstructed southerley aspect made possible by the open layout of the site and the pv wall has been inclined at 60° to the horizontal to maximise solar radiation and to reduce problems of glare for the driv-ers on the nearby A19 road. According to the architect "the building is in a business park with an established architectural language. We were asked to follow it, but the demands of a large photovoltaic array meant that, in certain areas we had to break away" (MacInnes, 1999). The building incorporates other low energy measures. Its 'V' shaped plan has two wings of 15m wide offices separated by an atrium, this allows good daylighting and the use of natural ventila-tion, the exposed nature of the site assists the natural ventilation strategy. A full-length rooftop trough together with eight wind baffles creates a negative pressure regardless of wind direction and draws air from the perimeter opening windows through the office spaces. The incorporation of exposed thermal mass in the ceilings assists in moderating internal air temperatures and the need for mechanical cooling. The building has been insulated to normal standards but has tightly sealed construction to reduce infiltration heat losses. Taken together, the target energy consumption for the building when occupied by a tenant with conventional power requirements is 85kWh/m^2/year (Winter, 1998). However, the building has been constructed in shell-and-core form only and allows the flexibility for tenants to incorporate a mechanical displacement ventilation system or even air conditioning. The overall performance of the building will therefore depend heavily on the tenant's choice of building service installation and the way in which they choose to use the building.

3.3 *Central Square Offices, Newcastle upon Tyne (see http://www.centralsquare.co.uk)*

The Central Square offices are a 7000m^2 speculative office development capable of accomodating multiple tenancy. It has been built by Parabola Estates, a Newcastle based Development Company. The building is located on a city-centre site in an area bounded by Newcastle's Central Station and the northern bank of the River Tyne. Accessibility is a key part of the buildings marketing strategy. The site is located immediately adjacent to Newcastle's main transport hub of Central Station with good access to rail, Metro (light transport system), bus and road links. The building also provides extensive facilities for cyclists in its basement car park. This 'brownfield' area has previously been occupied by a mixture of light industrial uses and the offices are the first stage in the redevelopment of the area which will include a mixture of uses, commercial, retail and residential. It is described by the developer as "the most exciting area of change in central Newcastle" (http://www.centralsquare.co.uk). The client and design team's ambition for the building was to "create a landmark building of exceptional quality" and "to create a building that could be distinguished from the norm by being environmentally aware in its approach"(http://www.centralsquare.co.uk). The building has been rated 'excellent' through the BREEAM accreditation scheme.

The five-storey building is a refurbishment of the old Orchard Street Post Office Sorting Centre, built in 1934. An additional floor with glass curtain wall construction has been added to the original building which is a steel frame / concrete construction with solid brick walls. As far as possible the original form of the building has been left intact with a 'U' shaped arrangement of office spaces enclosing a central atrium roofed with a tented PTFE translucent membrane structure. The key aspect of the building's environmental approach has been the pragmatic use of the original construction. Retaining as much as possible of the original building has meant that the use of new materials has been kept to a minimum. Where repairs were necessary to the original external facades, materials from an adjacent demolition site have been recycled and used. Where new materials have been used attention has been paid to address their environmental profile, for example by using steel rather than aluminium framed windows and specifying timber from renewable sources. The original building has been utilised as part of the building's low energy strategy. The generous floor to ceiling height increases daylight penetration into the plan and helps to reduce overheating in the occupied zone. The heavyweight construction of the original reinforced concrete floors has been left exposed and the thermal mass helps to moderate internal temperature swings. The positioning of the office spaces in the north, east and west of the building and the extensive use of solar control glazing helps to further reduce the risk of potential overheating problems. Unlike, the two buildings previously described the Central Square offices have not been designed to incorporate natural ventilation, except in the atrium space. The building service engineer was concerned that this would be a "risky' strategy" (interview) in this location where air quality and noise pollution might be significant factors. Instead they proposed a low energy mechanical displacement system with comfort cooling. Displacement ventilation is provided throughout the office spaces via grilles located in a raised floor system. Fresh air is supplied to the floor void by fabric textile ducts. Air entering the basement air handling units is pre-cooled naturally as it is ducted to the plantroom (9m underground) and the large thermal mass of the thick concrete sub-basement provides further pre-cooling, this can represent up to 4°C free-cooling in the office spaces (interview). Energy efficient condensing boilers provide heating and underfloor perimeter convectors supply the office perimeter zones. Comfort cooling is provided by air-cooled refrigeration units, which use refrigerants without any ozone depletion potential. When taken together these measures mean that the building's target energy consumption is set at 180kWh/m^2/year (interview) compared to good practice for an air-conditioned office of 225kWh/m^2/year.

Having described the three buildings above, it is important to be clear about how they should be interpreted. First, in highlighting these particular examples we are not suggesting they represent the 'ideal' or the only models of sustainable building, there are a whole range of possible sustainable design approaches that might exist beyond those described. Second, we are not questioning the relative merits of each approach or disputing that each is a commendable example of sustainable design. Each can be understood to make a contribution to reducing the environmental impact of development across a number of 'best practice' performance indicators, energy efficiency, non-renewable resource use, occupant health, ecology, environmental footprint, pollution, etc. However, it is our argument that a commitment to undertanding buildings and cities solely through a quantatative physical performance model can serve to limit our understanding of sustainability to the relative efficacy of different models or particular technologies. Third, rather than viewing the case studies as differing approaches to a pre-defined and homogenous definition of sustainability we suggest an alternative interpretive understanding that recognises the contrasting visions or competing pathways employed by development actors, each "pathway embodies quite different assumptions about the form, design and development of future cities"(Guy & Marvin, 1999). Seen in this way, what the case studies do highlight is that for particular sustainability issues there are likely to be to be different strategies or pathways that co-exist, supported by different coalitions of actors in response to a particular development context. Here, "the notion of a set of best practices is simply too narrow and static"and "instead a notion of competing environmental logic's is required to acknowledge the variety of pathways of innovation in turn reflecting the diverse context of environmental action" (Guy & Marvin, 1999). In comparing the three buildings we can apply the methodology of competing design "logic's" developed in our previous work to give a 'window' through which it is possible to identify the strategic priorities and differing forms of environmental value implicit in each approach. Looking back at the buildings we can begin to locate different and contrasting approaches to sustainability each informing a particular attitude to cities, infrastructure provision and the definition of appropriate technologies.

The Groundwork Trust building draws on an eco-centric attitude to sustainability. Here, the overall aim was to produce a building with a radically reduced ecological footprint in comparison to a conventional office building. To achieve this aim the holistic design strategy revolves around relatively small scale, de-centralised and autonomous techniques. An overriding emphasis has been placed on reducing or severing dependancy on centralised infrastructure services of water, energy and waste. This has resulted in the application of a hybrid mixture of low and high technologies combined with the incorporation of recycled, renewable, natural and where possible local materials. In relation to location we can identify an ambiguous attitude to the city. Whilst there is a concern for accessing public transport links, the city periphery site was selected primarily for its physical characteristics, a key factor in achieving self-reliance. Here, we can identify a vision of the city made up of independent, dispersed and sovereign buildings, each self-sustaining and free from the constraints of existing infrastructure.

In contrast, the Solar Office at Doxford represents a very different attitude to sustainability. Analysing the building we can identify a technocentric, modernist and future oriented approach in which the aim has been the incorporation and demonstration of the application of new, high technology techniques. Here, it is not the overall ecological footprint that has been addressed, the priority issue is energy efficiency and energy generation perhaps reflecting an overriding emphasis on contemporary concerns for global climate change. Although semi-autonomous in energy terms, the vision is not of a building severed from centralised infrastructure provision, rather one that can make a positive contribution to existing supply networks. In aesthetic terms the building celebrates its 'future-oriented' environmental credentials, the large photovoltaic wall expressed as the dominant feature of the building. Here, the attitude to the city is distinct, the city edge, business park location is distant from the main public transport hubs. The park incorporates the latest communication technologies, microwave, fibre-optics and a satellite earth station and promotes itself through its global communication networks. Here, there is the vision of the de-centralised and fluid city made possible by new technologies and not dependant on the physical constraints of locality.

Rather than a radical vision of autonomy or an overt demonstration of the potential of new technologies, the Central Square offices can perhaps be understood to embody a reformist approach to sustainability. Here we have a vision of incremental environmental change where a "progressive process of innovation mitigates the adverse effects of development" (Blowers, 1996). The approach can be understood to reflect an 'institutional' response to achieving sustainable buildings. The central goal in the development of the environmental approach has been the aim to achieve an excellent BREEAM rating where the building is rated across a range of 'best practice' issues. Overall, there is an emphasis on reducing energy consumption and efficient resource use. This has resulted in a pragmatic attitude to technology, reflected in the sensitive refurbishment and reuse of an existing building and an efficient integration of conventional technologies. In terms of location, this approach most closely maps onto the compact city model, the building is located immediately adjacent to a main public transport hub, it acts as a catalyst for the regeneration of an inner city 'brownfield' site that will be developed to incorporate a mixture of uses.

5 BEYOND MODELS: THE HYBRID NATURE OF SUSTAINABLE BUILDING

In highlighting the distinctiveness of each building we can begin to acknowledge that each element of these competing design strategies incorporates their own "logic" which can be justified in environmental terms by differing arguments. Each of these particular design logic's has mobilised biases in and out of the particular specification brief and has thereby shaped the subsequent development strategy. However, in highlighting the contrasts between different approaches we should also be aware that the logic's rarely surface in isolation. In the design of any particular development, environmental logic's may merge or co-inhabit debates about form, design and specification. In analyzing the three buildings we can also begin to identify overlaps and similarites as the different models mesh with a combination of technical, organizational and commercial considerations in the messy social context of development. Seen this way, the three buildings highlighted are not easily captured by static and universal models of sustainability. They would perhaps be better classified as complex hybrids in which design can be understood to incorporate competing social visions, differing ideas about our relationship to the environment, work, organizations, aesthetics, finance and so on. The three buildings can be interpreted to be the products of a variety of contrasting green logics that collide, clash and mesh to produce hybrid designs, situationally specific responses to the challenge of sustainability.

When viewed in this way the three case studies can serve as illuminating examples of the paradoxes that inevitably face planning and design strategies aimed at promoting 'sustainable' buildings and cities. Rather than relying on abstracted models that prioritise particular issues above others, we suggest that to understand why a building or city might be designed in a particular environmental fashion we have to understand the strategic priorities of those involved in its design and construction. Further, if we seriously want to locate opportunities for environmental innovation then we have to begin to more closely identify the ways in which particular logics of environmental innovation take root in changing development practices. This inevitably means rejecting any notion of buildings and cities as simply technical structures that can be more or less better designed related to an external model of accepted environmental standards. Instead we must accept that both are "part of the conflicting and contradictory struggle of differing forces, interest groups and movements" (Borden & Dunster, 1995) and therefore contingent on the particular strategic objectives of those design and development actors with the power to implement their chosen design strategy.

6 CONCLUSIONS

By demonstrating the flexibility and plasticity of environmental design strategies, our analysis of differing logics of environmental innovation raises significant questions about the framing of sustainable architectural practice in terms of urban compaction and intensification. By exploring how the interplay of competing urban visions and alternative design logic's shapes the techno-environmental profiles of sustainable building development, we have highlighted the contested nature of environmental innovation. Seen this way, alternative technological strategies are the result not of technical superiority, but of distinct philosophies of sustainable design. That is, the concept of sustainable building is fundamentally a social construct. In order to more fully understand green buildings we therefore have to account for the social structuring of both the identification of environmental problems and their resulting embodiment in built forms through multiple design and technical development pathways.

In understanding sustainable buildings and cities we therefore have to be sensitive not only to the widely differing motivations and commitments of actors, but also to the range of techniques or technical innovations employed, the variety of contexts and settings in which development occurs, and the social processes involved in the definition and redefinition of the nature of the environmental problem itself. In this way, we may begin to understand how different logics of sustainable design are mobilized by designers, developers and planners with distinct environmental strategies, and are then framed by the dynamic social and technical contexts of urban development. Adopting this way of seeing building design we might better recognize both the hybrid nature of sustainable building and competing pathways towards the sustainable city.

REFERENCES

Borden, I. & Dunster, D. 1995. *Architecture and the sites of history*. London: Butterworth Architecture.
Blowers, A. 1996. Environmental policy: ecological modernisation or the risk society? *Urban Studies* 34(5-6): 853.
Breheny, M. 1996. Centerists, decenterists and compromisers: views on the future of urban form. In M. Jencks, K. Burton and K. Williams (eds) *The compact city: a sustainable urban form?:* 13-35. Oxford: E & FN Spon.
Bunn, R. & Ruyssevelt, P. 1996. Ecological? *Business Services Journal*. December: 14-18
DETR. 1999. *Towards an urban rennaissance*. Final report of the Urban Task Force. London: E & FN Spon.
Evans, B. 1997. Solar power gets serious. *The Architects Journal*. 19 June: 44-45.
Fulford, M. 1996. The compact city and the market: the case of residential development. In M. Jencks, K. Burton and K. Williams (eds) *The compact city: a sustainable urban form?:* 122-133. Oxford: E & FN Spon.
Guy, S. & Farmer, G. 2000. Contested constructions: the competing logics of green buildings', in Fox, W. (eds.) *The Ethics of the Built Environment*. London: Routledge (in press - forthcoming).
Guy, S. & Farmer, G. 2001. Re-interpreting sustainable architecture: the place of technology. *Journal of Architectural Education*. Themed issue on Technology and Place (published February 2001).
Guy, S. & Marvin, S. 2000. Models and pathways: the diversity of sustainable urban futures. In K. Williams, E. Burton & M. Jencks (eds.) *Achieving sustainable urban form*: 9-18. London: E&FN Spon.
Guy, S. & Marvin, S. 1999. Understanding sustainable cities: competing urban futures. *European Urban and Regional Studies* 6(3): 268-275.
Jencks, M., Burton, K. & Williams, K. (eds.) 1996. *The compact city: a sustainable urban form?:* 122-133. Oxford: E & FN Spon.
Lloyd Jones, D. 1998. *Architecture and the environment: bioclimatic building design*. London: Laurence King.
MacInnes, K. 1999. Solar Office Doxford International. *World Architecture* No 74, March: 114
Pearson, A. 1998. Solar so good. *Building Services Journal*. August: 14-18.
Smyth, J. 1996. Running the gauntlet: a compact city within a doughnut of decay. In M. Jencks, K. Burton and K. Williams (eds.) *The compact city: a sustainable urban form?:* 122-133. Oxford: E & FN Spon.
Wilson, A. (eds.) *Green Development: Integrating Ecology and Real Estate*, Chichester: John Wiley and Sons.
Winter, M. 1998. Solar Synthesis. *Architecture Today* No. 89, June: 24-30.

People, perception and policy

Urban Lifestyles: Spaces · Places · People, Benson & Roe (eds)
© *2000 Balkema, Rotterdam, ISBN 90 5809 169 4*

A nice place to live? The role of urban livability rankings in the construction of public policy

E.J. McCann
Department of Geography, The Ohio State University, Columbus, Ohio, USA

ABSTRACT: Governments and business coalitions in urban areas throughout the Western world are increasingly focused on representing their cities as nice places to live. The desire to be seen as livable places has manifested itself in the development of city slogans and promotional drives. This form of urban boosterism often entails references to various rankings of cities as good places to live and invest. This has been particularly the case in the United States where periodicals such as *Money* magazine publish such listings annually. This paper examines the origin of these rankings and uses a case study of local economic development policy-making in Lexington, Kentucky to analyze their use in the formulation of public policy. It argues that these rankings problematically circumscribe the terms of policy debates over what makes a 'livable' city and that they limit the types of people whose views are represented in such discussions.

1 INTRODUCTION

Few cities lack an official slogan, these days. Mottos like "Glasgow's Miles Better," "Austin, Texas. Live Music Capital of the World," and "Must See Melbourne" have become central parts of local economic development strategies in the wake of the "I ♥ New York" campaign of the late 1970s. These slogans are part of urban policy-makers and business elites attempts to compete for investment and tax revenues by emphasizing the 'livability' and 'investability' of their localities (Short and Kim, 1998 provide an extensive list of United States city slogans). Paralleling the increasing use of marketing slogans as a weapon in inter-place competition in the United States during the last fifteen years has been the proliferation of published 'rankings' or 'league tables' that rate cities on a series of criteria reflecting their level attractiveness to potential residents and investors. For instance, *Money* magazine, a popular consumer affairs and investment periodical has been compiling annual lists of approximately three hundred US metropolitan areas since 1987. In each of these rankings, cities are evaluated on a series of criteria considered by the magazine's readers to be the most important factors when choosing a place to live (including, for example, 'low crime rate,' and 'high potential for future job growth'). The publication of *Money's* rankings, along with those of other periodicals such as the *Places Rated Almanac* which presents, in much more detail, a listing of criteria for choosing a city in which to live, *Fortune* magazine's annual ranking of the best US cities in which to invest and do business, and *Employment Review's* annual 'Best Places to Live and Work' list are highlighted in local and national news media each year. These more 'conventional' rankings – highlighting standard and generally unproblematized criteria for relocation familiar to most businesses and middle class residents – are now accompanied by others. For instance, the *Utne Reader* magazine, a periodical digest of the alternative media, published a list of the "Ten Most Enlightened Towns" in the US in 1997 and, as a supplement, identified one town in each US state and Canadian province that it considered 'most enlightened' in terms of such criteria as "access to alternative health care" and "diverse spiritual opportunities." While high rankings on the 'conventional' lists tend to be the most desirable goal for city governments and business groups, those placed highly in any ranking tend to feature them alongside their other marketing materials distributed to potential investors and residents in hard copy format or through web pages. On the other hand, a ranking near the bottom of one of these lists is a cause for consternation and indignation among local business groups and politicians (Moore, 1996; but see Ward, 1998 for a discussion of the London borough of Hackney's use of the slogan, "Britain's Poorest Borough" to make a political point about government funding priorities in the early 1980s).

Despite the current level of attention given to image-making slogans and prominent references to favorable positions on various livability league tables, place marketing is hardly a new phenomenon. As Ward (1998) shows, place marketing has occurred in various forms on both sides of the Atlantic since the middle of the nineteenth century, if not before. In the United States, the opening of new tracts of land after 1700 led to government proclamations about their high quality and the production of documents outlining incentives for those willing to settle them. With the development of the railroads in the nineteenth century, place marketing – aimed at encouraging the settlement of the westward-moving Anglo frontier through the development and sale of town properties laid out on land granted to railroad companies by the federal government – marked the beginning of an early version of the 'public-private' place marketing partnership using the print media. While the railroads and land companies marketed new towns on the frontier at this time, political and economic elites in existing frontier settlements saw railroad service as crucial to their future prosperity. This led to the practice of cities subsidizing railroads in return for the location of a line or a hub in their jurisdictions. As Ward notes, Winnipeg, Manitoba rose from an obscure settlement to a railroad 'gateway' through this process of municipal subsidy for private railroads, while in the US context, Rutheiser (1996) has discussed the importance of railroads to the rise of Atlanta.

In the late nineteenth and early twentieth century, resorts and newly-built suburbs became major foci of place-marketing efforts in Britain and the United States. In both contexts, images of healthy living, personal rejuvenation, and escape from the industrial city were central to the marketing materials. On the other hand, regions like the US South where urban business elites were gaining increasing power over rural landed elites were being marketed as locations for branch plants. Here, boosters tended to emphasize the importance and desirability of industrial development. The Forward Atlanta campaign of the mid-1920s led the way in promoting the South as an important market and the city as the region's "industrial headquarters" (Ward, 1998, p.45). After the Second World War, most cities in the South had followed suit. For example, Lexington, Kentucky's equivalent of Forward Atlanta, the Lexington Industrial Foundation, was constituted in 1954 in an effort to industrialize the city's economy by buying land and making it available to major firms interested in locating branch plants in the South. The LIF's marketing strategies attracted firms including IBM in the following years (McCann, 1998, ch. 4) and is still frequently referred to in the city as a model of efficient, targeted economic development strategy.

The fact that civic boosterism has a long history, especially in the United States, and that this has often been focused on the development of branch plant industrialism, as in the cases of Atlanta and Lexington before 1970, does not mean that these issues are irrelevant today. Indeed, there is broad agreement among political-economy analyses of contemporary cities that they have made a transition from 'managerialism' to 'entrepreneurialism' since 1970 (Harvey, 1989). This shift has entailed the development of policy-making frameworks based on private-public partnerships where the role of urban governance is increasingly seen to be primarily one of speculative place construction (including urban image-making and marketing), rather than on managing and improving social and economic conditions. A discussion of 'urban lifestyles' in the new century can be informed, to a great extent, by an understanding of how contemporary urban entrepreneurialism is related to past boosterism; how and why the development of public policy in the entrepreneurial city is increasingly predicated upon middle class concepts of livability and quality of life; and how the development of such polices shapes processes of social and economic exclusion in contemporary cities. In this paper, I will restrict my attention to the issue of urban lifestyles and quality of life concerns, while recognizing that this is only one part of contemporary civic boosterism strategies which not only emphasize urban amenities like parks, various cultural activities, attractive climate, low house prices, and so on to attract residents, but also use tax incentives, worker training schemes, proximity to major communications lines, etc. as bargaining chips in their competition with other places for corporate investment. Here I will seek to shed light, through a case study of contemporary economic development planning processes in Lexington, Kentucky, on why lifestyle-based place-marketing strategies have become increasingly popular among urban policy-makers in recent decades. I will also discuss the role the increasing number of popular urban livability rankings have played in the way that local economic development policy is formulated and implemented. I will make the following arguments: I suggest that the increasing role 'quality of life' indicators and urban livability rankings play in local economic development policy-making indicates a restructuring of urban planning as an institution of the local state in the United States; following on this I argue that this restructuring is tied up with a crisis of legitimacy in the local state and that the use of these rankings is part of an attempt to confer legitimacy on business-led policy-making efforts; in turn, I contend that the results of this move toward certain definitions of good lifestyle is fundamentally problematic in that it constrains the possible futures available to policy-makers but that, by definition, it excludes many groups in society with different views of the future from being part of the policy discussion.

In order to flesh these three related arguments out, I will discuss the nature of the contemporary entrepreneurial city. In doing so, I will suggest that the rise of entrepreneurialism in urban governance in recent decades has been a key process in the rise of lifestyle as something more than an afterthought in discussions of urban policy or a concern only in the context of suburban residential development and seaside resorts (Harvey, 1989; Short and Kim, 1988; Ward, 1998). In this section, I will also provide a brief outline of the rise of urban livability rankings as a certain manifestation of the contemporary atmosphere of urban place competition and entrepreneurialism. Following this I will provide an example of the use of urban rankings in the development of public policy. This example is drawn from a four-year research project in Lexington, Kentucky, conducted during a period of economic and institutional restructuring in the 1990s and based primarily on participant observation in various local planning processes. The paper will conclude with an analysis of this process and a discussion of the exclusionary nature of urban livability rankings in the context of public policy-making.

2 THE ENTREPRENEURIAL CITY AND URBAN LIVABILITY RANKINGS

The rise of the entrepreneurial city is set within an ongoing restructuring of economic and political relations at higher scales including the national and the global. It has entailed a fundamental change in the organization of public policy in the United States, Britain, and other parts of the Western world. As Harvey (1989, p.4) puts it,

> there seems to be a general consensus emerging throughout the advanced capitalist world that positive benefits are to be had by cities taking an entrepreneurial stance to economic development. What is remarkable, is that this consensus seems to hold across national boundaries and even across political parties and ideologies.

With the rise of entrepreneurialism there has been a related shift from urban govern*ment* – indicating the primacy of public officials and state institutions in the development of policy – to govern*nance* where the power over the future of places is increasingly located in private institutions that control governing coalitions where state agencies play a facilitative role. Furthermore, the fact that the risks of contemporary local economic development efforts seem to be absorbed largely by the public sector at the local level distinguishes the entrepreneurial city from previous rounds of civic boosterism (Harvey, 1989, p.7). A third key aspect of urban entrepreneurialism is a refocusing of urban policy away from territory – jurisdictions within which policy is intended to improve life for the majority through the provision and maintenance of public goods – to the construction of places in terms of the built environment or the labor market, for instance. The initiatory or speculative impulse at the heart of urban entrepreneurialism can, then, perhaps rather crudely be characterized in terms of the twin desires among urban elites to remain competitive in a zero-sum game of inter-place competition for investment from increasingly mobile international corporations and to increase local tax bases as funding from higher levels of the state dry up. It is in this latter regard, with its focus on the use of place image and amenity to attract new residents to cities, that urban livability rankings can play a major role in the formulation of public policy.

2.1 *Rating the entrepreneurial city*

"If you could live anywhere in the U.S., where would it be?" asked *Money* magazine as it introduced its first Best Places to Live ranking (1987, p. 34). The answer, according to a poll of its subscribers was, "in a city with little property crime, high personal safety, and an appreciating housing market, among other factors" (Table 1). In 1987, this meant cities like Nashua, New Hampshire, Norwalk, Connecticut, and Wheeling, West Virginia (the three top-rated places that year). The first two were experiencing the effects of economic expansion in certain sectors while Wheeling ranked surprisingly high in the listing due to its low house prices and crime rates. While the rankings were welcomed in these places, their publication led city business leaders in Flint, Michigan – ranked last out of the three hundred cities – to organize a rally at which copies of the magazine were burned by residents holding signs proclaiming, "*Money* is the root of all evil" (Moore, 1996).

Table 1. *Money* magazine readers' top three and bottom three criteria for choosing a place to live.

1987	1996
Three Most Important Criteria for Choosing a Place to Live	
• Safety of Property	• Low Crime Rate
• Personal Safety	• Clean Water
• Likelihood House Value will increase	• Clean Air
Three Least Important Criteria for Choosing a Place to Live	
• Proximity to Amtrak (Commuter Rail) Station	• Near Amusement Parks
• Availability of Household Help	• Close to Skiing
• Proximity to a Bus Terminal	• Minor League Sports

Source: *Money* (1987, 1996).

In the next decade, the major change in the criteria ranked as 'most important' by *Money* was a shift toward 'environmental' issues (Table 1). During that decade, the significance of these rankings in the wider discourse of urban policy and marketing grew dramatically as did the number and variety of similar rankings (Table 2). Two questions arise from the reactions to these urban livability rankings: why do people in cities ranked either high or low on the lists feel that they are important enough to be of concern, and how have they become part of the public policy process to a greater or lesser extent in many US cities? The first question can be answered in the context of the rise of neoliberalism at the global scale and the concomitant increase in discourses and practices of inter-place competition under the rubric of entrepreneurialism at the local level.

Table 2. Urban livability rankings published recently by four US periodicals (1 = best place to live).

	Money (1996)	*Places Rated* (1997)	*Employment Review* (2000)	*Utne Reader* (1997) ('Most Enlightened')
1	Madison, Wisconsin	Orange County, Calif.	Sarasota, Florida	Ithaca, New York
2	Punta Gorda, Florida	Seattle, Washington	Austin, Texas	Portland, Oregon
3	Rochester, Minnesota	Houston, Texas	Fort Worth, Texas	Durham, N. Carolina
4	Fort Lauderdale, Fla.	Washington, DC	Raleigh, N. Carolina	Burlington, Vermont
5	Ann Arbor, Michigan	Phoenix, Arizona	Salt Lake City, Utah	Madison, Wisconsin
6	Fort Myers, Florida	Minneapolis, Minn.	Atlanta, Georgia	Arcata, California
7	Gainesville, Florida	Atlanta, Georgia	San Diego, California	Portland, Maine
8	Austin, Texas	Tampa, Florida	Denver, Colorado	Iowa City, Iowa
9	Seattle, Washington	San Diego, Calif.	Orlando, Florida	Providence, Rhode Isl.
10	Lakeland, Florida	Philadelphia, Penn.	Portland, Oregon	Chattanooga, Tenn.

Source: Money (1996); Places Rated Almanac (1997); Employment Review (2000); Utne Reader (1997).
Note: *Money* magazine has not published its entire ranking recently. Instead, it asks readers to go to its web site and find their own 'best place.' Resultantly it is impossible to compile the current 'top ten.'

In recent decades, 'competitiveness' has become the watch-word of almost all aspects of public policy. Cities have been convinced that in order to stay 'on top' in the high stakes game of inter-place competition, they must reduce costs, assume risk formerly located in the private sector, and produce a polished image of stability, safety, and compliance in order to attract industry to their jurisdictions. Sports metaphors abound in this frequently masculinist discourse of urban competitiveness. As such, it resonates perfectly with a view of a national urban system as a 'league table,' the fluctuations of which become a significant media event at the national and the local level. Given the emphasis on competitiveness and image-making that permeates urban policy in the age of entrepreneurialism, it is not surprising that these rankings have become topics of discussion in the local state institutions of many cities in the US. In the next section I will provide a brief discussion of the way urban livability rankings have influenced policy-making in Lexington, Kentucky.

3 LIVABILITY RANKINGS AND THE FORMULATION OF URBAN POLICY

The shift from managerialism to entrepreneurialism entails, among other things, a restructuring of the form and function of the local state. In this process of restructuring, certain institutions of the state gain power and legitimacy while others lose out (although it would be wrong to characterize this process as a zero-sum game). Furthermore, the restructuring often entails a redefinition of the boundaries between the state and what might be called 'civil society.' In this later aspect of restructuring, associations such as business organizations and community activist groups frequently gain certain powers to create and implement policy. In the case of Lexington during the 1990s, one of the main foci for state restructuring was planning – the state institution charged with producing and managing the landscape of the city. Through the first half of the 1990s, planning decisions over the future of the city's economic development and environment had been the subject of a great deal of rancorous debate, while in the city more generally, planning was coming increasingly under fire as an institution implicated in the construction and maintenance of barriers that kept certain populations impoverished (McCann, 1997, 1999). As the decade progressed, these situations were at the center of a restructuring in which the city planning commission lost power to the city council and the Mayor and where the private sector, in particular, was given greater power to plan for future economic development.

Indicative of, and crucial to this restructuring was the development of new forms of planning ('open,' and 'inclusive,' according to the rhetoric of local politicians) and the hiring of private planning consultants from outside the city to come in and facilitate these processes and return the policy-making process to a degree of stability. For example, a planning process called New Century Lexington was instituted at the end of 1994. The intention of this process was to develop a set of goals for what the city should be like, economically, socially, and environmentally, in the future. These goals were to be developed through consensus-based decision-making, facilitated by a private planning consultant from Florida. The New Century process – sponsored by the Chamber of Commerce and the city government and developed with the intention of having a direct impact of future public policy – had two defining characteristics beyond its rhetoric of inclusion and consensus. First, it developed a competitive language of 'goals' and 'opponents.' In the meetings, the public was encouraged to set 'targets' for what it wanted the city to be like by 2015. Second, the planning consultant went about defining the 'playing field' by focussing on clear facts and rankings, outlining Lexington's position versus other similar cities in terms of job growth, property crime, etc. (McCann, Forthcoming). Through this process, New Century developed a vision of the future set squarely within an urban entrepreneurial discourse of competitiveness, and standard definitions of the 'good life,' developed through the use of various economic and social indicators and rankings. It also attempted to set the policy agenda in terms of larger objective 'facts of economic life' ('all cities that are winners at the moment have high technology sectors – that's just what the world economy requires!') rather than in reference to the interests of local business elites.

In the first planning meeting, the consultant outlined Lexington's current position with reference to its 'competitors' (largely other growing, mid-sized Southern and Midwestern cities) and attempted to show areas in which the city could 'do better.' In doing this, he distributed a large

215

array of photocopied business reports, crime reports, and spreadsheets to the gathered participants. In these, he highlighted Lexington's position in various categories (thirtieth in manufacturing, twenty-first in services, fifth in education level, number forty in murders, etc.). He also
distributed photocopies of *Money* magazine's 'Top Quality of Life Factors' (the criteria from
it's reader poll used to evaluate US cities) for 1992, 1993, and 1994 (Table 3).

Table 3 *Money* Magazine's top ten quality of life factors, used in the New Century process.

Quality of Life Factors	1994	1993	1992
Low crime rate	1	2	2
Clean water	2	1	1
Clean air	3	3	3
Plentiful doctors	4	5	4
Many hospitals	5	4	5
Strong state government	6	6	Question not asked.*
Low income taxes	7	9	9
Low property taxes	8	12	10
Housing appreciation	9	7	7
Affordable medical care	10	14	12

Source: *Money* Magazine (1992, 1993, 1994).
Note: * In 1992 the question on the importance of strong state government was not asked. Instead,
strong *local* government was ranked as the sixth most important locational factor. In 1993, good schools
and new-business potential ranked 8 and 10 respectively; in 1992, inexpensive living ranked 8.

The *Money* criteria and the other data became the basis for a discussion of the possibilities for
Lexington's economic future. They set the terms of discussion, *the conditions of possibility* for
visions of the future of the city and the implementations of these visions through the private-
public policy process. The outcome of the New Century process was a set of statements that
would be turned over to 'strategic planners' in the Chamber of Commerce who would, in turn,
develop specific policy prescriptions to be considered by the city government and local planners. While this part of the process is yet to bear fruit, the list of statements produced by New
Century can, I suggest, be seen as a direct reflection of the terms of the debate set at the first
planning meeting by the consultant's use of certain types of data and certain definitions of good
quality of life (Table 4).

Table 4. Summary of New Century Lexington's 'vision statement.'

- Healthy community, healthy people.
- Arts, cultural and recreational opportunities for all citizens.
- Preserving the best of what we already have.
- Harnessing the brainpower of our universities.
- Globally competitive manufacturing and high technology businesses.
- Retaining and expanding the best of what we have.
- Economic expansion that benefits everyone.
- A career focus in K thru 12 [*sic*] education. (Kindergarten until the end of Secondary School.)
- Lifelong opportunities for skill development.
- Excellence in the education process.
- Make the Lexington community responsible as the primary advocate of the region's world class
  cluster of colleges and universities.
- State of the art communications and industrial infrastructure.
- Integrated transportation system.
- Geographically dispersed, diverse housing.
- Clean and green infrastructure.
- A 'reinvented' government.
- An empowered government.
- A forward-thinking government.
- Private sector initiative.
- A new tradition of inclusiveness.
- Leadership development.

Source: New Century Lexington, 1995, pp. 5-13.
Note: These themes were not ranked in order of preference. The order here does not indicate a ranking.

The question remains: Does the use of urban livability rankings as a basis for urban policy-making contribute to social exclusion. I argue that, in the case of Lexington, the development of a vision of the future along the lines of *Money's* and in accordance with standard discourses of urban competitiveness coupled with a rather problematic notion of conclusion in the policy process reinforced existing marginalization along the lines of class, and so on. New Century's meetings were held on weekdays, from 8am until 10am, thus excluding those in the population without the ability to rearrange their own work schedules and privileging the voices of those who could. Furthermore, the terms of the discussion set by the rankings and statistics produced by the consultant made it very difficult to propose alternative futures. As one participant found when he proposed a vision of the city's economy based on cooperative economics and farming, visions of economic development using a language foreign to *Money* magazine and local business leaders were met with uncomfortable silence, the polite clearing of throats, and a hasty admonition from the facilitator against 'getting behind schedule' in the discussion. Finally, I will suggest that the exclusionary nature of the process can also be identified in the unproblematized acceptance of the criteria developed by *Money's* ranking and that of other publications. There was no room to question the definition of, means to achieve, and consequences of 'low taxes,' for instance. Thus, the process of planning the city's future did little more than reinscribe standard visions of the future of the city, its economy and society.

To summarize, I argue that the use of these livability rankings as the basis for the formulation of public policy has three interconnected characteristics: (1) It is indicative of a 'loosening' of the definition of what stands for urban policy-making, at least in the United States. The use of the rankings as the 'factual' basis for the development of certain policy trajectories with profound effects on the landscapes, economies, and socio-economic structures of urban areas is tied up in a shift in the power to plan cities (Dear, 1986, 1989; Beauregard, 1989). This shift entails a diminution of the power of professional planners trained in rational planning models and holding certain criteria for evaluating the veracity of information claimed to be pertinent to decision-making. Related to this is the rise of 'open,' 'inclusionary' private-public policy-making processes with a much more varied set of decision-making processes (more than merely the planning hearing) and the increased use of primarily business-oriented types of data for defining and analyzing the utility and 'success' of public policy. (2) Within this context of institutional restructuring, the use of livability rankings confers a degree of legitimacy and objectivity to local economic development planning procedures. This legitimacy is necessary given that the restructuring in the form of the local state characterized by the 'opening up' of planning and the development of private-public local economic development policy-making is always contested on the grounds that the increasing role of business coalitions in the development of public policy is problematic and undemocratic. Legitimacy is conferred through the presentation of the rankings as quantitative and objective, based on incontrovertible census data, and formulated by disinterested third parties usually located beyond the boundaries of the city in question. Therefore, it is more difficult for activists interested in articulating different visions of the future of a place or concerned with the undemocratic nature of business-led policy initiatives to suggest that the goals of a particular policy process are merely those of self-interested local business groups. At the same time, the types of criteria used by *Money* and other publications in ranking cities as good places to live tend to be hard to argue with, at least when taken at face value. 'Safe streets,' 'vibrant economy,' and 'high quality of education for our children,' might, in the American context, be termed 'motherhood and apple pie' issues – it is hard to suggest that they are *not* good things, but the very fact that they seem self-evidently desirable for any policy process often makes it very difficult to question the means by which these ends will be achieved. (3) While the use of these rankings as a way to identify policy goals is indicative of state restructuring and is central to the maintenance of a certain hegemonic order in the local economic development process, it also has the direct result of constraining the range of possible futures available in urban governance. Therefore, the dominance of middle class, business oriented criteria for what makes a city a nice place to live excludes, by definition, those in the community who, for various reasons, are not, or do not want to be, a part of conventional definitions of 'economy,' community,'' 'education,'' family,' 'quality of life,' and so on. In developing policies on the basis of what *Money* magazine or its competitors designate as the basic qualities of a nice place to live, urban policy-makers constrain the possibilities for the development of alternative futures and reduce the range of people willing or able to engage in community discussions of policy priorities.

In this regard, these rankings and the reaction to their periodic publication should be seen as more than entertainment. Their development and use in the policy process can be analyzed in the context of a shift from managerialism to entrepreneurialism in the governance of cities in the US and other parts of the advanced capitalist world. The crucial question in any policy-making process intent on developing a nice place to live in reference to these rankings is, "a nice place for whom?"

REFERENCES

Beauregard, R. 1989. Between modernity and postmodernity: the ambiguous position of US planning. *Environment and Planning D: Society and Space.* 7: 381-395.

Dear, M.J. 1986. Postmodernism and planning. *Environment and Planning D: Society and Space.* 4: 367-384.

Dear, M.J. 1989. Survey 16: Privatization and the rhetoric of planning practice. *Environment and Planning D: Society and Space.* 7: 449-462.

Employment Review. 2000. Best Places to Live and Work, 2000. www.bestjobsusa.com.

Harvey, D. 1989. From managerialism to entrepreneurialism: the transformation of urban governance in late capitalism. *Geografiska Annaler.* 71(B): 3-17.

McCann, E.J. Forthcoming. Constructing consent and producing place through privatized planning. *Professional Geographer.*

McCann, E.J. 1999. Race, protest, and public space: Contextualizing Lefebvre in the US city. *Antipode,* 31(2): 163-184.

McCann, E.J. 1998. *Planning futures: the restructuring of space, economy, and institutions in Lexington, Kentucky.* Ph.D. diss., University of Kentucky, Lexington, Kentucky.

McCann, E.J. 1997. Where do you draw the line? Landscape, texts, and the politics of planning. *Environment and Planning D: Society and Space.* 15: 641-661.

Money Magazine. 1987. Best places to live. August.

Money Magazine. 1996. Best places to live. July.

Moore, M. 1996. Flint and me: Michael Moore returns to our first last-place city. *Money.* July: 88-89.

New Century Lexington. 1995. *New Century Lexington: A partnership for developing a shared vision of the Lexington Community in the 21st Century and a strategic plan for achieving the vision.* Lexington, Kentucky: New Century Lexington/Lexington *Herald-Leader.*

Places Rated Almanac. 1997. *Places Rated Almanac.*

Rutheiser, C. 1996. *Imagineering Atlanta: the politics of place in the city of dreams.* New York: Verso.

Short, J.R. & Kim, Y.H. 1998. Urban crises/urban representations: selling the city in difficult times. In T. Hall & P. Hubbard (eds), *The entrepreneurial city: geographies of politics, regime, and representation.* New York: Wiley, 55-76.

Utne Reader. 1997. The ten most enlightened towns in America. *Utne Reader* Magazine, May-June.

Ward, S. 1998. Place marketing: a historical comparison of Britain and North America. In T. Hall & P. Hubbard (eds), *The entrepreneurial city: geographies of politics, regime, and representation.* New York: Wiley, 31-54.

Urban Lifestyles: Spaces · Places · People, Benson & Roe (eds)
© 2000 Balkema, Rotterdam, ISBN 90 5809 169 4

Opening up the suburbs for the urban poor: What types of localities will housing voucher recipients migrate to?

D.P.Varady
School of Planning, University of Cincinnati, Ohio, USA

C.A.Walker
Centre for Urban Policy Research, Rutgers University, USA

ABSTRACT

Over the past several years, the U.S. Department of Housing and Urban Development (HUD) has initiated a number of mobility demonstrations (e.g., Moving to Opportunity) designed to give families the opportunity to move from areas of high poverty and minority concentrations to neighborhoods that offer greater socioeconomic diversity and educational opportunities. The demonstration programs provide clients with extensive counseling, information on housing opportunities, and support services.

The experience of the Section 8 housing voucher program in Alameda County, California (Oakland and some of its suburbs) has been notably different from that of the counseling-driven mobility demonstration programs. HUD has observed relatively large numbers of housing voucher recipients exercising "portability" under routine administration of the program, relocating from areas under the jurisdiction of the Oakland Housing Authority (OHA) or the Berkeley Housing Authority (BHA) to areas under the jurisdiction of the Housing Authority of the County of Alameda (HACA).

This paper is part of a larger HUD-funded study, carried out through the Center for Urban Policy Research at Rutgers University, aimed at (1) determining the housing and neighborhood outcomes for renter households who received Section 8 rental vouchers, then relocated to various parts of Alameda County, and (2) to document and describe procedures used by housing agencies in their administration of the portability feature of the Section 8 program. This paper focuses on a related issue, the characteristics of the destination neighborhoods. To what degree are voucher recipients clustering in particular communities, and what are the causes of this clustering? What is the racial and ethnic composition of destination neighborhoods in Alameda County? Has the influx of Section 8 residents introduced problems in the destination neighborhoods? If so, what programs, if any, have been implemented to deal with them?

Using a case study methodology, we will combine: (1) a demographic analysis of population changes utilizing 1999 estimates prepared by the Claritas Corporation as well as 1990 U.S. Census information, (2) a GIS analysis of relocation patterns based on housing authority records, (3) an SPSS analysis of a telephone interview survey of 300 voucher recipients (divided roughly equally between those who remained in the older cities of Oakland and Berkeley and those who used their housing voucher to "port" to the newer areas of Alameda County), and (4) a qualitative analysis of informant interviews with local housing and planning officials (using a computerized program called NUD.IST).

Preliminary results available thus far deal with patterns of relocation from Berkeley/Oakland to southern Alameda County and are based on analysis of housing authority records for 489 "porting" households for the period, 1976 to 1999.

- Almost two-thirds (66 percent) relocated to four communities just south of the Oakland border (Hayward, San Leandro, Ashland, and Cherryland). These are areas developed in the 1950s and 1960s that, like other inner suburbs around the United States, are beginning to display problems commonly associated with central cities (e.g., increased crime and drug dealing). Relatively few relocated to the more southern parts of Alameda County, closer to Silicon Valley where housing prices are higher.

- Families moving from Oakland/Berkeley to southern Alameda County often moved from predominantly African-American neighborhoods to neighborhoods that were more ethnically diverse. Porters moved from neighborhoods in Oakland/Berkeley that were 45.8 percent African American and 21.9 percent Hispanic to destination neighborhoods in Alameda County that were 8.0 percent African American and 23.1 percent Hispanic.

- Porting enabled households to move to neighborhoods that were modestly better in socioeconomic status. In 1999 median income levels for destination neighborhoods were 45.5 percent higher than for origin neighborhoods ($51,455 versus $35,368), while median housing prices were 31.3 percent higher ($265,826 versus $202,368).

Thus, the results available to us thus far hint at a degree of reclustering of Section 8 voucher holders, but movement into better-off neighborhoods. The final paper will present a fuller treatment of the impact of voucher holders on these four suburban communities based on analysis of the household survey, published reports and newspapers, and informant interviews.

Urban Lifestyles: Spaces · Places · People, Benson & Roe (eds)
© *2000 Balkema, Rotterdam, ISBN 90 5809 169 4*

But would you live here? Researching attitudes towards Newcastle upon Tyne's urban area

T.G.Townshend
Centre for Research on European Urban Environments, School of Architecture, Planning and Landscape, University of Newcastle upon Tyne, UK

ABSTRACT: Over the past four decades major UK urban areas have lost considerable populations. Today the desire to revitalise these areas, plus a necessity for an extra 4 million homes nationally, has created official pressure for more urban living. Yet can our urban areas meet the desires and aspirations of future generations? This paper examines the attitudes of students who have lived in the city of Newcastle upon Tyne for approximately 3 or 4 years and who are due to graduate shortly. It explores their experiential and perceptual views of urban living and the city and further examines their aspirations of where and how they want to live after leaving University. It questions whether given the views and perceptions of these future household formers, plans to repopulate the city seem desirable and achievable.

1 INTRODUCTION

The need to accommodate an extra 4 million or so homes in the UK over the next two decades has stimulated debate over the future of our towns and cities and how we live in them. There has been much deliberation over how much growth can be accommodated in urban areas and whether this growth can repair 'tears in our urban fabric' (Urban Task Force, 1999a: 46). Plans to repopulate urban areas seem to appear contrary to the prevailing aspirations of UK citizens, however, illustrated by research into migration patterns, residential preference and causal factors for residential relocation. Work on migration patterns, for example, has shown a dramatic decline in urban populations, or 'counterurbanisation' over the past four decades (Champion, 1989; Boyle & Halfacree, 1998; Champion *et al.*, 1998). Newcastle upon Tyne has lost one fifth of its population since 1961, though decline elsewhere, for example Liverpool and Glasgow, has been even greater (Champion, 1996). Several recent reports of residential preference have also emphasised the continuing preference for suburban housing and lifestyles as an expectation of middle-class family life (Angle & Malam, 1999; Forest, Kennett & Leather, 1997) and that such preferences are often shared by single people too (Hooper *et al.*, 1998). Further, research into priorities of housing choice suggests the lure of the 'rural idyll' is extremely strong and is motivated by a desire for a more natural lifestyle and a perception that traditional 'communities' still exist in rural areas (Murdoch, 1997; Newby, 1985). Erroneously or not, people also associate 'quality of life' factors, for example perceived crime levels, pollution and access to good education, as being essentially anti-urban (MRAL, 1995; Burrows & Rhodes, 1998).

It is against this background that, as part of a wider remit of making practical recommendations of how our urban areas might be revitalised, the Urban Task Force has been researching the feasibility of making urban areas the residential place of choice for UK citizens. This work has been recently published in the 'But would you live there?' report (Urban Task Force, 1999b) from which this paper in part draws its inspiration. This research was undertaken by conducting a series of citizens' workshops in Manchester, Bristol and London, made up of a mix of people defined as 'cityphiles' and 'cityphobes', but all of whom were described as persuadable to choosing an urban lifestyle. The workshops concentrated on discussing perceptions of urban areas, how these were formed and whether they were open to change. The overall conclusions of this report were that there was no inevitability in a continuing depopulation of our urban areas and while people may value suburban characteristics of peace and quiet, they also miss urban characteristics of diversity and variety (op. cit. 39).

A central criticism of this report, however, is that it really does not make clear its own definitions of 'urban', or 'urban living', though interestingly it does discuss at length the problems of language and the value-loaded nature of words such as 'urban', 'city' and 'lifestyle'. The report does state that it excluded those who had already 'chosen' an urban lifestyle, defined as those for example 'already living in city centre apartments' (op. cit. 15) suggesting a city centre focus (though again there is interestingly no definition of 'chosen', or explanation of what factor had determined these persons' residential choice). The research also included areas which are not city centres, however, but which it also defined as representing 'urban living', for example the Clifton and Redland areas of Bristol, suggesting at least the inclusion of inner suburbs, as well city centres, in its remit. The lack of clarity is problematic since there would appear to be a large difference between populating city centres in Britain, many of which have had little or no population for several decades (some central areas have never had significant residential populations) and re-populating urban areas more generally where traditional communities may well have lost sizable populations, yet where remnant communities may remain.

Aligned to this issue is the proliferation of the use of urban frontier vocabulary in the report. Enthusiastically it labels the initial wave of new urban migrants as the 'urban pioneers' followed by another group the 'urban settlers' in their wake (op. cit. 15). While at first glance such terminology may seem innocent hyperbole, in fact frontier imagery carries considerable ideological weight. Pioneers and settlers displace, or at least overrun, whatever lies before them. This may seem acceptable enough if no one lives in the areas being 'pioneered', as in the case of vacant city centre property, but as Neil Smith pointed out the vocabulary of frontier myth was used to rationalise the more sinister aspects of gentrification resulting from the 1980s housing boom. Here middle-class repopulation of parts of UK and US cities often involved the displacement of poorer communities. Frontier imagery was used to justify the social differentiation and exclusion wrought by gentrification as 'natural' and the displaced communities as 'uncivil' (Smith, 1996: 17). In Smith's view the idea of 'urban pioneers' is as 'insulting (when) applied to contemporary cities as the original idea of "pioneers" in the US West' (ibid: 33).

The above is extremely pertinent to Newcastle since arguments over populating the city centre would largely appear to have been already won. Currently there is a high demand claimed for a range of properties from social housing to luxury private apartments in Newcastle historic core (Grainger Town Partnership, 1999). This small but steady increase in population is in sharp contrast to some of Newcastle's traditional housing areas where populations in some wards declined by over 40% in the two decades 1971-1991 (Newcastle City Council, 1997). Newcastle now contains some extreme examples of property devaluation and abandonment. In Newcastle's West End, large amounts of social housing stand empty, much of it low rise and relatively attractive. This includes local authority and housing association property and the effect extends into the private sector too. It is against this background that Newcastle has launched its 'Going for Growth' strategy, which aims to address long-term decline in many of its traditional residential areas (Newcastle City Council, 2000).

It is, therefore, important to be quite clear about the background against which the Newcastle research is set. In this context plans for repopulation and restructuring of the urban fabric necessarily have far reaching impacts. Some areas of housing in Newcastle may have been all but abandoned but there may also be remnant communities and in particular adjacent communities, fighting for survival. Thus the Newcastle research perhaps questions not simply 'would you live here?' but perhaps 'would you gentrify here too?'.

2 THE NEWCASTLE UPON TYNE RESEARCH

2.1 *Aims*

This paper draws on a qualitative study, the principal aim of which was to develop a greater understanding of students' attitudes towards Newcastle upon Tyne as a place in which to live and work after graduation. In achieving this the research had four secondary aims which were to examine students' perceptions of the city as a whole, i.e. not just the central area, or areas where they might live; the way in which such perceptions are formed, how realistic they are and whether there is a need to try and change prevalent perceptions; the aspirations of the participants in terms of their expectations of the city, their neighbourhood and also their own housing; and whether realistically Newcastle can meet these expectations.

2.2 Method

Eight focus groups of students were held, three from the University of Northumbria at Newcastle, four from the University of Newcastle upon Tyne and one mixed group. The groups contained between six and nine participants. Students were drawn from the disciplines of business management (two groups), computing science, marine technology, marketing, sports management and science and town planning. With the exception of the town planning students the disciplines were chosen to reflect key employment sectors and entrepreneurial skills identified as essential in the city council's economic development strategy (Newcastle, 1999) although an 'exact fit' was not possible. The town planning students were included to test to what extent these students were in tune with their contemporaries from other disciplines in their attitudes to urban living. Finally a mixed group of randomly chosen volunteers was also included to see whether the results from this group were less consistent from those drawn from single disciplines i.e. whether students drawn from particular disciplinary sets really did share common attitudes towards urban living and lifestyles.

The groups of participants were given a series of exercises covering mental mapping of the city, designed to find out how much the students engaged with the city as a whole; an area perception exercise where students were asked to discuss their attitude to neighbourhoods within the city; housing preference discussions where participants debated various types of housing and their aspirations for the future; a discussion on nature of neighbourhood and the desirability of local facilities; and finally a discussion about commonly used generic images of urban places, what meaning they conveyed and whether they related to Newcastle as a place. The exercises on mental mapping and area perception were plan based. The exercises on housing preference and generic imagery were based on reactions to appropriate illustrations. Each participant was paid £10. Discussions were recorded and later transcribed. To preserve anonymity where individuals are quoted they are identified only by group and the initial of their forename, quotes are verbatim, {…} indicating where material has been removed. The initial 'Q:' denotes a question from a researcher. This paper illustrates some key themes and conclusions that were drawn from the work.

2.3 The exercises and discussions

2.3.1 Mental mapping

This exercise was carried out individually. Participants were asked to draw a plan, which included as many areas, districts or neighbourhoods of the city that they could recall, i.e. a mental map of the city. The key issue that arose from this exercise was the limited knowledge the participants generally possessed of the city as a whole. The maps varied from the simple to the relatively sophisticated, including details for example of landmarks, transportation routes and nodes and directions to surrounding towns and cities. Even in relatively sophisticated representations, however, the number of neighbourhoods shown was relatively limited, an average of 7; the minimum number of areas identified was 2, the maximum 14 (a recent plan of identifiable neighbourhoods produced by Newcastle City Council included over 100). In terms of what areas were covered by the maps, the most frequently included area, apart from the city centre/university area, was unsurprisingly Jesmond, where over half of the students lived; this appeared on over 95% of plans. Heaton where just over a third lived was included on 68% of plans and Fenham where just under a quarter of participants lived, included on exactly half of all plans.

223

These plans were used as the basis of discussions of what might be called the participants 'experiential city'. These experiences were naturally mostly based on living in an area, or visiting it regularly, as in the case of the city centre, places where friends lived or areas visited for some specific purpose. For example, the Byker area was experienced by some students through a number of public houses where live music was played, but they would not go to this area for any other reason. Interestingly certain groups possessed much greater experiential knowledge of the city than others; for example the average number of neighbourhoods identified by the sports management students at 11 was much higher than the overall average. This resulted from their use of sports facilities around the city, the impact of which became clear in the following exercise.

2.3.2 *Area Perception*

In this exercise participants were shown a plan of Newcastle's neighbourhoods produced by the city council and asked in the group to agree on the status of area colour coding as to whether they were undesirable as somewhere to live after graduation (red), whether they were a desirable location (green), or somewhere in between (amber). In terms of the amber areas they were asked to discuss whether they felt these were likely to get better or worse and further they were also asked to discuss generally what factors might change their perceptions of places.

In this exercise both the negotiations involved in creating the maps and the end results were equally fascinating. It might have been expected that the starting point for these plans would reflect the mental mapping exercise, but this was not usually the case. The marketing students, for example, none of whom currently lived in the West End, began by colouring most of this area of the plan red. When one of the group questioned the designation of one of the neighbourhoods of Fenham as 'red' the following exchange took place,

R: "Well my friend has just bought a house there and she really likes it, actually its really nice with a garage and a big garden and everything."
J: "Well I hate Fenham! I lived in Fenham for a year and we got burgled 5 times and the burglars lived right across the road from us, I couldn't wait to leave Fenham!"
Q: "Where in Fenham was that?"
J: "Brighton Grove"
Q: "Um, isn't that the Arthur's Hill area?"
J: " Is it? Oh, I don't really know!"

The significance of this exchange is not simply that student J referred to the Arthur's Hill area incorrectly as Fenham, since this is actually a frequent ploy of letting agents. More interestingly she did not stop to question student R's description of her friends house; this could not possibly be the same area that she was recalling since there are no houses of this type near Arthur's Hill. Here the perceived city and experienced city images became confused, but overall the perceived image is much stronger, this was a general observation through this exercise and with all groups. The Benwell area was another case in point. Until the 1980s this was an area with a considerable student population. However, after rioting that took place in nearby parts of the West End in 1991, it has become all but abandoned by student residents. The result is that though few students have ever visited the area it has become associated with crime and disorder as has the West End generally.

A discussion about crime in the West End between sports management students is an interesting adjunct here,

J: "Well, crime in the west end is really bad"
Q: "What sorts of crime concerns you most?"
J: "Well, there was that student that got stabbed coming back from a night club..."
E: "Yeh, but that was in Jesmond!"
M: "That could happen anywhere..."
J: "Yeh, I know, but I was just saying..."

224

Here the blending of a related incident in Jesmond, a popular area with students and the idea of crime and the West End is a telling example of how stories might get confused before being passed round the student body. It was such stories (many also perhaps apocryphal) which were cited as the most important element of forming perceptions about areas of the city with which the students were unfamiliar, "I've been told" "...by word of mouth", " everybody knows" were phrases frequently used. Other forms of communication, essentially the media, were felt to be much less important, though publications aimed specifically at students were thought to have some impact.

The effect of having greater experiential knowledge of the city, for example with the sports management group, became evident in this exercise in two ways. Firstly the designations of colour coding might be described as far more location sensitive. This produced a map that showed a far greater insight to slight changes in status in general areas of the city and this group felt able to code a far greater expanse of the city than most other groups. More interestingly the sports management group produced a far more positive reflection of the city, with far fewer 'red' areas than many of the other groups.

Several of the groups made interesting observations regarding how areas may improve, or decline. One factor that was discussed by over half the groups was the proximity of areas to the city centre. In general they thought areas of sound housing close into the city centre might improve more readily than those slightly further out. Another interesting observation was the role that students and graduates have on areas. Here they recognised that too many students might detract from an area's desirability. Several observed that after graduation they would not wish to live in the Heaton area of the city, as it was "too studenty!" On the other hand some students from the Fenham area felt that many of the students who lived there enjoyed the area, might remain living here after graduation and this could have a positive effect on the area.

2.3.3 Housing Preference

In this exercise reactions to properties, though shown entirely randomly, could generally be equated to housing of differing historic periods even though the housing within these groups might varying quite considerably in terms of its size, quality, internal layout and other significant variables. Briefly these groups are early to mid-nineteenth century; high-Victorian and Edwardian; inter-war; 1950s and 1960s; and contemporary, including new-build and building conversion. There was also a clear divide between houses and flats in all periods with houses being more highly valued. Flat conversions were generally viewed negatively as participants felt these often entailed mean space standards and awkward room layouts.

The earliest properties, early to mid 19th Century town houses, received mixed reactions. Generally it was recognised that such properties had historic value, which was a positive asset, but the groups also correctly recognised that such property was likely to be in the core of the city and this was view negatively, "too urban", "congested" and "over-crowded" were expressions commonly used. It was also appreciated that given their general size and location, few of these properties would remain as single houses and as already mentioned this was viewed very negatively.

The most consistently popular property type was represented by later Victorian and Edwardian period. These houses were felt to be "solidly built" and "traditional" with attractive external features, such as bay windows. Mostly, however, it was the internal attributes of such housing which were felt to be most desirable, having "large rooms", "high ceilings" and interesting "period features", though the capacity for these houses for certain modernisation was also praised,

K: "I'd like a few historic features, but I wouldn't want it all frilly..."
J: "Yeh, you could have some nice old fireplaces and stuff, but a really modern kitchen and bathroom."

(sports management group)

Flats from this period were seen as less desirable. Tyneside is unique in that its standard by-law terraced properties were built as upper and lower flats, rather than terraced housing. Though the flats were purpose built a lot were constructed before internal bathrooms were standard.

225

Many of the students had experience of this type of flat and though generally property of this period was liked, the bathroom additions to this type of property, often being accessed through the kitchen were extremely unpopular.

Inter-war property was largely rejected being described variously as "boring" and "old fashioned" phrases such as "its like where your granny lives" were used,

> **T:** "You just know before you go in it, its going to have a really small bathroom."
> **W:** "And it'll be draughty!"
> **R:** Lets face it when you've been in one, you've been in them all…they're all the same."

(computing science group)

There were some positive comments however,

> **A:** "Now that house really says 'home' to me…"

(mixed group)

Such positive comments were very much in a minority, however, though other aspects of this type of property particularly gardens and off-street parking provision, were seen as redeeming features. The groups thought that all such properties would be quite some distance from the city centre and again this was viewed negatively, though in fact many of Newcastle's inner suburbs contain property of this type.

Property from the 1950s and 1960s was generally even less liked than that from the inter-war period. Both low and high-rise property were unpopular, though overall high-rise 1960s local authority flats came in for most vehement criticism, variously described as "prison-like", "hideous" and "inhuman". The prevailing opinion was people only lived in such buildings when they had no other residential choice. Even when it was pointed out to the groups that such refurbished property was commanding high rent and purchase levels in parts of London, participants were not swayed,

> **A:** "You might get away with that in London, but not here!"
> **P:** "No! People are not that desperate!"

(business management 2)

Perhaps most interesting, however, were discussions on contemporary properties. These included housing, flats and a locally well-known conversion of an Art Deco cigarette factory office block. Some of the most vehement reactions were towards newly constructed apartments on Newcastle's refurbished quayside. The only groups to feel wholly positive about these were the planning students,

> **R:** " I can see myself living there"
> **N:** "Yeh, I really like the look of that
> **I:** " Um, it'd be alright if you had the money!

Far more typical were comments from the computer science students,

> **W:** "It's too flashy it's not me at all…"
> **R:** "It's trying too hard, its saying look at me I'm trendy!"

Other doubts were raised at whether it represented good value for money. At £110,000 the quayside flat was the most expensive property shown to the groups and most felt the water front location was not worth the high price. The marine technology students also had an interesting discussion about whether such property would date quickly, and most groups expressed the views that they felt modern property was badly built and that space standards were mean. These latter points were applied not only to these flats, however, but all the contemporary property. Contemporary houses were frequently referred to as 'box houses', or 'little boxes',

> **L:** "…new houses look nice when they're new, but not in five years time…"

A: "I think they lack charm and character, I would never buy such a house, they just look ridiculous…"

(marketing students)

Perhaps more surprising was the reaction to the converted cigarette factory, which were almost entirely negative. The business management students' discussion was typical,

A: "It looks so institutionalised like a hospital, or school…
J: "That's it! It would be just like going to school everyday again!"
A: "…or prison!"

Perhaps unsurprisingly the one group who were significantly different were the town planners, who were very positively disposed to the re-use of what they felt was a historically interesting building and stated that at least the development had "a particular identity". It should be noted that both the 'Wills' flats and the Quayside flats in reality sold very well.

Generally, therefore, there was a huge amount of conservatism over housing choice. This might be seen as both positive and negative set against the Newcastle context. On the one hand, the participants did not seem to be particularly engaged by some of the interventions on the city, for example the regeneration of the Quayside area, however, Newcastle does have a substantial supply of sound late Victorian and Edwardian housing in areas perceived to be undesirable, which might prove significant.

2.3.4 *The nature of neighbourhoods*

Following the discussion on housing preference the participants went on to discuss the nature of neighbourhoods that they perceived to be desirable. The positive theme from this discussion is that they did indeed expect to live in neighbourhoods with locally available facilities. Given that this is a sector of society who are frequent users of the inter-net, ideas such as grocery shopping from home (or indeed any other type of shopping) were not discussed without prompting. What the students discussed mainly was the importance of local shops, the value of public transport, and access to some form of open space. The emphasis on local shops even if just a local corner shop and off licence, was interesting as it was contrasted to supermarket shopping which was thought to be only viable in conjunction with car use, so its proximity to residence was not seen as a priority. In terms of public transport the Newcastle Metro system was highly valued, while bus services were seen as a poorer alternative. This may be important since Newcastle's Metro system does not serve its West End and this is seen as detrimental to this area.

Issues regarding open space warrant further exploration. Newcastle has a range of open space close to the city core including the semi-natural 'Town Moor' as well as more formal public parks. Though the nature and quality of open space most valued was not investigated in any depth in this study, phrases such as "somewhere to relax", "a breathing space" and "somewhere to sunbathe!" were used, suggesting that a range of spaces may be acceptable.

2.3.5 *Images of urban living*

The final exercise, during which students were shown a series of generic images of urban living, perhaps produced less in terms of hard evidence of the participants' aspirations regarding lifestyle, but did reveal some interesting observations about how they felt about Newcastle as a place. Discussing a mobile phone advert, for example, in which a number of people are shown speaking into phones on a busy street against an urban backdrop, the marine technology students made these observations,

P: "Well this looks really busy, hectic, no one has enough time"
B: "But look, everyone is on a mobile phone, everyone has their own agenda, they're not speaking to each other... that's not Newcastle, people do speak"
S: "I'd agree it's not like the picture at all, it's more laid back...."
B: "Um, it's a city, but I think it still has a small town feel. When you go down the street you see people you know..."

Though not universal, a general emphasis on friendliness and intimacy was evident in many of the discussions. More disputed was the now infamous claim that Newcastle was the eighth party city of the world (Observer, 1995). The town planners' comments were representative,

D: "Its terrible there are no really good clubs, there is only the Quayside if you're pretentious, or the Bigg Market which is dead rough!"
N: "Um I think other cities are way ahead of us, Sheffield and Manchester, for example."

3 DISCUSSION

A number of themes have begun to emerge from the Newcastle research from which some preliminary conclusions may be drawn. The differences between what might be defined as the experiential and perceptual views of the city is an area that merits further exploration. The Newcastle work suggest that experiential views can be over-written by perceptions particularly when these are negative. The perceptions of the participants were drawn from the dissemination of stories within the student body and this seemed a remarkably powerful way of shaping opinion.

With regard to attracting more people to live in the urban area the students combined positive and negative messages which might be translated into policies. Their reactions to Newcastle as a place and their aspirations for traditional neighbourhood structures seemed particularly encouraging. Some interventions in the city, for example the regeneration of the Quayside, did not seem to be engaging most of the participants and the extremely negative images of parts of the city are deeply problematic. These points combined illustrate that even by narrowing the focus of this research to certain groups and to particular locations the considerable complexities involved in this area of work. The aim now is to take this research forward and begin to address at least some of these issues.

REFERENCES

Angle, A. & Malam, S. 1998. *Kerb Appeal: The External appearance and site layout of new housing.* Winchester: the Popular Housing Forum.
Boyle, P.J. & Halfacree, K. Ed. 1998. Rural Areas: Theories & Issues. Chichester: Wiley & Sons.
Burrows, R. & Rhodes, D. 1998, Unpopular places: Area disadvantage and the geography of misery in England. Bristol: Policy Press.
Champion, A., Ed. 1989. Counterurbanization: The changing pace and nature of population deconcentration. London: Edward Arnold.
Champion, A. 1996. Migration between metropolitan and non-metropolitan areas in Britain, Department of Geography, University of Newcastle upon Tyne.
Champion, A., Atkins, D., Coombes, M., & Fotheringham, S. 1998. Urban Exodus: A report for the CPRE. Department of Geography, University of Newcastle upon Tyne.
Forest, R., Kennett, T. & Leather, P. 1997. Homeowners on new estates in the 1990s, Policy Press.
Grainger Town Partnership. 1999. Interim Report. Newcastle: Grainger Town Partnership.
Hooper, A., Dunmore, K. & Hughes, M. 1998. Home Alone, vol. 1. The Housing Research Federation.
MRAL. 1995. Towns or Leafier Environments? A survey of family home buying choices. London: Mulholland Research Associates Ltd.
Murdoch, J. 1997. Why Do People Move to the Countryside? Report for the Countryside Commission, Cardiff: Department of City and Regional Planning, University of Wales.
Newby, H. 1985. Green and Pleasant Land (2nd Ed.) Harmondsworth: Penguin.
Newcastle City Council, 1997. City Profiles: Results from the 1996 Inter-Censal Survey, Newcastle upon Tyne: City of Newcastle upon Tyne.
Newcastle City Council. 1999. Competitive Newcastle, Newcastle upon Tyne: City of Newcastle upon Tyne.
Newcastle City Council. 2000. Going For Growth: a green paper. Newcastle upon Tyne: City of Newcastle upon Tyne.
Observer. 1995. Newcastle is ranked with Rio as world party city, Observer, 17 Sept: 13
Smith, N. 1996. The New Urban Frontier: gentrification and the revanchist city, London: Routledge.
Urban Task Force. 1999a. Towards an Urban Renaissance.
Urban Task Force. 1999b. But would you live there? Shaping attitudes to urban living. London: Urban Task Force.

Urban Lifestyles: Spaces · Places · People, Benson & Roe (eds)
© *2000 Balkema, Rotterdam, ISBN 90 5809 169 4*

People and their aesthetic tastes for streetscape

R. H. S. Rezazadeh
Iran University of Science and Technology, Tehran, Iran

ABSTRACT: The quality of streetscape has been the focus of attention during the last two decades. This has been true for the Iranian streetscape as well with an emphasis on the problem of lack of Identity. In response to this problem designers often seek specific qualities in the streetscape, which in their terms are manifested in specific physical features. While on the other hand some believe that culture is a determinant of the type of spaces and places that people prefer. Focusing the case on some streetscapes of Tehran, Iran, the preferences and the mental constructs of users were studied. The results show cultural differences between some user groups, but there are certain commonalities among their tastes. The most permanent preferred dimension of meaning in the environment is the organization. Diversity is the second dimension of meaning which is almost permanent and positive contributing to the preferences of all groups. The least permanent and most controversial quality is typicality/atypicality.

1 THE PROBLEM DEFINED

The streetscape is one of the major determinants of the life setting of residents. The visual quality of streets and especially the architectural design of the facades of buildings have been issues of concern for many architects and designers as well as researchers within this field, especially during the last two decades.

It is the task of the urban designer to find ways of creating a more enhanced streetscape. This involves mechanisms both to reduce and to eliminate the present problem and to prevent its recurrence in other places, either in redevelopment or in new developments. This needs an inquiry into the present situation, analyzing the positive and negative aspects of the existing streetscape.

The issue of the quality of streetscape has become a concern during the last few years within the Iranian professional environment. The Iranian streetscape also has been the source of many criticisms in recent years, especially for its poor quality and lack of unique identity (Pakzad, 1996). On the other hand, the dominance of the attached building type in Iranian cities as well as the scarcity and cost of land create a definite street edge in which the street facade becomes very prominent.

In general, the architects and urban designers' perspective is artistic and intuitive and therefore their approach to the issue is non-empirical. Architects are concerned with design issues and are obliged to suggest design solutions to problems at hand. Therefore their role is constructive and so their approach is prescriptive (Rezazadeh, 1999).

1.1 *The solutions adopted*

In response to the problem of lack of quality, and especially lack of identity of Iranian streetscapes, architects and urban designers have proposed some remedies. The major solution to the problem has come from the architects and that is a totally design oriented solution. In this solution the present street facades are analysed and an ideal state of design for streets is proposed, which is suggested as the ultimate state of the street after development. Also, the aesthetic values of the designer are taken as universal and applied to the environment. For instance in the design for Abbas Abad Street in Tehran, the diversity of the skyline is assumed to be aesthetically pleasing, therefore this is set as a design principle within this static approach

1.2 *Problems with the present solution*

The present solution is based on another assumption, that is as Porteous (1982) puts it 'the expert paradigm.' In this paradigm, the architect is the one whose taste is the ultimate, while the taste of the society has to be elevated. This is very similar to the romantic way of thinking (Brolin, 1980). In this paradigm, the architect sets the pattern and the society has to follow it. Hence, even when a static design solution is not proposed, and principles of design are considered to control the development process, setting the rules is based on the supremacy of the designer over people.

This solution, while quite innovative, also lacks a proper understanding of the processes involved in the life of the city. The city is not a static product such as some art objects including architecture may be. The city is a live entity in which its cells are born, grow, age and die. In other words it undergoes a natural life cycle, in which the cells which are the individual buildings within its overall entity each may be in one or other stages of their life cycle. Understanding this dynamic process would have helped proposing dynamic solutions which have been lacking in the Iranian context during this time period.

The Iranian architects have not considered this fact in their approach to the problem and hence have taken a static approach which may be appropriate for architecture projects, but not at an urban scale. In other words, Iranian Architects have seen urban design as 'architecture at large.' This is an inappropriate vision of the problem. Analysing the roots of this vision and the fundamental solutions to it is beyond the scope of this paper and should be dealt with somewhere else. Considering the dynamic vision of urbanism, and believing in the lifecycle of cells of the city organism, I would seek a different approach to the problem. This organism is shaped and reshaped by people and not by an organisation or governmental body. Therefore understanding the way people evaluate their environment is a crucial step in understanding the way people shape their environment.

The question has two aspects, one involves the taste of a society over their surrounding streetscape, itself being a byproduct of their cumulative effort. The other involves differences of needs and preferences among user groups within the society as a product of their age, qualifications and expertise. Therefore one aspect requires a focus of attention on the commonalities, while the second is a search for differences and the reasons for them.

2 A NEW APPROACH TO THE PROBLEM

Here an Empirical approach based on environmental psychology theory and techniques has been taken to find out more about these issues. The study has focused on several user groups including the public, the youth, the architects and the students of architecture. Therefore differences of the cognitive and affective responses of these user groups to the environment were analysed. This sets the ground for a detailed analysis of the processes involved in preference determination and in the long run on the formation and reformation of the built environment.

Focusing only on the environment and streetscenes would have revealed some facts about the type of streetscapes that users prefer, but this would not have revealed the processes involved in determining their preferences. Hence, in this study, instead of focusing on the streetscapes, the study was directed towards revealing the mental constructs of the users and their cognitive perceptions of the environment. The streetscapes were referred to as exemplary of Iranian streetscenes with due variations in physical qualities used for the experimentation.

Therefore, with the aim of revealing the mental constructs of the users and their major cognitive dimensions towards the environment, the semantic differential technique was used. This technique uses several bi-polar adjectives to rate photomontages of some street facades in Tehran. In the rating of the streetscenes, slides of nine photomontages of typical streetscenes were

Table1: Dimensions revealed and the adjectives contributing to these dimensions for each respondent group.

First year	Organisation	Diversity	Atypicality
	Ordered	Stimulating	Unusual
	Compatible	Bold	Unfamiliar (-F)
	Symmetrical	Ornate	
	Unified	Complex (-Si)	
	Uniform	Dynamic (-St)	
		Colourful	
Fifth year IUST	Organisation	Monotony	Diversity/ Atypicality
	Compatible	Unified	Colourful
	Ordered	Uniform	Ornate
	Symmetrical	Static	Unusual
	Neutral (-S)		
	Simple		
Fifth year MAU	Organisation	Diversity/ Atypicality	Monotony
	Compatible	Bold	Neutral (-S)
	Ordered	Ornate	Static
	Familiar	Colourful	Unified*
	Symmetrical	Unusual	
	Uniform		
	Simple		
	Unified*		
Professional Architects	Organisation	Diversity	Atypicality
	Ordered	Ornate	Unusual
	Compatible	Colourful	Stimulating*
	Symmetrical	Stimulating*	Bold*
	Unified	Bold*	
	Simple		
	Uniform		
	Familiar		
	Static		
Public	Organisation	Diversity	Typicality
	Symmetrical	Ornate	Usual (-U)
	Unified	Stimulating	Familiar
	Compatible	Bold	Simple*
	Ordered	Colourful	
	Uniform		
	Static		
	Simple*		

used. Factor analysis was then employed to group the adjectives which formed a dimension of meaning for every group. The results of factor analysis revealed three dimensions of meaning for every group, the first being Organisation, the second and third were Diversity and Typicality or variations and combinations of the two. Table 1 shows the dimensions revealed and the adjectives contributing to these dimensions for each respondent group.

The major dimensions identified were organization, diversity and typicality. The user groups examined were consisted of the general public, architects, first year students of architecture and two groups of fifth year students of architecture. This provided an excellent ground for comparison of the mental constructs of different user groups towards their surrounding streetscape. The importance of each dimension in the mental constructs of the user groups and the contribution of each dimension to the preferences of the user groups reveals the commonalties and variations across groups of people.

The dimensions revealed are comparable with the collative variables that Berlyne (1960) introduced previously. He introduced several major constructs as collative variables or properties of the environment. He explains collative properties as those which involve 'comparison between stimulus elements that may be present together or at different times' and mentions such properties as novelty, surprisingness, complexity and incongruity. He (1972) further explains that these collative variables include variations along dimensions of familiar/novel, expected/surprising, clear/ambiguous and simple/complex. Wohlwill (1976) identifies two related aspects for complexity, which are diversity and structural or organisational complexity. He also explains that all these collative variables relate to the uncertainty contained within a stimulus, or the conflict it engenders in the individual attempting to interpret it.

3 ORGANISATION DIMENSION

Organization was the most prominent dimension of the environment noticed by all subject groups. It appeared as the first cognitive dimension and explained over 30 percent of the variance in the data for all groups. This dimension was mainly determined by associating adjectives; symmetrical, ordered and compatible which together act as marker variables. Adjectives such as uniform, unified, static, simple and even familiar were also associated with this factor. The importance and contribution of the adjectives varied among different respondent groups.

The public group as well as the first year students had a very clear understanding of the Organization dimension of the environment. Symmetry, unity, order and compatibility of the scenes mainly contributed to this dimension while uniformity, being static and simple, was also considered to contribute to it. This finding was important since it showed that for the untrained public eye as well as for the first year students, the Organization dimension of the streetscenes, which is a formal dimension, is clearly recognizable and is the most important cognitive dimension. It also showed that recognition of the Organization dimension does not require any particular training. However, its importance increases in the cognitive dimensions of students of architecture and professional architects. This may be due to the increasing attention to and importance of the pure physical features in their cognitive schemata.

In short, Organization is the most important cognitive dimension for all the subject groups and refers to the structural order, the later aspect of complexity as proposed by Berlyne. Organization is the first dimension to be recognized and it explains at least one third of the variation in the data, which is far greater than the other recognized dimensions. Its contribution to the preferences of each group is discussed later.

4 DIVERSITY DIMENSION

Diversity is the second well-recognized dimension of streetscenes. The variables predominantly contributing to the Diversity of the streetscenes were ornate and colourful along with such variables as bold, stimulating and sometimes unusual. Diversity appears very strongly for first year students of architecture, professional architects as well as the public group as the second cognitive dimension and accounts for about 20 percent of the variation in the data. However, for 5th year students of architecture at IUST, as well as the same group at MAU, this dimension appears in a different way.

These two groups have identified a dimension to which the adjectives unified, uniform, static and neutral (-stimulating) contribute. For the 5th year students at IUST this appears as the second dimension on which the variables unified, uniform and static have high loadings. For the 5th year students at MAU it appears as the third dimension on which the variables neutral (-stimulating), static and unified, have high loading.

This dimension was only identified by the students of architecture in their final years of study. This shows sensitivity to lack of Diversity or the existence of Monotony in the environment. Such sensitivity is not observed among other groups, either first year students or the public who lack any professional training, or the professional architects who have achieved a state of maturity in their profession. However, for 5th year students of architecture at IUST as well as MAU, lack of Diversity, or as it is called here, Monotony, was less important and explained only about 10 percent of the variation in data.

For these two groups, the two adjectives colourful and ornate, which were markers for Diversity, are associated with the adjective unusual. The adjective unusual is considered as a marker variable for Atypicality of the streetscenes. Typicality which is identified as the third dimension of meaning of streetscape is an important dimension to focus upon. Typicality/Atypicality dimension is recognized with such marker variables as the adjective pairs usual-unusual, and familiar-unfamiliar.

5 ATYPICALITY DIMENSION

Atypicality is a dimension recognized in this factor analyses through the association of the marker variable unusual with other variables. Unusual was considered as the marker variable for the Atypicality dimension since it determines the fit of visual stimuli (streetscenes) to a knowledge-structure or schema. In determining the Atypicality of a scene, the usual/unusual adjective pair was the strongest concept among the variables. However, the other adjectives that were associated with usual/unusual, and creating the Atypicality dimension, were different among subject groups.

Usual appears along with variables such as familiar, stimulating, bold and simple for first year students of architecture, professional architects and the public. However, it appears along with colourful and ornate for the 5th year students of architecture at both IUST and MAU.

The public and the first year students of architecture in particular associated the adjective usual/unusual with the adjective pair familiar/unfamiliar. It must be noticed that both groups lack any professional training and use usual and familiar as a pure measure of Typicality/Atypicality. The emphasis of the public is on Typicality, while the first year students, emphasized Atypicality. This difference is mainly due to the age of the respondents and the effect of arousal on their preferences. For the professional architects, Atypicality was associated with the adjectives stimulating and bold. Their recognition of this dimension is also more affective and less dependent on particular visual qualities.

However, Atypicality for students of architecture in IUST and MAU was associated with the visual qualities, of colourfulness and ornateness of the streetscape. For both groups the adjective unusual was associated with ornate and colourful and with an affect which contributed less to the identified cognitive dimension. This dimension was considered to be a mixture of Diversity and Atypicality, and hence, is called the Diversity/Atypicality dimension. This dimension is close to Berlyne's collative property, novelty.

The first year students and the public must have had a clear schema of the environment; this is due to the association of the adjective usual with an absolute physical measure, rather than with a more affective variable such as familiarity. This is also the case for the professional architects who showed an independent cognitive dimension from the physical variables, for Atypicality.

However, the 5th year students of architecture were in the phase of changing their schema of the environment due to their particular training. The new schema was mainly based on physical attributes of the environment and the students needed more experience to become independent of it. These students were using some physical variables such as colour and ornamentation in the environment to create the Atypicality dimension. Therefore, they had to base their judgment of Atypicality on some physical variable.

For the professional architects, Atypicality was a very important factor in their cognitive schemata of the environment, explaining about 20 percent of the variation of the data and being independent of absolute physical measures. Depending on the importance of this dimension in determining the preferences of the group, it could be difficult to find the underlying processes affecting the preferences of the architects and therefore their influences on the physical environment.

6 DISCUSSION

In general, while the dimension of Organisation stayed clear and stable across all groups, the dimensions of Diversity and Atypicality showed differentiation among some groups. The first year students of architecture, the public and the professional architects recognized these dimensions in one way, while the 5th year students of architecture in both schools had a different understanding.

Organization is a purely physical dimension, which is defined by formal aesthetic variables. Understanding of this physical dimension is independent of age and professional training and hence remains constant among groups. However, the Diversity and Typicality dimensions are partially related to the physical attributes and partially related to the schema in mind, and this is the reason for the discrepancy in its recognition among groups.

The importance of each dimension of the environment in the cognitive schemata of the user groups is indicated by the percentage of the variance in the data that that dimension is explaining. The results show that Organization is the most important dimension of the environment accounting for about one third of the variations in the data.

Diversity stands as the second cognitive dimension for first year students, professional architects as well as the public. However, the recognition of Diversity for 5th year students of architecture has changed to a sensitivity to Monotony in the environment and hence they have identified this dimension at either second or third place in their cognitive structure of the environment.

Typicality also appears as the third cognitive dimension for first year students, professional architects as well as the public. Again the recognition of this dimension for 5th year students of architecture is different and is associated with physical attributes pertaining to Diversity. Therefore a dimension, which is called Diversity/Atypicality, is recognized. This shows the dependence of judgment of Atypicality on visual attributes of the environment, and not on a mental schema of the environment and proves the overt sensitivity of students of architecture in their final years of training to the visual qualities of the environment.

This study suggests that there are many qualities that are common among all user groups, regardless of their age, qualifications and expertise. Organization and to some extent diversity are among these qualities which here are known as dimensions of meaning. These are the constants,;on the other hand there are some qualities which are varied among groups in both their understanding and their evaluation of the environment. Typicality is the most well known of these which involves some complex issues. Whether a typical environment or an atypical environment is preferred is one issue. The other is that the physical manifestation of typicality/atypicality also largely depends on the life experiences of the person and not the inherent qualities of the environment. This creates the most controversial issues in aesthetic qualities of streetscape among groups.

REFRENCES

Berlyne, D. E. 1960. *Conflict, arousal and curiosity.* New York: McGraw-Hill.

Berlyne, D. E. 1972. Ends and means of experimental aesthetics. *Canadian Journal of Psychology.* 26:303-325.

Brolin, B. C. 1980. *Architecture in context: fitting new buildings with old.* London: Van Nostrand Reinhold

Pakzad, J. 1996. Hoviat va in hamani ba faza. *Sofeh.* 21 & 22:100-107

Porteous, D. 1982. Approaches to Environmental Aesthetics. *Journal of Environmental Psychology.* 2:53-66

Rezazadeh, R. 1999. *Shaping the streetscape, Developing design principles for street facades, Tehran, Iran.* Unpublished PhD dissertation. University of Sheffield.

Wohlwill, J. F. 1976. Environmental Aesthetics: The Environment as a Source of Affect, in *Human Behavior and Environment Vol.1,* Altman, I.; Wohlwill, J. (eds.), Plenum Press.

Urban Lifestyles: Spaces · Places · People, Benson & Roe (eds)
© *2000 Balkema, Rotterdam, ISBN 90 5809 169 4*

Sustainable living in high density cities: Pilot study in Hong Kong

O.Chung & P.Jones
Welsh School of Architecture, University of Wales, Cardiff, UK

ABSTRACT: The increasing world population is coupled to rapid environmental deterioration and social problems. Governments are realizing that sustainable development is necessary to improve the overall quality of life. High-density cities provide an option in which people potentially enjoy a higher level accessibility of social facilities and transportation. However, people also suffer side effects of this condensed habitat, for example, air and noise pollution, loss of privacy, etc. This paper is the result of a recent survey, which was conducted in February 2000 in Hong Kong. The objectives of this survey were to gain a better understanding of people's satisfaction with the living environment and the quality of life in this city.

1 ABOUT HKSAR

The British occupied Hong Kong Island from 1841 to 1997 on the basis of somewhat dubious trading activities in the nineteenth century and their victory over the Chinese in the First Opium War. From 1851 to 1999 the population of Hong Kong increased from 34,000 to 6,843,000. In current situation, with the change of political background from Capitalism to Specialized Socialism, further increases are likely, with the current rate at about 2.5% per annum. (The new population is assumed to range from 7.5 million to 8.1 million by 2011) To accommodate this projected increase, government targets for new housing are set at 85,000 units per year. HKSAR is a relatively small and high-density city, in which available land for building is scarce and there are minimal natural resources. The territory is so small that it may be thought of as entirely 'urban'. The population is aging, with the median age rising from 30 in 1988 to 36 in 1998. With its land area of only 1,097 square kilometers, the land population density per square kilometer is 6,330. Currently, most immigrants are coming from Mainland China. In 1998, 56,039 mainland residents came to settle in the HKSAR under the One-way Permit Scheme, most settling for family reunion purposes.

1.1 *History of housing development*

The disastrous fire in a squatter settlement at Shek Kip Mei, Kowloon in 1953, which, overnight, made 53,000 people homeless, increased government participation in the provision of housing. In the following year the Hong Kong Housing Authority 'HKHA' was formed. This replaced the Hong Kong Housing Society, which was an independent organization established in 1948 for planning and building affordable housing of high quality for rent or sale to specific target groups. The earliest type of accommodation was the Mark I apartment block. These were 6-storey walk-up blocks, which generally comprised back-to-back living units of 11.1m², each with access from an external open balcony where cooking took place. Each block contained two parallel wings joined by a link in which common toilets were provided, along with communal bathing and washing facilities in each wing. These resettlement estates were provided on the basis of 2.23 m² of usable floor space per adult and half that figure for children under the age of 10 years. Without a doubt, general living and environmental conditions were bad and modernization of these old estates began in 1968, with the installation of individual water taps, better lighting, improvement of toilet facilities and landscaping of common areas between blocks. In order to meet the insatiable housing demand, coupled with the restricted availability of sites for housing development, in 1972 the government introduced new policies designed to boost housing production. The aims were to accelerate development of new towns and restructure obsolete parts of the existing urban areas. Now, most public housing estates are 40-60 storey self-contained apartment blocks. Each block has at least two lifts and most have centralized mail-boxes in the lobby (or on each floor for the elderly). Many recently developed estates have their own retail, community and recreational facilities, coupled with a provision of access to transportation networks.

1.2 Housing policy

In 1972, the Governor announced a new housing programme with the target of providing enough permanent homes, self-contained with good amenities and in a reasonable environment. In 1987, the Housing Authority announced its Long-Term Housing Strategy (1987-2001) which aimed to provide adequate and affordable shelter for any one who needed it by the end of the century. The Authority was also given greater financial autonomy. In 1998 February, in a White Paper on Long Term Housing Strategy in Hong Kong, the Government pledged the following initiatives:

- Build no fewer than 85,000 flats a year (50,000 and 35,000 from public and private sectors), starting from 1999-2000, as a long-term target to meet the future needs of the community;
- Achieve a home ownership rate of 70% by 2007; and
- Reduce the average waiting time for the public rental housing to three years by 2005

1.3 About contemporary housing issues

Public rental housing accommodates about 2.3 million people (34% of the population), while another 298,000 families live in their own flats purchased through various home ownership schemes. According to the figures from the 1999 Policy Address, during the past two years, 73,000 families were provided with low-cost public rental housing. The waiting time for public rental flats has been reduced from seven to six years on average and over 100,000 families fulfil their wish of purchasing their own flats through various home ownership schemes. Beyond these achievements, there are still a lot of people suffering very bad living conditions. They are living in squatter and cottage areas, rooftop and 'bedspace' apartments. Most of them are elderly, unemployed or new immigrants, who are waiting for public housing, or they do not meet the requirements to apply for government housing.

2 SUSTAINABILITY IN HOUSING DEVELOPMENT

In 1995, Wackernagel and Rees published 'Our Ecological Footprint – Reducing human Impact on the Earth'. In relation to Table 1, they commented 'Hong Kong.. which has positive dollar

Table 1. Ecological footprint of different countries and cities

Country	Density (people/km^2)	Population (m)	Footprint	Avail. Capacity	Ecological deficit
USA	29	268.2	10.3	6.7	-3.6
China	131	1,247	1.2	0.8	-0.4
UK	240	4.4	5.2	1.7	-3.5
Singapore	5,624	2.9	7.2	0.1	-7.1
Hong Kong	6,373	5.9	6.1	0	-6.1

Source: Wackernagel and Rees

trade balances, provided little ecological productivity to the world, while importing a great deal from other places to maintain their high levels of consumption.. Hong Kong is densely populated and wildly prosperous yet has very little natural carrying capacity, while many African countries with much larger biophysical capacities suffer from famine'.

2.1 Sustainable Development in Hong Kong for 21st Century (SUSDEV)

The first public consultation of sustainable development was introduced in April 1998 in order to obtain from the public and a wide range of stakeholder organizations their view on which aspects of life in HKSAR they felt were important to their current well-being and to their future. These views contributed to the process of establishing the Guiding Principles and Indicators to be used in the SAR Government's Sustainable Development System, which is a tool to illustrate the economic, environmental and social effects of the SAR Government plans and policies and thereby assist in the decision-making process.

2.2 Application of Sustainability in Hong Kong Housing Authority

The Hong Kong Housing Authority 'HKHA' is playing an important role in providing affordable and comfortable homes for citizens, and is increasingly contributing toward sustainable development. In the light of social sustainability, their task is to provide on average 50,000 flats annually, and also help people to own their own flats. Besides that, the Housing for Senior Citizens Scheme (HSC) was implemented in 1994, which aims to foster a sense of security, belonging, health and worth among the senior population through housing design. HKHA is participating in the development of the Hong Kong Building Environmental Assessment Method (HK-BEAM) Residential Version. A major improvement in building design is the introduction of the Automated Refuse Collection System (ARCS), which has had a positive response from residents.

3 PILOT STUDY IN HKSAR

3.1 Research background

A future option for urban environment is the high-density city, in which many people live or work in a given area. Such cities are business oriented, have a high consumption, network transportation, better accessibility to shops or offices, etc. Indeed, economic development in these cities seems to be much better than less dense urban environments. However, the lifestyle in dense urban environments may not be sustainable in relation to quality of life, high levels of pollution, etc.

A pilot study was designed to explore socio-environmental problems and expectations on the living environment for those people living in high-density cities. The core element of the research was to study the determinants of quality of life in high density residential developments, and the relationships between quality of life, sustainable development, and built environment. The study included housing and socio-economic condition surveys of the current population, as well as informal interviews with professionals.

3.2 Research Methodology

The main part of the study was carried out using a questionnaire survey amongst residents of high-rise apartment estates. The purpose of the questionnaire was to explore the existing problems in high-rise housing. The questionnaire was in three parts, in addition to the interviewees demographic and geographic background. The three parts comprised, (i) asking residents satisfaction about their flats, (ii) their housing blocks and estates, and, (iii) their perception of sustainability and quality of life. During the pilot study, because of time constraints, interviewees were only asked to complete one section of the questionnaire. In addition, there are some open-ended questions to allow interviewee's to express their ideas and concerns about their living environment. Several informal interviews were carried out with housing professionals.

3.3 Hypothesis

The main hypothesis tested in the pilot study was:
- "Although people living in a high-density city benefit from the high level of accessibility, their quality of life is much worse than before in view of socio-environmental aspect."

Three sub-hypothesis tested were:
- "In a high-density city, people are satisfied with high-rise buildings in light of physical appearance, environmental aspects, health hygiene sanitation and safety"
- "In a high-density city, people are satisfied with the high accessibility to local facilities and transportation."
- "In a high-density city, people realize the elements of quality of life, but they behave in an unsustainable manner."

3.4 About the study area

This pilot study was mainly conducted in two government housing estates, Siu Lun Court, finished in 1993, and Tin Tze Estate (and Tin Lai Court), finished in 1997. Siu Lun Court comprises 12 housing blocks, each of 35-storeys, totaling 4,200 flats. Tin Tsz Estate comprises 4 high-rise housing blocks with 2 low-rise housing blocks (for single persons), of 38-storeys and 14 storeys, totaling 3,108 flats. The demographic backgrounds for these two government housing estates are a little different. As Siu Lun Court was designed under the Home Ownership Scheme, the target clients for Housing Authorities are people who are able to afford to buy a flat (under mortgage or fully-paid). Therefore the population in this area is middle-class. The target tenants for the Tin Tsz Estate are low-income population, especially the elderly and single people, and there appear to be more Chinese immigrants and their families living in this estate.

3.5 Media and duration of survey

Most of the questionnaires were conducted during office hours from Monday to Friday via on-street and telephone interviews. As a result, many of interviewees were housewives (who are more likely to stay at home), or residents on holiday or day-off. Besides this, the study was also conducted on one Saturday when more selected interviewees had full-time jobs.

3.6 Sampling

The level of response to the three questionnaires in this survey is presented in Table 2. Questionnaire I and II were mainly conducted in two government housing estates, that is Siu Lun Court (Home Ownership Scheme) and Tin Tze Estate (public rental). Also, there are some interviewees coming from the nearby public and private housing estates. Questionnaire III was randomly conducted through personal contact. As there were no exact figures available for the population living in these housing estates, an assumption of numbers in households was made. The average number of family members in a household in HKSAR is about 3. Therefore, the estimated populations of the study estates were about 12,600 living in Siu Lun Court, and 9,324 people living in Tin Tsz Estate. Based on this assumption, the sampling sizes of interviewees from these two housing estates are 0.67% and 1.42% respectively. 146 people were interviewed (0.002% of the Hong Kong population), and more than 62% of interviewees were from the New Territories.

Table 2. Summary of Study Area

Study Area	Questionnaire I – Flat satisfaction	Questionnaire II – Housing blocks & estate satisfaction	Questionnaire III – Quality of life
Tin Tze Estate	22	22	nil
Siu Lun Court	14	14	nil
The public	10	9	55
Total	46	45	55

3.7 Response rate and variations

An arrangement was made with the Housing Authority to carry out the surveys and both estate housing management companies delegated their staff to accompany the researcher for the whole process of the study. Before the conduct of a questionnaire interview, the estate manager and officer briefed the researcher about the existing problems and complaints about their estates. With this support, tenants and owners were quite positive and willing to finish the questionnaire and express their concerns and ideas. The rate of successful interviews was over 60%. In these Questionnaires, the levels of satisfactions are divided into 5 scores, in which 1 represents the least satisfaction, 5 is the highest satisfaction, and 0 is no consideration.

3.8 Analysis about residents flats

3.8.1 Physical appearance

The results are summarized in Tables 3 and 4. There was some dissatisfaction about the size of rooms and adaptability for furniture and interior design. During discussion with residents complaints were noted that the size of their bedrooms and kitchens were too small, and they had to spend more money to order tailor-made beds, clothes and dish cupboards. Some of them also changed their kitchens to the open style.

Table 3. Satisfaction on Size of rooms

Score	Tin Tze Estate	Siu Lun Court
1	0 (0%)	3 (21.4%)
2	8 (36.4%)	0 (0%)
3	5 (22.7%)	2 (14.3%)
4	9 (41%)	9 (64.3%)
5	0 (0%)	0 (0%)

Table 4. Satisfaction on interior design

Score	Tin Tze Estate	Siu Lun Court
1	0 (0%)	1 (7.1%)
2	4 (18.2%)	2 (14.3%)
3	6 (27.3%)	0 (0%)
4	10 (45.5%)	11 (78.6%)
5	2 (9.1%)	0 (0%)

Table 5. Satisfaction on humidity

Score	Tin Tze Estate	Siu Lun Court
1	2 (9.1%)	1 (7.1%)
2	16 (72.7%)	8 (57.1%)
3	3 (13.6%)	0 (0%)
4	1 (4.5%)	5 (35.7%)
5	0 (0%)	0 (0%)

Table 6. Satisfaction on outdoor noise

Score	Tin Tze Estate	Siu Lun Court
1	2 (9.1%)	4 (28.6%)
2	12 (54.5%)	3 (21.4%)
3	5 (22.7%)	0 (0%)
4	3 (13.6%)	7 (50%)
5	0 (0%)	0 (0%)

Table 7. Satisfaction on external pollution

Score	Tin Tze Estate	Siu Lun Court
1	1 (4.5%)	2 (14.3%)
2	10 (45.5%)	4 (28.6%)
3	4 (18.2%)	1 (7.1%)
4	7 (31.8%)	7 (31.8%)
5	0 (0%)	0 (0%)

Table 8. Satisfaction on thermal comfort

Score	Tin Tze Estate	Siu Lun Court
1	2 (9.1%)	1 (7.1%)
2	5 (22.7%)	5 (35.7%)
3	8 (36.4%)	0 (0%)
4	7 (31.8%)	8 (36.4%)
5	0 (0%)	0 (0%)

Table 9. Satisfaction on neigbouhood noise

Score	Tin Tze Estate	Siu Lun Court
1	1 (4.5%)	0 (0%)
2	7 (31.8%)	0 (0%)
3	4 (18.2%)	0 (0%)
4	10 (45.5%)	14 (100%)
5	0 (0%)	0 (0%)

Table 10. Satisfaction on Fungshui

Score	Tin Tze Estate	Siu Lun Court
1	0 (0%)	0 (0%)
2	0 (0%)	0 (0%)
3	4 (18%)	6 (27.3%)
4	2 (9.1%)	0 (0%)
5	0 (0%)	0 (0%)
0	16 (72.7%)	8 (57.1%)

3.8.2 *Environmental aspects*

The results are summarized in Tables 5 to 8. The typical weather in HKSAR has high humidity in spring, during January to April, which causes complaints associated with condensation. The main sources of noise pollution in both housing estates was the nearby traffic. In addition, noise and environmental pollution of the nearby construction in Tin Tze Estate was noted. Complaints of dust were also noted. Also, internally generated noise from neighbors was noted. There were frequent complaints of conditions too windy and cold in winter, particular for people who live in Siu Lun Court. Over half the respondents did not believe in Fungshui.

3.8.3 *Privacy*

Although there is minimum distance between housing blocks, people still complain their privacy cannot be protected. Their major concern is the visual distance between two flats, which are oriented at right-angles in the same housing block.

Table 11. Satisfaction on privacy

Score	Tin Tze Estate	Siu Lun Court
1	0 (0%)	0 (0%)
2	3 (13.6%)	1 (7.14%)
3	5 (22.7%)	0 (0%)
4	14 (63.6%)	12 (85.7%)
5	0 (0%)	1 (7.1%)

Table 12. Satisfaction on stair

Score	Tin Tze Estate	Siu Lun Court
1	0 (0%)	0 (0%)
2	5 (22.7%)	0 (0%)
3	4 (18.2%)	2 (14.3%)
4 .	13 (59%)	12 (54.5%)
5	0 (0%)	0 (0%)

3.9 *Satisfaction about their housing blocks and estates*

3.9.1 *Physical design*

In the modern housing estates, stairs are mainly used for fire or emergency exits and by tenants who live on the lower floors. Stairs are often located at the rear of housing blocks and not easily noticed, so they become a dangerous place in relation to crime and perceived safety (Table 12).

Table 13. Satisfaction on humidity

Score	Tin Tze Estate	Siu Lun Court
1	1 (4.5%)	0 (0%)
2	3 (13.6%)	4 (28.6%)
3	10 (45.5%)	3 (21.4%)
4	8 (36.4%)	7 (50%)
5	0 (0%)	0 (0%)

Table 14. Satisfaction on air ventilation

Score	Tin Tze Estate	Siu Lun Court
1	0 (0%)	0 (0%)
2	1 (4.5%)	1 (7.1%)
3	7 (31.8%)	2 (14.3%)
4	13 (59.1%)	11 (78.6%)
5	1 (4.5%)	0 (0%)

Table 15. Satisfaction on lighting

Score	Tin Tze Estate	Siu Lun Court
1	1 (4.5%)	0 (0%)
2	2 (9%)	5 (35.7%)
3	10 (45.4%)	1 (7.1%)
4	9 (40.9%)	8 (57.1%)
5	0 (0%)	0 (0%)

Table 16. Satisfaction on refuse collection

Score	Tin Tze Estate	Siu Lun Court
1	1 (4.5%)	0 (0%)
2	3 (13.6%)	1 (7.14%)
3	13 (59.1%)	2 (14.3%)
4	5 (22.7%)	11(78.6%)
5	0 (0%)	0 (0%)

Table 17. Satisfaction on privacy

Score	Tin Tze Estate	Siu Lun Court
1	0 (0%)	0 (0%)
2	2 (9%)	0 (0%)
3	6 (27.3%)	4 (28.6%)
4	13 (59.1%)	10 (71.4%)
5	1 (4.5%)	0 (0%)

Table 18. Satisfaction on elderly facilities

Score	Tin Tze Estate	Siu Lun Court
1	2 (9%)	0 (0%)
2	0 (0%)	0 (0%)
3	10 (45.5%)	3 (21.4%)
4	10 (45.5%)	11 (78.6%)
5	0 (0%)	0 (0%)

Table 19. Satisfaction on facilities for children

Score	Tin Tze Estate	Siu Lun Court
1	0 (0%)	0 (0%)
2	6 (27.3%)	0 (0%)
3	8 (36.4%)	4 (28.6%)
4	8 (36.4%)	10 (71.4%)
5	0 (0%)	0 (0%)

3.9.2 *Environmental aspects*

Tables 13 and 14 present satisfaction with environmental aspects of estates. Discussions with tenants also revealed complaints of not enough sunshine, and rainwater leakage during storms.

3.9.3 *Facilities and privacy*

The cleanness in Tin Tze Estate is problem (Table 16) with rubbish left in the lobby of some floors. This can be a serious problem on some estates. Privacy and facilities are summarized in Tables 17 to 19. Facilities for the elderly and children are not satisfied in Tin Tze Estate compared to Siu Lun Court. Some tenants complain that their gates are too easy to open. For safety, they prefer to close the door even though the ventilation with the door closed is not good.

3.9.4 *Accessibility*

Satisfaction with accessibility is summarized in Tables 20 to 23. It is noted the level of satisfaction in Siu Lun Court is better than Tin Tze Estate, where people need to walk at least 15 to 20 minutes to the nearest food market, shops and bus terminus to other districts. There is not much difference between two housing estates in relation to access to the countryside, in fact, countryside is a 'luxury' for every one in HKSAR.

Table 20. Satisfaction on food markets

Score	Tin Tze Estate	Siu Lun Court
1	4 (18.2%)	0 (0%)
2	9 (40.9%)	3 (21.4%)
3	7 (31.8%)	0 (0%)
4	2 (9.1%)	11 (78.6%)
5	0 (0%)	0 (0%)

Table 21. Satisfaction on shops

Score	Tin Tze Estate	Siu Lun Court
1	6 (27.3%)	1 (7.1%)
2	9 (40.9%)	6 (42.9%)
3	4 (18.2%)	4 (28.6%)
4	3 (13.6%)	3 (21.4%)
5	0 (0%)	0 (0%)

Table 22. Satisfaction on transportation

Score	Tin Tze Estate	Siu Lun Court
1	0 (0%)	0 (0%)
2	7 (31.8%)	0 (0%)
3	8 (36.4%)	3 (21.4%)
4	7 (31.8%)	11 (78.6%)
5	0 (0%)	0 (0%)

Table 23. Satisfaction on countryside

Score	Tin Tze Estate	Siu Lun Court
1	0 (0%)	0 (0%)
2	4 (18.2%)	1 (7.1%)
3	13 (59.1%)	9 (64.3%)
4	4 (18.2%)	4 (28.6%)
5	0 (0%)	0 (0%)

3.10 *Quality of life*

The purpose of Questionnaire III was to assess people's perception and understanding of concepts and principles of sustainable development, and to explore their expectation on quality of life in a high-density city. The followings are the findings of the survey:

• In relation to housing design, 78% of people agreed the existing facilities for children are not enough, and 69% of people complain of insufficient protection from crime. 72% of people realize the urgent need to have special housing design for the elderly.

• In relation to environmental issues, 93% of people realize environmental deterioration in HKSAR is much more serious than 10 years ago. Half the respondents agreed and half disagreed when asked whether 'Economic growth is the more important than good environ-

ment quality'. Positively, 99% of people realized environmental protection is a good step towards a good quality of life. 84% of people would pay more in order to improve quality of life.
- 91% and 89% of people agreed that HKSAR people spend too much time at work, and neglect to protect environment and participate in social activities. Half of respondents do agree that HKSAR is a good place to live because of the quality of environment and social welfare provided. In spite of the recent Asian Crises and economic restructuring of HKSAR, over 60% of people still believe there are numerous employment opportunities in this city. Because of the 97-handover and close relationship with Mainland China, the number of Chinese immigrants is expected to increase. 80% of interviewees think these new comers will affect the quality of life in HKSAR.
- From the behaviour analysis, it is found that nearly 62% and 56% of people did not take part in any social activities and environmental protection activities in the past 5 years, however, most of people, nearly 75% always make a conscious effort to save energy.

4 CONCLUSIONS

- In contemporary housing development, the techniques of sustainability are not yet well adopted and people are still not satisfied on many accounts of their flats and housing estates.
- Tenants and owners' were not satisfied with the thermal conditions, being too humid in spring, too hot in summer, and cold and windy in winter. There were also complaints of rubbish in lobby and corridor and dust and noise, and difficulties to dry clothes outside. There were insufficient facilities for recreational purposes and lack of security, low privacy and problems of perceived safety. There was generally poor accessibility to community facilities for daily necessities. So some of the benefits of high density living, such as accessibility, are therefore not being realized in practice. However, this pilot study was conducted only on two estates and so generalizations cannot be concluded.
- In general people are aware of issues of sustainability. They have a positive attitude towards environmental protection and recognize the link between the environment and quality of life. But there is a lack of perception of immediate benefits from individual action.
- Estate Management expressed difficulties for management and maintenance, so they have to spend more human and monetary resources because of poor design (in Tin Tze Estate), and on designs often not being realistic. In the past, housing design was dominated by architects, planners and engineers. However, estate management is now playing a crucial role. Because they are the people who know the problems in the housing estates, their contribution and suggestions are essential in the process of housing estate design.
- 'Sustainable living' needs to be encouraged in both the design and management of housing estates and in resident's attitudes and behaviour. Recent developments such as Hong Kong Environmental Assessment Method (HK-BEAM) and its adoption by HKHA show a positive response to government's growing awareness of the importance of sustainable development.

REFERENCES

Pryor, E.G. 1992. Housing in Hong Kong .
Hong Kong SAR Government. 1999. Hong Kong Report 1998.
Hong Kong SAR Government. 1998. White Paper on Long Term Housing Strategy.
Hong Kong SAR Government. 1999. Study on Sustainable Development in Hong Kong in the 21st Century: Topic Report No. 6.
Hong Kong SAR Government. 1998. Territorial Development Strategy Review: A Response to Change and Challenges.
Hong Kong SAR Government. 2000. The 1999 Policy Address: Quality People Quality Home - Positioning Hong Kong for the 21st Century.
Wackernagel, M. & Rees, W.E. 1995. Our Ecological Footprint, New Society Publishers.
Ng, M.K. & Cook, A.1997. Reclamation: an urabn development strategy under fire, Pergamon.
Bristow, R. 1989. Hong Kong's New Towns: A Selective Review, Hong Kong Oxford University Press.

People, cultures and diversity

Urban Lifestyles: Spaces · Places · People, Benson & Roe (eds)
© 2000 Balkema, Rotterdam, ISBN 90 5809 169 4

The quality of life for refugees: A challenge for governance

E.A.Ahmed
Welsh Refugee Council, Cardiff, UK

H.Thomas
Department of City and Regional Planning, Cardiff University, UK

ABSTRACT: It is very likely that refugees will form significant portions of urban populations, worldwide, in the next few decades. There are urgent practical questions to be addressed about how they are to secure a reasonable quality of life and equal opportunities. Addressing these questions throws an interesting light on more theoretical issues, particularly on the nature of contemporary urban governance, for the "refugee question" is one which appears well suited to be tackled by the more flexible governance structures allegedly characteristic of (at least) Western cities, and an issue which calls out for a sophisticated multi-level response by agencies of capacity to shape a just city, by analysing a British case study of responses to refugees, especially contemporary responses to asylum-seekers. It ends with practical recommendations for the short and medium term.

SUMMARY

It is widely acknowledged that profound changes have been occurring in the governance of countries in "the West" (Rhodes, 1997; Stoker, 2000). At all levels - from the nation state to neighbourhoods - there appears to be a shift in the nature and role of the state, with hierarchical, bureaucratic modes of government being replaced (to varying extents) by the "looser, more interactive administrative arrangements such as coalitions, partnerships or networks "(Cowell & Murdoch, 1999, p. 654) characteristic of governance. This shift, it is generally argued, is a state-led response to an increasingly complex and turbulent economic and social environment, sometimes encouraging the passing of tasks which might otherwise be direct state responsibilities to institutions and agencies more, or less, independent of the state. The institutional fragmentation which results, while possibly advantageous in terms of gaining flexibility, sensitivity and focus in addressing some policy issues also leads to the need for coalition and networks to define and pursue strategic goals both at particular levels of governance and between levels of governance. This picture of a shift to multi-level governance, as it if often called, is familiar; but certain aspects of it need to be highlighted.

First, networking and coalition building is inherently exclusionary; so whatever the breadth of an apparent multi-level governance consensus - eg in relation to urban renewal - there are likely to be groups and agencies excluded from it (Khakee *et al.*, 1999, Thomas & Imrie, 1999). Generally organizations representing racialised minorities have not featured, in the UK, as key parts of governance coalitions (Thomas, 1999). Secondly securing a governance coalition or effective network may be at the cost of incoherence or inconsistency in the policies being pursued (Boland, 1999). Finally, it has been argued that the shift to governance is limited to areas where "visions and goals can be shared between 'partners'" or local variations in policy can be tolerated or exploited (Cowell & Murdoch, 1999, p. 664). Consequently, the move to governance from government has, in fact, been rather patchy, and old-fashioned hierarchical government remains very influential in certain policy fields. These considerations make the current reconstructing of the UK government's policy in relation to asylum seekers of some theoretical as well as practical interest. On the other hand, dealing humanely with asylum-seekers, particularly if the flow is erratic as a result of unanticipated crises, is the kind of complex task, cutting across policy areas, which necessitates flexible governance structures.

There are very many reports which illustrate the ways in which the needs of refugees and asylum-seekers cut across bureaucratic divisions (eg Means & Sangster, 1998). The new UK government policy of dispersing asylum-seekers means that some sophisticated, and swift consideration is required between a variety of local agencies if a coherent and comprehensive package of housing in the UK of a spatial strategy for immigration of any kind (Smith, 1989), and while there may be a degree of congruence in the (racialised) values of agencies at various levels of governance about the 'threat' or 'problem' posed by asylum seekers, there are likely to be radically different views about the significance of specific proposals. At the most crude level, for example, a proposal to house asylum seekers in redundant college accommodation in a rural village, may strike some agencies (particularly those looking from the top down) as a rational use of resources, but to residents the proposal may appear to threaten a radical change in the nature of the locality. In these circumstances, consensus and coalition-building may prove impossible. In similar circumstances, traditional hierarchical modes of government have been used to impose solutions on a reluctant village (see Thomas, 2000, for details of the struggle for planning permission for the Hari Krishna Bhaktivedanta Manor in rural Hertfordshire); yet, such an approach may be counter-productive when a degree of local support is needed over the medium term if life is to be tolerable for asylum-seekers or, indeed, for immigrants in general.

This paper will examine how these tensions have been played out, and what they reveal about contemporary urban governance. This is a question of theoretical and practical significance, for while global refugee flows may ebb and flow, international migration remains relative and is a "potent force of social transformation" (Castles & Miller, 1998, p. xiii), particularly in urban areas.

In particular, the paper will consider the roles of agencies representing the interests of asylum seekers in the shifting sands of governance coalitions at one level rather than another and in their operations between tiers; do they contribute, in any way, to the creation of multi-level coalitions? It will suggest that networks become more permeable to influence by refugee organizations the higher spatial role (this, however, does not guarantee influence); however, the British government has sought multi-level agreement in an area of policy where there is a limit to value-consensus. Why this should be is explicable only in the light of a history of racialised politics (Solomos, 1993). The result, however, is to create a position where the scope for decisive action is shaped by the local politics of race and in some areas is difficult and where influence in networks at one level can be negated by exclusion at another. This imposes its own strains on relations between organisations representing refugees at the various levels of governance.

In the short term, therefore, reversion to government, rather than governance, maybe the best approach to securing a just response at the urban level to the plight of refugees and asylum seekers.

REFERENCES:

Boland, P. 1999."Contested Multi-Level Governance: Merseyside and the European Structure Funds". *European Planning Studies* 7 (5):647-664.
Castles, S, & Miller, M. 1998. *The Age of Migration.* 2nd. London, Macmillan.
Cowell, R. & Murdoch, J. 1999."Land Use and the Limits to Regional Governance: Some Lessons from planning for housing and minerals in England". *International Journal of Urban and Regional Research.* 23 (4):654-669. Urban Renewal, Ethnicity and Social Exclusion in Europe. Aldershot: Ashgate.
Means, R. & Sangster, A. 1998. *In Search of a Home.* Bristol: Policy, Press.

Rhodes, R. 1997 *Understanding Governance.* Buckingham: Open University Press

Smith, S. J. 1989. The Politics of 'Race' and Residence. Cambridge: Polity.

Solomos, J. 1993. *Race and Racism in Britain* 2nd ed. London: Macmillan.

Stoker, G. (ed) 2000. *The New Politics of British Local Governance.* London: Macmillan.

Thomas, H. & Imrie, R. 1999. "Urban Policy, Modernisation and the Regeneration of Cardiff Bay" in Imrie, R and Thomas, H (eds) *British Urban Policy* London: Sage.

Thomas, H. 1999. "Urban Renewal, Social Exclusion and Ethnic Minorities in Britain" In A. Khakee, et al (eds) *Urban Renewal, Ethnicity and Social Exclusion in Europe.* Aldershot: Ashgate.

Thomas, H. 2000. *Race and Planning: a UK Perspective.* London: UCL Press.

Urban Lifestyles: Spaces · Places · People, Benson & Roe (eds)
© *2000 Balkema, Rotterdam, ISBN 90 5809 169 4*

Landscapes of cultural production and regeneration

J. Foord & G. L. Evans
Cities Research Institute, University of North London, UK

ABSTRACT: Urban lifestyles increasingly reflect the breaking down of the barriers between spaces for living, working, recreation and consumption, in contrast to the traditional separation of social and economic life in cities. This is evident in the sphere of cultural production and consumption in areas undergoing revitalisation. Artists, designer-makers and producer services have colonized parts of the inner city/fringe, however resident communities of these poorer districts contain socially excluded groups who 'exist' on the fringes of these 'creative' and gentrified areas. These traditional cultural industry quarters have been commodified through the promotion of cultural consumption, exploiting their appeal for residential, employment and tourism use. Urban design has looked to flagship developments in pursuit of this mixed-use strategy. Drawing on experience in East London, it is suggested that the association of cultural with regeneration practices is an attempt to 'govern' local areas through self-reflexive governmentality.

1 INTRODUCTION

The development of cultural activities as integral elements of urban regeneration has been a feature of European (Bianchini & Parkinson, 1993) and North American (BAAA, 1998), post-industrial city strategies since the early 1980s. The combination of visitor-led animation and cultural industries as twin economic development opportunities, has placed cultural policy within the realms of both economic and urban policy. The associated notions of the 'creative city' and the 'innovative milieu' (Landry & Bianchini, 1995; Verwijnen & Lehtovuori, 1999) have become central to recent analyses of city development. For example Hall (1998) traces the importance of a vibrant cultural milieu to the economic ascendancy of particular cities over time. Such rich inner city areas have cheaper land and rents and have also traditionally been the 'cultural workshops' of cities with a high concentration of artist (visual, crafts, designer-making) activity. The areas subject to most intensive urban regeneration activity also tend to be those with high levels of unemployment and a combination of factors (health, housing, environment, education) that create acute and cumulative levels of social deprivation. However, as Cheshire & Hay concluded (1989), across Europe, urban and regional development strategies accessing structural investment programmes were seldom consonant with the most deprived inner city areas. Moreover, the needs of these areas have to date not been met by these flagship cultural *Grand Projets* (Harvey, 1993) nor by the improvement of central zones associated with cultural consumption and tourism. At the same time, the cultural context of these locations is more accurately represented as a locale of 'hybridity' (Hall, 1990). As a result of successive diasporas, a rich history and diversity in cultural expression emerges in such locations, reflected in the re-use of symbolic buildings - from Methodist Hall to Synagogue to Mosque.

2 CULTURE AND URBAN REGENERATION

This cultural geography is no more manifest than in East London, where over 75% of the UK's practising artists and crafts people operate (Evans, 1993), and where high proportions of immigrant and refugee communities have followed Hugenot, Jewish and Afro-Caribbean migrants. The rationales for culture-led urban regeneration policies and investment in this and other areas, have attempted to reconcile social welfare policy through community cultural development, and economic goals via the creative/cultural industries, and physically through property-based redevelopment of former industrial zones (Lim,1993). This has encompassed studio-based production, advanced producer (e.g. design) services, to street and market-based animation and consumption spaces. The extent to which these strategic policies and programmes have achieved these multiple goals is questionable. There are clear tensions between, on the one hand, cultural consumption and production and, on the other, arts participation and amenity, whilst the gentrification effect has had dramatic spatial and economic impacts on both residential and commercial property use values. The urban regeneration process has not however, been one left to the private market. Indeed, successive property growth and recession periods and the planning liberalisation during the 1970s and 1980s (i.e. 'change of use'), have taken place alongside a long history of regional - local, national, European - development funding and the support of cultural industry strategies by the public sector.

The current phase of urban regeneration exhibits aspects of both these earlier periods – the social exclusion agenda, access to the arts, neighbourhood renewal (Shaw & Evans, 1999) on the one hand, and the private sector partnership (e.g. Private Finance Initiative, mixed-use), small business development and creative industry initiatives, on the other. To an extent the patchwork of urban funding programmes (Audit Commission, 1989) converges, or at least purports to conflate, these social and economic rationales for culture within the urban policy agenda. However, whilst some critiques see the late-twentieth century post-industrial city as now no longer linked to the nineteenth century tradition of arts and the pursuit of cultural homogeneity (Ellmeier & Rasky, 1998), the concern for amenity, social exclusion and an economic creative industry base, has clear resonance with the Victorian rational recreation movement and the long established relationship between culture and commerce (Hall, 1998). Urban regeneration, which in itself has shifted in direct relation to global capital, geopolitical and supply and demand movements, continues to look to opportunities for adding 'value' and 'quality' to major development projects and areas, including design, animation and public realm (e.g. landscaping, public art), but as Robins claims: 'Urban regeneration reflects a more acceptable face of rationalism, and fails to come to terms with the emotional dimensions of urban culture' (1996: 8). This means, in Ellmeier and Rasky's view that: 'today the tasks of city planning also include compensating for differences and creating necessary community in order to allow the city to function at all. If inhomogeneity becomes visible, if the idea of the homogenous national or city culture is no longer tenable, then the city, the urban space, becomes important' (1998: 80).

The region of East London provides a particular case not only due to its historic and contemporary significance, but also as the unwilling "host" to earlier intervention (through the nineteenth century rational recreation social reformers, 'People's Palaces'), and the repeated claims that urban policy has so far failed this community. A key concern of the current government is to re-connect impoverished, socially disconnected areas and estates to mainstream society (Social Exclusion Unit, 1998). London, in common with the other 'world cities' of New York, Tokyo and Paris, has a central city core area of intense wealth generation based on the global command and control activities of finance and business services and the attendant sectors of business tourism, leisure and retailing (Fainstein *et al*, 1991; Sassen, 1990; Llewelyn Davis, 1996). These 'hot spots' of economic growth, as well as creating multiplier impacts on the commercial and residential property markets, also influence labour demand and skills. London has experienced areas of intense property speculation with labour and skill shortages in close proximity to locations dominated by economic disinvestment, relative poverty, high levels of unemployment and pockets of severe social deprivation. This spatial juxtaposition of wealth and poverty, social 'inclusion' and 'exclusion', is particularly sharply focused in the eastern core area of London. Here ethnic diversity adds a further layer of complexity to the socio-spatial dynamics of inclusion/exclusion. This socio-spatial context can be interpreted in two very different, though related, ways. One interpretation sees areas of socially excluded populations as a threat. The inclusion policy is therefore driven by a desire to minimize this threat. The other interpretation presents the same areas as an opportunity. Here the goal is to make use of wasted resources. Both interpretations however have led their protagonists to propose policies which fuse cultural initiatives with urban regeneration programmes. Both advocate the remaking of local cultures.

For those who construct socially excluded populations as a threat, this spatialized urban inequality highlights the increase in social isolation of those who are outside the organizations and networks of key institutions (work, education, 'community') and therefore the environments in which normative values are created, negotiated and absorbed. Such exclusion therefore does not simply pose moral questions of social injustice, it fuels more deep seated fears. Indeed Lord Rogers (1996), during a series of public lectures on the future of cities, called the inner suburban ring around London's prosperous core 'a powder keg'. He therefore suggested, in a manner somewhat reminiscent of the 19th century English middle classes, that these areas are going to explode into social unrest in the not too distant future. Yet unlike the Victorian middle classes, today's new (predominantly white) urban professionals no longer wish to escape the urban core. Instead they wish to reclaim the city for themselves as workplace and pleasure zone. As this vision of an 'urban renaissance' emerges into the forefront of urban policy debate (DETR, 1999), new regeneration strategies are increasingly suggesting that inner city 'cultures' as well as infrastructures need to be addressed in order to ameliorate such fearfulness. Thus when 'cultural' initiatives are fused with proposals for urban regeneration they are constructed principally in terms of building forms of local cultures which are safe. What must be created are controllable, socially responsible communities - ones which no longer threaten middle class sensibilities.

This urban debate coincides with widespread criticism of regeneration programmes which rely principally on infrastructure and property redevelopment. The vogue now is to advocate regeneration schemes which, in addition to physical renewal, provide community development, training and education, youth development, parenting support, art projects and local community economic development (Taylor, 1997; Comedia, 1998). It is in this context that some cultural initiatives, particularly those offering elements of job training or community capacity building, have found some favour. Furthermore the leadership of 'experts', either as individuals or institutions, including the local authorities, has been roundly criticized as unresponsive, inappropriate and wasteful of resources. Now local people are entreated to lead their own regeneration by proposing initiatives, taking central roles in the management structures, creating their own businesses, and organising self help groups. What appears to be taking place is an orchestration of local expectations as part of the wider goal of social inclusion. Porter (1995), drawing on evidence from North American cities, also argues that there are 'advantages of these close inner city locations which provide:

i.   strategic cheap sites for rent or development close to the overheating core;

ii.   local niche 'ethnic' markets which can be serviced and/or tapped for 'new' cultural practices/products to be introduced to 'mainstream' markets;

iii.   reliable, culturally literate and flexible labour which also happens to be 'cheap'; and

iv.   integration of local finance/business services and retail/ tourism services with successful firms in the core and therefore increasing overall regional competitive advantage.

Worpole & Greenhalgh (1999) suggest that the potential of inner city areas lies in the very intensity and diversity which others see as a threat. Cities, and especially those like London which have a global reach, are now home to diverse populations with a multiplicity of languages and lifestyles, behaviours and aspirations. Difference is often more familiar than sameness. This 'rich mix', it is argued, is a breeding ground for creativity. Individuals and organizations are more likely to succeed if they tap into cultural difference and make use of its opportunities - tastes, practices, interactions. Thus it is in these locations of intensity and diversity that one is able to "engage through imaginative awareness of new environments and new conditions, anticipating change rather than reluctantly responding to it" (p4).

Tapping into these areas has inspired initiatives which seek to support creative and innovative activity. Here local 'culture' has been translated into an asset for regeneration. Cultural diversity becomes the source of innovations and therefore new products (artefacts, events, food, music) which can be marketed by cultural industries.

3 NEW GOVERNMENTALITY

Currently these agendas of 'social inclusion' and 'local assets' are influencing the form and direction of regeneration policy at the local level. Cultural projects have been harnessed to meet both objectives. Common to both however is an overarching goal: to create new 'communities' of self-reliant, creative citizens. Indeed a particular form of local governmentality, in which the individual is encouraged to take up 'opportunities' to participate in mainstream society (via paid work) underpins local regeneration strategies today. Governmentality (Foucault, 1991) as an expression of power, includes the modes, rationales and techniques which seek to "shape, guide or affect the conduct of some person or persons" (Gordon, 1991, p. 2). Its purpose is therefore to "act on the conduct of conduct", influencing the actions of others through a process of self-regulation of behaviours. As such governmentality operates at arms length and not directly through coercion or consent. Burchell (1991, p. 145) suggests that notions of participatory individual citizenship "must, at the same time, address the question not only of how we are to be governed by others, but also of how we ourselves are to be involved in the practices of governing others".

Drawing from initiatives in East London it is suggested that the association of cultural with regeneration 'practices' is an attempt to 'govern' local areas by influencing how local people act on their own behaviour. Cultural and regeneration activities have become conduits for self-reflexive governmentality, which guide and affect the conduct of local residents in such a way as to promote notions of individual responsibility, through training and enterprise, and involvement in the agency structures of regeneration. It would appear that this form of governmentality, based on presenting individuals with opportunities for self-development, is becoming the pathway to 'inclusion' of erstwhile 'excluded' populations and communities. These examples are therefore used to illustrate a local, contingent 'art of governing' which rests upon creating opportunities for individuals who thus become capable of shouldering the responsibilities of 'making it' in post industrial/modern urban society. Yet such a form closes down possibilities as well as opening them up. The objectives are narrowly focused and by presenting new possibilities for successful social inclusion, it also carries with it the intensified risk of failure. In the following local case studies, some examples of the fusion of 'practices' of cultural and urban policy are traced and the implications of local governmentality are then raised.

3.1 *Pulling Stepney back*

Stepney's population is socially excluded though they live on the doorstep of the City of London. Survey work on the social composition, quality of life, health and housing conditions in Stepney present a harrowing picture (Evans *et al*, 1999). Poverty, poor housing conditions and fragile health add to the isolation and social exclusion of many living within the local area. Un/underemployment (in the restaurant/rag trades) and low educational achievement are exaggerated in a population dominated by minority ethnic groups (mostly Bangladeshi and Somali). High levels of economic dependency on state benefits is coupled with cultures of low esteem and dependency. Experience of and access to jobs, training and economic resources is disproportionately low. Local housing is overwhelmingly in the social rented sector. Many of the properties are arranged in estates of flats and have structural problems stemming from poor design, piecemeal modernization and inadequate maintenance. These estates have become the focus for local social tension, especially amongst territorially defined groups of young men and between older (white) tenants and those with teenage and younger children. Strain over the identity of Stepney - who belongs and who does not - occasionally erupts into running street battles. Crime and drug abuse are also increasingly visible elements of daily life. Stepney appears to conform to Roger's notion of a 'powder keg'. As a consequence of the multiple problems emerging from these estates and in Stepney as a whole, the area is currently the target for a large number of regeneration programmes and initiatives - SRB, New Deal for Communities, Estate Renewal, Health Action Zones et al. Despite criticism of property and infrastructure-led regeneration programmes, the overwhelming emphasis in current programmes is on infrastructural and environmental improvement and on building new homes. One specific goal is to erode the dominance of social housing by the development of co-ownership and privately owned housing. As such this is a covert strategy to alter the social composition and therefore to rearrange the local cultural formation.

Embedded within these regeneration programmes are individual and small scale initiatives which are indirectly aimed at remaking local culture. To date, there has not been a specific cultural strategy for Stepney. Indeed Stepney has suffered from a dominant bias in British local urban cultural policy generally, and in Tower Hamlets in particular, which emphasizes the economic potential of 'creativity and the cultural industries' to the exclusion of social arts programmes (Evans *et al*, 1999). Consequently local borough wide cultural policy has reinforced the western edge of the borough, abutting the City, in which there is considerable buoyancy around the economic growth potential of a 'cultural quarter' attracting high levels of investment from new-media firms, fashion, film and the music industries. Since Stepney does not have a high cultural industries profile, borough wide strategy simply did not apply locally. Stepney was wiped off the cultural map. Despite these difficulties some local 'cultural' initiatives have emerged through the community development funding attached to major rebuilding programmes, and through European (ERDF) and more traditional arts funding. Below are just three 'cameos' of small initiatives: what is of interest here is the use of such initiatives to suggest shifts local attitudes and aspirations while using the creative approaches of arts and culture-led projects.

3.2 *Public art project*

This involved a summer programme of participatory visual arts activity led by an artist residency. Located on one of the estates experiencing redevelopment there were several goals. At one level it aimed to produce decorative murals to screen and engage humorously with the building work. At another it was to engender amongst local youth a collective disapproval of the high levels of drug abuse on the estate and to signify this publicly (again through murals indicating drug free zones). Yet at another level the programme aimed to encourage multicultural participation and commitment amongst local residents, especially the young. Furthermore developing notions of responsibility for oneself and others and respect for the environment emerged in work to develop proposals for an installation which was to be located in the redeveloped estate.

3.3 *Women's photography project*

This developed out of women residents demands for additional security (grills, cameras, locks, entry systems) on their newly redeveloped homes. Instead of acquiescing to their demands, the housing development agency brought in an outside voluntary sector women's design service to undertaking a project to explore women's fears through photography. The output was not additional security but the identification of deep-seated fears of change being experienced by the women. Their experimentation with photography was then used to develop their self-awareness, confidence and sense of responsibility for their own and each others attachment to and security within the locality.

3.4 *Somali cultural project*

The principle focus of this Somali support group is cultural reinforcement for refugees and migrants who find themselves housed in the area. The project runs a programme of music and arts as well as facilitating contact with 'home'. Using ERDF funding and considerable support from a local Women's Business Advice Agency, a 'training package' including language skills, business skills, textile design and marketing was assembled and delivered. A key element of this programme was to mobilise women's existing craft skills for enterprise. Again a key underlying theme of this pragmatic training was encouraging women participants to think of themselves as potential earners and small businesswomen. Thus through building confidence in themselves as Somalis and in their belief that there was a market for their products, the *idea* of economic independence and self-determination was being promoted if not delivered.

Within each of these local initiatives, it is possible to identify how the fusion of cultural and regeneration practices in these local circumstances are creating a set of attitudinal expectations which challenge dominant everyday cultures of dependence and low esteem: self awareness, responsibility, economic independence, familiarity with change, acceptance of social difference and intolerance of anti-social behaviour. As such they are part of a movement towards encouraging a local form of self-government.

3.5 *Making it in Hackney*

Hackney is also a poor area. Approximately 26% of economically active men and 18% of economically active women are unemployed, more than twice the average for London as a whole. Black and other ethnic minority groups are disproportionately represented amongst the unemployed. Hackney also has a very young population: a third are under the age of 20. Despite massive declines since the 1970s, manufacturing still remains a framing element of Hackney's economy. Most manufacturing is in small enterprises and concentrated in clothing and footwear, paper products, and furniture production. This area of the economy is precarious, with poor pay and working conditions. This residual core is also 'backward looking' with many structural problems: it operates in declining sectors and targets the lower end retail markets; lacks finance; and has poor long term business planning. Yet this residual manufacturing provides an important entry point for local entrepreneurs and potential employees, especially newly arrived migrants.

Following a commissioned audit of cultural resources, 'a portfolio of cultural opportunities' for the arts and cultural industries was devised. This focused on elements of existing cultural activity which it was suggested was capable of providing a spur/new direction to the local economy - designer-makers (in craft based disciplines, furniture making, and domestic interiors), the production side of music and film/video, and the 'production' of fine and conceptual art. Unlike other arts and culture driven local agendas, a consumption based strategy was not initially constructed. Hackney was not the place, in the early 1990s to do much consuming of culture. There were a few key venues: Geffrye Museum, Angela Flowers Gallery, entertainment venues such as the Rio and the Hackney Empire, and a small restaurant economy - but not enough 'critical mass' or sufficiently developed/non derelict interesting spaces to warrant a consumption based strategy. In the last four years an embryonic consumption strategy has emerged, linked to a local market initiative to revive flagging street markets and support for evening activity through restaurants, clubs and arts events in strategic locations. However, cultural intervention in regeneration initially identified the underdeveloped capacity for production across a number of 'cultural activities/industries'. What they required was consolidation, promotion, marketing, business support and infrastructural investment. This construction of Hackney as 'The Cultural Workshop of London' became adopted as a component of the borough's rhetoric. This coincided with the beginning of major regeneration projects, including 'City Challenge' and European funding. What is of note here is that there were, in the borough, some key 'cultural intermediaries' (Bourdieu, 1989, 1993) who were able to mobilise the economic arguments for the 'cultural production' and shape it to suit the local condition and funding opportunities. These 'intermediaries' were drawn from a small group of well educated though not 'wealthy', middle class arts/media professionals living locally and/or working in local arts administration/consultancy. They operated on the fringes of artistic activity. They had high 'cultural capital' and were culturally literate in the conventions, tastes and values of the arts and crafts movements. They gained a powerful position enabling not only access to Challenge and, latterly European funds, but also to influence the direction of key elements of funding. This position was consolidated through facilitating networking - drawing together a new arts based constituency for regeneration including a range of cultural producers, critics and audiences/consumers which had hitherto been fragmented and not mobilised in regeneration initiatives. A 'creative' approach has been adopted by regeneration agents to engendering cultural production: 'there is no grand plan and no shopping list of projects'. The key agent for channelling European funds relies on local projects developing and being developed through networking and pre-bid negotiation. Stress is laid on the 'quality' of the organisation as well as the product. However it would seem that 'quality' is being used as a tool of both 'cultural' and 'economic' intermediaries to direct local regeneration in a particular direction: one which favours the middle-brow tastes and cultural values of London's (white) middle classes (Foord, 1999).

4 CONCLUSION

In this East London context much has come to be expected of the 'artist' /cultural producer: as well as providing the aesthetic meaning to/interpretation of (a rapidly changing) life, expectations have been increasingly made of 'artists' to become involved in community development and social work, the re-imaging of place and in local economic development. It is suggested that 'creative artists' are uniquely able to engage in participatory problem solving. Bringing in the artist to work 'creatively' on a housing redevelopment scheme, into the local schools and into derelict retail space on estates to use as workshop/studio space or as exhibition space is not only justified in terms of their potential to re-imagine both problems and solutions in new ways, but also because it can be developed quickly according to a local situation; it is flexible and can change as required; and it offers a potentially high return for low capital risk.

Moreover the adoption of this new fusion of regeneration and cultural practice has a particular appeal and intensity in this part of East London. The abandonment of welfarism at an institutional level and potential for cultural initiatives within the regeneration context to promote new forms of self reliant governmentality are particularly attractive. It is apparent that the objectives of urban regeneration and cultural policy are becoming locked together at the local level in Britain. In East London, a particular 'governmental rationality' is emerging which is advancing notions of self-regulation within constructed norms of individualized responsibility and liberal citizenship. As such there has been a significant shift in the mode of local governmentality within which arts and renewal programmes operate. Social arts programmes in the past sought to expose and persuade new audiences and participants of the benefits of cultural activity for enlivening and enriching the self. The role of 'experts' (intermediaries) was paramount in constructing both the knowledge and practice of culture. Likewise strategies to raise the profile and support for the 'cultural industries' relied upon compliance to an economic authority which circulated self-evident 'truths' of the benefits of the market. These strategies promoted everyday practices which legitimized private sector activity in opposition to public welfare. However what appears to be emerging in the current fusion of cultural and regeneration practice, is an internalisation of self-responsibility so that compliance to a governmentality of self-regulation is widespread. The 'message' of self-reliance and regulation is becoming a means of ordering peoples lives. As this governmentality becomes embodied in local cultural and regeneration practices, its power lies in its unquestioned acceptance by all 'stakeholders'. Yet this governmentality leaves little room for those individuals and urban neighbourhoods who fail to meet its expectations, remaining outside the mainstream and 'socially excluded'.

REFERENCES

Audit Commission. 1989. A Review of Urban Programme & Regeneration Schemes. London: HMSO.
BAAA. 1993. The Artist in the Changing City. London: British American Arts association.
Bianchini, F. & Parkinson, M. 1993. Cultural Policy and Urban Regeneration: the West European Experience. Manchester: Manchester University Press.
Bourdieu, P. 1984. Distinction: A Social Critique of the Judgement of Taste. London: Routledge.
Bourdieu, P. 1993. The Field of Cultural Production. Cambridge: Polity Press.
Burchill, G. 1991. Peculiar interests: civil society and governing 'the system of natural liberty'. In Burchell et al (eds) The Foucault Effect: Studies in Governmentality. London: Harvester.
Cheshire, P. & Hay, D. 1989. Urban Problems in Western Europe. London: Unwin Hyman.
Comedia. 1998. The Economic Importance of the Cultural Industries to the LB of Tower Hamlets.
DETR. 1999. An Urban Renaissance, Final Report of the Urban Task Force. London.

Ellmeier, A. & Rasky, B. 1998. Cultural Policy in Europe – European Cultural Policy?, Nation-State and Transnational Concepts. Ratzenbrock, V. (ed.). International Archive for Cultural Analysis: Vienna.

Evans, G.L. 1993. An Urban Renaissance The role of the Arts in Urban Regeneration. London: UNL.

Evans, G.,L. & Foord, J. 1999. Cultural Policy and Urban Regeneration in East London, International Cultural Policy Conference. Bergen, November: 457-494.

Evans, G.L., Foord, J. et al. 1999. Putting Stepney back on the Cultural Map: An Investigation into the Potential for Local Cultural Activity. CELTS for L.B. Tower Hamlets: London.

Fainstein, S. Gordon, I & Harloe, M. 1991. Divided Cities. Oxford: Blackwell.

Foord, J. 1999. Creative Hackney: Reflections on Hidden Art, Rising East 3(2): 38-66.

Foucault, M. 1991. Governmentality. In Burchell, G et al (eds) The Foucault Effect: Studies in Governmentality. London: Harvester Wheatsheaf.

Gordon, C. 1991. Governmental rationality: an introduction. In Burchell et al (eds) The Foucault Effect: Studies in Governmentality. London: Harvester Wheatsheaf.

Hackney, LB. 1997. Regeneration Strategy. London: LB Hackney.

Hall, P. 1998. Cities and Civilization: Culture, Innovation and Urban Order. London: Weidenfeld & Nicholson.

Hall, S. 1990. Cultural Identity and Diaspora. In Rutherford, J. (ed) Identity. London: Lawrence & Wishart.

Harvey, D. 1993. Goodbye to all That? Thoughts on the Social and Intellectual Condition of Contemporary Britain. Regenerating Cities 5: 5-16.

Landry, C. & Bianchini, F. 1995. The Creative City. London: DEMOS.

Lim, H. 1993. Cultural Strategies for Revitalizing the City', Regional Studies 27(6): 589-595.

Llewelyn Davis. 1996. Four World Cities. London: Government Office for London.

Porter, M. 1995. The competitiveness of the inner city, Harvard Business Review 5/3.

Robins, K. 1996. Prisoners of the city. In Carter et al (eds) Space and Place. London: Lawrence & Wishart

Sassen, S. 1991. The Global City. Princeton University Press.

Social Exclusion Unit. 1998. Bringing Britain Back Together: a National Strategy for Neighbourhood Renewal London: HMSO. Cmnd 4045.

Shaw, P. & Evans, G.L. 1999. The Arts and Neighbourhood Renewal: A Literature Review, Policy Action Team 10. London: Department for Culture, Media and Sport, pp.25.

Taylor, M. 1998. Unleashing the Potential. York: Rowntree Foundation.

Verwijnen, J. & Lehtovuori, P. (eds). 1999. Creative Cities: Cultural Industries, Urban Development and the Information Society. Helsinki: University of Art and Design.

Worpole K. & Greenhalgh L. 1999. The Richness of Cities. Comedia in association with Demos.

Zukin, S. 1996. Space and Symbols in an Age of Decline. In King, A.D. (ed.) Re-Presenting the city: Ethnicity, Capital and Culture in the 21st Century Metropolis. London: Macmillan: 43-59.

Urban Lifestyles: Spaces · Places · People, Benson & Roe (eds)
© 2000 Balkema, Rotterdam, ISBN 90 5809 169 4

Discovering 'lost voices' of the community in regenerating Hong Kong

A.H.S.Cook & M.K.Ng
*Centre of Urban Planning and Environmental Management, The University of Hong Kong, SAR,
People's Republic of China*

ABSTRACT: Redevelopment is rapidly changing the scale of the urban fabric in many old areas of Hong Kong. High rise office and residential buildings are replacing the old tenements and bringing with them a change in community composition and the types of commercial activities. In Hong Kong, emphasis by both the public and private sectors is on redeveloping physical structures for economic gain. The social and environmental aspects are neglected. The community is not a partner in the redevelopment process and its views are rarely sought. How does the community in an old urban area view the changes taking place around it? To shed light on community values and perspectives our study focuses on the district of Wanchai.

1 INTRODUCTION

Government rhetoric has been strong on the theme of sustainable development in the past year but the interpretation is narrowly based. The concept of sustainable communities encapsulates an enduring balance between the social, economic and physical attributes of our total environment. Of these three, only two are currently brought into the sustainability equation in Hong Kong: the economic and physical dimensions. The social dimension is largely ignored by government.

2 SUSTAINABLE COMMUNITIES AND SOCIAL CAPITAL

The ability of a community to take responsibility based on a shared vision, to have the ability to access expertise and knowledge for their own needs, and to have the capacity to influence the outcome of decisions that affect them is central to creating sustainable communities. The importance of 'social capital' was referred to by Jane Jacobs in relation to district governance and planning: 'If self-government in the place is to work, underlying any float of population must be a continuity of people who have forged neighbourhood networks. These networks are a city's 'irreplaceable social capital'...(1984, p. 148). Jacobs, in discussing the governing and planning of districts, refers to the lack of understanding that government officials have when they make decisions affecting districts, of what the citizens of those districts consider 'of value in their lives, and why' (p. 419). Further, her opinion is that 'the larger, the more impersonal, the more incomprehensible big-city government becomes, and the more blurred in the total localized issues, needs, and problems become, the more attenuated and ineffectual becomes either citizen action or citizen supervision'. And, that 'it is futile to expect citizens to act with responsibility, verve and experience' on big city-wide issues when they are powerless at the local level (p. 436).

Traditionally, in Hong Kong, agenda setting is by the government. Planning is very much top-down and the opportunity for the public to make inputs into planning decisions is lacking. Working for a sustainable community needs to be a team effort, a partnership between the different arms of government and those of the community. Initiative and leadership must come from within the community and the community must take responsibility for its own future. This requires a sea change in the socio-political system of Hong Kong. The social capital is weak in Hong Kong (Lau, 2000), attributable in part to the top-down paternalistic form of government that persists, despite the end of colonialism in 1997. He remarks that '[o]ver the years the voluntary sector has become so dependent on the Government that by now it is more a supplicating client than a resourceful and helpful partner'.

3 GENESIS OF THE 'LOST VOICES'

3.1 *'Borrowed time, borrowed place'*

When Hong Kong was a British colony (1842-1997) it was viewed as a 'borrowed time borrowed place'. WWII and the subsequent civil wars on the China mainland from 1945-49 brought an influx of refugees who abhorred politics, and as refugees, they had few expectations from the ruling class. Capitalists and workers alike settled in the city and started the territory's 'transferred industrialisation'. There was little communication between the ruling class and the ruled. The government did not realise the dissatisfaction of the community until the mid 1960s when riots broke out in the territory.

Although the riots were partly precipitated by the Cultural Revolution in China, the frustration experienced by the alienated mass in the process of economic growth was also a reason. Hong Kong then was like any rapidly growing third world city with squatters on hillsides, poor infrastructure, corrupt government, and maturing market practices which made the lives of the poor unbearable at times. After the riots, the government introduced a number of administrative measures to boost people's sense of belonging to Hong Kong. However, the top-down efforts aimed at pacifying, rather than nurturing the citizenry.

Because of Hong Kong's British connections and major trading companies, the post-riot economy quickly regained strength and expanded until 1973 when the stock market collapsed and the oil crises affected the world economy. Growth returned in 1976. The same year also marked the beginning of a period of vigorous new town construction. The physical dislocation of population through the movement of many people to the new towns contributed to the dismantling of many of the social networks built up in the post-war era. Economic take-off also played a part in the break up of communities. Many citizens became 'individualistic' economic beings as there was no alternative. Without democracy, politics was regarded as 'dirty', and without communities, people 'forgot' that they should be social beings. Hong Kong seemed to have only one reason for existence: making money.

3.2 *1980s: political transition and the divided society*

The strong economic growth experienced in the latter part of the 1970s was checked by the Sino-British negotiations on the future of Hong Kong. The state-level political negotiations saw the beginning of a divided society within the Hong Kong Chinese community. On the one hand, the political talks prompted some of the post-war locally born population to press for a better polity for the territory. The introduction of direct elections for the advisory district boards also gave citizens a taste of democracy. However, the pace of democratization was very slow. For many Hong Kongers 1997 was a threat. Under political, and hence economic, uncertainties people tried to emigrate or engaged in escapism of various kinds. Hong Kong became a divided society: a vocal minority and a silent majority.

The impact of China's Open Door Policy began to be felt in Hong Kong in the early 1980s. The availability of cheap land and labour across the border made one of the functions of new town development, the provision of cheap industrial land, almost redundant. The relocation of labour-intensive and low value-added industries from Hong Kong to China intensified economic restructuring in the territory and dramatically affected spatial development of the territory. The transformation to a tertiary economy made redevelopment of the urban fabric essential.

Political awakening opens a new perspective of involvement for some. However, the great majority have a mentality of dependence, brought about by a history of dis-empowerment and disengagement. Instead of recognizing their own rights and responsibilities to contribute to improvement of their environment, they expect the government to do everything for them. This is particularly evident in relation to urban regeneration.

3.3 The challenge of urban regeneration

Hong Kong may function well as a city economically because of its high density development, compact settlement, mixed land uses, high public transport usage and low private car ownership. Yet it is not a sustainable city because of serious air and water pollution, large areas of poor quality housing, low personal living space, little concern for nature, culture and heritage, a pedestrian-unfriendly environment, and low social capital. As argued elsewhere (Ng and Cook, 1999), Hong Kong is badly in need of a multi-dimensional urban regeneration strategy. Such a strategy should come out of the collective wisdom of the people, but in contrast to many other post-industrial cities, there is little engagement of the community in planning for developments in the different districts. The colonial style of government is still alive and well, with a top-down mode of decision-making persisting.

Policy makers today, because of political pressure, are required to consult the public, but few really believe in the usefulness of consultation. This is reflected in the lack of resources for local community building, education and development. The public is often portrayed as ignorant and uncooperative. Problems at the local level are not well understood by government, particularly those of the old communities, which are often seen as being mainly ones of physical deterioration. Human factors, such as compensation and rehousing are considered as constraints to be overcome. Financial viability is the over-riding concern in the renewal of these areas, which invariably means demolition and rebuilding with the original residents being moved elsewhere. Government officials still retain the mentality of the 1970s when they could move citizens around at their will. Unlike many other Western cities where regeneration strategies comprise broad ranging approaches including human resources training, economic revitalization packages, neighbourhood development strategies, physical restructuring and the provision of social amenities, etc., Hong Kong's urban renewal strategy seems to be limited to a programme of reconstruction of buildings in poor condition.

It is against this backdrop that we carried out a series of community workshops to explore the lost voices of the community in a district that is under substantial urban renewal pressure.

4 DISCOVERING COMMUNITY PERSPECTIVES

4.1 Introducing Wanchai

Wanchai is located east of the CBD between the northern shore of Hong Kong Island and the steep slopes of Victoria Peak. Its original shoreline has been pushed further north in waves of reclamation that have resulted in a quite stratified pattern of urban form with coarse grained and open form of development on the water front, dominated by the Hong Kong Convention Centre. As one moves away from the shoreline, there is a progression from large office towers, hotels and theatres, through medium office towers occupied by private firms with restaurants, night clubs and other service and retail activities on the lower floors, to mixed use residential, small business and industry, and retail. Many buildings in the original neighbourhood are old but redevelopment is beginning to occur, which is substantially changing the scale, appearance and other characteristics of the built form, as well as displacing local uses with up-market ones. Here the block pattern is comparatively small in scale and the street network tightly woven. High-class large residential tower blocks line the southern edge of Wanchai, on the steep slopes and are more apart from, than part of, Wanchai.

Wanchai has a long and colourful history in Hong Kong's development and is well known to both locals and tourists as a vibrant and interesting microcosm of Hong Kong life. Several major redevelopment projects have been undertaken and more are in the pipeline. The pressure for

redevelopment is great because of Wanchai's locational attributes and is threatened by a gentrification process that is bringing change where the new stands in stark contrast with the old. The
objective of our research was to try to discover the community's attitudes to the changes and to
identify their perspectives, within the context of planning for more sustainable communities.

4.2 *Finding the 'lost voices'*

The process was one of both building up a relationship with the community, and of awareness
raising within it of its attributes, the changes taking place, and the problems as it perceived
them. From this base, the objective was to encourage suggestions on the types of improvements
considered desirable, and to assess these in terms of their contribution to a more sustainable
community.

The approach taken was to target five different segments of the community: the elderly,
homemakers, business people, teenagers and tourists. It was considered that, although not comprehensive, these would enable a reasonable spread of the Wanchai community to be represented, and other input would be made through a series of three on-street community workshops. Social workers of a community organization, the St James Settlement, were instrumental
in providing introductions to different members of the community, particularly the elderly and
homemakers.

The project, of 12 weeks duration, commenced with interviews with people in the target
groups to find out what they thought was special about Wanchai, what the community valued,
the problems, and what needed changing. Those interviewed were asked if they would participate more fully, by taking photographs of the items they nominated, but very few volunteered as
they were not accustomed to this type of activity. A series of three informal community workshops sought to build up an agenda for improvement of the urban environment. These were held
outdoors in a busy pedestrian corridor near an entrance to the mass transit station. The results
were presented to the community in a more formal setting, the meeting hall of the St James Settlement. The process is outlined in Table 1.

To encourage people to express their opinions a number of techniques were used. These included a 'Wishing Tree' placard (I wish Wanchai could be.....); 'Post-it' stickers for writing

Table 1. Seeking the community perspectives

Community workshops	Purpose	Means
Understanding Wan-chai (week 4)	Raise awareness about the district; stimulate com-ments and discussion on community issues.	Photo exhibition of what people like and dis-like in Wanchai from the perspectives of the 5 target groups.
Issues, consensus building and improve-ment ideas (week 7)	Identify key community is-sues, the relative impor-tance of them, and sugges-tions for addressing them	Panels displaying community issues from the perspectives of the 5 target groups; discus-sion with community members, focus groups and other forms of input and feedback.
Options and sustain-ability impact assess-ment (week 10)	Information dissemination and feedback. Translate ideas into planning options; introduce the concept of sustainability impact as-sessment: social, economic and environmental impacts; show indicative results of the SIA.	Panel display. Showed suggestions from the community developed into practical propos-als. Broadly evaluated the social, economic and physical impacts on different sectors of the community. Sought feedback from the community.
Proposals (week 12)	To make recommendations for a more sustainable community. To disseminate the findings of the project to the community.	Powerpoint presentation, panel exhibition, Q&A, supper.

comments on; and coloured dots to indicate likes and dislikes, agreement and disagreement, and priorities and preferences, depending upon the context. The latter proved to be an effective method of creating a highly visual and dynamic record of opinion and of the polarization of it.Plans and developments that are products of civil servants, their agents and developers, and not based on community perspectives have given little consideration to the needs of the community and the impacts of their actions on the community. Discovering the lost voices of the community, when the norm is imposition of policy and plans from above, is a process of confidence building among the many and varied strands which meld together to comprise the community.

The adage '[s]eek first to understand then to be understood', popularized by Stephen Covey (1990) in his highly influential work *The Seven Habits of Highly Effectual People*, as the key to effective interpersonal communication, is highly relevant in this context. However, finding out people's views is not always an easy process, particularly when they are unaccustomed to giving them. While residents felt at ease to talk about their neighbourhood in an informal outdoor setting, a more restricted setting was found to be intimidating:

We went to places where housewives could easily be found, such as the St James Settlement, the markets and schools. At first we found that many housewives were not interested in discussing planning interests with us. Many housewives said they knew nothing about urban planning and they were not well educated, so they were not ready to talk. Therefore we interviewed the housewives informally. We asked questions about their backgrounds, families and daily activities. Through a story-telling format we obtained much information about the history and local characteristics of Wanchai, and how they felt about their living environment. Two of them agreed to help us make a photographic record of the things that were meaningful to them...and what they liked and disliked.

At the photographic exhibition other homemakers volunteered to take part in a focus group discussion. Information summarized from the photographic exhibition was distributed to these people in preparation for the focus group meeting. But, only one person turned up at the appointed time and she had found the information too difficult to digest. A change of approach was tried by suggesting that she talk about different places by looking at a map. 'However, Mrs. X was terrified when she saw the map. She said she did not know how to read a map...to an ordinary housewife a map was too technical and professional. She felt too nervous'. So conversation was focused on daily life which, in a more indirect way, revealed much about the issues in the community. A second focus group meeting was arranged with the help of a social worker from the St James Settlement, and although several people agreed to participate only three came, one of whom left because she was too nervous to stay without the presence of the social worker.

4.3 Discovered voices

Discussions with targeted groups in the community were initially limited very closely to their own personal spheres. However, these spheres broadened when they had the opportunity to see what other members of the community thought.

The outdoor community workshops resulted in comments by people from a wide range of interests and as the ideas presented became more concrete, people's interest increased. The process of starting by generating understanding of the district from the grass roots, of specifically targeting different groups among these to obtain different perspectives, and then opening out to the wider community at each stage has produced a wealth of local information. Discovering the perspectives is a first step in planning for a more sustainable community. These are summarized in Table 2.

Table 2. Perspectives of the target groups

Community group	Perspectives
Homemakers	Primarily concerned with the markets and public spaces. The market area is central to their daily lives and it is not only a place for purchasing goods but it is also a meeting place. The pros and cons of street markets versus indoor markets were put forward, but as each had different attributes, there was no clear preference. While the street market was open, friendly, lively, traditional and cheaper, but had conflicts between vehicles and pedestrians, the indoor market was more hygienic and protected from the elements. Public space criticized for being inappropriately located and designed. Even though public spaces often had facilities for children, the play equipment was rarely used, because the parks were occupied by drug addicts and street sleepers. Sites hidden from public surveillance did not fulfil their designed objective.
Elderly	Street life is an important part of their daily lives. Local food stalls and Chinese restaurants, markets, sitting out areas and parks, St James Settlement (community services) heritage buildings, and convenient public transport are valued. They disliked or felt threatened by street sleepers in parks and sitting out areas, drug addicts, bars and nightclubs, dilapidated buildings with poor hygiene, dirty streets, traffic congestion and air pollution.
Teenagers	Recreation and entertainment are their major concerns - computer arcades, shopping, cheap eating places, St James Settlement (a place to gather, entertainment facilities, nice staff). They were critical of dirty back lanes, dilapidated buildings, traffic congestion, air and noise pollution, and the poorly designed open space areas that attracted undesirable activities, such as gambling and drug dealing.
Business people	Their major concern is their business. Qualities that improve business were valued. These included a pleasant environment, good accessibility by public transport, good connectivity within the area, high pedestrian flow, a great diversity of businesses and shops, and choice of rent level. Considered traffic congestion, air and noise pollution as threats to their business.
Tourists and visitors	Asian tourists tended to be more interested in modern shopping whereas Western tourists liked the street shops, street markets, traditional Chinese culture, restaurants and the night life of bars and night clubs, pedestrian bridges, old buildings, the public transport (particularly the tram) and the 'hustle and bustle of life'. The need for a tourist information centre and better signage was stressed. Concerns were expressed about diminishing local character and the desirability of conserving small shop character, historic buildings, and street markets. Criticism was leveled at the inadequate pedestrian facilities – pavements, landscaping and street furniture.

5 'LOST VOICES': GIVE THEM SPACE!

An unforeseen difficulty was finding a suitable venue for holding the exhibition. The criteria for a suitable space were that it should be in a location well trafficked by pedestrians representing many walks of life, should be central to the study area, should be readily visible at street level and should have protection from the weather. No public space in the district met our criteria. Permission had been sought, and granted, to use the covered entrance area of a large commercial building situated in a busy shopping area. However, the permission was revoked two working days before the exhibition, the reason tendered being that such activity would be against the interests of the owner of the building, a large development company with development interests in the district. The only alternative seemed to be to hold the exhibition in the open air along a small pedestrian corridor outside the mass transit station. Even this was not straight forward as various government departments directed us to different authorities for obtaining approval. Another hurdle to overcome was falling objects. Not only did it rain on the three workshop days, we had to contend with 'unexpected falling objects' from a nearby high-rise building. Protection from the rain was possible at the entrance to the station, although this area was very poorly lit, and did not have a good ambience. Subsequently, after taking stock of possible alternative sites, no improved venues were found and this location was used for the two ensuing community workshops.

The dearth of suitable venues was identified as a major weakness in the process of community involvement. The venue used was the St James Settlement premise because this organization has its headquarters in Wanchai where it is very well known. However, the meeting hall was on the fourth floor of the building and attracting people to such a location proved difficult. This highlights the lack of physical space for engaging the community in such activities. There is no community hall or meeting room at street level, or other facility, such as a school, in a location that could create a central focus for community activity. A lack of community space severely limits community involvement and is itself indicative of the society's own values.

Publicly owned land offers most opportunity for meeting this need. Several public facility sites including a temporary and permanent market building, a sports ground, and a large site amalgamated by the Land Development Corporation for redevelopment, offer such a potential. As part of the market area is currently being redeveloped it presents a very good opportunity to discover how the community values and uses the facilities and to design a new market which incorporates the attributes which the community values and needs.

6 CONCLUSION

The 'discovered voices' have led to a number of suggestions for making Wanchai a more sustainable community. These include pedestrianisation of several of the narrow market streets and of a section of a major commercial street; more innovative design in the redevelopment of the indoor market currently being planned, including the incorporation of community facilities; new uses for old buildings with architectural or historic merit; redesign of parks and recreation areas; a tourist information centre and a cultural trail.

The Wanchai District Office and District Council are actively considering the feasibility of these ideas, which complement their plans to launch a 'Hygienic, Dynamic and Healthy City Project'. The timing has been most opportune. The message has also spread beyond Wanchai. Other districts have expressed interest in similar projects being carried out.

The community planning workshops demonstrated that the lay public is a valuable resource for a better understanding the restructuring context, and is a source of insights and ideas for possible solutions to various planning problems. Hence it should be properly nurtured so that social capital can be accumulated. Resources are needed to enable communities to understand their districts better and to be able to contribute meaningfully and fully to the planning process. It is important for residents to know the strengths, weaknesses, opportunities and threats of their district before they can share their aspirations about its future development.

Awareness raising, first in their own personal sphere, then more broadly about what is happening in the environment around them, is a key step in building social capital among members of a community. The project revealed that there is much latent social capital in the community of Wanchai. The observation of Jane Jacobs some 40 years ago holds a positive message for Hong Kong:

'Once a good, strong ...network does get going in a city district, the net can enlarge relatively swiftly and weave all kinds of resilient new patterns....But to get going, a district network needs three requisites: a start of some kind, a physical area with which sufficient people can identify as users; and time' (Jacobs p.146).

The start has been made.

REFERENCES

Covey, S. 1990. *The seven habits of highly effective people.* New York: Simon and Schuster.

Hughes, R. 1968. *Hong Kong: borrowed place – borrowed time.* London: Deutsch.

Jacobs, J. 1961. *The death and life of great American cities.* New York: Random House. Re-issued by Penguin Books, 1984.

Lau, S. K. 2000. 'Short on Social Value' *South China Morning Post.* 21 May: 10.

Ng, M.K. & Cook, A.H.S. 1999. 'Urban regeneration in Hong Kong – Questions of partnership', *Town and Country Planning*, 68(7):227-230.

Urban Lifestyles: Spaces · Places · People, Benson & Roe (eds)
© *2000 Balkema, Rotterdam, ISBN 90 5809 169 4*

Outsiders in the urban landscape? An analysis of ethnic minority landscape projects

R. MacFarlane, D. Fuller & M. Jeffries
Division of Geography and Environmental Management, University of Northumbria,
Newcastle upon Tyne, UK

ABSTRACT: Just as historical antecedents are often analysed at length in determining appropriate management strategies for designated and protected conservation sites, such histories may be all-important at a personal and community level in determining the level of interest and involvement with conservation projects. Endogenous environmental initiatives by ethnic minority groups in the UK, which have embraced community gardens, sacred lands and food gardens, are fundamentally about the creation of meaningful areas of 'nature' and cultural landscapes within cities. These often communicate ideas about ecology, landscape, nature and belonging, which cut across the lives and ideal lifestyles of dominantly urban ethnic minority populations in the UK. These ideals, aspirations and motivations need to be accommodated in the wider thinking about landscape management, ecological restoration and urban conservation initiatives to promote both their overall momentum and wider inclusiveness.

1 INTRODUCTION

Dominant discourses of nature and the natural landscape, belonging and the appropriateness of certain environmental management strategies are being increasingly contested by a wide range of interest groups in UK society. How people are defined and constrained by, and react against landscapes that are reflections of a dominant culture is an area of growing significance, perhaps most notably in urban conservation circles. This paper arises from an ongoing research project which seeks to analyse the motivations and socio-cultural constructions of landscape which underpin a variety of urban conservation, community garden and landscape genesis projects around Tyneside, that are either multi-cultural or from within specific ethnic minority groups. The primary focus of this work is the way in which people construct urban landscapes, both at a conceptual level and also with particular reference to ethnic minority projects to physically create meaningful landscapes at a variety of different scales and across the range of social spaces, from the private to the public. Ethnic minority groups have been widely analysed as 'others' in the British landscape, both urban and rural, somehow disassociated from the cultural connotations that are held to be so resonant with dominant groups in society. This paper starts with an analysis of the predominantly rurally-focused literature on the cultural associations of landscape and nature, and how the constructs of nationhood and the 'rightness' of particular environmental features have intertwined to provide an implicit rationale and framework for nature conservation and landscape management initiatives.

The paper goes on to discuss the place of minority groups in constructing an agenda for local conservation and environmental management strategies that flow against, or at a tangent to, 'mainstream' thinking about conservation and landscape projects. The objective is in no way to de-bunk the 'scientific' rationale and framework for conservation, but to critically evaluate how landscape initiatives from within ethnic minority communities are perceived both internally and externally, and tied in with projects such as Local Agenda 21 (LA21) and the Biodiversity Action Planning (BAP) process. There is clear evidence that the multi-cultural composition of the

United Kingdom is not evenly engaged with these projects, for a variety of different reasons, yet conservation and landscapes are attributed meaning as activities and environments by socio-economic frameworks and cultural values, and there is a growing acceptance of the value of the experience of 'nature' in the everyday landscape.

2 THE UNITED KINGDOM: MANY CULTURES, BUT HOW MANY LANDSCAPES?

The place of landscape in the definition of Englishness, both as a source for self-definition and also as a point of distinction for the non-English, has been widely discussed (for a key review see Matless, 1999) and the enduring power of images such as church steeples, thatched roofs and cricket on the village green, however isolated in reality and hackneyed in popular use, remains considerable. Indeed dominant narratives of the English countryside have, both explicitly and implicitly, 'naturalised' the landscape and the socio-economic, political and cultural forces that have shaped it.

However, such popular imagery has never drawn evenly upon the variety of regional landscapes of England, let alone the wider diversity of Britain as a whole, and the source of the imagery is dominantly a Southern one. The influence of literary and artistic associations such as Constable (East Anglia), the West Country (Thomas Hardy) and the Scottish Highlands (Landseer) in constructing iconic landscape images is well known (Short, 1991). It is too simplistic to claim that the iconic landscapes of Southern England have been appropriated to represent the English landscape, and by extension in certain narratives, the British landscape as a whole, for the enduring appeal of the landscapes of the primarily upland National Parks remains strong. Cosgrove et al. (1996) argue that the 'national landscape' embraces a range of places and regional environments, including both 'lowland gardens' and 'upland wilderness'. Such a construction of the whole that is at ease with internal diversity has been carried forward by 'The Character of England Map', created as a joint venture between English Nature and the Countryside Commission (now Countryside Agency). It identifies regional landscape and natural area zones within which local authorities and other agencies are encouraged to pursue regionally consistent policies. Such a process, it is hoped, will conserve and reinforce the matrix of regionally distinctive landscape types that contribute to the overall character of the English landscape. While this is widely accepted as a principle of good practice in land-use planning, the relationship of the English to that landscape is less clearly defined. The Self that Matless (1998, p.17) refers to equates with those for whom the English landscape, in its iconic, regional or overarching form, represents a focal cultural point in their self-identity as English, or as an Other where it may carry little positive cultural symbolism within a framework of self-identity which draws upon non-English histories and values.

> 'National identity, even in acknowledging regional variation, by no means exhausts the significance of landscape values, for there are local meanings too which may at times resist the national' (Cosgrove et al., 1996, p.549).

Certain groups in society are 'excluded from popular images of the countryside' (Scutt & Bonnett, 1996, p.1) and as such have limited power to contribute to the development of the English national identity which, Scutt and Bonnett argue, is situated in rural life and rural landscape. The centrality of the rural landscape to the self-definition of the English seems long established, and this is indeed part of the appeal, but Lowenthal (1991) points to the critical role of the enclosure movement in the creation of an 'idealised medieval vision' (p.213). Short's (1991) coining of the phrase a 'perfect past to an imperfect future' has been widely cited in explanations of the landscape aesthetic and cultural attachment for the English, but Scutt and Bonnett (1996) develop the line of argument which asserts that part of that uncertainty and perceived imperfection in the future is due to the growth of non-White elements of the English population. They comment that 'contemporary ideologies of Englishness are firmly fixed within the White space of the countryside. Indeed, it may be argued that the exclusion of ethnic minorities from the rural has been intrinsic to the survival of the countryside as the visual foundation of Englishness' (p.12). That foundation is illusory in many respects, and perhaps most significant is the selective 'naturalisation', with overtones of nationalism (see also Toogood, 1995), or appropriation, of elements of the physical and cultural landscape to represent the essence of Englishness. Lowenthal (1991), Paxman (1998) and a number of other commentators have described the mixed ethnic origins of the British as a whole, which is overlooked in the myopia of much of the nationalistic analysis of the all-important heritage landscapes. Further to this, Muir (1999) observes that the coherence and historical continuity of those landscapes are in fact the result of different episodes over history, some quite recent, 'which have endured for different lengths of time for different reasons' (p.43). It is clear that the cultural context from which landscape conservation stems is heavily constructed around ideals and histories that are variously selective and muddled. The next section traces a very different set of concerns, ideals and identities which underpin conservation and landscape projects in urban areas, where the ethnic mix is often highly diverse.

3 NATURE AND LANDSCAPE IN URBAN AREAS: ISSUES OF RARITY, QUALITY AND COMMUNITY.

In his book 'Ecology, Community and Delight', Thompson (1999) argues that beauty, usefulness and ecological integrity should be woven together in the landscape design process wherever possible, although he recognises that forcing a particular aesthetic, functional capacity or ecological design on an unreceptive community can be unacceptable. In Figure 1 some of the tensions that make consensus building around landscape design so fraught are identified.

For instance, reconciling what Nassauer (1997) has termed 'aesthetic conventions for the display of care' with a growing interest to reintroduce wilder elements into cities and the countryside, is likely to find little common ground. As a further example, 'expert' definitions of rarity and significance relating to a conservation site, are likely to find little resonance with a local community if access to that site is restricted and positive interest is not actively encouraged (Harrison & Burgess, 1994). The difficulties of achieving a balance, even where a balance is

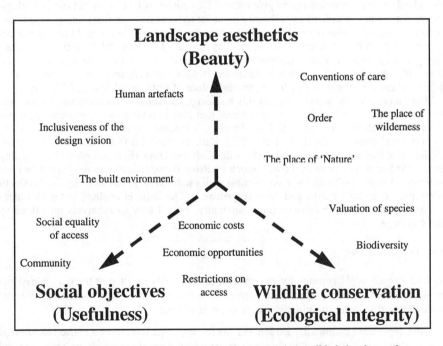

Figure 1. The concerns of the landscape designer: an impossible balancing act?

held to be desirable, are compounded where the community of interest is highly differentiated along grounds of, for example, age, ethnicity or ability.

> 'If landscape is a site of value, it is also a site of anger; at buildings, against authorities, developers, different pleasures. Statements which might at first appear to be taken-for-granted as to the architectural character of a place rest upon cultural judgements as to what and who belongs there' (Matless, 1999, p.10).

A range of obstacles to participation in countryside and green space activities have been identified by Agyeman (1990), including the economic costs (summarised by Malik (1992) as 'working class plus'), cultural associations of rural spaces, time availability and racism, both experienced and anticipated. Malik (1992) proposes a number of strategies to address the barriers that have developed for ethnic minority groups. These focus on the imagery, language and physical transmission of information about green spaces as 'the [dominant] images of rural life that are often portrayed … probably do more to exclude than to entice those who do not see themselves fitting into this scene' (p.39). It is perhaps inevitable that the 'urban countryside' (as green spaces within and around cities are increasingly being promoted) carries similar associations. Yet it is in the cities that around 85% of the population, and a disproportionately large amount of the non-white population, lives. Given the economic and time costs of access to the rural countryside, projects to engage ethnic minorities with conservation and landscape resources and initiatives, such as Malik (1992) urges, should be focused on areas close to the home. Multi-cultural and highly inclusive urban countryside projects are gathering pace, yet the cultural barriers to participation and involvement may be more subtle.

4 'ALIEN' NATURE AND CREATIVE CONSERVATION.

Barker (1996) examines the sometimes thorny issue of what is native and what is alien, and what is judged to be appropriate in any given place. He comments that 'there is little in ecological science with which to defend any arbitrary point set to separate organisms into groups based on length of residency under the circumstances which hold in Britain' (p.19). Although the circumstances to which Barker refers are dominated by the last glaciation which essentially 'wiped the slate clean', a more cultural interpretation of the environment begs the question of the 'rightness' of particular species, habitats, micro-landscapes and environments, especially in urban Britain where the ethnic mix is drawn, through place of birth or cultural self-identity, from many different parts of the world. Against this backdrop, the debate over alien and native, and the appropriateness of each in local environments, and also in relation to mainstream environmental projects such as LA21 and the BAP Process, is interesting as a window on the values underpinning such projects (Harrison *et al.*, 1998). Barker (1996) illustrates some of the flexibility in values that has permitted species such as the Collared Dove (first recorded as a breeding resident in 1955 and now present through much of Britain) and the Sycamore (judged to have been introduced in the 1400s and to have become well established 'in the wild' by the 1700s) to be widely judged as both native and alien respectively. The logic is unclear, yet such judgements have resonance for the conservation community, even if they go relatively unnoticed by the public at large.

There are two issues here:

- To what degree might community gardens that are explicitly an attempt to create a particular environment, however 'alien' or contrived in 'national' and 'natural' terms, run counter to the values that underpin initiatives such as the BAP process?

- To what degree are community garden and micro-landscape initiatives a conscious attempt to reflect and celebrate ethnic difference against a backdrop of values about landscape and nature that are 'British' or 'English' to the point of being exclusionary?

5 THE BLACK ENVIRONMENT NETWORK.

The Black Environmental Network (BEN) describes itself as 'a multi-racial organisation that works to enable the missing contribution of black and ethnic minority communities to come forward in environmental work' (BEN, 1998, p.1). In attempting to reach its goals BEN articulates the two-way nature of the communication process. Whilst one major aspect of its function is to provide support and advice to black organisations and individuals who are new to environmental work, BEN also highlights the role it plays in recognising that actors from more mainstream organisations require help too:

> 'The enabling has to work from two directions for the co-operation to happen. BEN is not about separating off ethnic communities, but about being a catalyst for opening up the environmental movement so that ethnic communities can make their enormous missing contribution' (1998, p.1).

These aims are articulated and enacted on a variety of scales. On perhaps the most general level, BEN seeks to emphasise the role of the 'countryside experience' as an 'essential basis for participation in the environmental movement', highlighting problems of access that ethnic communities often face. Importantly, the countryside experience is seen as an essential factor in furthering enthusiasm and participation amongst ethnic communities in the environmental movement at large. At the more local scale, the 'cultural garden' is highlighted as a key vehicle in allowing ethnic communities to engage more with their local environment, and 'nature' writ large, whilst simultaneously providing the local community with a multi-cultural resource. The cultural garden involves the cultivation of plants from around the world, but does not only do so through the introduction of foreign species, but by using plants already available in the 'English' garden. As Judy Ling Wong, founder of BEN has noted, following the development of a school cultural garden, '[t]hey began to notice the diversity of origin of the plants around them and discovered that the natural elements they have come across have been multi-cultural all the time. Tulips in window boxes or on road islands, so famous for being Dutch, came from Turkey. Red Hot Pokers glowing in front gardens come from Southern Africa. Indian Bean Trees stand against the Houses of Parliament...It was just that they never knew' (BEN, 1998, p.9). This new awareness of the multi-cultural foundation of much of the landscape we see around us, especially in urban areas, may also lead to multi-cultural themes more generally being extended into more public spaces. In this manner, projects, such as the development of cultural gardens within school environments, can 'extend developmentally into the community and break into avenues which transform local life and local environment' (BEN, 1998, p.10).

6 SOCIAL SPACE AND GEOGRAPHICAL SPACE.

A critical issue in understanding the dimensions and limitations of the involvement of ethnic minority groups in environmental schemes and initiatives, whether endogenous or externally initiated, is the social construction of space. Particular places and different spaces in an urban area are not neutral in terms of their perceived characteristics by both dominant groups in society and amongst minority groups. Social dynamics such as the differential access to resources, including travel, racism, fear of crime and orientation towards the range of different spaces for leisure, consumption or work, combine to effectively exclude different groups from some areas, or positively reinforce their focus on other spaces. Figure 2 presents the range of such spaces as a basic continuum from the highly intimate and personal spaces that may be described as forming the bedrock for most peoples' lives, and a space where free expression of personal and cultural values can be made in relative security from external judgement, interference or harassment. It is a key objective of this ongoing work to research the degree to which expressions of environmental values and landscape preferences that are made across a variety of such social spaces conform to or conflict with dominant discourses and values about nature and landscape in an urban setting.

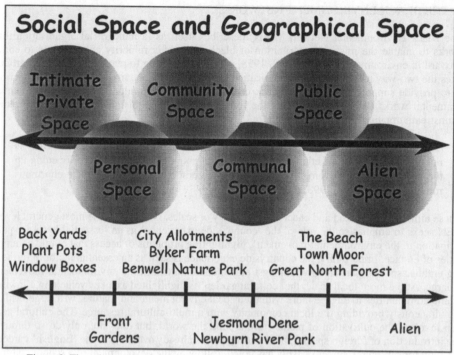

Figure 2. The spheres of social space and equivalent places around Newcastle upon Tyne.

In Figure 2 personal spaces are defined as those where individuals or small groups, such as households, have the freedom and control to create and produce specific micro-landscapes, yet where those landscapes are in the public view, with potential implications for the creative process (this may be constrained by the very fact of being in the public gaze) and the management process (being a potentially larger area and abutting wider public spaces there are additional constraints on what is feasible as well as desirable). Community spaces are defined as those where the landscape creation process is driven by a substantially larger group, yet within which there are dominantly shared values and visions about that landscape. The space will be more extensive than the gardens of individual households, but the interface with wider public spaces is that much more open and there are instances in Newcastle where community gardens in dominantly Bangladeshi areas have been repeatedly vandalised and thus rendered untenable. The distinction between communal and public spaces is more blurred than the previous, but communal space is proposed here as a category where different communities may overlap, but where there remains a sense of ownership of that local space. Public spaces are those which may be more extensive and more remote from the home, but critically they are perceived as being for free and open access to all sections of society, a characteristic which in reality may be relatively exclusionary.

Abu-Gazzeh (2000) has analysed the transmission of environmental messages across a range of different social spaces in Jordan. A number of factors are identified as significant in the meaning and personalisation of intimate and personal spaces as territory. These are a desire to define boundaries around private and personal space; concern about neighbour perceptions; the influence of social relationships beyond the family on the perception and use of space around the home; a psychological commitment to the home, in terms of ownership and availability of time for management; access to financial, as well as time and space, resources for management of personal spaces. Abu-Gazzeh (2000) observes that:

'Primary territories (areas under private control) served as extensions of the owner's sense of identity, so that markers included important, personally meaningful symbols re-

270

flecting the owner's style and decorative tastes... Public territories were less central to the owner's self-concept and so markers displayed less variety and included objects which were less personalized and represented explicit claims to space (e.g. no trespassing signs)' (p.108).

Alien space is included as the opposite pole to intimate space. The debate over alien and native species in the landscape is a highly relevant one to this research, yet alien is potentially a very loaded term, with implications of not belonging and even the denial of permission to entry. It is not used here in such a stark fashion, rather it is used to describe a range of landscapes and spaces where individual may feel uncomfortable and out of place. The 'bubbles' in figure two that represent roughly discrete categories of social space and equivalent scales of geographical space are not, of course, distinct or hard points on this continuum of space. In reality, experiences of individuals may impose significant boundaries and social barriers to participation in recreation, amenity or conservation activities in urban green spaces as well as the wider countryside. Sharma and Arlidge (2000) comment on their research findings that 'for many participants, however favourably and rationally the wider countryside may be perceived, how they felt and were treated in their local green areas (indeed, from the front door onwards) was a deciding factor in wider countryside participation' (p.3).

7 CONCLUSION

Hinchcliffe (1996) has argued that environmental policy has had to accommodate a multiplication of foci in recent years, whilst simultaneously dealing with a shift in the representation of environmental issues through the media away from narratives and images of catastrophe (which characterised the mid to late 1980s) to a rather more low key, but relatively constant level of coverage. Against this backdrop initiatives such as LA21 and the BAP Process have been initiated. LA21 is fundamentally rooted in the development of consciousness, participation and action, both individual and community, relating to the multi-dimensional objective of sustainability. The BAP process is a complementary project, which, it is hoped, can build on mechanisms for participation, consensus building and positive action for community-based conservation (the adage 'think global, act local' is often used in this context). This paper has attempted to describe some of the tensions which limit the participation, consensus and action which these projects aim to stimulate. The very fundamental issues of relating the effective conservation of environmental resources that are judged, through reference to 'objective', 'scientific' criteria, to be of regional, national or international significance, to value systems that may not recognise the validity or the relevance of those knowledge claims (Macnaghten & Urry, 1998; Watson & Alexander, 1999) have not yet been adequately addressed. The socio-cultural value of conservation in an urban context where the species may not be rare or of any particular conservation significance has been widely reported, and the benefits of communicating environmental messages, especially to children, through such a medium is widely accepted as a way of effecting culture shifts in environmental responsibility over time (Kong et al., 1999).

However, just as geographical space is not uniform in its contribution to landscape quality, the conservation of rare species or recreational potential, social spaces are not uniform in respect of different individuals' and communities' perceptions of the everyday, the valuable, the threatened and the scope for effecting change that will have a positive outcome for them. Agyeman (1990) has referred to 'the professionalization of environmental issues' which has tended, however unwittingly, to marginalise the environmental concerns, resources and interests of ethnic minority groups. BAPs are largely underpinned by dominant conservation concerns about native species, threats and rarity, although guidance documents stress that the plans should 'include targets which reflect the values of local people, and which are based on the range of local conditions, and thereby cater for local distinctiveness' (HMSO, 1995, p.5). Such distinctiveness does not explicitly embrace 'the alien'. Harrison et al. (1998) comment that 'the science of biodiversity should not be about replacing and discounting original sources of knowledge, but about adding new ones and employing them wisely' (p.319). Such a challenge clearly invites much closer attention to the potential contribution of multi-cultural and ethnic minority landscape projects to the inclusion of a wider section of the British population in local environmental initiatives and supporting projects within community and more private spaces may be a critical element in this. Urban conservation policy must demonstrate a greater level of sensitivity to social as well as geographical space.

REFERENCES

Abu-Gazzeh, T.M. 2000. Environmental messages in multiple-family housing: territory and personalization, *Landscape Research* 25(1): 97-115.

Agyeman, J. 1990. Black People in a White Landscape: social and environmental justice, *Built Environment* 16(3): 232-236.

Barker, G. 1996. Alien and native – drawing the line *ECOS*, 17(2): 18-26.

BEN. 1998. *Ethnic environmental participation*, Vol. 1 Llanberis: Black Environment Network.

Cosgrove, D., Roscoe, B. & Rycroft, S. 1996. Landscape and identity at Ladybower Reservoir and Rutland Water, *Transactions of the Institute of British Geographers* 21: 534-551.

Harrison C.M. & Burgess J. 1994. Social constructions of nature: a case study of conflicts over the development of the Rainham Marshes. *Transactions of the Institute of British Geographers* 19: 291-310.

Harrison, C.M., Burgess, J. & Clark, J. 1998. Discounted knowledges: farmers' and residents' understanding of nature conservation goals and policies. *Journal of Environmental Management* 54: 305-320.

Hinchliffe, S. 1996. Helping the earth begins at home: the social construction of socio-environmental responsibilities, *Global Environmental Change* 6(1): 53-62.

HMSO. 1995. *Biodiversity: the UK Steering Group Report*. London: HMSO.

Kong, L., Yuen, B., Sodhi, N.S. & Briffett, C. 1999. The construction and experience of nature: perspectives of urban youths, *Tijdschrift voor Economische en Sociale Geografie* 90(1): 3-16.

Lowenthal, D. 1991. British National Identity and the English Landscape, *Rural History* 2(2): 205-230.

Macnaghten P. & Urry J. 1998. *Contested Natures*. London: Sage.

Malik, S. 1992. Colours of the countryside – a whiter shade of pale, *ECOS* 13(4): 33-40.

Matless, D. 1998. *Landscape and Englishness*. London: Reaktion Books.

Muir, R. 1999. *Approaches to Landscape*. Basingstoke: Macmillan.

Nassauer, J. 1997. Cultural sustainability: aligning aesthetics and ecology. In J. Nassauer (ed.), *Placing Nature: culture and landscape ecology*. Washington: Island Press.

Paxman, J. 1998. *The English: a portrait of a people*. London: Michael Joseph.

Scutt, R. & Bonnet, A. 1996. *In search of England: popular representations of Englishness and the English Countryside*. Working Paper No. 22, Centre for Rural Economy, University of Newcastle upon Tyne.

Sharma, P. & Arlidge, S. 2000. *Ethnicity and leisure in the English countryside*, Paper presented to the Institute of British Geographers January 2000 Conference, University of Sussex.

Short, J.R. 1991. Imagined country: society, culture and environment. London: Routledge.

Thompson, I. 1999. *Ecology, Community and Delight: sources of values in landscape architecture*. London: Routledge.

Toogood, M. 1995. Representing ecology and Highland tradition, *Area* 27(2): 102-109.

Watson, D. & Alexander, L. 1999. *Recommendations on the first ten Local Biodiversity Action Plans in NE Scotland*. Report to the NE Scotland Biodiversity Steering Group, Environmental Network Ltd, Tarland.

Urban Lifestyles: Spaces · Places · People, Benson & Roe (eds)
© *2000 Balkema, Rotterdam, ISBN 90 5809 169 4*

Open use for open spaces

D.Grimm-Pretner
Institute for Landscape Architecture and Landscape Management, University of Agricultural Sciences, Vienna, Austria

L.Licka
KoseLicka, Landscape Architects, Vienna, Austria

ABSTRACT: This paper explores the impact of social, spatial and gender-specific issues on the usage of public open space in an urban renewal area in Vienna. Due to the intensive use of these spaces a large range of conflicts arises resulting from a multitude of causes. The challenge for designers is to find a spatial solution for improving the interplay of space and activity. Particularly for small spaces, such as Yppenplatz, design concepts have to be revised and changed into open ones with versatile, multi-purpose areas.
The aim of this paper is to study the characteristics of public open spaces in an urban renewal area in Vienna and examine how these spaces function to serve residents. The goal is to define key issues in a spatial, social and gender-specific context which are to be translated into design in the second part of the paper.

1 INTRODUCTION

Public open spaces are an important part of urban life; they provide sites on which different generations, social groups, and cultures can meet and intermingle. Social planners and sociologists have stressed the importance of public open space in daily life (Jacobs, 1961; Gehl, 1987; Spitthoever, 1989). They view public open space in terms of its symbolic and cultural aspect and emphasise the difference between life-cycles (age, family structure, employment) and social groups (income, education, profession). Especially for young people, they open up a much wider range of social and communicational experiences than is possible in private and institutionalised places (Deutsches Jugendinstitut, 1992; Emmenegger, 1995). Due to social segregation within the city of Vienna the public open spaces under investigation have taken on an important function in the lives of children of immigrant families from Turkey and Ex-Yugoslavia. Financially and socially underprivileged, they are the main users of the few existing parks and squares in areas of dense 19th century housing. But many inhabitants are dissatisfied with the maintenance, the equipment and overuse of these spaces and often blame this on the immigrants. This polarising view covers up the reasons which emerge from a wider spatial and social context: city structure and lack of open space, different values and forms of usage of open space, prejudice against foreigners, the socio-economic situation of the inhabitants and the design of these spaces.

The quality of urban space depends amongst others on urban structure, spatial and social criteria and the design of the space. Research concerning the use of open space generally analyses social behaviour in the context of specific spatial surroundings. The scope of this paper is limited to the study of the 'physical design characteristics' of the public open spaces and how people use them. Suggestions are based on field studies done in an urban renewal area in Vienna. Activities were observed, users were interviewed and their pattern of outdoor space use was recorded. These findings and the results of a participation project are the basis for the design project for Yppenplatz.

The hypothesis for the following is that the spatial concept of a design by itself already influences the mixture of users and their range of activities.

The first part of this paper poses the following questions: For which activities and persons/groups do the public open spaces under investigation offer space and possibilities? Which uses are encouraged, discouraged or made impossible by the existing design? In other words, to whom does public open space offer an opportunity for experiences and activities and what impact do design decisions have?

Therefore, if we are to learn to improve our designs in the future, it is important that we see how people use space and how space determines the uses and attracted users. While research and design were worked out separately, an informal exchange of ideas and experiences took place before as well as during the design process and will continue after the opening in June 2000.

1.1 *Urban Renewal Areas in Vienna: The Urban Fabric*

The urban renewal areas of Vienna are still dominated by the built structures of the period of industrial growth and housing construction of 1850 to 1910. These city quarters can be characterised as described below: A high percentage of the buildings are old, poorly equipped and densely inhabited apartment houses in closed block structures. Many apartments still consist only of a kitchen and one room - the kitchen having no window to the outside, only to the hallway. Often apartments on one floor have to share a single separate toilet. In these areas a lack of public and private open space is evident (1.3 m^2 of green area per inhabitant – while the Vienna average is 22.5 m^2). The social make-up of these areas shows a higher percentage of foreigners and - in connection with this - a higher percentage of young people than on average in Vienna. The unemployment rate is also higher. One reason for social segregation occurring within the city is that Austrian citizenship is needed to be able to live in public housing (25% of all apartments). So immigrants concentrate in privately owned apartment houses in urban renewal areas. In the mid-eighties, immigration to urban renewal areas reached a peak because of families moving together. This led to overcrowded (overpriced) apartments and a great strain on social and educational institutions as well as to an intensive use of public space. It also led to tensions with the remaining Austrian inhabitants, who very often belonged to socially underprivileged groups, seeing foreigners as rivals for workplace and living space.

This short overview shows that in urban renewal areas spatial, social and economic problems overlap.

1.2 *Public open spaces - quality of life*

Small open spaces in urban renewal areas are important for everyday use for less mobile inhabitants like children and the elderly but are also significant for the character of and orientation in the town borough. Open spaces in urban renewal areas are more lively, and the line between in- and outdoor life is blurred. In the ground-floors, small shops and businesses have been opened by immigrants. Around Yppenplatz there has been a growth in urban life: Vienna´s biggest street market, shops and cafés work successfully. Many of those companies are owned and run by family-members. This is how networks are being formed and neighbours stop being only the next-door-tenants. But with the intensive use of public open spaces a lot of problems have also arisen. Yppenplatz is a representative example for a number of similar public spaces in urban renewal areas.

2 METHODOLOGY

2.1 *Public spaces under investigation*

The research involved eight squares and parks and drew on different sources of information, covering design analysis of the sites and observation on site (recorded in user-graphs), interviews with experts, a group discussion, discussions with users and photographic documentation. We will show the site-related methods of analysis more closely by the example of Yppenplatz.

The design analysis of the site covered the spatial and functional organisation and structures, accessibility, design elements and equipment. Each design element is shown separately (= decomposition plans). Combining these layers, the design of the site can be made more transparent. At the same time the range of used design elements and their contribution to the characteristics of the location can be shown.

The central question which developed as a result of site observations was: what opportunities does this square offer to users. The behaviour of users was observed, documented and interpreted within their spatial and social context. Two different observation methods were used:

1. 'Survey of the moment' investigated all activities of all users on a site. In a map of the site all users (age, sex), their activity and their position was recorded. Repeating this at hourly intervals, a general view of the situation could be obtained and the framework necessary to reflect the activities of the target groups was built.

2. 'problem-orientated survey' focused on the target groups, female and male users between 10 and 14 years ('girls' and 'boys') and from 15 to 18 years ('female' and 'male adolescents'). Here, their activities, their precise position within the site and their relationship to each other and to the other groups of users were investigated.

2.2 Participation process and development of the design for Yppenplatz

The necessary renewals of the Yppenplatz area could finally take place within the framework of the EU-program called URBAN WIEN GUERTEL PLUS ("Guertel" being the outer ring-way around the inner districts of Vienna). An URBAN-office was opened at Yppenplatz as a platform of information for the public.

Since many attempts to improve the area had failed, the intention was to integrate the public, planners and administration in the planning process. Before redesigning Yppenplatz a one-year-participation-process took place. A work-group of 46 people was established. Beside representatives of various departments of the city's administration, representatives of interest-groups, of political parties as well as of inhabitants participated. Five businessmen/women from the local market and five residents were chosen to represent their interests. The process was guided by a planner and supported by experts of the necessary professions, such as architects, traffic planners and landscape architects. The group met and discussed intensively on a monthly basis. The results of every meeting were drawn into model-maps and rediscussed.

The outcome of the process was transcribed into the "Framemap", showing a rough spatial structure as well as definitions of interests and functions which had to be considered in the new design. The framework also dealt with the surroundings of Yppenplatz and defined some general objectives.

KoseLicka, landscape architects, were commissioned to redesign the square while the market stalls and the surrounding streets were to be designed by Maczek & Mateovics, architects. The traffic concept was commissioned to Rosinak & Partners. The main intention was to reduce functional predefinitions and to keep the design as modest as possible in order to allow users the freedom of choosing their own activities within the space.

During the more detailed design-process KoseLicka arranged several meetings with the workgroup to explain changes of the "Framemap" emerging from the spatial translation of the objectives.

3 FINDINGS - THE SPATIAL CONCEPT OF DESIGNS AND HUMAN USE

The most common design concept practised in urban renewal areas is a concept which divides the site into highly specific spaces.

Within the site, spaces are designated for one specific use; for example a football field, a playground or a sitting-area. Physical activities are clearly given priority and the lack of spatial differentiation leads to spatial discrimination of non-sports activities. Spaces for communication - in a broader sense - as well as spaces that offer a variety of different uses are few.

This designation of space favours the already more assertive boys and male adolescents. Even at times when the squares are less busy, huge activity areas like football courts are seldom used by female users, or for pastimes other than proposed by the design. Even when other areas of the site are crowded, sports-courts are often left unused. The dominance of football courts also leads to a segregation of male and female groups since sports activities tend to cause homogeneous group structures in sex and age. On the other hand there is hardly any space for communication, an activity where the groups are more heterogeneous.

Options for activities beyond the conventional use of the facility are extremely limited. Female adolescents are forced to use areas designated for other user groups, like the playground, or to claim space on the periphery such as entrance areas. Due to the lack of activity options many female users simply stay away from these locations which also means that their range of experience and their options for interaction are limited.

4 DISCUSSION

4.1 *Functionalised design concepts - the need for an alternative approach*

Inadequate designs of public open spaces in urban renewal areas in Vienna seem to be the rule rather than the exception. This is not because the designer was ill-intentioned but because concentrating on designing a space for clearly defined uses meant ignoring those factors that make a neighbourhood space suitable and liveable (Grimm-Pretner, 1997).

There is a need to introduce alternative designs that will stem from social needs for improving the site. They must be based on a spatial concept that meets the different interests of various user groups and should offer a variety of spaces and possibilities. In order to ensure a fair distribution of space, the design must be an open one with versatile, multi-purpose areas. This is the only way of achieving a wide range of uses and allowing interaction between different user groups. And last but not least - the needs of girls and boys must be considered separately during all planning stages in order to respect the girls' rights to utilities and space.

4.2 *Quantitative expansion of open space*

Problems resulting from a lack of open space cannot be solved by a design concept, nor in one single small site. Even sports activities represent more than just playing the game: watching, chatting and socialising belong to them and must be spatially considered. When a small site has to be restricted to one activity or user group this must occur within an open space concept for the whole borough.

Existing spatial resources must be mobilised, like opening up school-grounds or the temporary use of empty sites as well as establishing safe and lively routes between parks and squares (Kose & Licka, 1992).

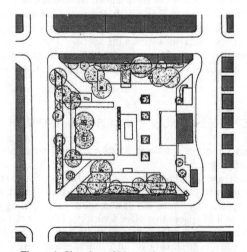

Figure 1. Site plan of Yppenplatz before rebuilding

4.3 Social exclusion and safety

Safety includes both physical and social dimensions. Designs which exclude groups of users influence the way people feel about a public space in their neighbourhood. The dominance of football fields is not only a spatial one, but also influences the atmosphere of a site because of the often aggressive way of playing. Due to this and the lack of other opportunities, user groups stay away. However, only the presence of heterogeneous user groups can ensure a certain amount of social control.

5 YPPENPLATZ – REDESIGNED FOR OPEN USE

5.1 Objectives resulting from the participation process

5.1.1 General objectives
Since the decision-making for the framework was an intensive discussion process with the users of the square it contains a detailed description of their demands. In the framework for the new Yppenplatz the following main objectives are defined:
- The square has to meet a wide range of demands for a variety of different users.
- The square will be used for all kinds of recreation by many age and interest groups with different cultural backgrounds.
- The square is important for the basic recreational needs of local people.
- It has to meet the social requirements of all age-groups, playing needs of small children and (mainly) their mothers recreational demands.
- It has to have a high quality as a place to stay and relax but also as a place for sports.
- The vicinity of the market means an increasing number of people cross the square choosing a more pleasant route or using it as a place for a short rest in passing.
- The problem of safety has to be solved. Not only physical threats but also feelings of unsafety have to be avoided. Especially girls and women react sensibly to these aspects.

5.1.2 Spatial objectives

The framework also formulated objectives in relation to locations within the square.

The central area of the square being the concrete roof of a former air-raid shelter is defined as the "moving area" containing sports courts as well as unspecified spaces with plain, more or less hard surfaces. Different kinds of sporting activities should be possible in order to support girls as much as boys: Space for volleyball and streetball adds to the football field. The zones north and south of the central area should contain facilities for smaller children and for adults. The space surrounding the market office-building is planned to be the rest-area with benches. This is the only space where flowers are planted (climbing roses and lavender). Facilities such as the old toilet, which is historically protected, drinking fountains and public phones are to be restored and situated in the entrance areas to the square. The road east of the square functions as a temporary market street, which should be integrated into the new concept. The diagonal crossing from south-east to north-west is defined as the main footpath connecting the street market with an important housing area. The route to a green park nearby has to be improved, so the spaces can complement each other.

5.2 Design principles (objectives)

The landscape architects based their design objectives on the framework. Working on the spatial translation of the framework, it became obvious that some of the demands had to be defined more precisely in order to find an overall solution meeting all the requirements. In some cases it turned out to be more sensible to even skip a prerequisite in favour of higher spatial quality.

It was necessary to build a solid, robust structure for multifunctional use in order to achieve equal opportunities for all groups of users. Clear visibility and a generous spatial concept meet prerequisites concerning the feeling of (un)safety. One of the basic objectives was to make use of the potentials of the site. The roof of the shelter in the centre allowed best for a hard surface whereas the zones along the market stands should be planted with trees. Other green areas should be avoided because they would soon be ruined by the pressure of intense use. The new design of the square had to improve the functional structure and reduce wear and tear as far as possible. The goal was an unobtrusive design: materials as well as colours should be calm and modest, forming a background for the lively action on the square.

5.3 *Spatial Concept*

Three zones provide the square with different spatial characteristics based on the existing potential: the hard covered centre and the soft border zones.

The centre is covered by hard surfaces (concrete, asphalt, tiles and rubber), since most of the movements are expected to take place here. Walking routes cross the central area, sporting activities are likely to be carried out in the open middle part of the square. The roof top of the bunker does not allow for plants or trees to be planted here. The spatial structure of the central area is produced by small concrete walls to sit on. They divide the open space into differently sized fields. The structure aims not only at promoting one single sporting activity - football for the boys - but also at suggesting different (ball)games for girls. The different sizes of possible sports court divisions (without strictly marked lines) allow smaller groups to perform their favourite sport even if other fields are occupied. The square also provides for meetings and festivities. Part of the hard area is defined as a ballgame court within a fence. A basket is fixed outside this fence, so that groups or single people not belonging to the team inside the court also have sports equipment available.

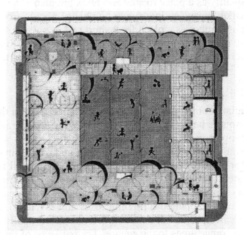

Figure 2. Multifunctional layout of Yppenplatz

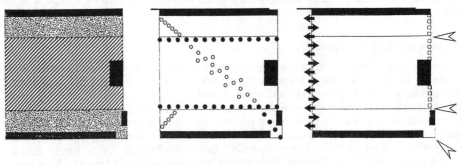

Figure 3 - 5. Zoning, permeability and edges

The areas along the north and south borders of the square lie outside of the underground bunker along the back walls of the new market stands. Existing trees are added to using the same variety of species. The soft surface (sand) is shaded by a green roof of leaves. The bordering walls give shelter to (people sitting or playing in) the soft zones. More passive activities are expected here, such as playing marbles or boccia or sitting and chatting.

The southern space is open and equipped only with benches and tables. The entrance from the market takes the form of a small square containing infrastructural facilities such as public phones, water and the restored toilet. The playground for younger and older children is in the northern space. The existing playground installations had to be reused and are combined with new ones. The entrance square in the west is designed as a place to rest, allowing for parents to watch their children in the neighbouring playground.

Two large passages are provided along the soft borders. Those paths fulfil the requirements for a safe and practical footpath: sufficient lighting, plain surface and good visibility. There is no diagonal footpath despite the workgroup's wishes. It can still be used as a crossing, yet is not emphasised as such in order not to disturb the centre. There are, however, small lights installed in the sitting walls to mark the line of the diagonal path.

The north and south borders are formed by the market stalls. The western border is supposed to be functionally open to the street market but still visible. A visual border is created by espaliers planted with wisteria, forming a vertical growing wall above head level. The passage to the street market remains open. The transition is flowing. In the east the square has a definite border to the street used by market and garbage-lorries. The slight slope of the square is levelled to increase the height between street and park. A wall closes the park but retains an open view and allows for communication between inside and outside. Entrances are built as stairs or ramps.

5.4 Design Elements

The zoning of Yppenplatz is mainly created by the varying surfaces and the trees. The size of the surface treatment is related to the expected speed of pedestrian movement in that area. Large

Figure 6. Model of Yppenplatz
size: 4.554 sqm; costs: 363.370 Euro; commissioned by the Garden Department of the City of Vienna, subsidised by the EU; design: 1998; construction: 1999 – 2000

tiles suggest faster movements than smaller ones.

All materials are chosen to resist the pressure of frequent usage of the square. There are two types of benches: some are fixed to the concrete walls, some are movable. Tables are fixed to the benches.

The walls in the centre are equipped with poles. It is possible to create a badminton court by fixing a line or a net onto them or to install bulb-lines to light the square colourfully for festivities.

6 OUTLOOK

The opening of the new square will take place in June 2000. During summer the authors will observe the users and uses and thus evaluate the suitability of the new design.

REFERENCES

Gehl, J. 1987. *Life between buildings.* New York: Van Nostrand Reinhold.
Grimm-Pretner, D. 1997. *Parks und Plaetze als soziale Interaktionsraeume von Kindern und Jugendlichen – Oeffentliche Freiraeume in Wiener Gruenderzeitgebieten mit besonderer Relevanz für Kinder und Jugendliche aus Migrantenfamilien.* Diss. University of Agricultural Sciences Vienna. Vienna.
Grimm-Pretner, D. 1999. *Oeffentliche Freiraeume in Wiener Gruenderzeitgebieten – Ein Potential zur Verbesserung der Lebenssituation von Kindern und Jugendlichen ODER Verschaerfung sozialer Gegensaetze?* Vienna: Kammer fuer Arbeiter und Angestellte fuer Wien.
Kose, U. & Licka, L. 1992. *Der Weg ist das Spiel – Verknuepfung von Freiflaechen durch bespielbare Wegeverbindungen.* Vienna: Stadtplanung Wien.
Kose, U. & Licka, L. 1995. *Bespielbare Stadt.* Vienna: Stadtplanung Wien.
Muchow, M. & Muchow, H.H. 1935. *Der Lebensraum des Grosstadtkindes.* reprint 1980. Frankfurt/Main: paedex-Verlags-GmbH.
Deutsches Jugendinstitut (ed). 1992. *Was tun Kinder am Nachmittag? Ergebnisse einer empirischen Studie zur mittleren Kindheit.* Muenchen: Deutsches Jugendinstitut.
Emmenegger, M. 1995. *Zuerst ich denke: Schweiz ist Schwein, aber jetzt ist besser. Neuzugezogene fremdsprachliche Jugendliche, Situationen - Orte - Aktionen: eine sozialgeographische Studie in Basel.* Bern: Peter Lang.
Spitthoever, M. 1989. *Frauen in staedischen Freiraeumen.* Koeln: Pahl-Rugenstein.
Jacobs, J. 1961. *The Death and Life of Great American Cities.* New York: Random House

Poster summaries

Urban Lifestyles: Spaces · Places · People, Benson & Roe (eds)
© 2000 Balkema, Rotterdam, ISBN 90 5809 169 4

A development programme for urban fisheries in England and Wales

M. Diamond, M. Aprahamian & M. Atherton
Environment Agency, Warrington, UK

1 INTRODUCTION

In England and Wales the Environment Agency issues licenses to fish for migratory salmonid (salmon and migratory trout), and trout and coarse fish species. Income generated from the sale of trout and coarse fishing licences provides the sole source of revenue and capital available for the regulation and management of these fisheries. Thus the amount of work that can be carried out in order to maintain, improve and develop coarse and trout fisheries is dependent on licence sales. The aim of this study was to determine what factors affect the sales of coarse and trout fishing licences and how this information could be best used to improve income.

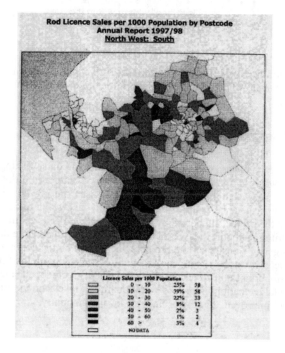

Figure 1

2 ANALYSIS OF FISHING LICENCE SALES

In England and Wales the vast majority (>99%) of all fishing licences are sold through the post office. Information available from the post office includes the number of licences sold by each post office. These were totalled for each postcode district and compared with demographic information for each postcode.

The analysis of licence sales by postcode indicated that sales per capita were not distributed evenly (Figure 1) and that sales reflected availability of fishing (Figure 2).

This correlates with the fact that the majority of anglers travel < 10 km to go fishing. Though density of water bodies explained a high proportion of the variability in licence sales, other factors were also important. In particular; the level of licence evasion, the presence of main post offices (the main outlet for licence sales), whether the waters contain fish and the accessibility of the water – i.e. whether the fishery is open to the public.

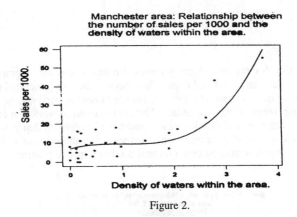

Figure 2.

The conclusion from the study was that the most effective way of increasing the proportion of people who fished was to improve fishing opportunities in densely populated areas, such as in cities or large towns.

3 DEVELOPMENT OF THE URBAN FISHERIES PROGRAMME

The aim of the programme was "to increase the availability of coarse fishing in urban areas". In the first instance it was important to set down a number of criteria in order to be able to select and prioritise which sites have the greatest potential. These criteria were; are there fisheries in the vicinity? will the fishery be open to the public? how accessible is it? is the project good value for money? is the project supported by a partnership? and is its future assured?

The first three criteria support the overall aim of the programme, while the latter two support the Environment Agency's desire for the project to be owned by the community and, in particular the Agency is keen to have existing angling clubs associated with the future management of the fishery. Other important objectives of the improvements include; enhanced biodiversity, improved environmental education, improved water quality in lakes and in terms of discharge into efferent streams and improved "quality of life" for local community.

4 CONCLUSION

In conclusion it is too early to say whether the schemes have increased participation in urban areas. The project has, however, generated enthusiasm, support and commitment towards future development.

It is certainly the Environment Agency's belief that through working in partnership with others such as the local councils and anglers it will be possible to provide good quality angling and angling facilities in urban areas. It is also the best forum to reduce user interaction by integrating anglers and other park user groups and also provides an opportunity for environmental education. The benefits also include increasing the profile and respect of the Agency.

Urban Lifestyles: Spaces · Places · People, Benson & Roe (eds)
© *2000 Balkema, Rotterdam, ISBN 90 5809 169 4*

A multi-cultural perspective on urban green space

C. Rishbeth
Department of Landscape, Sheffield University, UK

ABSTRACT: This research explores design issues of neighborhood parks in the UK where there has been a conscious response made to the cultural heritage of an ethnic minority group. The study looks at different approaches to reflecting ethnicity in landscape design, and how these relate to the requirements of ethnic communities in Britain.

1 INTRODUCTION

"(Man) creates around him an environment that is a projection into nature of his abstract ideas" writes Jellicoe (1975). British urban green space is inevitably the projection of the ideals of a Northern European culture. However, over the last half century people from many different backgrounds have moved to Britain, often settling in urban locations adjacent to Victorian parks. What is the value of these parks as seen through their eyes, and how might their cultural heritage be reflected in park design and management?

1.1 *Parks and Ethnicity, review of current literature.*

Initial research suggests that people from different ethnic groups have differing patterns of use in urban parks. Hutchinson (1987), studying parks in Chicago, found notable variations with regard to stationary and mobile activities and in the average group size of park visitors. In Los Angeles, Loukaitou-Sideris (1995) additionally reported differences between ethnic groups with regard to the importance they attached to social, physiological and aesthetic aspects of parks. Whilst it is important to be cautious of generalities, design professionals need to be aware of expectations of open space when working in a multi-cultural environment.

In Britain, work with Asian woman's groups found that the women enjoyed memories of open space in their native country and had a real desire to use British parks in a similar way for social occasions and relaxation, Burgess (1988). Other studies focus on feelings of alienation and fear of racist attack, Madge (1997) and Northampton County Council (1997).

1.2 *Cultural Gardens*

The rise of community-led design has started to test ideas about ethnicity and landscape in tangible form. Usually on a small, local scale 'Cultural Gardens' have been developed by and for people from ethnic minority communities.

The reference to different cultures can take many forms. One possibility is for areas of a garden to take on the design style and planting character or one or more cultures, for example in Chumleigh Gardens, Southwark, London. Another is to respond to cultural heritage using the arts, picking up on religious or national themes in mosaics, floor paving, murals or street furniture design. A third approach is primarily functional and responds to activities that are common uses of outdoor spaces in the home culture. This could be vegetable growing or large family gatherings for picnics and barbecues. These approaches are, of course, not mutually exclusive. The Calthorpe Project in Camden, London has used mosaics and murals to reflect the multi-cultural nature of the area and also created allotment plots which are primarily tended by the local Bangladeshi community.

2 PROJECT OUTLINE

2.1 *Aims of research*

1. To understand the strengths and weaknesses of the different approaches to the design of Cultural Gardens.
2. To understand the motivation and aims of members from ethnic communities when making decisions regarding the development of a Cultural Garden.

2.2 *Scope of project*

The project will focus on people of ethnic origin who have had some involvement with creating Cultural Gardens. The issues explored will include:

- Differences between the traditional character of British parks and that of parks of the home country.
- The importance of different aspects of the park; social, ecological, physiological and aesthetic.
- The strength of the symbolic nature of Cultural Gardens as an embodiment of a communities cultural identity.
- The potential of these gardens to be an educational resource, both to children with ethnic backgrounds and to white British children.
- How their use reflects activity patterns found in the home countries.

3 METHODOLOGY

The research is being carried out by two methods. A brief face-to-face questionnaire survey of users will be carried out at two different Cultural Gardens. This will aim to establish what people from ethnic communities value about different design approaches. In addition, focus group discussions will take place with two ethnic community groups who are beginning to develop their own Cultural Gardens. These discussions will aim to draw out more specific hopes and aspirations for these projects.

REFERENCES

Burgess, J., Harrison, C. & Limb, M. 1988. 'People, Parks and the Urban Green: A Study of Popular Meanings and Values for Open Spaces in the City', *Urban Studies*, 25: 455–473.
Hutchinson, R. 1987. 'Ethnicity and Urban Recreation: Whites, Blacks and Hispanics in Chicago's Public Parks'. *Journal of Leisure Research*, 19(3):205-222.
Jellicoe, Sir G. 1975. *The Landscape of Man*. London : Thames & Hudson.
Loukaitou-Sideris, A. 1995. 'Urban Form and Social Context: Cultural Differentiation in the Uses of Urban Parks'. *Journal of Planning Education and Research*, 14: 89–102.
Madge, C. 1996. 'Public Parks and the Geography of Fear', *Tijdschrift voor Economische en Sociale Geografie*, 88(3):237-250.
Northamptonshire County Council. 1997. *Countryside Access for All: A Millennium Project at Brixworth Country Park and Pitsford Water, Northamptonshire*: Northamptonshire County Council.

Urban Lifestyles: Spaces · Places · People, Benson & Roe (eds)
© *2000 Balkema, Rotterdam, ISBN 90 5809 169 4*

Big value from small public spaces – Lesson from New York

E. Knighton
School of Art, Architecture and Design, Leeds Metropolitan University, UK

ABSTRACT: Recent visits to New York have brought me into contact with a range of inspirational small scale urban spaces, their creators and users. Based on field research in Manhattan and reflecting upon a theoretical underpinning, this paper focuses on the collective value of contemporary small-scale interventions to city design and their range of roles in improving urban lifestyles.

1 INTRODUCTION

A rich tapestry of planned, pragmatic and opportunist interventions have created quality spaces relevant to human needs. A range of theorists and practitioners - including Alexander (1987), Jacobs (1961), Koolhaas (1978), Papanek (1995), Venturi (1966), Zion (1963) - support the need for a "hybrid of ideas in the urban landscape" (Jencks, 1995) to create diversity, chaotic vitality and experiment. This is of relevance beyond the Big Apple, particularly so to today's trends and issues in UK cities. It addresses our current anti-urban ethic and the urgent need to make city living attractive and inclusive to a diverse and ethnically rich population. Recent debate in the UK has frequently focused on the need for high-density cities, without sufficient consideration of the value of "breathing spaces" to create healthy city environments. Perhaps we need to be reminded that the word "city" is derived from Latin "civilis" meaning "benefiting a citizen".

2 PERCEPTIONS

Looking down at Manhattan from the World Trade Center or the Empire State Building is an awesome sight. Memories of Andreas Feininger's (1941) photographs or the opening sequences of the Cary Grant movie "Mr. Blandings Builds His Dream House" (Dir. Potter, 1948), where people are packed like sardines on the sidewalks reminds one that this is an extreme urban environment. With the notable exception of Central Park, it would appear to offer little in the way of relief from dense buildings and the cacophony of city sounds. At this macro scale, it is all too easy to overlook the importance of a finer grain of detail; yet it is the micro scale that has a major impact on the human experience.

In the UK, creating attractive cities where people choose to live is one of our most pressing challenges. Manhattan's attractiveness is not diminished by high-density living; its density of housing units is twenty times that of London, and double that of Paris or Barcelona. An important part of the experience of living in Manhattan is the collective value of small spaces and their significant contribution to creating sensory-rich environments. Indeed, this context of high density enhances their value that is inversely proportionate to their size. Hough (1984) supports this view, stating that "the former is only enhanced by the latter".

3 VALUE

Historically, quality of life has been strongly associated with contact with nature. Appleton (1995) argues that proximity to nature is important to man's psyche. Today, in the world's larger cities such as New York, contact with nature beyond the city limits has become more difficult. This helps justify the need for open spaces within the city and not just around it. It also helps explain why Manhattan's small open spaces are a most treasured public resource. Their physical representation on plan as a negative gap between buildings belies their true value: that given by their users, as evidenced by Whyte (1979). The contribution of Manhattan's small open spaces can be summarized as follows:

Psychological (relief, contrast, refuge, sanctuary, memory of nature); physiological (walking, breathing fresh air, not in an air-conditioned mall); environmental (microclimate amelioration, enhanced ecological diversity and sustainability); social (meeting, trading, resting, social inclusion, personalization); economic (value added to neighbouring real estate); cultural (a forum for cultural expression where social, environmental and aesthetic values are articulated)

4 WHY DOES IT WORK ?

The poster presentation will illustrate innovative practices through selected case studies. The following key characteristics are identified as being significant to their success:

Frameworks - Pluralistic responses through public action and private philanthropy have created a unique framework for interventions appropriate to human needs for urban living. Investment in this resource is symbolic of positive attitudes about urban living that can be measured by the public response.

Processes - Realization of projects through a range of processes in their planning, design, management and governance. State interventions have created meaningful and accountable public art spaces; novel funding techniques (e.g. Business Improvement Districts) have financed open space projects. Planning incentives for private real estate development have created public gain of over five hundred public plazas whilst urban dwellers have appropriated vacant lots and humanized neighbourhood spaces.

Designers - Hybridization, innovation and accountability of landscape architects activities challenge traditional professional practices in the creation of public space design. The evolving role of the professional designer as catalyst (Paley Park), facilitator (community gardens) or public artist (Javitz Plaza) has blurred and extended professional boundaries.

If "Cities...exist first and foremost to satisfy the human and social needs of communities"(Rogers, 1997) a major contribution in Manhattan is being made by small scale, yet spectacular, open space interventions. Their special features make them a model for meaningful open space interventions beyond the Big Apple.

REFERENCES

Alexander, C. et al (1987) A new theory of urban design. New York: Oxford University Press.
Appleton, J. 1995. The experience of landscape. London.:Wiley.
Beardsley, J. 1998. Earthworks and beyond. New York: Abbeville Press.
Feininger, A. 1941. Life Magazine. New York.
Hough, M. 1984. City form and natural process. London: Croom Helm.
Jacobs, J. 1961. The death and life of great American cities. New York: Random House.
Jencks, C. 1995. The architecture of the jumping universe. London: Academy Editions.
Koolhaas, R. 1978. Delirious New York. New York: Oxford University Press.
Papanek, V. 1995. The green imperative. London:Thames and Hudson.
Potter, D. 1948. Mr. Blandings builds his dream house. RKO.
Rogers, R. 1997. Cities for a small planet. London: Faber & Faber.
Urban Task Force Report. 1999. Towards an urban renaissance. London: Spon.
Venturi, R. 1966. Complexity and contradictions in Architecture. New York: Museum of Modern Art.
Whyte, W. 1979. The social life of small urban spaces. Washington DC: The Conservation Foundation.
Zion, R. & Breen, H. 1963. New parks for New York. New York: Architectural League.

Urban Lifestyles: Spaces · Places · People, Benson & Roe (eds)
© *2000 Balkema, Rotterdam, ISBN 90 5809 169 4*

Cities, people and social exclusion

M. K. Bhogal
University of Central England, Birmingham, UK

1 INTRODUCTION

The focus of urban policy from Central Government in the 1980s to date has clearly concentrated on physical development and property led initiative in order to counter urban decay (Stewart, 1994). As the manufacturing sector has steadily declined, successive governments and many local authorities have turned to the service sector as the answer to urban decay. The decline of the manufacturing has left many of our cities, particularly in the north and the Midlands with high pockets of deprivation. Empty warehouses now stand in run down estates, which were once vibrant with people and jobs. Prosperous communities are now a rarity, and academics and people who lived in this era, recall stories of a golden bygone era.

The challenge facing governments, of any political dimension, and local authorities is how to bring back life to these run down areas. As well as creating jobs, both central and local governments face the challenge of bringing life back to these areas. The infrastructure also needs to be adapted to accommodate new industries. These industries need to be attracted into an area. Buildings need to be able to accommodate their needs. Also, houses are needed to house their employees and a variety of social facilities are required to attract people to live and stay in these areas.

The problem facing many local authorities is how to bring about this urban renaissance. Their existing labour force most likely has skills in the manufacturing sector. The new sector is the service sector. This sector does not require 'metal bashing' skills. So, local authorities have a problem of skills mismatch. Furthermore, our society, which is continuously changing, has a new problem: social exclusion. Groups of people in society are becoming increasingly marginalized from mainstream society. These groups of people tend to live in poverty and are concentrated in deprived communities in inner city areas. They tend to be made up of the following groups: single parent families; ethnic minorities; the elderly; the disabled; the homeless; and in some cases young people. This list is not exhaustive.

However, it is important to realize that none of the above is ground breaking information. The research undertaken has examined a flagship project: the international conference centre in Birmingham. This particular development has been chosen because it was funded and undertaken by a local authority. The development was marketed in a number of different ways. For instance, local people living in the Ladywood ward adjacent to the international conference Centre were told by local politicians via the media and at public meetings that they would benefit from the development in a number of ways, including job creation.

2 METHODOLOGY

The development of flagship projects and the re-use, refurbishment and expansion of existing historical buildings has been seen by many as a successful way to market an area, encouraging tourists and creating employment by the service sector. Birmingham City Council attempted to create an arena for this scenario, and it has been seen as an excellent example of urban renaissance.

However, key questions need to be asked: who does actually benefit form these types of developments, do local people gain jobs? Is it money well spent, or could it have been spent otherwise? Who actually benefits: the local unemployed manufacturer, the single parent with no formal qualifications or the recent graduate living in a suburb within easy commuting distance of the city centre. What about social exclusion and community spirit; are local people, who live in close proximity to the new development in favour of it? Are the results here applicable to other similar developments, or is it a localized scenario.

The results so far have indicated that local people have not benefited from full time jobs. Furthermore, many are unaware of what is happening in the area with reference to new developments. Hotels in the area are sometimes unwilling to employ local people from 'trouble' estates, in case they will cause mayhem in the workplace. Local people are increasingly becoming resentful, as they feel alienated from the new developments.

3 RECOMMENDATIONS.

The way forward can only be with partnership with local people. Tailor-made training schemes need to be set up at the early stages of the developments to ensure that local people do actually have the right skills for the new jobs. The changes in the physical environment, be it open spaces or new social facilities, need to be inclusive and cater for all sections of the population. Only then can urban renaissance take place. However, with bidding for central funds by local authorities, local authorities may be more interested in employing the best consultants to produce a successful bid, rather then looking at the needs of their local population. Whilst physical urban development is applauded for bringing about positive changed in the environment in a relatively short period of time, the people who really matter, who live in these areas, must not be side stepped. Only if funds and manpower are made available, will we have a truly inclusive society, which the Government advocates.

Urban Lifestyles: Spaces · Places · People, Benson & Roe (eds)
© *2000 Balkema, Rotterdam, ISBN 90 5809 169 4*

Cybercity – An urban matrix of the information society

V. Petresin
Faculty of Architecture, University of Ljubljana, Slovenia

ABSTRACT: The electronic information space, also referred to as cyberspace, is generated by the new media. The built environment melts with the media landscape thus forming hypersurfaces containing phenomenological or perceptional experiences of space-time-information. Being a combination of electronic data and physical architecture, a hypersurface is not in binary relation to space: it exceeds the categories of the real and the virtual by integrating them. Today, as a consequence of the processes of digital urbanism, cities are changing their structure as well as their function of transportation, economic, political and cultural intersection. They comprise the visualisation of transportation and services as well as data networks. A cybercity provides equally valid functions as does its real-life city-space counterpart. It does not entirely relate to form but rather to an urban matrix of the new information society, initiating complex social and economic processes.

Urban Lifestyles: Spaces · Places · People, Benson & Roe (eds)
© 2000 Balkema, Rotterdam, ISBN 90 5809 169 4

Intervening with history: Sandeman House/Netherbow Closes, Edinburgh

K. Horner
Turnbull Jeffrey Partnership, Landscape Architects, Edinburgh, UK

Edinburgh's Old Town exemplifies history as an evolving urban fabric. Whilst the distinctive imprint of the medieval street pattern remains, layers of subsequent urban evolution have diffused the genuine, the restored and the imitation into an historical haze. Wrapped within this urban fabric are found the city dwellers 'gifts' – crucial spaces which act as focii for social interaction and as reinforcement of the neighbourhoods identity.

Within the dense, history-laden context of the Old Town, a design dilemma crystallizes – how to generate a contemporary sensibility to history which lies outwith the sentimental and blinkered agendas of restoration and revival. The essence of this dilemma lies not with history itself, but rather with the presence of history in the present, and also with formulating a contemporary design response to a centuries old, richly layered urban grain.

In the closes and courtyards behind John Knox House, a new realm of interventionist thinking has emerged. Firmly rooted in the artisanal traditions of craftsmanship, materiality and detail, it rejects a simplistic return to the repetition of historical methods and forms which pose as authentic constituents of the locality. Rather, a thoroughly contemporary adaptive and interpretative response is pursued, revolving around the juxtaposition of both traditional and modern materials with the texture and grain of the old. This approach results in an urban oasis, bearing the strong personal signature of its authors whilst engaging, informing and exciting its users.

Comprising a sequential series of individual spaces, the user is presented with a continuous design narrative, offering varied itineraries for those intrigued to explore further. Successively, the layers of gift wrapping are revealed, initially through tantalizing glimpses from the busy High Street down narrow closes, then through a spatial sequence which slowly unfolds as the user penetrates deeper into the hinterland. Recurring themes are unveiled on this journey – the celebration of thresholds; the expressive power of details; the juxtaposition – visual and physical – of materials; and a procession of discreet incidents orchestrated into a coherent design statement.

Sweeping away the existing features of the steeply sloping garden, yet retaining the maturing tree cover, significant manipulation of the changes in level were undertaken which emphasize the robust underlying geometric layout and exploit the opportunities for outlooks. The central circular lawn, enclosed by a striking drystane Caithness stone wall, is the hub of the design layout, forming an 'in the round' area for performance, exhibitions and relaxation. Urbane design detailing, inspired by Scarpa, Lloyd Wright and Murase, creates a highly crafted, boldly articulated scheme with its own distinctive design vocabulary. At night, recessed uplighters highlight the massive corbels of Moubray House and emphasize the texture of the drystane wall stonework. Neat unobtrusive luminaries in the closes act as alternatives to the ubiquitous reproduction lanterns used elsewhere in the Old Town.

Through shared commitment and partnership between funding agencies, neighbours, designers and constructors, and emanating from a concern with how to respond to historical context in a thoroughly contemporary manner, a stimulating, accessible and modern urban space has been created from a design language fusing tradition, craftsmanship and invention. Quickly adopted by city dwellers and visitors alike as a focus for activity or relaxation, it has achieved its aspirations as an urban 'gift' which contributes to the wider resurgence of the locality. However, it will be the signaling of a contemporary sensibility to historic settings and its associated contribution to the enrichment of local identity and sense of place by which the project will ultimately be judged.

Urban Lifestyles: Spaces · Places · People, Benson & Roe (eds)
© *2000 Balkema, Rotterdam, ISBN 90 5809 169 4*

Speak to me in a language I can hear

M. Maple, R. Milligan, S. Handley & L. Handley
Manchester Metropolitan University, UK

1 INTRODUCTION

A letter published in "Landscape Design" recently (by a member of P:3:5) introduced the idea of a "parallel framework" free of existing constraints of postmodernist landscape and architectural philosophy. It is this same framework that the members of P35 have committed themselves to exploring, searching ultimately for a popularist dialogue between space and user. A "creative parallel framework on which to consider the vastly complex relationships inherent within landscape design" will form the central pillar of our presentation.

Current debate concerning the impact of information and social comment generated by traditional media, such as TV, film, and newsprint and latterly new phenomena such as e-dialogue and the Net are well aired and the debate continues.

Equally well documented is the perception of failure on the part of 20th Century landscape design techniques to address an evermore media empowered / media enslaved public. Commentators from Tom Turner (City as Landscape) to Adriaan Geuze (Beyond Darwinism) have long espoused the need for more radically updated design thinking, producing spaces which connect with the impartial public psyche.

We observe an indisputable phenomenon within the day to day forum, that of demand and acceptance of the 'comfort–dialogue' which is spewed out daily to the news hungry masses. Could we envisage a design language that replicates this uncomplicated 'dumbed down' discourse? Could we embody the thrills and excitements of the Hollywood blockbuster or latest 'Tomb Raider' game within an urban park or even an A.O.N.B.? The answer to these preposterous questions is almost always negative (although it does not require much imagination to envisage an electronic interactive mega space within the inner metropolis – Millennium Dome?). Yet if we consider the essence of the earlier questions in a theoretical rather than a literal application the answer becomes a tantalising proposition in the affirmative. Would media language and media devices enable us to access the 'creative parallel framework' we have previously identified? Will a populist dialogue between place and user be introduced?

Could landscape designers be more aware of the potential of the elements currently used in the built environment, e.g. CCTV and advertising billboards?

There seems to be an emerging perception of a "Dome" syndrome – the Millennium Dome acknowledges the need to compete with multimedia entertainment inside peoples' houses, and yet it should not compete but offer alternatives, which are just as engaging.

Communication and interaction should be explored. The Public is already familiar with the complex media format, and is in contact with it every day. They are no longer fooled by subliminal advertising messages, but rather take delight in unraveling and exposing them.

Children are Internet aware - will it become second nature to them in the next ten years? Probably. We must explore comprehensive Internet access within the public realm.

Public intervention can be used as a positive element –slogans, graffiti, positive "vandalism" – the public is instrumental in defining and evolving space.

Explore "parallel framework" as opposed to landscape design techniques – make spaces to be inhabited by people with their own agenda, do not provide activities.

POSTER FORMAT AND CONTENT

FORMAT
The poster will be interactive and undergo constant change. It will be smart, i.e. Using digital text to update the debate throughout the conference, the matrix will be a contemporary skin constantly changing colour.

CONTENT
The installation will examine these issues –
The exploration of communication using constituent elements within built environment
    Interactive space, Internet access in the public realm
    Specific user groups and multimedia assistance
    Sound storage of past, present, and future history

Urban Lifestyles: Spaces · Places · People, Benson & Roe (eds)
© *2000 Balkema, Rotterdam, ISBN 90 5809 169 4*

Urban forestry and its contribution to a quality urban lifestyle

A. Simson
Faculty of Health and Environment, Landscape Architecture, Leeds Metropolitan University, UK

SUMMARY

The end of the 20th century marked the definitive shift from a rural society to a predominantly urban society throughout the world. In 1900, only one third of the world's population lived in urban areas, but by the end of the century, this had increased to more than half. In Europe, over two-thirds of the population now live in urban areas (EEA, 1995), and with this ongoing urbanization process, the pressure increases on politicians / planners & designers / developers to maintain and/or develop "liveable cities".

Many cities in Europe face a wide range of problems, which include environmental threats from air and noise pollution and waste management, social issues such as overcrowding, social exclusion and conflict, and the economic issues created by the need to successfully compete in an increasingly global market.

In recent years, the role of "urban green" has increasingly been acknowledged as being able to help combat some of these problems (CEC, 1990,1997; Inter-American Development Bank, 1997). Urban forestry in particular can play a vital part in the pan-European new urban thinking that seeks to improve the quality of urban life - so much so that the EU has now recognized urban forestry as a separate scientific, multi-disciplinary domain, largely as a result of the work of COST Action E12 : Urban Forests and Trees .

"COST" is a loose acronym for "European **CO**-operation in the field of Scientific and Technical research". COST E12 was approved by the EC in June 1997, and now has 22 countries signed up (June 2000). The objectives of E12 are:
- To improve the knowledge base and understanding of urban trees and woodland;
- To promote better planning, design, establishment and management of urban woodland and trees throughout Europe;
- To establish urban woodland and trees as a recognised scientific domain in Europe;
- To place urban woodland and trees on the European political agenda.

In order to deliver these objectives, COST's initial task was to establish a clear overall picture of the amount, type and location of all urban forestry research across Europe. Accordingly, three working groups were created to collate the information:
- Working Group 1 explored the objectives and functions of urban forests and trees, including policy, land-use planning and design;
- Working Group 2 examined the establishment of trees in urban areas, with reference to site conditions, identification and selection of appropriate species, provenance and cultivars;
- Working Group 3 looked at the management of urban forests and trees, including appropriate IT solutions.

Each country has produced a "State of the Art" report, which details the extent of their nation's urban forestry research. The combined document, totalling some 350 pages, has been published by the EU (Forrest, Konijnendijk & Randrup, 1999).

Current E12 projects in progress include:
- An urban forestry inventory of selected European cities;
- A study on attitudes and values of urban people towards urban forests;
- Criteria for the selection and breeding of urban tree species;
- Overview/ongoing testing of the Dutch elm hybrids;
- Research on methods of planting and establishment;
- A study of the use of structural tree soils in Europe;
- Computer/information systems used for urban forest management;
- A survey of the main pests and diseases of urban forests and trees across Europe.

In addition to the above, a three year research project entitled *"NeighbourWoods"* has been submitted to the EU's Framework 5 programme. This project, which will involve researchers from eight European institutions, seeks to develop tools to enhance the planning, design and prospective management of urban woodlands, applicable to the diversity of European contexts and inclusive of all stakeholders, so that the contribution such woodlands can make to the quality of urban life and the urban environment is improved.

The project will use an integrated approach, and will involve experts from a range of disciplines in considering the urban forest as a one of the first principles of urban green space and land-use planning. It will focus as much on the social aspects of urban forestry as on the strategic aspects of urban forestry conservation and development. The starting point of the project is the role of urban woodland as a *"NeighbourWood"* – the urban forest on people's doorstep that offers them a wide range of social and other benefits.

The first part of the project will concentrate on current best practice in urban woodland planning, design, management, public participation and education. How such best practice informs the decision-makers will be identified and analyzed by thematic, multi-disciplinary task forces. Based on this analysis, a combined set of tools for urban woodland planning and design in Europe, adaptable to local conditions, will be developed and then tested in six European urban areas – Helsinki (Fin), the Oeresund area (Copenhagen/Malmo), Telford (UK), Ghent (B), Florence (I) and Stara Zagora (BG). Testing will be done in close collaboration with local stakeholders, and the results fed into the development of a comprehensive *toolbox*, which will be presented to key players throughout Europe by way of a conference, via the internet and other existing urban forestry networks.

REFERENCES

Commission of the European Communities (1990) Green Paper on the Urban Environment. COM(0)197, Brussels.
Commission of the European Communities (1997) Towards an Urban Agenda in the European Union. COM(97)197. Brussels.
EEA (1995) Europe's environment: The Dobris Assessment, edited by Stanners, D. & Bourdeau, P., European Environment Agency, Copenhagen.
Forrest, M., Konijnendijk, C.C. & Randrup, T. (eds) (1999) COST Action E12 : Urban Forests and Trees – Research and Development in Urban Forestry in Europe, EC, Luxembourg.
Inter-American Development Bank (1997) Good Practices for Urban Greening. Social Programs and Sustainable Development Department, Environment Division, Washington DC.

Urban Lifestyles: Spaces · Places · People, Benson & Roe (eds)
© *2000 Balkema, Rotterdam, ISBN 90 5809 169 4*

Urban life styles in global-local life: With special reference to the City of Izmir, Turkey

S.G. Dündar & Z. Ersoy
Department of City and Regional Planning, Faculty of Architecture, Dokuz Eylul University, Turkey

ABSTRACT

There is no doubt that a most discussed matter is globalization and localization. With respect to the magnitude of its effects, there remains plenty of matters to be discussed, especially when "urban lifestyles" are to be scrutinized. This poster aims at elaborating the subject of globalization, fragmenting the phenomenon until the "style" of the impact upon the individual within his/her spatial environment can be decoded.

The first statement to be examined refers to the relationship between the global and the local. Though much has been said about this around the world, the supportive mutual relationship seems to be always agreed upon. Accordingly, the economical, political and social aspects of the highest stage of capitalism, the advances in information and technology, the augmented value of "knowledge", the increased importance of the "image" and "identity" of cities and the autonomization of all local/urban political processes from those of the nations, all have striking impacts on the local and at the same time are supported by the global as well.

Thinking about the "local" or the "locality", and focusing on the existing meanings of the term, there exists *a dual perspective*: On one hand, it is *the local being bargained* around the rest of the world; the local values, the local spaces and everything that symbolizes the phenomenon. It is as if there exists a completely different face of the locality among all others being represented globally. On the other, there takes place *the real life within the local;* the lifestyles of those who live at that specific place, and the cultural infrastructure, all that makes that space a place of the "real" world, not just an image. Thus, this dual relation and its social impacts constitutes the general framework of this paper and the manifestations of the spatial organization in the case of Izmir are explored.

The life within this "real" world is subject to many problems since the post-industrial era. The consequent distinctions among the different strata of society have tended to become even more intense, in terms of the lifestyles, spatial organizations and the ability to communicate among each societal group. This, apparently, can be attributed to the process of globalization. This poster focuses on various life styles of number of different groups present within the society, and their interactions with the urban space.

The different groups constitute a whole where individuals manage to achieve some kind of coherence within the global modern world. This coherence surely bears different levels and forms of adaptation. There are those who can comply with the modern institutions and reflect the global lifestyles diffused through all segments of his/her life, but others who have a hard time to adapt to it, but who do benefit from the global style of life. There will always be others who prefer to reject it all, but this, at the present time, remains only a possibility. Thus, this grouping can undoubtedly be multi-fold. No major groups can be homogeneous within the society. The main point to be made here is that the locality is not just a picture taken from the global arena. The reality is far more than this, supported by a variety of groups experiencing a variety of lifestyles in the same locality.

This is the actual reality of the "locality", as can be demonstrated in the case of Izmir. However this surely accounts for many other cities of Turkey, as well. As a consequence of such multi-dimensional realities of "urban life", inevitable resistances in nearly all parts of cities have emerged. In the case of Izmir, these refer to all kinds of the urban areas present: residential areas, public spaces, recreation areas, and production areas. The resistance can be conspicuous on even the overall form and identity of the city, not just on public spaces or the lifestyles of the dwellers.

Thus, supporting the afore-mentioned argument, what we can call "local" in terms specific to Izmir, or in other words, what Izmir is recognized by in the global arena, does not actually represent what Izmir really is. The represented locality refers only to some bits of cultural values and geographical characteristics since the actual locality is far more than just an image. This poster, then aims at setting forth all these bits and pieces within the context of a resistance between the real local and the bargained image of it.

Miscellaneous

Urban Lifestyles: Spaces · Places · People, Benson & Roe (eds)
© *2000 Balkema, Rotterdam, ISBN 90 5809 169 4*

Email addresses

Abbaszadegan, M. M.Abbaszadegan@hotmail.com,
Abrams, Robin Fran. robin@taz.tamu.edu,
Ahmed, E A,
Aprahamian, M. miran.aprahamian@environment-agency.gov.uk,
Atherton, M. mark.atherton@environment-agency.gov.uk,

Barrett, C,
Bassand, M,
Bell, G, graeme.bell@tcpa.org.uk,
Bhogal, M K. minni.bhogal@uce.ac.uk,
Blackie, Jonathan,
Bohrer, J, j.bohrer@unl.ac.uk,
Bussey, S C.

Carradice, I,
Chung, Olivia,
Cipriani, R. rcipriani@psrc.org,
Coles R W. richard.cole@uce.ac.uk,
Cook, A H S. alcook@hkucc.hku.hk,

Deelstra, Tj. iiue@urban.nl,
Diamond, M. mark.diamond@environment-agency.gov.uk,
Dickinson, J. dickinson@enigma.rider.edu,
Dimitrova, E. ELDIM_far@uacg.acad.bg,
Dundar, S G. sebnem.gokcen@deu.edu.tr,
Durack, Ruth. RuthDurack@cs.com,

Ersoy, Z,
Evans, G L. g.evans@unl.ac.uk,

Farmer, G. g.m.farmer@newcastle.ac.uk,
Farrell, T. jtobin@terryfarrell.co.uk,
Filor, S W. s.filor@eca.ac.uk,
Foord, J,
Fuller, D. duncan.fuller@unn.ac.uk,

Gowans, P. paul.gowans@sunderland.gov.uk,
Grimm-Pretner, D. dgrimm@mail.boku.ac.at,
Guy, S. s.c.guy@newcastle.ac.uk,

Handley, L. L.Handley@mmu.ac.uk,
Handley, S. steve@camlinlonsdale-m.demon.co.uk,
Harman, J,
Herrmann, M. michael@isustain.com,
Horner, K. keith@tjp.co.uk,
Howes, H R. hugh.howes@environment-agency.gov.uk,

Jeffries, M,
Jones, P. jonesp@cf.ac.uk,
Juvara, M. Martina.Juvara@arup.com,

Kathlene, L. lkathlen@unlserve.unl.edu,
Kitchen, M. mkitchen@psrc.org,
Knighton, E. E.Knighton@lmu.ac.uk,

Licka, L. kose@licka.vienna.at,
Lynn, J,

MacFarlane, R. robert.macfarlane@unn.ac.uk,
Maple, M,
McCann, Eugene J. mccann.80@osu.edu,
Milligan, R,

Ng, M K. meekng@hkucc.hku.hk,

Ozdil, Taner Recep,

Petresin, V. vesna.petresin@arh.uni-lj.si,

Rezazadeh, R H S. r_rezazadeh@hotmail.com,
Rishbeth, C. c.rishbeth@sheffield.ac.uk,

Simson, A. a.simson@lmu.ac.uk,
Soygenis, S E. soygenis@akbank.net.tr,

Thomas, H. ThomasH1@cf.ac.uk,
Thwaites, K. k.thwaites@lmu.ac.uk,
Townshend, T G. t.g.townshend@newcastle.ac.uk,
Turner, J. ajt@ajtec.globalnet.ac.uk,

Varady D P. varadtdp@email.uc.edu,

Walker, C A. cawalker@rci.rutgers.edu,
Westphal, J M. westphal@pilot.msu.edu,
Woods, D A,
Worpole, K. worpole@dircon.co.uk,

Zepf, M. zepf@dasun1.epfl.ch,

Author index